D0071457

"Imana yirirwa ahandi igataha i Rwanda."

"God travels around the world during the day but returns to Rwanda at night."

Rwandan proverb

Since 1994 many Rwandans say that God has forgotten his way home.

* * *

"I thought I knew most of the highlights of the Rwanda story. But this — one of the most riveting gospel accounts of our time — makes utterly compulsive reading, superbly researched. Ruin and revival run hand in hand as a member of an extraordinary Christian family tells her fascinating story." — Rev. Richard Bewes, Rector of All Souls Church, Langham Place, London

"How can a country which has known periods of life-changing revival then experience one of the worst atrocities in human history? Meg's book brings immensely helpful insights into this question, tracing in a most readable way the history of Rwanda, and in particular the remarkable story of the Guillebaud family. It will challenge, inspire, disturb and move you. You won't be the same again!" — Lesley Bilinda, author of *The Colour of Darkness*

"The Guillebauds are a remarkable missionary family who have worked tirelessly to bring the good news of Christ to the land of Rwanda. In this book Meg gives us a vivid and personal

account of missionary witness in a land which has known not only the triumphs of faith but also the terrible events of the genocide in 1994 which led to the deaths of some 800,000 people. I congratulate Meg on her honesty in facing up to the questions that arise from that terrible event, in which church leaders were implicated. Only the cross can heal those wounds."
— Most Rev. Dr George Carey, Archbishop of Canterbury

"This is the story of a succession of incredibly gifted individuals spanning four generations of missionary commitment with few parallels anywhere. Meg Guillebaud, like her parents and grandparents before her, carries the joys and pains of all the peoples of Rwanda in her soul. The book makes for compelling reading." — Emmanuel Oladipo, International Secretary, Scripture Union

RWANDA:
The Land God Forgot?

Revival, genocide and hope

Meg Guillebaud

MONARCH
BOOKS

Mill Hill, London and Grand Rapids, Michigan

Copyright © Meg Guillebaud 2002.
The right of Meg Guillebaud to be identified as the
author of this work has been asserted by her in
accordance with the Copyright, Designs
and Patents Act 1988.

First published in the UK in 2002 by Monarch Books,
Concorde House, Grenville Place, Mill Hill, London NW7 3SA.

Published in the USA by Monarch Books in 2002.

Published in conjunction with Mid-Africa Ministry (CMS)

Distributed by:
UK: STL, PO Box 300, Kingstown Broadway,
Carlisle, Cumbria CA3 0QS;
USA: Kregel Publications, PO Box 2607,
Grand Rapids, Michigan 49501.

ISBN 1 85424 576 7

All rights reserved.
No part of this publication may be reproduced or
transmitted in any form or by any means, electronic
or mechanical, including photocopy, recording, or any
information storage and retrieval system, without
permission in writing from the publisher.

Unless otherwise stated, Scripture quotations are
taken from the Holy Bible, New International Version,
copyright © 1973, 1978, 1984 by the International Bible Society.
Used by permission of Hodder & Stoughton Ltd.
All rights reserved.

British Library Cataloguing Data
A catalogue record for this book is available
from the British Library.

Front cover: Photo of girl: Richard Hanson, Tearfund
Background photo: Peta Guillebaud
Back cover: Photo of Meg: Paul Howard

Book design and production for the publishers by
Gazelle Creative Productions Ltd,
Concorde House, Grenville Place, Mill Hill, London NW7 3SA.

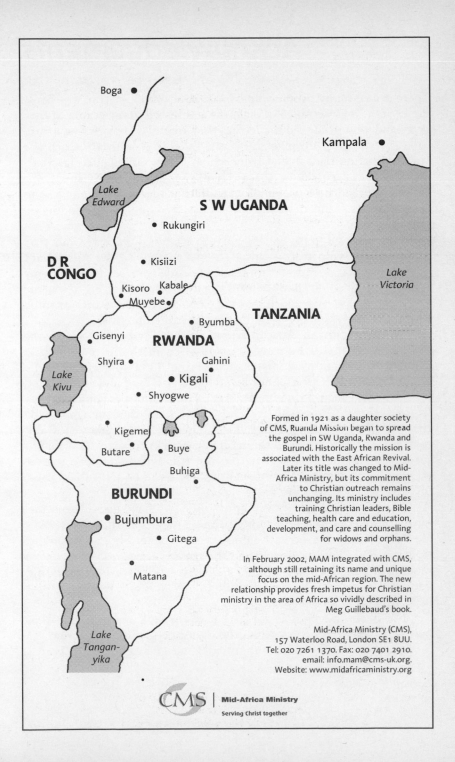

Boga •

Kampala •

Lake
Edward

S W UGANDA

• Rukungiri

**D R
CONGO**

• Kisiizi

Lake
Victoria

Kisoro Kabale
•   •
Muyebe•

TANZANIA

• Byumba

• Gisenyi

RWANDA

Shyira •   Gahini
•

Lake
Kivu

• Kigali

• Shyogwe

• Kigeme

Butare• • Buye
•

Buhiga
•

BURUNDI

• Bujumbura

• Gitega

•
Matana

Lake
Tangan-
yika

Formed in 1921 as a daughter society
of CMS, Ruanda Mission began to spread
the gospel in SW Uganda, Rwanda and
Burundi. Historically the mission is
associated with the East African Revival.
Later its title was changed to Mid-
Africa Ministry, but its commitment
to Christian outreach remains
unchanging. Its ministry includes
training Christian leaders, Bible
teaching, health care and education,
development, and care and counselling
for widows and orphans.

In February 2002, MAM integrated with CMS,
although still retaining its name and unique
focus on the mid-African region. The new
relationship provides fresh impetus for Christian
ministry in the area of Africa so vividly described in
Meg Guillebaud's book.

Mid-Africa Ministry (CMS),
157 Waterloo Road, London SE1 8UU.
Tel: 020 7261 1370. Fax: 020 7401 2910.
email: info.mam@cms-uk.org.
Website: www.midafricaministry.org

CMS | **Mid-Africa Ministry**
Serving Christ together

Acknowledgements

There are so many people who have helped me in writing this book. Firstly, my Aunt Veronica who got me interested in my grandparents' story and who produced the letters they wrote. Granny wrote a running commentary through the years, called her journal, which she sent to praying friends and from which I have culled such fascinating details of early life in Africa. Thanks too to the archivist at Bible Society who let me loose on all grandfather's letters. Thanks also to the archivists at CMS and MAM who answered queries and found me photos.

I am grateful to my colleagues who are missionaries in this part of the world, who were willing to spend time at the missionary conference at Kumbya in reading and commenting on my Afterthoughts. Their many helpful suggestions sparked off new areas of research, but the conclusions I came to are all mine. Antoine Rutayisire was also very helpful over the Afterthoughts.

My thanks to my African friends of both tribes, who read the book and commented on my interpretation of the history of their country. Any remaining mistakes are mine! I am so grateful to my Bishop, the Rt Rev. Onesphore Rwaje, who also read and commented on the book, sparing time in his busy schedule and encouraging me in this venture. I am also grateful to the many friends who made time to talk about their stories, despite many painful memories, and to check that I understood their Kinyarwanda properly. I am thankful that I got their stories written down before it was too late — already five of those I interviewed have gone to be with their Lord. Any remaining errors are mine.

Above all I want to thank my family who have encouraged me, have allowed me to reveal some intimate details of their lives, have checked their memories with mine and have generally supported me. How grateful I am that I have had the chance to record my mother's memories of a fascinating life in this part of the world. I pray that her story, and that of the rest of our family, and of our friends, may be a blessing to all who read.

I dedicate this book to the people of Rwanda and pray that they may work their way through all the pain to a lasting reconciliation. May God bless you — I know that he has never forgotten this land.

Meg Guillebaud
Byumba
January 2002

Contents

The Guillebaud Family Tree

Harold Guillebaud
(29.9.1889 – 22.4.1941)

Margaret Edwards
(8.10.1889 – 10.7.1961)

(m. 25.9.1912)

Peter Guillebaud
(19.4.1914 – 7.11.1996)

Elisabeth Sutherland
(11.1.1915 – 12.9.2001)

(m. 24.4.1940)

John Guillebaud
(19.1.1941)

Gwyn Jones

(m. 15.4.1972)

Jonathan
Lisa
Christopher

Margaret (Meg) Guillebaud
(12.10.1943)

Rosemary Guillebaud
(4.6.1915)

Lindesay Guillebaud
(16.11.1917 – 16.12.1971)

David Guillebaud
(20.2.1946)

Peta Steele

Tracy
Simon
Rebecca
Katy

Phillippa Guillebaud
(13.12.1918 – 10.10.2000)

Christine Guillebaud
(26.6.1950)

Ross Paterson

Deborah
Hannah
Sharon
Joanna
Esther

Mary Guillebaud
(15.6.1921 – 8.1.1999)

Tom Stockley

(m. 31.3.1950)

Jane
Andrew
Phillip
Rachel
Paul

Veronica Guillebaud
(15.6.1921)

Dick Madeley

(m. 29.8.1953)

Susan
Richard
Mark

Those marked in bold have visited or lived in Rwanda

Glossary of Terms

There are three tribes in Rwanda: Tutsi, Hutu and Twa.

Tutsi is the tribe; a **Mututsi** is one member and **Batutsi** are several.

Hutu is the tribe; a **Muhutu** is one member and **Bahutu** are several.

Twa is the tribe; a **Mutwa** is one member and **Batwa** are several.

Rwanda is the correct spelling for the country; a person from the country is a **Munyarwanda**; two or more are **Banyarwanda** and the language they speak is **Kinyarwanda**. although in this book I have used the English term **Rwandan**.

During colonial days until independence in 1962, the spelling was different and these were the terms used at that time. I have used the modern spelling but where I have quoted other people I have used the spelling of the time.

The country was known as **Ruanda**. During colonial rule it was united with Burundi as **Ruanda-Urundi**; a person from Ruanda was called a **Munyaruanda**; several were **Banyaruanda** and **Lunyaruanda** was their language. A person from **Urundi** was (and is) a **Murundi**; several were (and are) **Barundi** and their language was (and is) **Kirundi**. In this book I have used the English term **Burundians**.

Terms commonly used in this book

Abaka	"The ones on fire." The name originally given to those affected by Revival
Abazimu	The spirits of the dead
Binego	Cruel and powerful controlling spirit, son of Ryangombe
Imana	Creator God who Rwandans believe dwells in the Virunga mountains
Imandwa	Controlling spirits

Interahamwe	"Those who join together." It was the term used of the bands of killers who killed with machetes and hoes
Inyenzi	"Cockroaches." The term used to describe Tutsi who were to be exterminated. Originally it was a term the Tutsi used of themselves as they attempted to return to Rwanda during the 1960s
Kazu	A small hut. In Revival days it meant a prayer hut but during the latter part of President Habyarimana's regime it referred to the coterie surrounding his wife
Kubandwa	To bind yourself with an oath to the imandwa, the controlling spirits
Longdrop	A pit latrine
Masunzu	The towering hairstyle of aristocratic Tutsi
Mukecuru	An old woman
Muzungu	A white person
Nyabingi	Spirit worshipped in the north of Rwanda, especially near the Virunga mountains
Rugo	The enclosure round a Rwandan hut
Ryangombe	Chief of the controlling spirits
Shebuja	Master or Lord
Ubuhake	Feudal rights
Umuganda	Work done for the government in lieu of tax
Umurinzi	Watchman — usually used of the tree planted outside a homestead so that the spirit of an ancestor can watch over his family

The magazine which informed supporters of the work of the Ruanda Mission, later called Mid-Africa Ministry, was originally a collection of letters sent by missionaries to the Friends of Ruanda. Later these letters were collected into a magazine called *Ruanda Notes*. When the mission changed its name, the magazine also changed to *Partners Together*. At present it is called *MAM News*.

Introduction

Sleepily I turned over and looked at my watch. 6 a.m.! Whoever could be ringing at this hour? I listened as my father's voice rose in alarm. Grabbing a wrap, I went through to my parents' room as he put the phone down. It was Thursday 7th April 1994. I was staying with my parents in their cottage near Reading, on my break following a busy Easter in my parish in Swindon where I was the curate.

My father looked up as I went into the bedroom. "That was Harold," he said. "He was listening to the World Service. The presidents of Rwanda and Burundi were both in a plane which crashed last night at Kigali. It is feared there are no survivors."

Horror-struck, we all stared at each other, fearing what this would mean. Just two days ago my parents had received another early morning phone call, this time from Rwanda, inviting them to join in the celebrations in August to mark the Scripture Union silver jubilee. Twenty-five years earlier my father had started the work of SU in Rwanda and they were looking forward to returning to the country where they had spent so much of their married life. Whatever happened now, there was likely to be a period of unrest, and it was unlikely that this trip would be feasible — but our worst fears fell far short of the horror that unfolded on our TV screens over the next few days.

My parents had spent much of their lives in Rwanda, where I had been brought up. How was it possible that the people we knew and loved could have been turned into the savages we saw night by night? I saw horrific pictures of bodies floating down the river, of people being hacked to death in the streets, of refugees streaming out of Rwanda. One reporter described it as an exodus of biblical proportions. The stories we heard increased the horror. It seemed that the killers were not content to do the killing themselves. They wanted to make a nation of murderers.

One interview on television encapsulated the horror. A young Hutu woman stood there holding a child in her arms.

With wooden face she described how a man with a machine gun had ordered her to kill a neighbour because she was Tutsi. "I refused," she said, "but without any hesitation the man clubbed the baby on my back to death with his gun. Then he pointed it at my other child and ordered me to kill my neighbour — what else could I do?"

My brother heard from a friend of a man who had fled to Burundi. "The killers came and ordered me to kill my wife," he wrote. "I refused, saying that I loved her. They said that if I didn't kill her they would kill me and my wife and then our little children would be left as orphans to fend for themselves. My wife told me to kill her so I did. I managed to get away with the children — but I can't live with what I have done."

Daily, I heard the news of the death of friends. My earliest childhood playmate, together with his Belgian wife and his father, Eustace, who was my father's closest Rwandan friend, were all killed that first day, as was Israel Havugimana, another friend, the head of African Evangelistic Enterprises, who had worked tirelessly for reconciliation. Geoffrey, the dearly loved pastor of Kigali, who ought to have been enjoying a well-earned retirement, was first reported dead, though later we heard that he was alive, having been beaten up and left for dead. John, Edith, Pierre, Denis... the list of those missing for whom I was praying grew longer and longer. What had happened to them?

As I watched and listened to the news, I was full of questions. "Where are you, Lord? How are you allowing this? How can the unity we saw as children have turned to this ugly hatred?" I found it more and more difficult to continue my work in a busy parish when I was aching inside.

One friend I visited spoke of the troubles in Rwanda and then said, "My troubles seem very small in comparison."

"But they are big to you and your pain is real," I replied. "God wants to help you as much as those in Rwanda."

I knew it was true — but I needed to keep reminding myself of its truth. Another friend said she was trying to imagine what it would be like if a tenth of her home city was destroyed. But people like that were rare. More often, if I spoke of friends being killed, they would respond, "I thought all the Europeans had been evacuated from Rwanda", as if it were impossible for me to have Rwandan friends. And I was told that I was mentioning

Rwanda too much in sermons — people were beginning to switch off.

A deep anger began to fill my life. Anger at comfortable Christians who did not seem interested in the problems of Christians on the other side of the world; anger at seeing the life-work of my parents disintegrating and feeling their pain; anger with the United Nations who had apparently walked out of the country and left them to the killing but were now trying to help the millions of refugees who included many of the killers; above all, anger with God who was seemingly powerless to stop it.

One day I heard a news report that fighting had broken out in the Yemen. I screamed at God: "I can't take any more bloodshed!"

I heard the Lord speak gently to my heart. "I'm not asking you to," he said, "I have my own people who are bleeding for Yemen in the way that you are for Rwanda."

I thought of friends who had worked in Yemen and realized that this was true. I began to accept that the anguish I felt was a type of prayer, and that I was feeling what others could not; this was a prayer-burden for Rwanda — yet it appeared to be consuming me. For years I had visited a senior clergyman to talk about problems I was facing and to gain spiritual insight into my life. How I thank God for my spiritual adviser. He was a lifeline at this time, but my anger still grew.

Already that year I had coped with the emotional demands of a major operation as well as deciding unexpectedly that the Lord was calling me to be ordained into the Anglican priesthood. In December 1993 I had had a hysterectomy, just as news came through that the president of Burundi had been assassinated. Although this had not affected me as deeply as the later events in Rwanda would, I was still worried and upset about what it would mean for friends there. I went to recuperate at Burrswood Health Centre in Kent where the care and concern of so many people enabled me to share my worries, firstly about what was happening in Burundi and then about my future. I had always felt happy and fulfilled as a deacon and had no desire to be an ordained priest. But now, suddenly, I felt as if the Lord was calling me to take this next step. As I talked it over with the counsellors at Burrswood, I came to realize that what was holding me back was fear. I did not want to face the antagonism of so many over this question.

On my last Sunday at Burrswood I went down to the chapel. It was the Feast of the Annunciation. The chaplain described various Christmas cards he had received depicting the Annunciation. One was the familiar Botticelli painting with a demure Virgin accepting the astonishing news the angel had brought. But the other was by an Italian painter, with an enormous angel in the forefront of the painting and a terrified Mary cowering in the corners and a cat to one side with every hair standing on end. The first words the angel said were, "Fear not." Why? Because Mary knew that those who had been chosen by God had something to fear. As I have studied the lives of Isaiah and Jeremiah, I have known how true that is. Yet the message was, "Fear not, for the Lord is with you." How those words spoke to my heart! I knew that God was indeed calling me to take this next step in my career.

I felt that it was too soon after the emotional upheaval of my operation to be ordained with the very first women in March, so my ordination was arranged for July. I little dreamt that by then all my emotional energy would be concentrated on Rwanda.

As the news came through that April that Rwanda and Burundi had lost their presidents, in Burundi's case for the second time in a few months, and then as the horror unfolded on our television screens, I felt battered by too many emotions. Should I withdraw from ordination while I battled with my anger? I could not decide either way so went ahead, mainly because I lacked the energy to decide to withdraw.

Before my ordination I had to go away for three days on retreat with the others to still ourselves before God. My retreat at the beginning of July 1994 was an oasis of peace where at last I was able to face my grief and anger. The first night at evensong we read from 1 Samuel 4, the story of the capture of the ark of the covenant. I thought of the feelings of the Israelites when they realized that the symbol of God's presence with them had been captured by their enemies. Did this mean that the gods of the Philistines were more powerful? The news of their loss killed old Eli, the priest. Now they were leaderless — and God had apparently forsaken them. I thought about the Rwandan refugees now flooding into Tanzania and Zaire. Did they feel like that? Alone in my room I read on. Dagon, the god of the Philistines, was unable to stand in the presence of the living God. Not once but twice it fell before the ark — and the second time it lost its head! A glimmer of hope warmed my heart — perhaps this was not the end of the story. Next day, in the beautiful gardens of the retreat centre, I meditated. The Creator God, who loves beauty, endured the ugliness and pain of the cross. He shared the pain of our humanity in order to redeem the ugliness of human self-will. He too was bleeding over Rwanda.

The ordination service next day was wonderful. I had a feeling of rightness, of hope and of purpose.

News continued to come: on TV, radio, through phone calls and letters. We began to hear news of miraculous escapes. All but one of the people for whom I had been praying had escaped — often quite inexplicably. But then I had a new set of questions. If God was powerful and concerned enough to respond to my prayers, why had he allowed it in the first place? What about the estimated million dead — didn't he care for them? And what about those dying in the refugee camps, homeless and hopeless?

That autumn I went to a conference on spirituality. I arrived late, having taken the funeral of a friend whom I had visited almost daily in hospital for three weeks. I was emotionally and physically at the end of my tether. I overslept and arrived late for a talk on Ignatian spirituality. As I sat down, the speaker said, "Let's do an exercise." I didn't know it but he had just been speaking about the Mount of Transfiguration.

"Shut your eyes," he said, "and think of a mountain, any mountain." I thought of Mount Kigali on the outskirts of the capital of Rwanda. "Picture yourself walking up it... Can you see the twelve disciples?... Join them... Where is Jesus?... See him stop and look out over the view."

In my mind's eye I saw the torn and broken city below.

"Can you see the glory?"

I don't think I screamed aloud, but I was screaming inside. All my anger rose to the surface. How could there be any glory in what had been happening there over these past months?

That night at a meeting, the Holy Spirit met me. As I experienced his love, the pent-up tears began to flow and I wept, and wept and wept. All sorts of activity were happening round me but I was only aware of the gentle Presence helping me to pour out my grief and anger, and beginning to heal my battered emotions.

My parents, meanwhile, had been watching all the aid agencies flooding into Rwanda. So many did not know the language or the culture, and many did not know the Lord. My parents knew all three — surely there was something they could do? My father had had a stroke some four years before. In the hospital ward, I had had the privilege of anointing him and praying for his healing. He had said then that he was ready to die, but that if there was still a ministry for him to do then perhaps the Lord would restore him. Following the way that Aaron had been dedicated as high priest in Leviticus, I had anointed his and Mum's right thumbs as a symbol of their preparedness for what the Lord had in store. Now, as they considered the possibility of returning to Rwanda, they wondered. Was this why the Lord had restored him? Could this be another phase in their long connection with Rwanda?

My parents had gone as missionaries to the small country of Ruanda-Urundi, as it was then known (now two separate countries: Rwanda and Burundi), and had been there during the days of the famed East African Revival. They had gone as brash young missionaries wanting to teach the uneducated Africans — but found that it was they who needed to learn the true message of Christianity. Those uneducated men and women had learned the secret of walking close to God, never allowing sin to create barriers, but rather coming quickly to repentance, and soon they were challenging the missionaries to a fresh understanding of how they lived out their faith. My parents found a joy in the Lord they had never known before, and during those years they made lasting friendships which transcended all natural barriers of race, education or tribe. My grandparents had also been missionaries in that part of Central Africa, and my grandfather is buried in Burundi. My parents were married there and all four of their children were born there, though we grew up in neighbouring Rwanda where my father started a large Protestant secondary school. Our family connections with the country spanned more than 70 years.

On my mother's 80th birthday in January 1995 she read of the call of Moses to serve the Lord — aged 80! It seemed to be confirmation that this was right. I was unhappy at them going into a war-zone on their own at their age and asked my archdeacon for leave to travel with them.

"Is it wise for two 80-year-olds to travel to Rwanda at this stage?" he asked.

I replied that it wasn't a bit wise, but that it was probably right, as many of those now in power would have been taught by Dad years before. If anyone could help the broken people of Rwanda it was probably my parents. I was granted compassionate leave for a month.

We left for Nairobi in February 1995. Friends met us at the airport where they sang a spontaneous hymn of praise. We were taken to the provincial guest house where, over the next ten days we met many Rwandans who wanted to tell their stories. We heard of those who had lost entire families, of others who had done all they could to rescue Tutsi even though they were Hutu, of a Tutsi friend whose husband had been killed, who said she no longer felt free worshipping with Hutu Christians. We were able to join with Rwandans as they worshipped on Sunday. Dad was asked to say a few words, and we heard of the efforts of reconciliation going on among the refugees in Nairobi.

After ten days we left for Rwanda in a battered transport plane, noisy and cold. Soon we were flying over Rwanda. The hills still looked green and beautiful. It looked no different and yet how much had changed. My parents had permanent visas from their long years in the country. Under the new regime we wondered whether these would be accepted. I had been told that there would be no problem getting a visa at the airport and so it proved. Impressed by the Kinyarwanda spoken by my parents, we were welcomed and passed through customs.

Waiting for us was Sylvester from Scripture Union who had come to welcome back Emmanuel, their general secretary who had travelled with us. We were taken out to SU headquarters, where we briefly met the few workers and then we were taken to the Presbyterian guest house, which showed the effects of war. Next door, the church was pocked with bullet holes and had a badly damaged roof from grenades. Everywhere we looked we could see the marks of the conflict. Over the next few days as people came to see us and shared their stories, we heard of the horror but also of courage and heroism.

During that time, I met many of those for whom I had been praying. I heard amazing stories of faith and self-sacrificing love and began to see a glimmering of glory in the horrific events of the year before. At the same time I heard the questions: Isn't Rwanda a Christian country? How could the place where Revival started have turned to genocide?

I also heard many replies. The Revival message was only personal, it never tackled the root evils in society. We baptized many Rwandans but we did not produce disciples. Most chilling of all was this comment from a Pentecostal pastor: "When the Holy Spirit left a man he became worse than the worst of the killers." Is it possible for the Holy Spirit to leave a true believer? Was Christianity in Rwanda really only skin deep? What was the real impact of Revival?

Since 1994 I have read many books trying to explain the genocide. This is not going to be an exploration of the history and politics of the country, though I will briefly touch on that. Rather, through my family experience over 70 years, and through stories of some of their Rwandan friends, I hope to explore Revival as it affected a few people I knew and how its effect lives on even now, following the bloody events of 1994.

Chapter 1

Early Days in Africa (1925-1928)

Family history

I never met my grandfather but I was brought up on stories of his absent-mindedness. There was one occasion when Granny was ill upstairs and asked Grandfather to get her the foul-tasting medicine which she had left downstairs. Time passed and eventually she called out, "Harold, what happened to my medicine?" There was the sound of a book shutting in the library and then a conscience-stricken, "Oh bother! I've gone and drunk it!"

His dislike for rice-pudding was well known. One day, in the absence of his wife, it was served burnt and his daughters found it almost uneatable. One by one they passed their plates up the table and swapped them for their father's as he emptied his. He was engrossed in reading some learned tome at the time, something that he never did at table when his wife was present! Finally his eldest daughter Rosemary asked, "Would you like some more, Daddy?" "Oh, no thank you, dear. I've had enough." The family erupted in gales of laughter for, without knowing it, he had eaten the whole burnt pudding!

Descended from Huguenots who fled to England after the revocation of the Edict of Nantes in 1685, Harold Ernest Guillebaud came from a long line of clergy in the Church of England. He was a studious, frail young man who, from an early age, had been fascinated by stories about Uganda. He had taken a double first in classics at Pembroke College, Cambridge, and followed this by doing a second degree in economics in a year to please his uncle, the famous economist Alfred Marshall. The hard work entailed resulted in his having a breakdown, and it took years to recover his health. He virtually had to learn to read again by means of children's books and comics. It was said that one never knew what he would be found reading — *Tiger Tim* or *The Odyssey* in the original Greek!

His father was vicar of Yatesbury, in Gloucestershire, and died while Harold was still at school. His mother used to invite the neighbours in for afternoon tea. Usually Harold would ignore these gatherings, but one day, while he was still recovering from his breakdown, he heard that a girl was coming who was interested in Uganda. He met Margaret Edwards and was intrigued by her vigour and sense of purpose. She wanted to go to Oxford University but was fearful of the entrance exams. He offered to coach her. In July 1911, while she was far from well, she sat the exam but knew that she had not done herself justice. Harold comforted her and found himself stammering out a proposal of marriage. Although she failed the exam, Margaret had no regrets. She had found the mainspring of her life's work, and to care for and encourage the diffident young man in whom she saw the seeds of greatness, was at the front of all she did.

The following spring Harold's mother died, and Margaret's father, Rev. Philip Edwards, invited Harold to accompany him on a cruise to Palestine. Unfortunately, when they reached Cairo, Philip became ill. Harold wired to Margaret and started for home. They reached Bordighera, near Monte Carlo in Italy, where Philip's illness developed into pneumonia. Thankfully Margaret and her mother met them there and were with Philip when he died, and he was buried there. The strain of all this was too much for Harold who had a recurrence of his breakdown. Margaret wanted the right to care for Harold, and so, although it was not considered the done thing because they were both in mourning, they were married on the 5th September 1912. Both were 23.

They settled down with Margaret's mother in Combe Royal, a large house near Bath which had been bought by her father when he came into some money in 1900. They built a small house in the grounds of Combe Royal which they called "Homefield" where their son Peter was soon born, and later their daughters Rosemary and Lindesay. When war came, Harold was not well enough to be called up and they continued quietly at Homefield. In 1916 he became the curate at St Michael's Church, Bath, and three more daughters, Philippa, and the twins, Mary and Veronica, were born. Harold's health

improved but he had given up hope of going abroad. He continued his interest in missionary work by joining the Church
Missionary Society, while Margaret wrote two children's books
which were published by CMS.

Early days of the Ruanda Mission

Harold was on the CMS Committee when, in 1919, two eager
young doctors, newly arrived from Uganda, came seeking backing for a new venture into Ruanda-Urundi. As a result of the
war, CMS was facing heavy expenses and was considering cutting back on their work. It was not a good time to ask for more
funds. Yet certain members were impressed by the conviction of
Dr Len Sharp and Dr Algie Stanley Smith that God had called
them to this part of Africa. Harold was one of those who considered that this was from God and that He would provide the
means. The two doctors were told that they would need to find
their own finances, but that if these were forthcoming, CMS
would back their venture.

They managed to interest a group of friends, to be called the
Friends of Ruanda, who pledged themselves to pray and to give
to this new work. Harold, who had been at Cambridge with the
two doctors, became one of this group. The doctors returned to
Uganda with the blessing of CMS and believing they had the
backing of the Belgian government, who had been awarded the
mandate of Ruanda-Urundi after they fought the Germans
there during the war. When the doctors reached Marseille however, they found a letter from CMS informing them that the
Belgian foreign office had withdrawn its permission for work in
Ruanda-Urundi. The Belgian government was committed to
making Ruanda-Urundi a Roman Catholic country, and the only
Protestants they were allowing to work there were Belgian
Protestants who took over the three German Lutheran mission
stations in the country. In some dismay, the young doctors continued their journey wondering why God had so clearly called
them if they could not enter the country. Frustrated, they went
as close to the Rwanda border as they could and began medical
work in Kabale, in South-West Uganda. This was an area where
Kinyarwanda was spoken, as one of three tribal languages, so
they set themselves to learn the language of Rwanda while they

waited to see what God would do. They also wrote letters home asking the Friends to pray.

Towards the end of 1921, Britain asked Belgium for a large section of Eastern Rwanda, so that they could build a railway from the Cape to Cairo entirely on British-administered territory. As soon as this happened, Dr Sharp, with the permission of the British administrator, an old friend, went over the border and established various dispensaries at a number of small sites in Eastern Rwanda, which were staffed by African evangelists from Kabale. He found many chiefs were interested and wanted to hear more about Jesus. A few months later the Cape to Cairo railway project was abandoned and in October 1923 Eastern Rwanda was handed back to Belgium — complete with some British missionaries in their tents. The Belgian resident in the capital, Kigali, granted permission for the missionaries to continue their work though it was to be some years before they were officially recognized by the government in Belgium.

The call to Bible translation

There was an urgent need for more personnel, and Dr and Mrs Sharp returned to England in 1924. They spent much of that year speaking at different churches, telling how God had opened the way and asking for help to expand the work. Several clergymen responded to this call, including Rev. Jack Warren, who was suffering from a lung condition which it was hoped that the mountain air of Kabale might help. Sadly he was only to work there for four years before returning to England and dying on 20th January 1930, but in that time he had done much to help the infant church grow in South-West Uganda.

Another who responded was Captain Geoffrey Holmes, who spent three months in 1925 visiting and encouraging the evangelists in Eastern Rwanda and exploring the area before settling on Gahini at the northern tip of Lake Muhazi as the best centre for medical work.

As they travelled around, the Sharps particularly spoke of the need for the Word of God in Kinyarwanda. At one such meeting in Bath, Harold once more felt God calling him. He wrote:

By that time I had a family of six children, and both my wife and I had been medically rejected for any part of the mission field so that I should not have thought of the possibility of going out to Ruanda but for one thing. God gave to my wife, quite independently of myself, a strong call that we should go out for this work, and this call He afterwards confirmed to us so clearly, both inwardly and by a remarkable combination of circumstances, that no doubt it was possible.

Margaret's mother had just died, freeing them to go, but Harold's health was still uncertain and CMS would not hear of sending him out, particularly as they wanted to take their six children with them. Mary was sickly and the doctors warned that she was unlikely to live to reach Uganda though Veronica was strong enough to go. Margaret would not think of separating the twins and arranged for them to be cared for by Mary's godmother. Peter was at Monkton Combe Junior School and would keep an eye on them. Despite the wrench, they believed that they would be well looked after and they only intended to go for two years. Their sense of call was such that they felt they must go, despite the disapproval of most of their family.

Years later Margaret described the winter of 1924-5,

when all our closest friends strongly opposed our going to Africa, when much loved members of my family threatened to (and afterwards actually did) ostracise us, when we were solemnly told by a very beloved friend in high office in Salisbury Square, that it would be for the good of CMS and even for the glory of God that we should give up this mad idea, when dear Dr Jack Cook warned us that we should shortly return "sadder and wiser" people.

They went for a few days to the Isle of Wight to pray and think the whole situation through. They were walking down a hill between Shanklin and Lake when Margaret turned to Harold, acting (as she describes it) as Eve with Adam.

"Shall we give it up?" she asked.

"Margaret, if we give it up of ourselves, we shall never have any happiness in life again."

Margaret wrote,

I knew in my heart he was right, even though to go meant turning our backs on what for me at least represented earthly happiness and gain, the bringing up of our children in the home of my childhood, as against the leaving of our twin babies then aged three years and our only boy. But the outstanding memory of those dark days is his quiet <u>certainty</u> (and that at least I share to the full) that this was GOD'S CALL and that <u>we</u> had no choice save to obey and leave the responsibility with God.

So, Combe Royal having been sold and their affairs put in order as best they could, on Thursday 25th June 1925, at their own expense, they boarded ship en route for Uganda, with their three elder daughters and governess. They took a vast amount of luggage with them, including a piano, all of which was conveyed by train from Mombasa to Kampala in Uganda, and then had to be carried to Kabale by lorry over very rough roads.

Margaret revelled in the adventure. She had a strong personality and her journals show her to be the ideal pioneering missionary. Once at Kabale, she set about making a home for them, organizing a classroom where the children could be taught, and unpacking their boxes where to her dismay she found many breakages which she attempted to repair. Harold was no handyman. His one attempt at carpentry, a stool, collapsed when Philippa sat on it, to the amusement of the whole family. So it was Margaret who made all the furniture for the house, constructing cupboards from a wooden frame to which were tacked African woven mats.

Harold meanwhile was soon immersed in learning the language. Dr Sharp had found a Christian who came from Rwanda to be his assistant. Samsoni Inyarubuga, was a cousin of the king of Rwanda, a Tutsi who spoke clear Kinyarwanda. He was a grandson of King Rutarindwa who had been defeated by King Musinga, and all his remaining supporters had fled to their lands in Bufumbira which were now part of South-West Uganda, then known as British Ruanda. At Mbarara in Ankole, Samsoni received a little education and was baptized a Christian. The British government then gave him a small chieftainship in Bufumbira. Here he slipped back into old habits of spirit and ancestor worship, practically renouncing his Christianity.

When Dr Sharp returned to Uganda, early in 1925, he went

to find Samsoni. After a long talk, Samsoni repented and renewed his Christian vows, but insisted that he could no longer continue as a chief, because his duties involved immersing himself in ancestor worship and the temptations were too great. Dr Sharp suggested he might like to help the new missionary who was coming to translate the Bible, and so began a long and fruitful partnership.

Left to himself, Harold would have spent all day poring over his books, doing a job that he loved, but probably making himself ill again in the process. This Margaret would not allow, hauling him out to walk round the gardens with her or play with the children.

Responsibilty in British Rwanda (Bufumbira)

Before long Harold was speaking the language better than any other missionary, and this brought a new challenge. Len Sharp asked him to take responsibility for the Bufumbira area of Uganda where they spoke Kinyarwanda, thus relieving Rev. Jack Warren of some of his vast area of supervision. The work would involve going round the district three or four times a year, for two or three weeks at a time, encouraging the readers there, listening to their problems, arbitrating in disputes and making sure that candidates had been properly prepared before baptizing them.

There were also deeper problems, described by Dr Stanley Smith and Dr Len Sharp in their booklet, *Ruanda's Redemption*, which made closer supervision an urgent need. "The first Christians to be baptized there fell into deeper and deeper sin, until even a charge of murder lay perilously near their door. This terrible example has been a blight upon the work during the last three years, and has caused many to stumble."

Harold was horrified at the idea of going to Bufumbira, despite the opportunity for immersing himself in the language. He had always shrunk from responsibility, having no confidence in himself apart from his books. However, when the bishop visited Kabale and also asked him to take this responsibility, he reluctantly agreed to visit to see what would be involved, provided Dr Sharp went with him on his first safari to show him the ropes.

While they were still discussing when they should go, a letter came from Gahini asking Harold to visit them and baptize their first eleven candidates. Pleased to get away from the idea of Bufumbira, Harold and Margaret began to prepare for their first safari, no easy task. It involved collecting together a team of porters, sorting out what each would carry, making sure that there was a headman to supervise them all and that there was sufficient food, tents etc. At last all was ready and in great excitement they were having lunch the day before they were due to leave when another letter arrived from Gahini. They had misunderstood. The candidates were only being prepared and were not ready for baptism.

In consternation, they took the letter round to Dr Sharp. What were they to do? The porters were all ready. Should they dismiss them? Dr Sharp suggested they go to Bufumbira instead, although he was unable to accompany them. Harold vetoed this, feeling that they desperately needed a holiday and he could not relax while facing the challenge of Bufumbira. Someone suggested that they go to Behungi, a place 8,400 feet up, with a glorious view of the whole of Bufumbira and right into Belgian Rwanda and the edge of the Belgian Congo. The snag was that Behungi was only a short day's march from Kisoro, the central station of Bufumbira.

"Surely you will not go so near, and not go into Bufumbira at all," someone said.

It was suggested that they go down to Kisoro for the Sunday so that Harold could take the services there.

"But there are many baptism candidates at Kisoro, who have been waiting a long time for someone to go down and baptize them," said someone else. "Oh Harold, if only you could go just for two or three days and examine and baptize them, it would be of real value to the work."

Harold spent a few minutes quietly thinking while the discussion continued. Suddenly he knew that this was of God. There were the porters, all ready. A place was available for them to have their first real holiday, which they all needed. If God was asking him to do this then he would give the strength and take the responsibility. "It might be," he wrote, "and assuredly it has so turned out, that this short visit among the Bufumbira Christians would give me the little bit of experience which I so badly needed before the regular visitation, and give me the needed confidence so that I could set out without feeling I was going into the unknown." As always, once he felt that it was of God, he obeyed.

It was a wonderful time. To Margaret's disappointment, and Harold's relief, although they could smell the elephants they did not actually see more than their footprints. For two days they rested in the beautiful Behungi Camp with marvellous views, although they found it very cold. While the children played and Margaret sketched, Harold and Samsoni translated the communion service and revised the adult baptism service in the Anglican Book of Common Prayer. At last they descended the 2,000 feet into the Bufumbira plain.

On the way to Kisoro they were met by the teacher of one small church, and turned aside so that Harold could hold a little service and say a few words. "It brought a lump into one's throat to hear the Christian hymn from that line of readers," Harold wrote, "and to know that they were looking to me, humanly speaking, for help. This teacher is very keen, and his readers are keen too, it was a most cheering church to visit."

At Kisoro he questioned some 52 adults as to their understanding of the Christian faith, discussed doubtful cases with the teacher and ended up baptizing 42 on Sunday. He also dealt with some discipline problems. After a few more days of real rest by a lovely nearby lake, they returned to Kabale with Harold feeling that he had gained the necessary confidence to supervise this area of Uganda.

Bible translation

Before they had left for Uganda, Harold had spent time at the British and Foreign Bible Society headquarters in London. There he had discovered that there already was a version of the four gospels translated by a German missionary, K. Roehl of Bethel Bielefeld Mission, and printed in 1913. Roehl had written to the Bible Society after the war saying that his Mission had been expelled from Rwanda, but he still wished to translate the whole New Testament. This would not be possible from Europe, so he asked the Bible Society to consider sending him back to Rwanda to continue this work. They felt it would not be politically expedient for them to send a German to what was now

Belgian territory, but several letters had shown the need for a translation. The Belgian missionaries in Rwanda did not have the necessary expertise, so the Bible Society was delighted to learn that Harold had offered to go to Uganda for this purpose. They urged him to co-operate fully with the Belgian missionaries who had taken over the old German stations.

In Kabale, Harold used this German translation of the four gospels into Kinyarwanda as a means of learning the language. He would sit down with Samsoni in their office. In front of Samsoni would be the Bible in Lunyoro and Luganda, both languages of Uganda but kindred languages to Kinyarwanda, the language of Rwanda, together with the four gospels. Harold would have his Greek New Testament. He would tell Samsoni where they had reached last time and Samsoni would begin to translate into Kinyarwanda the next verse, frequently stopping to say, "The Luganda and Lunyoro say so-and-so, but the Lunyaruanda says so-and-so, what does the Lugiriki (Greek) say?" Samsoni spoke no English and Harold would try to explain with signs and gestures what the two alternatives meant and then decide which most nearly represented the Greek. Samsoni would then give the Kinyarwanda. Sometimes the translation given was not at all what was in the Greek and then, in halting Kinyarwanda, Harold would try to explain what the original meant. Often they had to leave it for a time, but a day or so later Samsoni would come up with the right phrase. Harold recorded, "This is the most delightful work, I have never in my life enjoyed myself so much." As he learnt each new word he would write it down, forming a dictionary, and great was his joy when he discovered new tenses and classes, which he wrote in a grammar.

He found that Samsoni had difficulty in understanding the German translation of the four gospels. At first, he thought that this was because they had been written with the help of Hutu translators. He thought that the Hutu and Tutsi had different dialects, but as he came to know the language and country better, he discovered that this was not the case. Both tribes spoke the same language, with variations being regional rather than tribal. He decided to revise the four gospels, primarily as a means of learning the language. Before long he found that it was a really bad translation, being largely unintelligible to most Rwandans.

For example, in a letter to the Friends dated 11th October 1925, Harold wrote,

> Apart from very serious defects in grammar, a surprisingly large number of words, including many of the key words of the Gospel, such as "righteousness" and "devil" are hopelessly wrong. Some ludicrous mistakes have been made. Lunyaruanda does not express the word "our" in the phrase "our Father": it is necessary to say "Father of us all" if it is desired to emphasize the universal Fatherhood of God. But if the word "our" is put in, it has the unlooked-for effect of turning "father", into "uncle". So in the present Gospels we read words which mean "uncle who art in heaven".

At the end of May 1926 they finally went to Gahini, leaving Samsoni in Kabale as it was still considered too dangerous for him to venture into Rwanda. The journey was on foot with a team of porters carrying everything on their heads. The rivers were flooded and several bridges washed away which involved long detours, so it was with some relief that they finally reached Gahini. There he baptized the first eleven candidates, whom he describes as "splendidly prepared and deeply in earnest". He adds that it was "a thrilling moment, that baptism service in the open air in front of our tent, when those eleven young lives were solemnly dedicated to the service of the Lord Jesus".

After a few days at Gahini, they set out to visit other churches in Belgian Rwanda. Wherever they stopped, they would play their records on the safari gramophone.

> The people enjoyed enormously the laughing records, and one which gives the voices of various animals. But there were also hymn records, which gave one an opportunity of explaining them, and telling the story of the love and saving power of the Lord Jesus to the crowd: I always found that they listened eagerly, and I am sure that there are very great possibilities in Ruanda, but the direct evangelism by the European is essential at the present stage.

Harold also tried reading passages of his version of Mark's gospel to see whether it was understood. He asked the people to criticize freely, and especially to tell him if there was any word which they did not know. To his delight, he found that even the most critical audience was able to understand what he had written. "Of course this only means the Lunyaruanda is good (which it ought to be, coming from Samsoni), but a native audience would not detect errors in representing the true sense of the original," he wrote.

Missionary co-operation

Harold tried to gain the co-operation of the other missionaries in Rwanda, both Germans and Belgians. They were using the four gospels perfectly happily. Not unnaturally, they wondered who this young man thought himself to be, that he should dare to consider his translation to be better. He was living outside the country, and had been in Africa for only a year. Despairingly, in February 1927 he wrote to the Bible Society saying he did not think he would ever be accepted by the other missionaries, and requested that they print a tentative version of Mark's gospel. This could be circulated in Rwanda and hopefully it would speak for itself. The Bible Society agreed to print Mark, but asked Mr Roome of the East African Bible Society to convene a conference with the other missionaries from Rwanda, together with Harold and Margaret, to discuss their differences. They had just heard from England that the twins were experiencing problems, but reluctantly agreed to stay on for the conference, then return to England in August, intending to come back the following year.

This conference took place from 11th to 19th April 1927 at Kirinda, a Belgian Protestant mission station in Rwanda. Present were representatives of the Belgian Protestant Mission, the Seventh Day Adventists, Harold and Margaret from CMS, and a number of Africans as their assistants, all under the chairmanship of Mr Roome. The first two days were very difficult. In a letter to the Bible Society, Harold described how they discussed various problems of orthography and principles of translation. "Although personally very kind," he wrote, "the other members of the conference evidently regarded me as a person who not only knew very little but thought he knew a great deal, and they seemed strongly prejudiced from the outset against anything I might say."

Several times, Mr Roome advised him to give way or the

conference would go nowhere. On the second day, the atmosphere began to change and soon they were having very profitable discussions. On the final day, Harold and Margaret were asked to leave the room for a time. They returned in some trepidation but were amazed to hear M. Durand of the Belgian Protestant Mission make a speech in which he said that he believed that Harold was God's special gift to Rwanda, and expressing their unreserved confidence in his translating ability. He asked that they consider spending a part of each year in Rwanda and offered him a home at Remera, the Belgian Presbyterian Mission.

Mr Roome returned to Kenya where he sent a cable to the Bible Society in London: "RWANDA CONFERENCE COMPLETELY SUCCESSFUL. IF MARK UNPRINTED AWAIT REVISIONS."

This cable caused some irritation at the Bible Society who had only agreed to an early printing of Mark in response to urgent pleas from Harold. They stopped the printing process although they felt that it was too far advanced to do alterations. A month later Harold's letter arrived and he made it clear that revisions would be substantial and there was still a need for the printing. Probably he was hoping that some of the orthography decisions that he had given way on during the first day could be reversed by the sub-committee which had been appointed to discuss his translation.

The conference had urged Harold to do all he could to complete the translation of Luke and John before returning to Europe. It was hoped that during the year that the Guillebauds expected to be in England, the sub-committee would read all four gospels and criticize them so that there could be a further revision conference soon after his return.

A passage was booked for Harold and Margaret to return to England from Mombasa on 3rd September 1927. When they arrived in Bath, they found that the twins, Mary and Veronica, were rather withdrawn, and Peter, who had visited as often as he could from his nearby school, reported his horror at finding that at six years old they did not even know their alphabet. Harold and Margaret both felt it right to return to Africa the following May, this time with the whole family. They were determined to keep all the girls with them as far as possible, and, although they knew that Peter would eventually need to continue his schooling in England, they felt he would benefit from a year in Africa, provided Harold gave him a little help in his education. Peter's relationship with his parents, however, never totally recovered from this separation at an early stage of his life. He always felt slightly apart from the rest of the family.

During their eight months in England, Harold spent time in further discussions at the Bible Society, and with experts in African languages, W. A. Crabtree and Professor Westerman. Harold was anxious not to go against the spirit of the Kirinda agreements, yet he was unhappy about some of the decisions on orthography, and wanted other opinions. He and Margaret went to Belgium as the guests of M. Anet, the head of the Belgian Protestant Mission, who approved of the fact that he was seeking expert advice. M. Anet was delighted to build a house for them at Remera. He made them thoroughly welcome and even arranged an exhibition of Margaret's African sketches at the Belgian colonial office.

Finally in May 1928 the whole family set off back to Uganda, taking with them this time a large station wagon which proved to be invaluable on their safaris.

Chapter 2

Bible Translation (1928-1932)

Early history of Rwanda

The Africa that my grandparents knew was very different from the country I now live in. I once asked my father what his most vivid memory of that time was and he said "the noise of skins rubbing against each other as people walked", for only the wealthiest had clothes made of European cloth.

The people of Rwanda were divided into three groups, with the king over all. The Tutsi were proud and aristocratic, for the most part with fine features and very tall, with their hair cut so that it accentuated their height; the Hutu tended to be shorter, with flatter, more negroid noses; and the Twa were pygmoid. Although they are called tribes, they should rather have been divided on class lines, as cattle-herders, cultivators and hunters. There was much intermarrying and movement between the first two groups, though the Twa were despised by the others as "non-people". Any Hutu who became wealthy or who rendered a special service to the king could be "tutsified".

It is important to remember that although there were several chiefs and sub-chiefs who ruled the country under the king, together with an elite of the wealthier Tutsi, there was also a large majority of poor and downtrodden Tutsi as well as wealthy Hutu. It was only at the time of the census ordered by the Belgians in 1933 that their tribes became fixed, with anyone who owned more than ten cows being regarded as Tutsi. Thereafter the tribe followed the father's line and there could be no further movement between tribes. It was these identity cards that were the means of identifying Tutsi at the infamous barriers where hundreds were slaughtered during the genocide.

The physical characteristics of the different tribes fitted in with theories of racial supremacy current in Europe at the end of the previous century, and many Europeans, missionaries included, assumed that the Tutsi, with finer features, were superior to the Hutu. Right through the early writings of the mission there was a perception that the Tutsi were the natural leaders, intelligent and active, and that the Hutu were passive servants: indeed they were sometimes described as slaves. The Twa were hardly ever mentioned. This view of Tutsi supremacy was only partially broken down during Revival which began in 1936.

John Hanning Speke, who camped on the river Kagera in 1861 but never crossed it into Rwanda, was the first to propound the theory that the Tutsi were superior to the Hutu. He wrote that the rulers of the various kingdoms in the Great Lakes region of Africa must have come from a conquering race, and brought a superior civilization. In chapter 9 of his *Journal of the Discovery of the Source of the Nile* (London, 1863), without a shred of evidence, according to Gerard Prunier, he decided that these conquerors had migrated south, probably from Ethiopia. This idea was taken up by other explorers and European missionaries until it was accepted as fact (*Rwanda Crisis*, Prunier, London, 1995; p 7). The theory had an impact on the Rwandans themselves since the Tutsi began to see themselves as "born to rule" even if they were thoroughly disadvantaged, and the Hutu developed a massive inferiority complex which made them very resentful of even the poorest Tutsi.

The statement that the Tutsi were descended from the Ethiopians, or indeed that they migrated from any other country, is a matter for some debate in scholarly circles today, but it was this belief that led to thousands of Tutsi being thrown by Hutu into the Nyabarongo River during the genocide of 1994 so that they could "return to Ethiopia".

Most modern historians agree that the monarchy arose from a Tutsi clan called Nyiginya which achieved political supremacy over central Rwanda, gradually extending their sphere of influence over several centuries, until by the time the first European explorers reached Rwanda, they were in control of most of modern-day Rwanda, although there were several Hutu princedoms, mainly in the north and west of the country, which were autonomous and resisted this central rule.

After Speke, the next European contact with Rwanda was in 1875, when Stanley tried to cross the Kagera but was greeted by a hail of arrows. In 1884, when the Conference of Berlin met to apportion African land among the European Powers, Rwanda and Burundi were allocated to Germany with Tankanyika, even though, as yet, no European had set foot in Rwanda.

The Germans finally entered the country in 1897 and found it administratively easier to rule through the king and his chiefs, and they insisted that the Hutu princedoms be incorporated into Tutsi rule. In 1912, less than ten years before the start of the Ruanda Mission, there was open revolt in Ruhengeri and Byumba areas, which was defeated by the king, with the assistance of the Germans, and many Hutu were slaughtered afterwards. Although they were defeated, they submitted with a deep sense of grievance, never fully accepting Tutsi rule. They also tended to despise the Hutu from the south whom they considered inferior because they had accepted Tutsi rule whereas it had been forced upon the northerners. This became a factor of some importance in the genocide as many of the *interahamwe* were northerners supporting the northern president, and many Hutu from the south, who had formed political parties in opposition to him, were killed on the first day of the genocide.

The Germans had arrived in Rwanda shortly after the death of King Kigeri IV Rwabugiri who had succeeded in conquering much of central Rwanda. There was no clear system of succession, and he had nominated one of his sons, Rutarindwa, as heir to the throne, with one of his wives, Kanjogera, as queen mother. She was not Rutarindwa's mother and was soon plotting, with her brother Kabera, a powerful chief, to have her own son as king. Within a year of the old king's death they had killed the young king and most of his supporters in a battle near Shyogwe, and in his place proclaimed her son as King Yuhi V. Musinga. It was then that Samsoni Inyarubuga, Harold's translator, fled to Uganda. The new king, Musinga, was only a lad at the time, and for years his mother, Kanjogera, was the real power in Rwanda. When the Belgians took over as the colonial power from the Germans, they found Musinga rather a thorn in the flesh. He never accepted them nor did he ever accept Catholicism and they finally deposed him in 1931 in favour of his son Rudahigwa who was French-speaking and already baptized as a Roman Catholic. Musinga went into exile in Congo with some of his chiefs, and there he died.

My grandmother's journals contain a fascinating description of her family visit to the Tutsi court at Nyanza. She describes Musinga as "a giant even among this race of giants, for he is about seven feet high." She adds that, about thirty years before her visit,

> Musinga's power was every bit as absolute as that of the old kings of Uganda. Many are the hundreds of unfortunate people who have been put to death at his orders, often to gratify some trifling whim or merely to show his kingly power. Indeed one of the Ruanda proverbs runs thus: "He who goes to court need not make provision for his cattle", the idea being that his heirs will see to all that as he is not likely to return. And the forms of death provided by his royal highness were by no means specially merciful. One of the last occasions when he used this power, which of course was taken from him under Belgian rule, was to punish someone who had robbed the mails (this was towards the close of the period of German rule when the king was still in supreme command over his people) and for this offence which might well have been met by a fine or a flogging, the luckless man was impaled alive. One of the king's great grievances against European rule is that they have deprived him of this power of life and death, for what is a king worth who cannot do as he will with his subjects.

The Guillebauds return to Africa

Margaret and Harold returned to Africa in June 1928 accompanied by all six of their children. Margaret had been quite ill on the voyage, and they needed time in Kampala for her to recover before the long journey to Kabale. The older girls were wildly excited to be back, and eagerly pointed out familiar sights and remembered landmarks to their brother and younger sisters.

In Kampala they arranged for two cars to take the whole family and their luggage to Kabale. Harold went ahead with Rev. Lawrence Barham who had travelled out just before them, together with the luggage, and Margaret drove the second car, with the family. Some distance away from Kabale she met M. Monnier of the Seventh Day Adventists in Rwanda. They stopped and had a long chat. To her dismay she heard that all was not well with the gospel revision. One of the sub-committee members, M. Durand from the Belgian Mission, was saying that he had been forced to concur with the conference decisions. Apparently he agreed with older missionaries that the existing four gospels were perfectly adequate and there was no need for a new translation. They were continuing to use them despite the fact that many Rwandans could not understand them and those who had read the newly-printed Mark infinitely preferred it. M. Monnier himself had been very busy and unable to revise the gospels sent to him. He was on his way back to Europe and would not be returning for another 18 months.

Harold was very discouraged when he heard her report and immediately wrote to the Bible Society and to M. Anet in Belgium seeking their advice. Mr Roome wrote encouraging him to continue with the translation but saying, "Every quality of tact and diplomacy which you possess should be put into action to secure the friendly co-operation of the other missionaries, especially those who have been so much longer in the field than yourself."

M. Anet wrote saying that M. Honoré of Remera was interested in working with Harold and would he visit and see what could be arranged. So a safari into Rwanda was planned, taking with them the older children but leaving the twins at Kabale. Peter was very excited at this, his first safari, which, unlike others, began by car with the porters going ahead with the bulk of the luggage.

The roads were not much better than cart tracks and it was not possible to make much speed but it was quicker than walking. Almost before they knew it, they were climbing the long hill to Gatsibo where fellow missionary, Captain Geoffrey Holmes, was now living in a simple African hut. When the early missionaries had first entered Rwanda, Gatsibo was a government post and Geoff had made his base there while he explored the surrounding area before finally deciding that Gahini, on beautiful Lake Muhazi, would be the best site for a hospital. He had been accompanied on that first visit by Kosiya Shalita who was returning to his home for the first time since his family had had to flee when he was a child. Captain Holmes had returned to Gatsibo when a new missionary, Dr Joe Church, had arrived at Gahini in June 1928, so as to leave him a free hand with the hospital. Legend says that he shared the hut with his motor-bike and a pig! His original hut can still be seen near the parish church at Gatsibo. The family spent the night there and then set off on foot, thinking that the road further on would be no good. In fact they regretted this when they found that there was now a road all the way to Nyanza in the south.

Eventually they arrived at Remera, feeling very uncertain as to what M. Honoré's attitude would be since he had said very little at the Kirinda conference. However, they need not have worried, as Margaret wrote in her journal:

> We had originally planned to spend ten days or so at the outside, thinking that even if he was willing to give a certain amount of help that would be amply long enough, but when we arrived we found that although he is a very busy man, quite singlehanded with many out-stations to look after, yet he was so keen about the translation that he had put everything aside and was prepared to give up the whole of his time and wished to go carefully through the four Gospels, verse by verse, with a chosen band of natives to help. And you will easily see that that is a pretty big task. Anyway the net result was that we stayed a fortnight, during which time they went through Matthew and Mark, working often eight to nine hours a day, never stopping except for meals. After that M. Honoré said he would be obliged to break off to arrange his work etc, but he was very keen as, needless to say, was Harold to finish, and that if we would wait he would be willing to give the necessary time.

They returned to Kabale for four days where they learned that M. Durand had resigned from the sub-committee and M. Honoré had been appointed by M. Anet in Belgium, so that it was in high spirits that they went back to Remera, this time travelling the whole way by car. Margaret was thrilled to realize that she was the first British driver to go further south than Kigali. Her pioneering spirit was very much in evidence as they crossed the Nyabarongo River:

> First of all of course we had the crossing of the Nyabarongo to negotiate, no easy matter. To start with the ferry pontoon is merely made of two canoes lashed together with a few boards across and is so short that there is considerable danger that in driving one's car on one will go off into the water on the opposite side. Also the approach is at such an angle that it is next to impos-

sible to get the back wheels straight with the front ones, and when you have only a couple of planks to drive along that is a matter of no little importance. As it was I got one of my back wheels off the plank and had a good deal of difficulty in getting on at all, but M Honoré being there made all the difference as he could tell me exactly what to do. Then too one must get sufficiently into the middle of the raft not to overbalance. Eventually the raft is pulled hand over hand across the river on a steel cable, very hard work for the current is frightfully swift, the river incidentally teems with crocs which adds to the excitement, though I've never actually seen one. The opposite shore is an almost precipitous sandbank and the only way of getting off is to have the car dragged up by ropes, with the danger that the pullers thereof will fall down or let go or something at the critical moment. Altogether it is a somewhat hair-raising job.

By the time I was growing up in Rwanda, a bridge had been built across the Nyabarongo near Kigali, but I remember several crossings of rivers on ferries similar to the one Margaret described here. Journeys were always adventures, though not so dangerous as in those earlier days. Often passengers had to get out and walk to relieve the weight in the car. Once on a hill near Byumba, Margaret missed her gear and suddenly the car began to slide backwards, gaining speed as it went. Seeing that it was heading towards a steep drop, Harold said to Peter, "She's dead, she must be", but somehow she kept her head and managed to steer the car until it came to a standstill.

The family stayed at Remera for a month while Harold and M. Honoré did a complete revision of all the work thus far translated. Harold was delighted at the way they worked together. They also chose a site, with a wonderful view, for a small house to be built for them so that they could have their own place for what looked like being frequent trips to Remera.

The royal court

It was during this time that they visited the court at Nyanza for the second time. Although Margaret realized what a cruel man the king had been, by the time they met him he was older and half blind and he gave them a royal welcome. The king and his chiefs were all in brightly coloured robes consisting of a skirt, in red or yellow or blue, with a long white cloth wound Grecian fashion over their shoulders. Although the family was tired after driving fifty miles, they were immediately taken to see a display of drills.

All the boys of the big government school in their white robes, for they do not discard the national dress in their schools as we do, were lined up and went through most graceful exercises. One was a Belgian sword drill, an extraordinarily graceful exercise, done in this case with sticks. Then there was throwing the spear, and after that shooting with bows and arrows, and the distances they were able to send both spears and arrows were amazing.

This was followed by high jumping, with the Rwandans taking off from small ant hills. Once they had completed the jumping, Harold went to stand beside the posts and found to his amazement that the crossbar was well above his head and that these schoolboys of between 12 and 17 had been jumping about seven feet, once the height of the ant hill had been taken into consideration.

Following the display of sports they were taken to the palace where they saw a display of *intore* dancers. Sitting on either side of the king, with the children at their feet, they watched entranced.

They are specially trained, and begin at quite an early age, you always find one or more quite small boys amongst the troupe, copying the others and usually very funny. This time there was a darling kid not more than seven or eight years old. He had a bow and arrow instead of the spear carried by the rest. [...] The "dance" consists of endless movements, usually beginning from a distance and coming nearer and nearer to the king, or else as in this case beginning close to the throne and then going gradually away and ending up close to the front again. Almost every movement ends with a terrific chattering from one to the other in very shrill tones, probably some kind of war cry as these are war dances, and the movements themselves consist mainly of rhythmic stamping and springing into the air, while the spears are waved round and round the head. Now and again one or other comes to the front and executes a *pas seul* as it were to excite the rest. The whole effect is bizarre and weird in the extreme and yet extraordinarily rhythmical. One only wonders how on earth they escape knocking one another down.

The onlookers were equally interested in them and especially with the children. Peter scored a real hit when he started imitating animal noises and even getting the neighbouring cocks to respond to his crowing. King Musinga was so pleased that he gave Peter the title *Bwana isaki*, "Lord of the fowls", which they were told was a tremendous honour. "After this we went in state to call on the queen mother, a real old villain who must have the blood of hundreds on her hands." They had with them a brown doll which Margaret had dressed in national dress, making for it the high towering *masunzu* hairstyle of the Tutsi. Very reluctantly, for the twins loved it, this doll was presented to the queen mother, who was delighted with it.

The next day Margaret was asked to take her car up for the queen mother to see it. Her journal gives a fascinating picture of life for a high class Tutsi woman at that time.

Like all the Batutsi women she lives almost a "purdah" life and must never be seen by outsiders, only certain men are privileged to be allowed into her presence. The interior of the royal hut like all other huts, is practically pitch dark. When you have been in there for sometime and your eyes get accustomed to the light, it becomes possible to see a certain amount, but imagine living nearly all one's life like that. When she comes out for any purpose, either to go to a different hut or to see anything, everyone is chased out of the courtyard and a mat is held in front of the gateway, while another beautifully woven mat is held carefully round her so that she walks as it were wrapped up from the outer gaze. On this occasion when she found that it was quite impossible for me to get the car through the gateway into the "urugo" (enclosure), the entrance being only a couple of feet wide at the most, she actually dispensed with the covering mat, and, after the court had been entirely cleared of everyone except the king himself, she hobbled right down to the gate leaning on my arm. I did wish I could have had a photo. She was dressed in her state headdress, a very high affair made of goatskin with a sort of tail standing up about a foot high and a fringe of white beads entirely covering her face. On her legs she wears masses of anklets made of woven fibre or bamboo, so many that they are like high gaiters coming right over the knee and make walking quite a difficulty. I brought the car as close as I could to the gateway, and she and her ladies pressed close to the mat and poked their fingers through so as to be able to see. I then suggested that she would probably like to see it close to, and we got a number of mats held all round the car like a wall and I tried for a very long while to get her into the car but with no success as she simply couldn't get up the step because of these anklets. She was quite disappointed as I had planned to put up mats all round the windows and take her for a drive.

As I was reading this description I remembered a man I used to know at Shyogwe who had inadvertently seen the queen mother and had had his eyes put out as a result. He was a leader in the revolution that overthrew the monarchy and Tutsi rule in 1959 and one could hardly be surprised. Musinga had a reputation of careless disregard for the life of his subjects and many acts of cruelty are attributed to him. Apparently someone in Uganda asked a missionary if Jesus had been crucified by the Rwandans, since impaling was a favourite form of execution of Musinga.

Peter returns to England

In January 1929 Harold and Margaret took Peter and the three older girls for a trip round Uganda to give Peter something to remember when he returned to England. They had a wonderful trip round the Ruwenzori mountains and Lake Edward, ending up in Kampala where one Saturday afternoon Peter and Rosemary were confirmed in the Hannington chapel of Namirembe Cathedral. Margaret described it as

> a beautiful little service and they both looked so nice. Rosemary has grown into such a tall girl and looks very sweet with her long mane of fair hair. She looks much older than Peter, and he gets very disgusted at being asked about his elder sister. She is very nearly as tall as I am already. It was so nice having their Confirmation at such a time and they were able to go to their first Communion at Makindye on the Sunday morning.

Peter remembered it somewhat differently. He had not wanted to be confirmed since he was not yet sure of his beliefs, but Rosemary was very eager and his mother so keen that they should both make their promises at the same time, with their parents present, that reluctantly he gave in, but as a result felt consumed by guilt since he could not keep the promises he had made. Back in England he shared a study at school with Harold

Adeney and had many discussions about faith with him. Eventually Harold told him that it was not a matter of trying to do your best to keep a set of rules; rather it was a case of recognizing that you are a sinner, but that Jesus had died to take your sin, and he would enable you to follow him. The peace that Peter felt as he relinquished his struggle and handed his life over to his Lord was something he never forgot, nor his gratitude to Harold who became his oldest and dearest friend. Years later Harold travelled out with him to work as a doctor primarily in Burundi but also Rwanda.

The New Testament is completed

Meanwhile, the Guillebauds continued life in Kabale. Harold spent his days translating with Samsoni, while Margaret made a home for her children. They made friends with the children of the Stanley Smiths and shared their governess with them. Periodically they would make a safari to Remera to do revision with M. Honoré. On one occasion Lindesay was badly bitten by his dog and the wound turned gangrenous. During her illness they thought she would die but with careful nursing and much prayer she pulled through.

Despite certain reservations over changes Harold had made, with M. Honoré's agreement, to decisions taken at the Kirinda conference, M. Monnier of the Adventists was anxious to get the new gospels into print as soon as possible. He had made some objections whilst in Switzerland, but once he returned to Rwanda in June 1928 revision continued well.

On 5th March 1930, less than five years after Harold had sailed for Uganda knowing no Kinyarwanda, the first draft of the New Testament was completed. Harold called Margaret to hear the last few verses of Revelation being translated. They had a special thanksgiving service in church when both the newly-arrived gospels, and the rest of the manuscript of the New Testament were solemnly dedicated to God. Margaret commented, "It was a moment worth all that it has ever cost for us to be here."

They went to Remera for the first revision, expecting it to be too great a task to be completed at one visit.

However, to everyone's utter amazement and joy, the whole thing was finished in ten days, as most of the epistles went straight through with barely a comment, M. Honoré and his people simply saying that the Lunyaruanda was so good it needed no alteration. And that for a translation which is done in the first place out of the country. We do indeed realise it is due to all the prayer that has been backing it up.

However, in August 1930 there was another time of anxiety necessitating another conference between M. Monnier, M. Honoré and Harold over issues of real disagreement, particularly over Adventist theology. Various changes were agreed and the conference concluded amicably. Harold wrote,

> M. Monnier's attitude has been most helpful, he could easily have made things most difficult and caused very grave delays, but he has taken the line that the thing he wants above all else is to get the New Testament out as soon as possible, and therefore, while he has presented his criticisms and argued strongly for them, he has made it clear that his support of the translation was not conditional on their acceptance.

Then came the long hard business of checking the translation. The whole manuscript was read aloud in the school at Kabale, seeking criticisms. It was also read to Samsoni who was very critical. Before the days of word processors, Margaret labouriously had to type all criticisms and alterations, which was a very lengthy job. Then she and all the children took turns to read the whole New Testament slowly in English so that Harold could compare and check that no word or sentence had been omitted or that any turn of expression had not got its full value. The twins, Mary and Veronica, were really excited the day they were told that their reading was good enough to help in this task. These notes had again to be checked with M. Honoré before the final fair copy was re-typed for the printer.

Margaret had copied the smaller epistles on the Gestetner, and they put a very small edition straight on to the market. Although it was expensive, it sold well. She wrote,

> Even this is a good deal of work, as each Epistle takes me nearly 24 hours steady work (I mean actual hours) including the binding.

For the latter I am using old wall papers, of which luckily I had brought out odd pieces left over from Combe Royal. Little did we ever think when Father used to put away all the spare pieces so carefully into a trunk in the attic, how they would eventually be used. I came across them turning out and thought they might be useful for the children so shoved them into a packing case as stuffing, and now scraps of them are flooding Ruanda.

Finally, on 27th November 1931 Harold wrote, "The New Testament is here!! It arrived at the end of October. The fact is of course known to you, but I doubt if you can realize what the fact means out here. I had not dared to hope that it would come so soon, and so it came as a delightful surprise." It had arrived at the end of October and he had immediately sent a few copies to Joe Church, the doctor who had arrived at Gahini in June 1928 about the same time as the Guillebauds had arrived back in Kabale, and to Dora Skipper, the headmistress of the girls' school who had come to Gahini after several years as a missionary in Uganda. He received a letter from Dora in the next mail telling of her delight at seeing the New Testament: "she had but spoken the word 'Isezerano Rishya' (New Testament) when the workmen on the roof came hurrying down the ladders in great joy and excitement: but woeful was the disappointment when it was found that there were no copies for sale."

Harold had found it surprisingly difficult to find the porters to send a large consignment.

Then suddenly the idea occurred to us that surely we were justified in going down to Gahini in the car with a load of books, so that we might have the great joy, as the crowning happiness of six years, of seeing the New Testament in the hands of the real Banyaruanda, most of whom could read no language but their own. The very next day (Saturday November 7) we started off, and arrived at Gahini at dusk. We were greeted with joy by the Banyaruanda who happened to be about when we arrived, and that night, as we were dining with Dr Church, his boys came in and lined up in a row, as house-boys do when they have a petition. Their request was that they might be allowed to buy New Testaments at once, as they could not go to sleep without them.

The next day was Sunday but they felt justified at selling "the Lord's own Book on the Lord's own Day". Over 100 books were sold before the service, and as the books were being sold, many of the purchasers went off and began to read aloud to a little group of eager listeners.

> Altogether it was an experience not to be forgotten. Then came the service, held in the church, although it was not really ready for use, and piles of bricks had to be moved out of the way earlier in the morning. Dr Church estimated that 1000 people were present, although as I have said there had been no notice of anything out of the ordinary. I preached on "The sword of the Spirit which is the Word of God", and we had three lessons from the New Testament, the third being the "armour passage" from Ephesians, read in the pulpit before the sermon. Then we had another equally crowded service in the afternoon, after which those who wished to go departed, but nearly all stayed, while I read from *The Pilgrim's Progress* for over an hour. In the evening a happy and memorable day was finished with a service in the Hospital: and next day we returned, having lost only one day and a half from the translation work.

Medical and evangelistic safaris

During the various safaris to Remera the family used to go through Gahini where, during 1928-9, famine had the country in its grip. Dr Joe Church paints a vivid picture of those years in his book *Quest for the Highest* where he describes people dying by the roadside, and his utter despair that there was so little he could do. That famine brought him to the end of his resources and caused him to seek God in a new way. In 1929, he had brought the famine to the attention of the international community who responded with food aid, and the Belgian government were spurred to build roads and so open up the country for the food-producing areas to be more accessible.

On a safari with Dr Church which was described by Margaret as "the perfect trip, medical and evangelistic combined", she and Harold spent one night at the village of a chief Dr Church wanted to meet.

> We spent the night camped in the long grass a stone's throw or so from this chief's hut. It really was great fun. Dr C had a tiny one-

man tent which he pitched in front of the car and H and I slept in the car, which makes an excellent bedroom, mosquito net and all. Washing in the morning is the only difficulty, at least for me as I can't strip in the open like the men, but have to manage as best I can. We had a very jolly supper by firelight and then sent word to the chief and his friends to come along, and after a little gramophone and chat, H read to them from the newly arrived gospels. Oh the joy of having those gospels, you need to have done without to know it. He chose the story of the Woman of Samaria, and it was simply fascinating to watch the effect on these folk of hearing it in their own tongue for the first time. They were enthralled and when it came to our Lord telling her that she had spoken truly "he whom thou now hast is not thine husband, thou hast had five husbands" one of them turned to his friend and slapped his shoulder and said "Yampay'inka Data" (lit. "My father gave me a cow" their way of expressing extreme amazement or surprise). It was all so new. After that they started asking questions and gradually got on to the ever-present question of the R.C. teaching. They brought forward lots of R.C. arguments which H answered. They were particularly struck with the words he quoted from the Magnificat "in God my Saviour". The idea that Mary herself saw her need of a Saviour impressed them at once. It was a wonderful evening. I got sleepy at last and went to bed in the dark while they were still talking.

In those days before Vatican II, relationships between the Roman Catholics and the embryo Protestant Church were not easy. Margaret wrote: "There is real persecution in this part of Ruanda, chiefs find themselves turned out of their hills and absolutely ostracized by the government if they dare to favour the Protestants." As a result, Harold wrote a booklet outlining the Protestant arguments which he called *One Mediator*. Following Vatican II when the strained relationships had eased, this booklet was revised, taking out some of the contentious material, and it is still a useful discussion book.

To keep his hand in with the translating while the revision work was going on, Harold had started translating *The Pilgrim's Progress*, which he loved, considering it to be the gospel acted out. He found that it appealed to the African mentality and he was delighted with the number of metaphors and proverbs that Samsoni produced which exactly expressed the meaning of Bunyan's allegory of the Christian life. This book, which was completed in October 1933, became much loved, with the characters as familiar as the Bible characters. For years it was the only Christian book printed in Kinyarwanda.

The safaris that they went on with Dr Church were wonderful times when Margaret would go "sketching" as she called it, while the doctor treated patients, and Harold would chat with the elders, reading from his gospels or manuscript of the epistles, preaching, but also learning more local idioms in the language.

Margaret was an accomplished painter, having taken lessons in her youth from her cousin, Lionel Edwards, RA. One story of her determination to paint comes from Innsbruck when she was about 17. She wished to paint in the abbey, and had her easel all set up when the mother superior came to stop her.

"No one may paint in here without permission," she said.

"Well, who can I get permission from?" asked Margaret.

"Only the emperor."

Undaunted, Margaret returned to her hotel and wrote to the emperor asking permission to paint in the abbey. Later, an envelope was received: "To the well-born Miss Edwards" from the palace, giving her permission to paint where she wished. That letter is now a treasured family possession! Her many paintings give a fascinating commentary on life in Rwanda at that time.

Those safari journeys could have their hair-raising times. One day they went to a village where a man-eating lion had devastated the neighbourhood.

Chinsovu which is a well populated little village beautifully situated overlooking the shyamba [scrubland] on the road to Rukira, is simply becoming deserted like a village of the dead. We went to hut after hut, and in every one they showed us where the lions had entered. Here they had got a cow, there they had dragged it through a hole, we even found tufts of hair on the bushes. Here was a hut in ruins, all the people had been eaten, here a deserted hut whence they had fled and so on. And almost before dusk no one will stir out. Dr Church has been called for again and again to this village to try and get the lion. It was here where only the other day a man was taken while hoeing in broad daylight, a young strong fellow. The old chief told us almost with tears that all his people were being killed, hardly a week passes without the loss either of a man or of cows. He himself has sent away his wife and children for fear of the lions.

An old woman showed them her hut where there was a hole in the side and she described how the lion got his head through. She had taken her hoe and beaten him over the head till she drove him back. "'Like this I hit him,' she said, banging on the ground. And there on the bullet-shaped head of the instrument were the teeth marks of the lion. It was a scene one will not readily forget." They felt that they should do all they could to try to kill this lion and prepared a trap for it, camouflaging the car while Margaret and Joe sat in front with their guns. Harold was not interested and slept in the back!

It was quite eerie in the dead silence waiting and waiting, hearing the soft tread of various beasts as they came up to inspect us. However, as we had more than half expected, nothing happened. These man-eaters are awfully cunning, and although they are supposed to take no notice of things such as cars, yet one knew it was but an off chance. The creepy part was the feeling it might be anywhere quite close by, watching us.

The next night, they were on their way back to Gahini and felt it would be worth sitting up for another few hours in the same village, as it was by then three nights since the lion had last killed and it had been seen in the neighbourhood. They had their supper by the side of the car, watching the sun set rapidly in all its magnificence. When it was dark they turned on the lights of the car and discovered to their horror that they would not light!

So that ended all our plans, as one cannot shoot in the dark and we were dependent on the spotlight. But it meant finishing supper etc by firelight and all the while one had the creepy feeling that that old lion might be behind the next bush. I shan't forget that supper in a hurry.

Margaret was a good shot but would never go out for sport. She wrote in that same letter,

We feel very strongly that there is all the difference in the wide world between missionaries going big game hunting and running into real danger when it is not <u>necessary</u>, and between missionaries either hunting for food, or still more trying to destroy animals which are preying on the lives or property of the defenceless native, as in this case.

Shortly after this, Joe was trying to kill a leopard which was terrorizing the neighbourhood. His gun jammed after he had fatally wounded it. The animal jumped on his back and he was terribly mauled by it. Kosiya Shalita, who later became a missionary to Burundi and the first African clergyman in Rwanda, was with him and with great courage managed to haul the leopard physically off Joe until finally Joe was able to shoot it dead. Joe had been virtually scalped and was seriously injured in the back. Kosiya had never driven a motor-cycle but he managed to get Joe on to the bike and together they drove it back to Gahini, with Joe giving instructions! At Gahini they found Mrs Stanley Smith visiting and she was able to clean his wounds, but he needed a doctor so he was taken in a rickety lorry on a terrible journey to Kabale where he was finally hospitalized, and was seriously ill for some time.

Margaret's youngest daughter, Veronica, remembers one night at Remera when they heard a leopard roaming around coughing outside their small house. Suddenly the door crashed open. The children were terrified, expecting the leopard to come in. Margaret, however, calmly walked to the door and, going outside to get a hold of it, she pulled it shut, telling them that it was only the wind and there was nothing to worry about, although all the children knew that it was a leopard and were impressed at her bravery.

Visiting and hymn-singing

Despite the fact that her language was not good, Margaret enjoyed visiting round Kabale, taking Robert, her head houseboy as her interpreter. Margaret wrote,

It is appalling how much absolute heathenism there can be at one's very door. I went the other evening to a hut only a few hundred yards from one of the European houses. Here I found some small boys, and a woman or two, most of the men were out getting in their crops. They were very delighted with the gramophone and gathered round and chattered away. But none of them had ever been inside the church. They had never heard of Jesus Christ, and the idea of God as a Father was something quite new.

Years later, during the genocide, Simon-Pierre, the Scripture Union schools worker, looked at the gangs of killers nearby and said, "This is our fault. These are our neighbours. We knew the gospel of peace and we did not tell them."

Robert had come to them in 1925 with no knowledge of European ways, but he was a quick learner and soon picked up English from listening to the children talking. After five years he told Harold that he had passed the exam to go to Budo, the top secondary school in Uganda, saying that he wanted to be ordained. Harold said that if this was so he needed more grounding in the faith and suggested that he continue working for them for another 18 months while he taught him. Then when they left for England in 1932, Robert went to Budo, where he did extremely well. In 1929 he had married Eseri, the Stanley Smiths' nursemaid, and lived nearby. When he left Budo he was sent to Bufumbira as an evangelist.

On Sunday evenings Harold and Margaret continued their family practice of hymn-singing round the piano. One evening Margaret looked up and saw Robert standing at the doorway, and invited him and the rest of the staff to join in. Harold roughly translated each hymn as they sang and, after they had gone, tried to get the words to fit the tunes. Margaret then typed out the translated hymns, the children helping her by fastening them with paper clips so that more pages could be added as Harold translated another each week. So from the mixture of English and Kinyarwanda hymn-singing, the first hymn book was born. Years later, Peter was to compile the hymn book which is still in use throughout the country, incorporating those hymns translated by his father.

Soon Margaret invited other African workers on the station to join them on Sunday nights and this became a regular feature of their life, somewhat to the dismay of some of the other missionaries who disapproved of the idea of inviting "natives" into the living room. It was simply "not done". Those early missionaries were a product of their time and there was an unconscious arrogance of the white as superior to the black that comes over very strongly in their writings and is hard to read with our perceptions now. This was something which began to be broken in Revival. I remember the horror of some of my friends at school in Kenya when I talked of Africans coming into our home and sharing our meals. How I thank God that from my earliest childhood Africans were seen as friends, something that my father had learned from his parents.

Yet my grandmother, along with other missionary wives, attempted to create the atmosphere of an English village out there in Uganda. The missionaries still changed for dinner when they invited guests from the Government Hill of Kabale (though not when they were on their own), silver tea-services were polished lovingly by their "house-boys", who might be men but were always called "boys", and the "native" was to be helped in every way but hardly to be thought of as a friend, just as the "poor" in England were considered unfit friends for the children of the "gentry". This was all part of the culture which was exported along with the gospel, but when the Holy Spirit breathed new life in Revival many of these attitudes were blown away.

Return to England

In February 1932 Harold and Margaret left Kabale to return to England for the sake of the children's education. Although some missionaries had sent their children back, Harold and Margaret would not hear of this, believing that their first responsibility was to the children God had given them. On their return they bought a house in Cambridge, where Peter was to start at university, so that they could be near him and give him the family life he had missed during their years in Africa. Despite longing to see him again, Margaret wrote, "It is terrible to think we are coming home so soon, we are all dreading it. Life in England after this will be a very empty affair I fear. Still it has to be. We do not know yet what the future may hold, but doubtless we shall be shown."

On their way they all caught flu and had to break their journey in Limuru, Kenya, which meant that they missed their boat, but also meant that they had time for a real rest and holiday before facing the upheaval of the return. During the seven years they had been in Africa, Harold had accomplished a phenomenal amount.

Harold's review of the years 1925-1932:

The following are the books which had been translated or revised since August 1925:-
St Mark's Gospel
The Four Gospels
The New Testament
The Prayers and Hymns (Morning Service with 8 Psalms and 25 Hymns)
Catechism for Catechumens
Catechism for those about to be confirmed
Umuhuz' Umwe (One Mediator) Protestant defence book

The above had already been printed. The following were translated but not yet in print:-
The Psalms
The Pilgrim's Progress (Part I)
Prayers and Hymns Revised (Greater part of Prayer Book with 113 hymns to date)
Kinyarwanda Grammar

What a number of big things we have to give thanks for, and to invite you to join us in praising God, as we look back over seven years to the call that came to us in November 1924. First for all the unseen and silent preparation which the all-wise Foreseer had been making all through our lives till the appointed hour struck. Then for the call itself, given with special clearness and definiteness, so as to give us firm ground to stand on when the difficulties and opposition began. Then for the truly miraculous way in which difficulty after difficulty was overcome. Though both in 1925 and in 1928 we were several times brought into places where the way before us appeared humanly speaking barred by insuperable obstacles, He who had given the call quietly but irresistibly made the way through all difficulties and brought us out to the work. Then again, our large family has been protected from dangers and from serious illness during all these years. There is not one of us who has not enjoyed, on the whole, far better health during our time in Africa than during any similar period in England before we came out. It is true that Lindesay had a serious attack of dysentery two years ago, but praise God she made a complete recovery; and my wife has had appendicitis, but this has been known to happen to people in England! We can look back to many occasions where God's protecting hand has shielded us in circumstances where there were possibilities of very serious disaster — notably on that safari to Remera with the family during the Ruanda famine. I do not say for a moment that we are unique in all this, not at all, our God is a God that doeth wonders and He delights to protect His children when they are on His errands. But in view of the fact that humanly speaking we did take grave risks (believing that we were called to do so) we do want to offer up thanks to God for having brought us through.

Chapter 3

Revival Starts

Joe Church's despair is turned to hope

In Margaret's review of the year 1930 she had written of the discouragement at Gahini where they were still recovering from the famine. Partly because so many had died or fled to Uganda during the famine, and partly because of Roman Catholic pressure on the chiefs, there was no inclination among the local people to help in the extensive building programme. However, a year later things were improving. She wrote,

> It was lovely to see Gahini again and such a refreshment in every way. The work there seems so "alive"; real conversions going on amongst the hospital boys and others; and every sign of real spiritual growth. There was a big gathering at both the services on Sunday, so big that they had to be held outside as the church is not yet finished and the old school building not large enough, it reminded one of old Kabale days. The buildings are going on apace, and the trees are growing fast.

Something had changed. God was at work through his Holy Spirit. The seeds of Revival were being sown.

Dr Joe Church had found those famine years really difficult. He had newly arrived and there were few resources at Gahini with which to meet the appalling demands. Several times he wrote of waking up to see up to 20 corpses in the road, of people who had died in the night. On top of that, white ants had destroyed his house and he knew he must build a new one for his fiancée, Decie, who was due to come out in 1930 for their wedding.

In September 1929, tired, unable to sleep, worried about the problems in the hospital even though the rains had finally broken and the famine was over, worried about finances and about how Decie would cope with the strains of life at Gahini, and feeling a failure both as a doctor and a missionary, Joe went to Kampala for a much needed rest.

On his first Sunday there he went to the vernacular service at Namirembe Cathedral. A Ugandan called Simeoni Nsibambi ran to meet him with just the encouragement he needed. The previous time he had been there, Joe had spoken at a Bible study about surrendering all for Jesus. Nsibambi had taken these words to heart and had found a new joy in the Lord, but as he looked at the Uganda church he felt there was something lacking. Joe too was discouraged by the state of the church in Rwanda, describing it as "paganism in Christian dress". For some time he had been praying for one African who truly believed, with whom he could have deep fellowship. God heard his prayer.

Over the next two days, Joe and Simeoni embarked on an extensive Bible study, tracing references to the work of the Holy Spirit, using his Scofield Reference Bible. Together they knelt in prayer, "deciding before God to quit all sin in faith, and claiming the victorious life and the filling of the Holy Spirit". There was nothing spectacular or dramatic but each was aware of the holiness of God and the transforming power of the risen Lord Jesus. They then prayed the costly prayer, "Lord, send revival, beginning in me." Simeoni returned to his work in the public health department while Joe went to Nairobi to collect a new car for Gahini. On his return to Kampala, a lady missionary spoke to him about the extraordinary change in Simeoni.

"He's gone mad," she said. "He's going round everywhere asking people if they have been saved."

Joe tried to explain what they had discovered together about the Holy Spirit but she would have none of it.

"Go back to Rwanda," she advised. "The Africans here are not ready for this teaching about sanctification and the Holy Spirit."

Dr Algie Stanley Smith was staying near Kampala so Joe drove out to meet him and talk through his experiences and this missionary's reactions.

"If this is what happens when you have asked God for a new filling of his Spirit," said Algie, "then we must trust that what follows must be his will."

On 19th May 1930 Joe and Decie were married in Namirembe Cathedral, Kampala. Back at Gahini it seemed as if there really was a new spirit at work. The buildings were going up at last and, more important, several people were coming to faith in Jesus Christ, including a sub-chief and a man who had been skilled in witchcraft. But Satan was counter-attacking. Opposition from Roman Catholic chiefs caused the building work to stop for a time; white ants caused severe problems in older buildings, which seemed to be falling down while they looked at them. The new converts were going through real difficulties in their homes and there were problems with the hospital staff.

The arrival of Blasio Kigozi

In October 1929 a young Ugandan called Blasio Kigozi, Simeoni Nsibambi's younger brother, had arrived at Gahini as headmaster of the boys' school. He was from a wealthy, high-born family who refused secondary school education because he felt that God wanted him to work with Apollo, a Ugandan missionary, among the pygmies of Congo. The way to Congo was constantly blocked but then he heard a request for help in the newly started work in Ruanda-Urundi and knew that this was where God was calling him. In preparation he went to Bufumbira where he requested a Rwandan schoolboy to come over to teach him Kinyarwanda. Misaki was chosen to go and was very impressed by Blasio who truly lived out his Christian faith. Their household also included another lad called Yohana Bunyenyezi who had been Harold and Margaret's cook-boy. After six months of intensive language study they set off for Gahini, walking all the way. They spent one night in a makeshift shelter. As it grew dark, they saw a leopard. The two boys were terrified and woke Blasio.

"How can you sleep when there is a leopard around?" they asked.

"Would you be frightened if there was a soldier here with a gun?"

"No."

"Well, we have better than a soldier. Jesus Christ is our protection. Go back to sleep."

They could not but were very impressed to see Blasio roll over and sleep peacefully. Later both boys were ordained and became fully involved in the Revival movement.

When Blasio got to Gahini, like Joe he was worried by the nominalism he saw all around him and he had a particular burden for a young hospital dresser called Yosiya Kinuka. Yosiya used to sit like a stone at the back of the prayer meetings and never take part in discussions on the Bible. By the end of 1930 he mentioned to Blasio that he was considering leaving hospital work and returning to Ankole in Uganda where he would be a chief. As Yosiya wrote in *Ruanda Notes*, one of the things that bothered him was that Joe "was always trying to make us work like the church teachers, but we thought it was 'not done' to work like the poorly paid evangelists".

Blasio took him on a holiday to Kampala where he stayed with Simeoni Nsibambi. Yosiya wrote:

I had never seen such a fervent Christian before. We kept talking about the subject of being born again. Simeoni had heard that the spirit of the hospital was bad and he asked me the reason. When I began to tell him, he turned to me and said that it was because of the sin in my own heart, and that that was the reason why the others on the staff were bad. I agreed with him that I was not right, and he taught me many more things, but my heart was still unchanged.

As he returned to Gahini bumping along in the lorry, Yosiya felt that his heart was a heart of stone bumping along inside him. As they waited in "no man's land" at the border between Uganda and Rwanda, he suddenly felt he could not go on as he was, and he yielded to Christ, asking him to take away the heart of stone and give him a heart of flesh. Back at Gahini people ran up to Joe.

"Have you seen Yosiya? His whole expression has changed."

Yosiya began telling everyone about the change that had come over him. He had been a trusted hospital dresser and it was costly to confess openly that he had stolen regularly from the hospital. One member of staff threatened to burn his house down since he was exposing their sin as well as his own. Before he could carry out his threat, he too was truly converted and became a close friend. Blasio, Yosiya and Joe found a unity in spirit as they prayed together and worked together as a real team.

The mission was expanding and one of the last safaris that Harold and Margaret had done in Rwanda was to join Joe Church, the Stanley Smiths, Sharps and others in the search for the new sites of Kigeme in the south of Rwanda and Shyira in the west. They spent three nights at Gahini in August 1931 and Harold wrote to *Ruanda Notes*, "We were struck by the evidence of the Holy Spirit's working. It was something to warm one's heart through to see that place, to give one renewed joy and courage in the work, and to rebuke feeble faith."

Characteristics of the Revival

While they were at Gahini one man confessed to stealing 90 francs from another the year before, and he came to repay the debt. Samsoni was also very impressed because for two nights he had no sleep. People came to him all through the night wanting teaching from the Bible. Both of these factors were characteristic of the Revival — repentance with costly restitution; and a hunger to be taught from the Word of God. Although they now had the New Testament and this meant that they could read it for themselves, they needed teaching from it as well.

A third characteristic came to be known as "walking in the light". As the team of Joe, Blasio and Yosiya expanded to include other like-minded people, they would challenge each other if they saw behaviour which did not live up to the life of Christ. Frequently Joe had to repent of loss of temper and ask forgiveness from those he had hurt. As he says in *Quest for the Highest*, "I was helped to see that the very 'root of bitterness' had to go as well in order that no trace of the 'rasp' would be left in my voice." But this aspect of Revival brought opposition, when challenges were brought to those who had not experienced this filling of the Holy Spirit. Senior church leaders resented a new, untaught Christian telling them how to live. "I have been a baptized and confirmed Christian for many years. I can read. Why do I need to be born again? Who are you to tell me how to live?" they would say. Sometimes they would hear the Holy Spirit reinforcing the challenge and would repent. Often they would harden their hearts in pride and oppose those whom they saw as challenging their authority.

A fourth characteristic of Revival was prayer. Joe wrote to *Ruanda Notes* at Christmas 1933, "A few days ago I suggested an early morning prayer meeting to the hospital staff, and when I said 5 o'clock they smiled and said they were always up earlier than that praying. At 4 a.m. I found them all on my verandah waiting, and we had a wonderful two hours of prayer until it was light." Often little huts of straw were built where people could join together in small groups to pray. Blasio built a two-man hut in his garden and would spend many hours in it alone. To many church people this seemed excessive zeal.

A final characteristic which may be mentioned here was the emancipation of women. Many high class Tutsi were not allowed to be seen outside their *rugo* (enclosure around their houses). When they insisted on joining fellowship meetings and going to church, it was misunderstood and led to much persecution. Even now, men are always given chairs while the women sit on mats, and at a recent convention to commemorate the Revival at Gahini, I was horrified to find that not a single woman was allowed to speak. During Revival days it was impossible to muzzle the women. Once they experienced acceptance in Christ, they wanted to tell everyone what he meant to them. They joined teams going to other villages to tell of what God had done for them.

Conflict in the church

I have mentioned the conflict when a senior church member was challenged by a younger one about his way of life. There was another source of conflict particularly among the missionaries, which Dr Stanley Smith wrote about in his little booklet *The Road to Revival* in 1946.

> One form of conflict requires mention in some detail; it may be called the parson-layman controversy. In a mission which comprises so many laymen this is bound to come, especially when the laymen in the Revival begin to take an active interest in the church. Partly through the tactlessness of the laymen, and partly through the novelty of the idea to clergy of the Church of England,

some of the ordained missionaries felt that the laymen were interfering in matters outside their sphere. [...] The Church of England "parish system" places nearly all the authority and initiative in the work of the church on the clergyman. It is too great a burden for one man, and it ignores the immense reserves of spiritual power latent in the laity. It became clear that God's purpose in this apparent rivalry was to teach the mission the importance of team work. Team work is a wonderful ideal. It calls for great humility and self-effacement on the part of the clergy, and tact and humility on the part of the laity. But it is indispensable to a revived Church.

Yet CMS, and therefore the Ruanda Mission, as an Anglican society, had a policy that the head of a station had to be a clergyman. This caused real problems for senior doctors who had been in the country for many years, when they were expected to accept decisions made by a younger clergyman who had only been out for a short time and didn't know all the circumstances. The church/laity divide became a real issue in the life of the mission. Some missionaries opposed the ordination of Kosiya Shalita for fear of perpetuating what they saw as wrong traditions within the African church. It has to be remembered that people like my grandfather, Harold, came from the evangelical wing of the Anglican Church in Britain in the 1920s, at a time when they were a very small minority. Grandfather was a convinced Anglican, seeing the Prayer Book as thoroughly biblical, although there were some aspects, for example the baptism service, that he felt were inappropriate for an infant church. In the last 20 years or so, the role of the clergyman described by Dr Stanley Smith above has largely given way to "every-member ministry", but in the 1930s there were real tensions for the Revival movement in the Anglican Church.

Spreading the message of Revival

Those who had experienced new life at Gahini had a compulsion to share it. They went out in twos and threes all over the area spreading the good news that the Christian life was not a matter of trying to follow the rules and regulations of the church, but that God had come down to us in Jesus Christ. He had shared our life and eventually died for us, bearing our sins and sorrows on the cross. He had borne the penalty for sin for us. There was no need for us to try to atone — he had done it for us. Our part was to accept that we are sinners, that he died for us, and ask him to take away our sins and live within us, giving us his power to follow him.

As these teams travelled, they found that God was dealing with them at a deep level. They could not live closely together under those circumstances unless they brought into the open things that troubled them, such as a loss of temper which needed to be repented of quickly, or when someone failed to do something and that failure irritated another, it was talked about, the irritation confessed, the forgetfulness explained and forgiveness sought and received. This came to be known as "walking in the light" and became the source of the deep relationships that developed across all racial and tribal barriers. The verse 1 John 1:7 became the key verse of Revival: "If we walk in the light, as he is in the light, we have fellowship one with another, and the blood of Jesus Christ his Son cleanseth us from all sin" (KJV).

The teams travelled further — to the new stations of Shyira and Kigeme, to the tse-tse fly-ridden area of the Bugesera, into Uganda and Kenya. In 1934 the call came to open up new stations in Burundi. Archdeacon Pitt-Pitts had recently moved from Kenya where he was the CMS field secretary to do the same work in the areas covered by the Ruanda Mission. He wrote to the Friends of Ruanda quoting the slogan which was known everywhere in Inter-Varsity Fellowship circles at that time, "Evangelize to a finish", and used it to challenge new missionaries to come out and move into the unevangelized areas of Rwanda and Burundi. But the first to respond to this call came from Gahini. Bill Church, Joe's brother who had been working with him for the past three years, and Kosiya Shalita who had recently been ordained in Uganda, together with over 30 Christians from Gahini, set off with 70 porters to walk the length of Rwanda and cross the narrow gorge of the Kanyaru river into Burundi. Some stayed with Bill at the new site of Buhiga in the north but others walked on for another 100 miles to Matana with Kosiya who was the first Rwandan missionary to another country.

Kosiya was a Rwandan, born near Gahini, whose family had

incurred the wrath of the king, Musinga, and had fled to Uganda. There he had met Bishop Willis who was struck by his intelligence and arranged for him to attend Budo Secondary School, the best boys' school in Uganda, where he learned fluent English and also became a Christian. He had volunteered to accompany Geoff Holmes when the opportunity first presented itself for the mission to move into Rwanda and had remained at Gahini where he became Joe's right hand man in his early days there. "It meant a big wrench for him to come away from his Gahini home, to a strange people," wrote Dr Stanley Smith in *Road to Revival*. "He had a hard time at first, living in a tent. It was cold and wet and lonely; food was scarce and workmen refused to come. But he kept steadily on, built himself a little round hut and then a mud and wattle church school. He made friends with the local chief who gave him his two sons to teach and soon began to find openings for out-schools." Another problem he faced was hostility from Roman Catholics who had told the local people to expect pygmies to come from Rwanda. They were amazed when Kosiya appeared since he was over six foot! But this did not remove the hostility. Rosemary Guillebaud wrote about Kosiya whom she had got to know when she was a child. She described him as "great fun and a tremendous tease", and added: "He was at Matana for about a year all alone, trying to make contact with the Barundi, who were shy and very wary of him and did all they could to make him give up. They put charms and spells on his house and cultivations to make him leave, but he went right on loving them, and bit by bit won over a number of the younger ones." By the end of the year, when Dr and Mrs Sharp went to join him, they found a school of twenty boys, a large number of adults had been taught to read, and three out-schools had been established. Dr Sharp was also a tall man and this tended to remove some of the early suspicion among the local people.

Blasio seeks deeper holiness

Meanwhile back at Gahini there were problems between the hospital staff and the church workers, also between Joe Church and the hospital sister who, with a hospital to run, did not relish it when the doctor disappeared for days on end, often taking some of her staff with him. Blasio was filled with a sense of inadequacy and failure. In 1932, despite the fact that he had not had the education usually required for ordination, he had been accepted for theological training at Mukono. On 27th May 1934 he was ordained deacon in Namirembe Cathedral, Kampala, and returned to Gahini to lead the evangelist training. The first term ended with a student strike, and despite all that he could say, six of his students decided that they had had enough and left for home. Coupled with the tensions on the station and spiritual apathy in the village churches all round, Blasio was overwhelmed by his own shortcomings. As soon as term finally ended, he shut himself into his house to pray and seek the Lord. When he emerged, it was with a new sense of urgency. Many people could not cope with his zeal and made accusations against him. He would listen, repent of anything he felt was wrong, and then take his accuser home for tea and general chat, showing that he still loved them.

Some even reported him to the government as a bad and rude teacher because he was always accusing them of sin. On the way home from the hearing where he had been reprimanded, Blasio said to his accusers, "You have defeated a Ugandan but you have not defeated the Holy Spirit."

A young evangelist called Yona Kanamuzeyi was challenged by Blasio's lifestyle, yet he could not understand his message. Yona had come to Gahini when he was ten, during the famine which his whole family somehow managed to survive. He saw some schoolboys playing with a tennis ball and desperately wanted one for himself. He pleaded with his father to send him to school so that he could have one. When he left school he taught others in his village to read and write, and then returned to Gahini to train as an evangelist. There he met Blasio, who showed a keen interest in him. But although Yona admired and respected him, he did not understand when Blasio tried to show him that Jesus rather than the church was the means of salvation.

Yona was baptized and confirmed at the end of his course, which he passed well, and was posted to Rubona, a trading centre ten miles from Gahini. But the temptations of this trading post were too much for him. He began to drink in the many drinking houses and fell into immorality. His case was brought to the church council in January 1936 and he was suspended.

He returned home wondering why he could not live the sort of life that Blasio lived. What was his secret? He knew what Blasio would answer but it didn't make sense to him. Then he heard some devastating news. Blasio Kigozi was dead.

During his weeks of prayer, Blasio had been seized with a burden for the dead church of Uganda. He wrote to the bishop asking that some important questions be raised in the next synod and he was invited to come and address them. There were three questions which burdened him:

1 What is the cause of the coldness and deadness of the church of Uganda?
2 Why are people allowed to come to the Lord's table, who are living in open sin?
3 What must be done to bring revival to the church of Uganda?

He had been asked to speak at the Mbarara convention for church teachers and clergy, and he preached with a sense of urgency on the need to repent. He spent the nights talking to people and pleading with them to be saved. During the night he must have been bitten by a tick, because by the time he reached the clergy retreat before the synod, he had a fever which steadily rose. He was admitted to Mengo Hospital with virulent tick fever. The following Saturday, 25th January 1936, he died with his wife and brother singing hymns beside him. On his gravestone near the cathedral is written one word in Luganda: ZUZUKA! meaning AWAKE! Even though he was not there to address the synod, his questions were discussed and his death emphasized the challenge.

Back at Gahini, Yona was not the only one to be devastated by the news, but it was as if Blasio's death gave his message added urgency. Many of those who had opposed him now remembered his love and the consistency of his life with the message he preached, and they too came to the cross in penitence and tears. But still there were those who felt that this was all excessive. Some of the missionaries thought that the mission was going off course. A pamphlet was published in Britain telling what God was doing and the different reactions to it and calling on the Friends of Ruanda to pray.

In June 1936, at the bishop's request, Joe led a team to the

Anglican Training College at Mukono, Uganda, where there had already been severe differences with some of the students who challenged the more liberal teaching at the college. The atmosphere was tense but the team taught from the Bible, taking a day for each subject, sin, repentance, new birth, separation from the things of the world, the victorious life and the Holy Spirit. About 40 people responded to Christ but several members of staff were unhappy with what they called an "unlovely gospel" and warned that this message was unsettling their baptized and confirmed students. In 1941 these divisions came to a head when 26 committed Christians, including William Nagenda who was to have such an influence worldwide on Revival, were expelled from the college because they refused to obey an order to stop the 4 a.m. prayer meeting. This led to bitter divisions among senior Christians in Uganda and Rwanda.

The Spirit descends in power

When Joe returned to Gahini, it was to find that dramatic events had happened in the girls' school during his absence. On Sunday night, 29th June 1936, Dora Skipper and Joy Gerson, newly arrived to help in the school, were woken by an extraordinary noise coming from the girls' dormitory. When they investigated, they found a scene of utter chaos. Several girls were crying out, some were rolling on the ground, others were making noises like animals. One girl was kneeling apparently in a trance with tears running down her face, crying out, "Can't you see him — look, there — Jesus is on the cross, dying for me."

Apparently it had all begun when four of the senior girls had joined together in prayer. At about 9 p.m. they were suddenly very conscious of sin and began to cry out and to weep. Others, coming to investigate, felt the same mysterious power and also began crying out the things they had done wrong. Some teachers' wives were staying at the school and, hearing the noise, came to investigate. They too were stricken in the same way. One fell to the floor unable to find peace because she had stolen a new cloth off the dead body of her mother-in-law and had substituted an old one for her burial.

The noise had then attracted a group of girls who had been dedicated to the cult of Nyabingi. Seeing similarities to their form of pagan worship, they had begun their own rites and ended up growling like animals on the floor. Such was the scene when the missionaries came to investigate. Joy Gerson described what she saw,

> The girls seemed to have gone mad. Some were on the floor. They were all throwing themselves about, they were absolutely uncontrolled, some were laughing, some weeping, most were shaking very very much and they seemed to have supernatural strength. The powers of darkness seemed to be right on us. It felt like being in hell as though Satan had loosed his armies.

With difficulty the two missionaries had been able to calm things down and restore order.

Changed lives

Over the next few weeks similar scenes began to happen all over the hill. Hymn-singing went on through the night and there was weeping in prayer meetings. In church services people began crying out and weeping; some fell to the ground motionless for several minutes. The Roman Catholics began to say that they had been bewitched and that the Protestants were now encouraging devil-worship.

While it is undeniable that Satan was counterfeiting some of the genuine signs of the work of the Holy Spirit, since Nyabingi worship also involves shaking and falling to the ground with loud crying, it is equally undeniable that those who had had experiences of the Holy Spirit, however bizarre, now showed genuinely changed lives. They were peaceful and the joy of the Lord Jesus shone from their eyes.

Dora Skipper, the headmistress, felt very confused by all that was happening. Initially she was convinced that the events in the dormitory were satanic, but some who had been there were undeniably changed. She had refused to allow Blasio or Yosiya to speak at the girls' school, fearing what she saw as emotionalism and sensation-seeking. In fact, one schoolgirl had confessed to her that she had put saliva round her eyes to simulate weeping, confirming her fears. But there was no arguing with the genuine article.

Dora was a down-to-earth person, very protective of her schoolgirls, and not above physical action if she felt events warranted it, as ex-schoolgirl Marian Kajuga told me.

Marian had developed appendicitis when she was eight years old. Her parents wanted to take her to the local healers but her brother had heard good things about the hospital at Gahini and persuaded her father to take her there where she was operated on by Bill Church.

Her father said, "Because they have saved your life, you now belong to them", and allowed her to join the boarding school there. But he died soon afterwards and when she returned for her first holiday her mother refused to let her return.

After some weeks Marian suddenly heard her mother shout, "Quick, hide yourself, they mustn't find you." As she was being hustled into the hut, she caught a glimpse of three people getting out of a car at the foot of the hill. Lying in the darkness of the hut, her heart sang when she heard Dora Skipper's voice outside. She could not contain her joy but ran out to greet her.

"Do you want to leave school?" Dora asked.

"No," she replied.

Dora physically dragged her away from her mother and took her back to the school where she began to hear the news of Jesus Christ. Yet she was puzzled by the inconsistency of some people who professed to be Christians and yet their lives seemed no different from the pagans among whom she had grown up. Then came that exciting night in June, and she saw lives changed.

Marian was sleeping in the junior dormitory that night. She told me that she had been woken by an earthquake and the sound of a rushing wind, and then heard a noise from the senior dormitory. She and several friends ran out to find girls lying on the ground all over the place. Several were crying out, "We are perishing, we are perishing. Jesus has told us that if we don't trust him, we are perishing!"

Marian was particularly impressed by the difference in those who had been in the senior dormitory that first night and soon she too had asked Jesus to be her Saviour. She joined a group of school boys and girls in a prayer meeting, among whom was a fourteen-year-old boy called Eustace Kajuga who had been led to the Lord by Blasio the year before. Little did they know, at that stage, that they would later marry and form an effective team for Christ.

Although Dora could see that lives were being changed, she found it hard to let down her own defences. During the following year she had many differences with Joe Church, who wanted to speak about what the Lord was doing on every possible occasion. Finally, during Holy Week 1937, she accepted what the Lord had been trying to say to her. She and Joe testified together in church that Easter, side by side. Next morning she made a round of several of the senior Christians to put things right and was amazed at how obvious their lack of agreement had been. She was to say several times in the future that although she had been a missionary for many years, she had never accepted the Lord in a personal way until that day at Gahini.

Dora was not the only missionary to fear emotionalism. Several believed that this was hysterical activity, or worse, but as time went on there was no denying changed lives and the total commitment to the Lord. One of those who was doubtful about the emotionalism was Harold who had returned to Rwanda alone to do further translation work on the Old Testament. He was very shaken when, during a visit to Gahini, his loved and trusted translator Samsoni, together with his wife, Lindesay, both wept in a meeting and produced heathen charms, confessing that during all those years as trusted Christian leaders they had at the same time been practising witchcraft.

William Nagenda

It was at this time (at the end of 1936) that William Nagenda arrived at Gahini. He was a converted government clerk, the son of a Ugandan chief, who had been to Budo School and Makerere University and who spoke excellent English. He had been converted through Simeoni Nsibambi and wanted to be considered for training for the Anglican ministry. But before he could enter theological college he was asked by the bishop to consider going to Rwanda where he took Blasio's place running the Evangelists' Training School at Gahini.

Although committed as a Christian, when the disgraced church teacher, Yona Kanamuzeyi, came to see him, telling him that he was defeated by secret sin in his life, William had to confess to the same sense of defeat. He went away to pray all night. During this time he read again 1 John 1:7, and he began to see that bringing into the light one's secret sins was God's way of restoring and delivering one from them, but that this was not a once-for-all event. It had to be daily cleansing for sins, however small, committed daily, and daily forgiveness.

Yona was immensely impressed by the immediate and obvious change in William and began to hunger for it himself, but it was to be another three years before the day when, in a prayer meeting, he was singing the hymn, "Rock of Ages":

> "Be of sins the double cure
> Cleanse me from its guilt and power."

Yona knew that it was the Word of Life for him. He sprang to his feet, and with many tears, made a clean breast of his sins before that little gathering. He claimed cleansing in the Blood of Jesus, cleansing from the two things, the guilt and the power — the guilt that had been dogging his footsteps for so long, and the power that had been holding him enslaved. (*Forgive Them* by Dr J. E. Church.)

Joe wrote in *Quest for the Highest*:

Those who had passed through a new experience of repentance and cleansing from sin and were freed from nagging guilt and binding debts and sometimes longstanding unforgiveness began to meet together for fellowship and mutual encouragement and for team witness.

This quality of fellowship swept away all natural barriers, between Tutsi and Hutu, between the educated and uneducated and between black and white. It was very precious to those who experienced it but it began to seem exclusive to those who were still not sure of what was happening. The teams of witness spread out further and further, an unsung band of unknown Christians spreading the gospel of grace throughout the country and beyond.

Revival spreads to Burundi

In Burundi, too, Revival broke out. A letter from Bill Church at Buhiga, in the *Ruanda Notes* in December 1936, records,

> On several occasions recently when quite unemotional addresses were being given, people have broken down under conviction of sin and have begun to tremble and cry out, and have been taken out and dealt with by some Christians. Much of the blessing, humanly speaking, has resulted from visits of keen Rwandan men, women and girls, who have come down and told the good news. Some have given up their holidays to do this 100 miles on foot.

Fellowship crossed denominational boundaries as well. They often used to say that at the foot of the cross there is level ground, with no room for anything that divides. Everyone who comes there is merely a sinner saved by grace. Mr Hans Emming, a Danish Baptist missionary, told how one day three boys, totally unconnected, all heard their names called out while they were on the hills tending their cattle. Each time there was no one to be seen. Each time they panicked and ran to Hans to ask what was happening. He asked each of them if they had spoken to anyone else that day but they denied it. He told them that God was calling them and led them all to the Lord. Later each became a pastor.

The blessings of Revival

In 1946 Dr Stanley Smith wrote a summary of the blessings he had seen in Revival in his book *Road to Revival*. He said that sometimes the Lord had moved through large gatherings, but more often it was through small groups of people.

> The church was becoming a repentant church, and maintaining a high level of spirituality and practical holiness. The joy of the Abaka [meaning "on fire", the nickname given to those touched by Revival] was unquenchable. During the months of famine at Gahini for example, when all classes were on famine rations, the fellowship meetings still went on with unabated enthusiasm, and the songs of praise night after night amazed the people around, oppressed as they were with misery and despair.

He gave practical examples of the way in which this vital faith was expressed.

> A poor dying woman said to two keen nurses attending her "I can't understand you people. You do things my own mother wouldn't do for me." [...] There was a great deal of conflict in the church, but constantly there was news of conversions, many of them of the most striking character. The standard of morality and honesty was very high. Perhaps the most striking proof of the reality of the conversions was seen in the homes of the Abaka, where married life was completely transformed. As for honesty, the practice of public confession and restitution powerfully impressed even government officials and commercial men. The ideal of honesty was carried to its limit.

I remember my parents telling me of one man who had divorced his very difficult wife. The Holy Spirit convicted him of this and he set off to find her. All he knew was that she had gone to Uganda. He trusted the Holy Spirit to lead him and had just arrived in one town on his way to Kampala when he met her in the street! He took her back and cared for her for years despite the fact that she remained extremely difficult and abusive. Another man, who worked for a shipping company on Lake Victoria, took all the things that he had stolen from them, wrapped up in a blanket, and deposited them on the desk of the European manager. "Who caught you?" asked the manager. "The Holy Spirit", was the reply and the whole story was told. After a pause the manager sighed. "I would need a lorry to return all that I have pilfered," he said.

Because drunkenness was (and is) such a curse in the country, those affected by Revival, on their own initiative and without any prompting from missionaries, decided that they would no longer touch alcohol and in one area the government receipts from the beer tax were down by 20 per cent!

> Underlying it all and the inspiration of it all was the profound understanding of, and constant emphasis on, the cross. This proved it to be without doubt a deep rooted and real movement of the Spirit. (*Road to Revival*)

Chapter 4   # A Wedding and a Funeral (1932-1941)

University days

News of the exciting spiritual revival reached the Guillebauds in England. They settled down in Cambridge to be near Peter who had started at St John's College in 1932. They knew that it would be some time before they would be free to return to the work they loved in Africa, but wanted to keep themselves available to return when God opened the way again. Harold refused to tie himself down though he was offered a job as a vicar. He accepted various curacies and spent the time in England writing books, notably *Why the Cross?* which was to be a tremendous blessing to countless people.

He and Margaret also became involved in the life of the students. The Cambridge Inter-Collegiate Christian Union (CICCU) met for tea every Sunday afternoon in the Henry Martyn Hall before going on to the evening service at Holy Trinity. Margaret began opening their home for Sunday lunch to help those students who lived too far away to return home between morning service and tea. Those Sunday lunches became a feature of life for many Christian students. Margaret, called Mrs G. by the students, would provide a simple meal and Harold would spend time discussing problems students had with the Bible. Out of these discussions came the idea for the Bible study series, *Search the Scriptures*, as well as the book *Some Moral Difficulties in the Bible*. He firmly believed that the best way to study the Bible was to search out answers to questions oneself, with only a notebook in which to record one's findings. He thought that reliance on Bible aids made people lazy. He also thought that evangelical scholarship was seriously lacking, so he was one of the committee who founded Tyndale House in

Cambridge, as a centre for serious theological study for evangelicals.

It was at a Sunday lunch that a young lady called Elisabeth Sutherland first met the Guillebauds, when she started at Girton College, Cambridge, in 1933. She had become a Christian at 16, when she went with a school friend to a Christian meeting in London. Soon afterwards she went to the Keswick Convention and became involved in the Holiness Movement, wanting above all things to conquer sin and be filled with the Holy Spirit. She had asked God to fill her with his Spirit but felt no different, so she asked him for a sign. Next morning her Bible reading was in Luke 1 and she read in verse 41 that "Elisabeth was filled with the Holy Spirit". From then on she never doubted that she was!

One day she attended a CICCU meeting where a missionary from China was expected to speak about his work. He started his talk by explaining that he had scrapped his previously-prepared talk on China and was going to speak rather about mission work in general, "because", he said, "I believe that there is someone here whom God wants to serve him as a missionary". Right through his talk Elisabeth had an uncomfortable feeling that he meant her. At the end of the talk she saw Mrs G. coming towards her.

"Do you think that he might have been referring to you?" Mrs G. asked.

Elisabeth returned to her room at Girton in some turmoil. There she said, "Lord, if you really are calling me, you must make it clear." Then she resolved to put the thought out of her mind and picked up *The Times* newspaper. Written across the front page, as usual in those days, was a Bible text. It appeared to be written in letters of fire: "Go ye therefore, and teach all nations, baptizing them in the name of the Father, and of the Son, and of the Holy Ghost" (Matthew 28:19 KJV). She threw the paper across the room as if it had burnt her. Then after a pause she retrieved it, and knelt by her bed, accepting that God was indeed calling her.

She joined the Cambridge Volunteer Union, for those who believed that God was calling them to work for him. At a meeting one day she saw a young man come into the room and said to herself, "If I ever marry it will be him." It was love at first sight for her, but for Peter, whom amazingly she had not previously met at the Sunday lunches, she was just another pretty girl surrounded by so many young men that he felt there was no chance to get to know her.

Elisabeth was concerned about how her parents would react to her desire to go abroad as a missionary, since she was their only child. She need not have worried. Before she was born, her mother had had two miscarriages and when she was pregnant for the third time they had prayed, "Lord, if this baby is born alive, we will dedicate her to you, as Hannah dedicated Samuel." They had given her the name "Elisabeth" which means "gift of God", and were fully expecting her to serve God, although they had not told her this until she came to tell them what she believed God was saying to her.

Elisabeth's background

In 1999 my brother David took my mother round Scotland to explore her roots. She visited the small "butt and ben" where *her* mother, Christina Fraser, had grown up. Chrissie's parents had been converted on the same night during a time of Revival in the Inverness area. Her father had died when she was small, leaving her mother with five children to bring up. Her mother was so poor that she gave two daughters to a relation to care for. Chrissie used to describe walking barefoot over the hills because they couldn't afford shoes. She frequently carried her sister, Annie, piggyback over the pebbles to save her feet. Even in 1999 the small hut was little more than a cattle-shed with no electricity and no running water. Granny Fraser, Chrissie's mother, used to say, "All we had was the Lord's blessing but it was sufficient." After about three years she was able to make a home for the re-united family in Inverness, where her eldest daughter had started nursing, and eventually Chrissie followed suit. It was in church in Inverness that she met George Sutherland.

George had also lost his father when he was young. His mother was stone deaf and he was the eldest of six children. At fifteen he therefore had to give up all hopes of university and got himself a job as a ticket collector at Inverness station. There he entered a competition for railway employees on the subject: "What will the London and North Eastern Railway have become in ten years time?" He won first place and so came to the notice of the chairman, Mr Whitelaw, who kept his eye on this promising young man, and when a suitable job was offered in the accountancy department, George was put forward. Chrissie and George were married in Inverness in 1908 and within four years another promotion meant that they moved to Edinburgh where they made a home for Granny Fraser and Annie. When Elisabeth was born on 11th January 1915, Annie said, "She was born with a silver spoon in her mouth!" When Elisabeth was eight, George moved to London where he eventually became chief accountant of the LNER.

At Cambridge Elisabeth gradually began to think that God was calling her to work with the Ruanda Mission — but this was an Anglican society, which did not please her parents, particularly when Mrs G. said that she ought to be confirmed. She had already been received into the Presbyterian Church and saw no need for a bishop to lay his hands on her. Her father had brought her up on stories of the Covenant and how Jenny Geddes had thrown a stool at the preacher in St Giles' Cathedral, Edinburgh, whereupon the whole congregation had left the church and signed the Covenant against bishops imposed on Scotland by England. Her parents did not at all like the idea that she could even consider being confirmed.

"Why can't you go to Manchuria or, if you want, Africa, why not Malawi or Kenya where there are good Presbyterian missions?" they asked.

Her mother came to Cambridge to talk things over. As she stood in the waiting room at Cambridge station, Elisabeth prayed that the Lord would make it abundantly clear if he wanted her in Rwanda, and confirm it independently to her parents. As she opened her eyes, she saw on the table in the waiting room a copy of the CMS magazine *The Gleaner*. It was open on a spread about Rwanda! She saw the train arriving, certain now that God was calling her to Rwanda but still uncertain how her parents would react. But God had answered her prayer. The day before, her mother had been at a meeting when someone had pressed a copy of *Ruanda Notes* into her hand saying that she had two copies. As she and George read it, they felt that it was indeed right for their daughter to go there, but they were still unhappy at the thought of confirmation. However, at the mission board meeting which considered Elisabeth's application the subject was never raised and to the end of her life Elisabeth was not confirmed as an Anglican.

Peter's future

In 1935, Peter took his final exams. On the day the results were posted, Peter could be seen by his parents, returning from the Senate House, dragging his feet. Although they had been expecting him to be a Wrangler (ie, to get a First in mathematics), Harold immediately turned to Margaret.

"Whatever the result we must not show him our disappointment," he said.

Peter came through the door. Margaret could not wait for him to tell her.

"Well?" she asked.

"Wrangler," he replied glumly — and then allowed his delight to show as they scolded him for his faked disappointment.

He was elected Scholar of St John's College and also awarded the Wright's Mathematical Prize. He could have achieved great things in Britain, but he knew that God was calling him to serve him abroad. Although he had loved his year in Africa, like so many, he did not believe that God could really want to give him the desires of his heart, and so did not think God could possibly want him to work where he felt at home, and so he set his eyes on China. Peter decided that the best thing he could do was to train as a teacher, so he studied for a year at the Cambridge Training College for Men, gaining his Certificate of Education.

Harold returns to Rwanda alone

Towards the end of 1935, letters from Africa were telling of the need for the whole Bible in Kinyarwanda. Harold was asked if he could possibly return to continue the translation of the Old Testament. Margaret felt that she needed to continue to make a home for their daughters and so reluctantly they decided that Harold should go alone for one year only. He travelled to Lobita in Portuguese West Africa (Angola) and got a river steamer up the Congo River and then across Lake Tanganyika to Bujumbura where he was met by Jim Brazier, later to become the first bishop of Ruanda-Urundi, who drove him to Kigeme. There he was based with the Stanley Smiths where he and his translator, Samsoni, immediately got down to work. King Musinga had been deposed by the Belgians in 1931 and it was now safe for Samsoni to return to Rwanda.

Harold wrote for the *Ruanda Notes*, the magazine for the Friends of Ruanda, "It is a great joy to be living in Ruanda itself, to hear the language which I love next to my own spoken around me all the time... Being in Ruanda I can discuss the meaning of disputed words with highly interested crowds, who enjoy the discussion as much as I do. For example the other day we had a long animated discussion as to the word which expresses the time in the early morning when it is just not light enough for one person to recognize another (Ruth 3:14)." He took great delight in reading the newly translated story of Ruth to crowds of appreciative listeners. In order to take a break from the intense work, he translated some English nursery rhymes and sang them to groups of delighted children for a short time every day!

Engagement

Meanwhile, Elisabeth was elected president of CWICCU (Cambridge Women's Inter-Collegiate Christian Union) and was involved in discussions about amalgamating the two Christian Unions. She felt it was a bad witness to have such segregation among Christians but the move was defeated at that point, one man arguing against it because "the women have an unfortunate knack of winning arguments"!

Mrs G. continued to take a keen interest in the Christian students, particularly Elisabeth who was now committed to going to Africa with the Ruanda Mission, possibly initially to Burundi. However, her strong personality upset some people who considered that she was having too much influence in the affairs of CWICCU, which was intended to be run entirely by students. Members of the National Committee of IVF (Inter-Varsity Fellowship, the forerunner of Universities and Colleges Christian Fellowship) came to see Elisabeth, telling her to ask Mrs G. to stand back from student affairs.

Elisabeth dreaded the task, but the opportunity came when

they both attended a conference at Swanwick in Derbyshire. As tactfully as she could, she conveyed the message to Mrs G, who was terribly hurt. Peter was also at the conference and soon asked Elisabeth to go for a walk. Her heart leaped, for this was the first time he had singled her out, but he soon disillusioned her. He spent the whole walk scolding her for what she had said to his mother. She had made her very unhappy and she had no husband to stand by her — on and on he ranted. When they finally reached the house again, Elisabeth could take no more and hurried off, close to tears. But as Peter watched her go, his own heart lurched.

"I love that girl," he thought, "and now I've blown it. How could I have made her so unhappy?"

Elisabeth thought it was the end of all her hopes, but Peter decided he must put things to the test. Very correctly he wrote to her father, asking to see him to discuss an important matter, and the following weekend drove to London. George guessed what was coming and with a wicked sense of humour fed him an enormous lunch before allowing him to speak. He then sent the two of them into the sitting room, where Peter asked Elisabeth to marry him and discovered to his amazement that she had been in love with him for two years.

Back in Cambridge he announced his engagement, to the great delight of his family. He had inherited his father's absent-mindedness, and his engagement made it worse. One day he was asked to play tennis with Elisabeth and two of his sisters, so he went up to change. After a long delay, one of them went up to find out what was happening. Peter, forgetting why he was changing, had got into his pyjamas ready for bed!

Elisabeth got her degree in history although at that stage, as a woman, she was only given the title of a degree and was not awarded a degree proper! Years later she was told she could get the degree if she paid £10, which she did because of the need in Belgian administration for proof that she was qualified to teach. In 1998, Cambridge made a public apology and had a degree ceremony for women who had graduated in those early years. Elisabeth would have loved to have attended but she was in Africa at the time.

Peter went to teach at Seaford College, Sussex. Most weekends, Elisabeth would use her railway pass to travel to Brighton where Peter would meet her and they would talk about the future. They were always so glad that Elisabeth had had a clear call to Rwanda before she had even met Peter. He only knew that God wanted him to work overseas and he now happily set his sights on Rwanda.

Years later, at his memorial service, my sister Christine said she liked to think that she was fulfilling that missionary call which he did not take up, as she and her husband, Ross Paterson, are now serving the Chinese church.

Margaret spends two months in Africa

In May 1937, Margaret and Lindesay travelled out to meet Harold. They planned to spend two months in Africa and then all three would return to England. The mission had now been working for two years in Burundi and had come to realize that Kirundi, although very similar to Kinyarwanda, was different enough to warrant a translation of the New Testament of its own. Initially, Harold had thought it would only be a matter of revising the Kinyarwanda text, but the more he studied the language, the more he realized that it needed a new translation. For example, the word used for Holy Spirit in Rwanda meant "holy steam" in Burundi, resulting in serious misunderstandings! The mission considered the need to be urgent, so, once he had finished the translation of the Pentateuch at Kigeme, he moved to Matana and began the work with a Danish missionary called Mr Anderson, who had already begun the work of translation but could not really spare the time. He gladly handed over to Harold the work he had done on Matthew and John, and was willing to revise the work in the way that M. Honoré had done in Rwanda.

Margaret and Lindesay arrived in Kampala on Whit Sunday 1937 in time for the Coronation celebrations which Margaret described as "splendid". The rains had been torrential, and everyone warned her that the road to Kabale would be difficult, but she had such a limited time in Africa and it was over a year since she had seen her husband so she decided to press on. The road was every bit as difficult as she had been told. At one point they reached a bridge where they could only see the white markers above the water.

The whole road had gone, the water was rushing across like a mill race and it looked impossible, it was a sheet of water for several hundred yards — I asked a man if we could get through and he said he thought so and as we could not sit and look at it indefinitely we had to try — you could see the road only by the tops of the white bridge a good way off. About 20 or 30 men held the car, they were waist deep themselves and often more, and we started. The real difficulty was to keep on the road as it winds a lot and there is swamp on both sides and we had to get in line for the bridge. They simply had to hold the car on the road. However we managed it, truly the Lord was watching over us for I have seldom done a more dangerous bit of driving. And when we got to the next bridge it was a repeat performance, the only difference being it was a bit shorter and the road was straight!

Eventually they reached Kabale where things had changed beyond recognition. Their old house was now one of the wards in the hospital. After a night or two at Kabale they travelled on to Seseme in Bufumbira where their old house-boy Robert Serubibi was now a church teacher and evangelist. They stayed with Robert and Eseri and their family, and were delighted to see what the Lord was doing. Robert had been asked to consider going as a missionary to Matana but he told Margaret that he was afraid to witness or to preach, and that much of his Christianity was in his head rather than his heart. After a long talk their first evening, they went on a picnic over the Congo border and that afternoon Robert "took the plunge at last and told them he had been holding back and been dishonouring the Lord. Tonight he told the local teacher and tomorrow he is going to tell the whole station. He has all along been fighting the Revival especially on the question of any open confession and this is a real victory and witness." The next day Robert and his wife Eseri both confessed their disobedience and sins of self-righteousness and fear to God.

A short time later he offered to take his family to Burundi, to help at Matana. This involved walking through Rwanda and most of Burundi for 32 days. Eseri had just given birth to their third child and the journey had to be taken in slow stages. At one point their eldest child fell into a stream and it was with great difficulty that Robert managed to rescue her. They finally reached Matana where, like any European missionary, they had to learn the language and try to understand the strange customs of the Burundians.

Margaret and Lindesay travelled on to Kigeme where they spent two days. She wrote of her impressions:

It is simply marvellous to see what God has wrought out here — talk of changed lives. The first morning I spent an hour or more with Samsoni and Lindesay who are simply <u>radiant</u>: both simply <u>full</u> of joy and of what it means to be a "new creation". There is a considerable amount of confusion esp among younger ones as to the difference between being "born again" and being "baptized with the Holy Spirit". Samsoni was <u>very</u> sure he had been "born again" but he had never before come into a life of victory or "abiding". If ever one had any doubts of the <u>reality</u> of a "second blessing" (I use a phrase which I really do not like but use it for lack of a better) one need only come out here and see the Holy Spirit at work changing lives.

But she also found that many of the church teachers had been resisting this new message. One such teacher had been smoking and drinking heavily and was very much against the Revival teaching. That night she had a long talk with him and "found the Lord had been preparing the way and instead of active opposition I found he had already been under conviction in his heart. Anyway when I left next morning his face was radiant and he said, 'Yes now I can say "pe" (=really, truly) I believe Christ can do everything in my life.'"

Finally they reached Matana where they found Harold with a worrying chesty cough and difficulty breathing. She decided to ask Dr Sharp to give him a real overhaul. Harold had been so absorbed in his work that he had neglected his health and Margaret soon took firm control of his days, insisting that he come on walks with her into the fresh air. He had managed the revision of the four gospels and had started on several of the epistles as well as translating dozens of hymns, taking an hour or so on that task every morning.

Margaret was soon absorbed into life at Matana, being put to work with Kosiya Shalita. He had been ordained since she had left for England and she wrote of the joy of receiving Communion at his hands. On her first Sunday morning a whole crowd of 70 or 80 people came forward in response to an invitation to accept the Lord Jesus as their Saviour. For the next week she joined with Kosiya in teaching them the basics of their new-found faith. She spent a wonderful week teaching church leaders, and then had the joy of going on safari with Kosiya to an area some distance from Matana, where for the first time in her missionary career she stayed in a grass hut.

> I am writing in a native hut which I am sharing with Teresa! Great fun, luckily it's a nice new one and I've got a mosquito net... Its rather fun staying like this — only native food but I get very stodged up with nothing but an enormous plate of potatoes (I hate potatoes anyway) and nothing to drink. I spoilt myself tonight and had a cup of marmite. There's a wee hut in the teacher's "urugo", a new one, and I'm in that on the ground (the Lilo is being a real boon these days) and Teresa has the other half, she is snoring away.

They were asked to go to another church area, and had intended going just for the day, but on the way the car misbehaved and they had to spend the night in it, in the bitter cold, huddled down as best they could. The next day they set out for the church area, walking for $1^1/_2$ hours, and at one stage wading through an icy-cold, very fast stream. When they arrived, they found a packed church and for the first time Margaret preached an evangelistic message with Kosiya interpreting. After a further teaching session in the afternoon they spent time with individuals. "One of the three teachers who at first said not only was he certain of everything etc but seemed very surprised at being asked, suddenly broke down and realized that he had been trusting entirely in head knowledge and had never been born again and he is just radiant."

Finally in August the three of them, Harold, Margaret and Lindesay, left Matana to return to England. Harold wrote, "It has been a terrible wrench for both my wife and myself to leave Matana, for it has meant leaving fruitful work right in the middle; for me in particular it has meant leaving when another eight or nine months at most would, humanly speaking, have meant the completion of the New Testament for Urundi."

During the thirteen months he had spent in Rwanda and Burundi, Harold had accomplished much but he asked people to pray that they could return soon to complete the work, and that he would have no problems preparing what he had completed for the press while in England and away from his translators. The four gospels and the epistles were in fact printed in 1939, as was the work he had earlier done in Rwanda, the Pentateuch and Ruth.

Harold and Margaret had their Silver Wedding on board ship from Cape Town and arrived back in England in October 1937 and were soon settled back in their Cambridge home. Peter was still teaching at Seaford but was considering going to the Missionary Training Colony as soon as he had completed two years.

Elisabeth goes to Africa

Meanwhile Elisabeth had successfully completed her teacher training course and was now living at home. Knowing she was shortly to get married, she attended a Mabel Liddiard Baby Care course. Harold started drilling her in grammar exercises in Kinyarwanda so that she would have at least the basis when she got out there. Her parents were by now quite happy with the thought that she was to go to the Ruanda Mission. They had met and been impressed by the Sharps, Chrissie particularly enjoying Mrs Sharp's down-to-earth manner.

George, Elisabeth's father, was quite a student of politics and, as the Munich crisis developed, he knew that war was inevitable. As Rwanda and Burundi were former colonies of Germany, he thought that Hitler was quite likely to try to get them back. He thought that it was unlikely that Peter and Elisabeth would ever get there once war broke out, so he was quite receptive to a suggestion from Mrs Sharp that, rather than kicking her heels in London waiting for Peter to finish his training, it would be a good idea for Elisabeth to accompany the Sharps back to Burundi. A year in Africa acclimatising herself to the language and culture before the upheaval of marriage would be good for her. The idea was that Elisabeth would spend a year at Matana helping the Sharps start a new primary school. Then she would return to England, get married, and then, if possible, go with Peter to the newly opened station of Buye in the North of Burundi.

So, on Christmas Eve 1938, Elisabeth set sail with the

Sharps. Esther Sharp told her all she could about life in Africa. She described the scourge of jigger-infested toes, telling how the burrowing-fleas get under the skin where they lay their eggs in a pea-shaped sack. "You will be public enemy number one if you ever allow one of those to develop to the point of bursting so that they spread thousands more jiggers into the dust," she warned. Some days after arriving in Kabale, Elisabeth was horrified to find a pea-shaped bulge in one toe. She was frightened to show it to Esther, fearing that she would be branded antisocial, but once Esther saw it she reassured her that it had a long way to go before it burst. The jigger was skilfully removed with a safety pin. Happily these days the sight of people hobbling on jigger-infested feet is a rare one. The humble safety pin and cement floors in houses have both done much to eradicate the scourge. (When I got fourteen jiggers soon after I went to Byumba, this was considered a huge joke — though friends were careful to remove them as gently as possible. It was almost enough to prevent my wanting ever to return to Byumba — but not quite!)

Elisabeth's first night in Rwanda was spent at Shyira where she stayed with Joy Gerson and Hilda Langston, both very involved in Revival. In the evening there was an urgent call from a lady who wanted to confess. Saying to Elisabeth, "You'll be all right won't you? Don't wait up — we might be late", they disappeared leaving her alone in the house. She was terrified! Her main fear was of jiggers and she gingerly made her way to her room trying not to step on earth. Lying in bed, she thought of all she had been told about the Revival. Dr and Mrs Sharp were very disapproving of the excesses that they had seen. They considered that some of those affected were verging on heresy and that this could be the work of Satan. "What am I doing here?" she wondered. "Why have I come?" She was still awake when the others returned, full of what had happened.

They had visited a woman who was under conviction of the sin of drunkenness and wanted them to pray with her, but realized that God was telling her that first she needed to destroy all the beer she had so recently brewed for sale, so they had gone with her to help her tip out the vast containers of banana beer in her back yard. Then with a light heart she had gone back to the house and asked the Lord Jesus into her life. As Elisabeth listened, the first doubts about what she had been told about Revival entered her mind. "Would Satan have told this woman to destroy beer?" she wondered. "Is this really of Satan or could it be the Lord?"

Ever since her conversion, from time to time she had had a vision of a great crowd of people with miserable faces staring at her. She had no idea what this vision was about or who the people were, but next day when she went to the hospital evening service, she sat in the front and looked at the people gathered there, mainly relatives of the sick who had come to look after them, and with a start she recognized her vision. It was a tremendous confirmation to her that she was where God wanted her to be, but it was also a feeling that God was in the work at Shyira Hospital where so much spiritual life had been brought in Revival.

Finally she arrived at Matana where she soon settled down, sharing a house with Margaret Clayton, and also sharing a car which they called "Miss Mattie". She learned Kirundi as she taught the children numbers, repeating with them the different classes of nouns. Eseri and Robert Serubibi, having walked there from Bufumbira, were living nearby and Eseri was a great help in her language study, frequently translating for her.

Questions continued to trouble her about the Revival. One man who had allegedly been filled with the Spirit seemed to her to be merely provocative. He knew that one missionary considered the dancing that sometimes broke out in church to be pagan and should be repressed. It seemed to Elisabeth that this man took great delight in provoking the missionary by dancing whenever he came near him. Yet she was unhappy at the contrast between people who had been involved in Revival who genuinely welcomed Africans into their home and the attitude that she sensed in some other missionaries who were against Revival. They seemed to endure, rather than welcome, the presence of Africans in their homes and would rather that they kept their place.

Rev. Bert Jackson came over from Buhiga one day and was describing an all-night prayer meeting he had attended. A missionary spoke harshly about the loud and excessive singing that accompanied such nights. "If you came to one," said Bert, "you would see that the singing is spontaneous and not inappropriate." Elisabeth determined to go and see for herself.

Then she went to a missionary conference at Gisenyi. She was given a room with Hilda Langston and Joy Gerson. Elisabeth could not but see that their love for the Lord was joyful and real. They had something that she wanted for herself. The messages from Joe Church, too, were vital and she could not fault them theologically.

Back at Matana she was teaching in the newly started girls' school and gaining confidence in Kirundi. She also planned to have a weekend training teachers. "In my pride I announced that I had spent four years learning how to do this," she said. "Pawulo Rutwe [one of the Revival young men] came up to me and said, 'Those four years are no good to us. We want to hear about Jesus.' I was furiously angry but it was my ego that was deflated and it was good for me."

Often when Pawulo preached, he spoke against missionaries who built churches and houses but did not preach the gospel. This aroused antagonism, but one day Julia Barham (Lawrence Barham's wife) heard him and said, "Keep your eye on that young man, he will go far one day." True enough, he became a much-loved evangelist who often joined Peter and Elisabeth at Scripture Union camps in later years.

He loved to tell the story about how, during those early days in the headiness of Revival, he had gone with a friend to proclaim the true gospel at a Catholic church. The priest had graciously given him permission if he would wait until after they had finished mass. Waiting under the trees, they had looked at each other. "We compromised," they said. "We ought to have gone into the mass now." Squaring their shoulders, they marched into the church shouting out that ritual was unimportant. It was only Jesus and his cross who could save sins. Not surprisingly they were manhandled out of the church, tied up and later frog-marched back to Matana. They congratulated themselves on being found worthy to suffer for Christ. "But we didn't suffer for the gospel," Pawulo would say later to young people who were themselves experiencing the headiness of Revival. "We suffered for our impoliteness. Just imagine that you have an important visitor to stay and you smell the wonderful savours of the meal your wife is preparing. But when she brings it she puts it on a tin plate on the floor and kicks it in — would you want to eat it? Just so we must be careful how we present the wonderful news of the gospel of Christ."

Elisabeth was so grateful to Pawulo and other Africans who showed her the truth of 1 John 1:7. All her life she had been seeking an experience that would change her spiritual life. Through them she came to see that it was not an experience she needed but a Person, the Lord Jesus Christ. They seemed to have a living relationship with him as they repented quickly of their sins and found that all that separated from him was removed daily, clearing the way for good relationships with others. She knew that this was what she wanted.

Although life was very fulfilling at Matana, every night as they listened to the news Elisabeth began to worry. What should she do if war broke out while she was in Burundi? She had already been engaged for three years and the thought of being separated from Peter for the duration of the war was unthinkable. She made contingency plans with another missionary, Winifred Cox, whose sister was visiting her, to drive to the coast and take the first boat back.

On 3rd September 1939, listening to the crackling radio, they heard the news of the declaration of war. Immediately they set about making arrangements to leave. Next morning as she had her usual quiet time with the Lord, Elisabeth read in her *Daily Light* the words: "Sit still, my daughter" (Ruth 3:18 KJV). She felt this was a message for her from the Lord and so she stayed in Matana, waving goodbye to Winifred and her sister. It was just as well that she did stay, because Peter, as an accepted missionary candidate, was allowed to leave Britain. He travelled out by boat with his close friend from school, Harold Adeney, who had just got married to Isobel, who was, like Harold, a doctor. They were also coming to work in Burundi. Had Elisabeth left when she planned, their ships would have crossed at sea and they would indeed have been separated for the duration.

Peter travels to Africa

Meanwhile, Peter had been completing his missionary training at the Colony. When war was declared, he helped at a local stretcher post while awaiting permission to emigrate. He finally boarded ship on 23rd November 1939, sailing as part of a large convoy, which was dispersed by rough weather off Dover so that in fact they sailed alone, and were thus able to make better time than if they had stuck in the convoy. On board, Peter, who had been much influenced by Hudson Pope, and had taken part in several beach missions with him, sought permission to hold a daily service for children. Because of bad weather this didn't get started until after Gibraltar, but between 12 and 18 children enjoyed his simple Bible teaching, and eagerly learned Bible texts every day. On the last day before they reached Mombasa they had a special service for parents and handed out prizes for those who could recite all the verses. They also held a daily evening service and, on Christmas Eve, a gospel service by moonlight on deck. Despite all this Peter felt that he had not been an effective witness during his time on the ship. As I was reading this in his journal, I thought how typical this was of my father. All his life he never felt that he was achieving as much as he could, and my mother commented after his death, "How wonderful that at last he is free from all sense of guilt."

On arrival at Mombasa he went for a walk and was over-whelmed by the remembered smells and sights of Africa. He wrote in his journal that night:

How all this brings back memories; it's as though the intervening ten years had rolled away — rather a disturbing experience. One's principal reaction to it all, I'm afraid, is one of fear and inade-quacy, rather than anticipation or the desire to get to work. I con-fess to having no great love for Africa or the Africans — yet; the reminiscences aren't of that kind at all. Why am I here? Simply because I'm called, that's all. One must accept this as a fact — as it is, even though one has little if any feelings on the subject — no impelling sense of one's own mission and the needs of the Africans. Frankly, my chief feeling is of my own need. "Lord, there is none beside Thee to help, between the mighty and him that hath no strength: help us, O Lord our God; for we rely on Thee, and in Thy Name are we come against this multitude" (2 Chronicles 14:11 KJV).

They finally arrived in Dar-es-Salaam on Wednesday 3rd January 1940 and had to wait for two days for the train up-coun-try. After a tedious train journey they reached Kigoma on Lake

Tanganyika where they discovered to their dismay that the steamer only went once a week, because of the war. This meant two nights in a comfortable hotel but it also meant that they were able to visit Ujiji where Stanley had met Livingstone some 68 years earlier. "How much has happened to Africa since that meeting!" said Peter.

The last stage of their long journey was on the small steamer which would take them up Lake Tanganyika. The steamer was towing two barges which Isobel Adeney promptly christened "Goodness" and "Mercy", which followed them all their days. Peter was in a state of some trepidation. Would Elisabeth be there to meet them? They had not met for over a year. Would they still be the same? When they got to Uvira, in the Congo, they were very disappointed not to see anyone waiting for them, but they went below to collect their belongings, intending to hire a car to drive the last stretch to Bujumbura. Meanwhile Elisabeth and Winifred arrived and were equally disappointed to see no European on deck! Peter wrote, "Harold looked out and saw them coming up the gangway — Elisabeth and Winifred Cox — so that was all right; so much for a year!"

Preparations for the wedding

For the next few weeks they were at Matana, sorting out plans for their wedding. Then Peter was sent to Buye in the north of Burundi where he was to concentrate on language study and also to teach English and French to the deacons in training, while Elisabeth was sent to Buhiga to start a girls' school there. Peter was also preparing a site for their eventual home at Buye after their marriage. "As one looks out over the neighbouring hills and into the valleys 1,000 ft below, from the site of our house, one can see vast banana plantations on every hand — the sign of many kraals, revealing the presence of thousands and thousands of people. Ibuye (now called Buye) is in a position of great opportunity and so of great responsibility."

He also accompanied some of the deacons on visits to churches. "We stayed in a village church for about three hours — the first being taken up in learning (to read) and collecting the people together. For the rest of the time, we had a somewhat protracted service, due to the rain! As one item, I had to speak by interpretation — which is not easy. My companion was Yosiya, one of the Revival leaders and a deeply spiritual man."

Like Elisabeth he was uneasy about some of the excesses of Revival.

> In the evening we had hymn-singing in the Barhams' house, as usual, but this time it got rather out of hand owing to the presence of some pretty lively people from other stations: there was a lot of shouting and swaying and one began to wonder where it would end, but the Barhams spoke to them pretty directly about it and they began to see that a good deal of these antics were only done for effect and were not to the glory of God. They ended by singing "Down at the Cross" in a quiet and thoughtful spirit and the prayers that followed showed that some at any rate were convicted about it.

One day he was driving Yosiya Kinuka somewhere and they started discussing the meaning of the words "walking in the light" from 1 John 1:7. Peter argued that the Greek implied walking in the light of God with no sin to darken fellowship with him, but it was not intended to reflect fellowship with other people as the Revival people were teaching.

Yosiya put his head in his hands for a moment and then sighed. "You missionaries can defeat me with theological argument, but it is sterile, unless your lives show the truth of what you teach," he said. "You are like a soldier with a whole caseful of ammunition but no gun to fire it from. I have only one round of ammunition, my testimony, but it is effective when I fire it."

These words affected Peter deeply. Was all his Bible knowledge truly ineffectual because he did not know how to make use of it?

On Easter Day, thousands attended the service, overflowing into the open air. Peter commented,

> I think Ibuye is going through a sticky time just now and all of us, African and European are feeling it; there used to be great power in the services and great zeal for souls but somehow there is a bit of a lull just now. For myself, I feel it extraordinarily hard to feel as interested in the African and his salvation as I long to. One's lack of language doesn't exactly help, of course, but that's not a very good excuse — after all one can pray. We need a constantly

renewed vision of the Cross to quicken our love for Christ and so burn in our hearts a real love, a dynamic love for those for whom He died — even though at first one may not feel much natural love for them; [...] Woe betide us if we allow earthly things, however worthy and necessary in themselves to sap our zeal for His glory and the extension of His kingdom. But yet it is so _easy_ for this to happen — what with a language to learn, a house to build, educational problems — not to say a coming marriage.

Meanwhile the wedding was drawing closer. Because of the war it was difficult to get all the legal documents the Belgians required for a wedding in their territory, so it was decided that it would be wiser to have a legal wedding on British soil. Yet both wanted to be married in Burundi.

They drove up to Kampala where on 12th April 1940

we went in for a farcical ceremony at the D. C.'s office [District Commissioner] — rather a necessary one, though, to be sure. It took about five minutes, I think, and consisted for the most part of injunctions not to commit bigamy under pain of I don't know what penalties. Anyway she emerged Mrs Guillebaud in the eyes of the law but not in mine! The morning's _Daily Light_ caused her considerable amusement (Hebrews 10:1 KJV) — "The law having a shadow of good things to come"!

Just before they left for Uganda, the sad news had come of the death in Kenya, on Good Friday, of Archdeacon Pitt-Pitts, leaving a deep void in the church of Rwanda, for he had been a much-loved leader whose wisdom had kept together the divergent views on Revival among the missionaries. Peter and Elisabeth were to have their church wedding on 24th April 1940 at Matana and it was arranged to have a church council on the following day, to decide whom to ask to take up the leadership of the church. This meant that most of the missionaries were able to attend the wedding, as well as many of the government officials — and even the king of Burundi and several of his chiefs.

Bill Butler, Peter's best man who had been at the Colony with him, was a tutor at Mukono Theological College, and one of the students there was William Nagenda from Gahini who came over to see them before they left Uganda. Peter described him as "a deeply spiritual man; Bill says he's deepening all the time. He may have been a bit woolly in the past, but now he's turning into a real humble man of God — a delight to meet: so also is Yosiya Kinuka."

Finally the day of their wedding dawned. They had wanted Kosiya Shalita to marry them but because so many government officials were there it had been considered more politic for Lawrence Barham, newly made canon, to marry them, though Kosiya preached in Kirundi explaining the difference the love of Christ can make in a Christian marriage. Hymns were sung in both Kirundi and English, and Lawrence also preached, in English, on the text: "That in all things Christ may have the pre-eminence" (Colossians 1:18 KJV).

After a somewhat riotous send-off, they drove off in the new car they had collected in Kampala for a month's honeymoon in the Congo and Uganda, which was marred only by worrying news from the war in Europe.

Harold returns as archdeacon

The church council at Matana decided that there was only one man who could help them at this time, so Len Sharp wrote to Harold in England, knowing that it would be hard for them to come out in war time, but begging him to do what he could to come as archdeacon of Ruanda-Urundi. After much prayer, Harold and Margaret felt that it was right and that they could be of more use in Burundi, where Harold was longing to continue with the translation of the New Testament, than in England. Despite his reluctance to take responsibility, he felt this was of God and they began to make arrangements to leave. He wrote to his fellow missionaries before he left for Africa:

> I would like first to explain briefly to you all why the Bp.'s letter asking me to be Archdeacon in succession to Arthur P-P came to my wife and myself as a call from God which could not be disobeyed. We had originally hoped to return for the translation work somewhere about the end of this year or early next year, but the war and Lindesay's illness combined seemed to close the door as far as this year was concerned, and we had come to the conclusion that we should have to wait till the autumn of 1941.

Then last winter, just as I was turning down an offer of a living lest I by my own act should bar the way of return to Africa, came the Alliance wire asking me to return as soon as possible. The next thing was the minute of your own executive committee, confirming the Alliance minute, followed by an urgent letter from the archdeacon, the last I received before his death. Still we could not see our way to return this year, but we were deeply impressed by the cumulative calls, and went away for a short holiday to think and pray over the whole question. Then came the news of the archdeacon's death, and though the idea that I might be asked to take his place did not enter my mind, we realized that the need of another ordained man was greater than ever. Then came the Bp.'s letter. Well, what could I do? It was as though for months God had been saying to me, "Are you coming? Are you coming?", and we both felt that though the difficulties were as great as ever, we must accept God's call and leave it to him to deal with them.

Who is sufficient for these things? You all know that translation is my special line, and that any form of taking the lead is not congenial to me. And to follow one so gifted and so devoted as Arthur P-P. is a formidable matter. But if God has given the call, I can look to him for wisdom and strength. One thing I want to say from the outset. "Archdeacon" means chief servant; and I want to be from the first the servant of the Ruanda-Urundi church, both European and African. My great prayer (in which my wife joins me) is that you may always find us ready and glad to be of service to any of you.

I hope to be able to go round the mission shortly after my arrival, which we hope will be about the middle of October, and subsequently to arrange if poss. regular visits to each station every year, of sufficient duration to enable me to get real personal contact with the African leaders as well as with the Europeans.

You will all realize that the present grave war situation greatly increases the difficulties of our getting away, and that humanly speaking we might even be prevented altogether from coming this year. But such impossibilities are only a call to prayer and faith. Please pray us through. Our own faith is that God has called us and will not let us be stopped.

War conditions have brought about an entirely new set of problems in which we shall all share sooner or later and we can none of us see how far-reaching the problems will be. One thing is certain: that new problems and new difficulties are the prelude to new and deeper experiences of God's wonder-working power. And such new experiences should lead us on to new witness to this power and to a still deeper fellowship with one another. I come to you in critical days. I trust that the Ruanda Mission may buy up our opportunities in every direction, that we may go forward in new confidence in the Lord who always leads us in triumph, with a new song on our lips, and an ever-growing testimony to His all-sufficient grace. We know how helpless we are of ourselves to accomplish anything of the task committed to us, but I say to you as to myself "Our sufficiency is of God". Therefore let us take courage and all the glory be to Him. He must triumph.

Your friend and fellow worker

H. E. Guillebaud

Rosemary and Lindesay had both completed their university courses and were allowed to accompany their parents back to Burundi. Veronica had learned to type so that she could act as her father's secretary and was planning to travel with them when suddenly they heard that the government had refused her permission to leave the country, saying that her skills "were of use to the war effort". At short notice, George found her a job in the LNER offices. He and Chrissie also offered her a home where she could live until she was called up and joined the WAAF. She was only 19 at the time, and it was a real wrench to leave her in those unsettled times but they had to accept the decision. Philippa, rather to the dismay of her mother, had felt that God was calling her to teach in the Sudan rather than Ruanda-Urundi. She spent most of the war years teaching in Cambridge before doing her missionary training with CMS and leaving for the Sudan in 1945. Mary had studied the piano at the London School of Music and gained her LRAM, but at the outset of war had felt it right to train as a nurse at St Thomas' Hospital, London where she met Dr Tom Stockley, whom she later married.

On 3rd August 1940 Harold and Margaret, with Rosemary and Lindesay, set sail on the *Llangibby Castle* for Cape Town. There were several missionaries travelling, as well as a large number of unaccompanied children, and Harold described the voyage as "a cross between the taproom of a bar, a school playground during break, and a monastery". They had to carry their life-belts with them wherever they went on board and there was the constant fear of attack. They disembarked at Cape Town on 23rd August and set about finding out about trains north as well as arranging for the heavy luggage to go via Dar-es-Salaam. After a long and tedious train journey up through Africa, they caught the lake steamer up Lake Tanganyika to Uvira where they were met by Peter and Robert Serubibi on 9th October.

Peter had two pieces of news for them. He and Elisabeth had finally moved to Buye where they were living in the house built for the servants, while supervising the building of their own home, and Elisabeth was expecting their first child.

Harold and Margaret had a wonderful welcome at Matana, where there was a baptism of 80 candidates their first Sunday, and Harold had the privilege of preaching. They stayed for only a week before setting off for Uganda where Harold was installed as a canon of Namirembe Cathedral and made archdeacon of Ruanda-Urundi. He had started a cold on the way to Uganda and this developed into bronchitis so he was ill for about ten days, but seemed to have made a good recovery when they set off to visit all the stations and see what was happening. Finally they arrived back at Matana in time for Christmas when Harold preached. He began working on the Kirundi New Testament and also translated most of the Prayer Book before leaving for Buye on 10th January in time for the birth of their first grandson, John, on the 19th. Elisabeth had a very difficult birth and took some time to recover from it.

Ordination of the first African clergymen in Burundi

They had hoped to go to a convention at Buhiga, but Harold developed a cough again and it was considered wiser to stay at Buye. He was much better by the time the bishop arrived for the ordination and he was able to give three addresses at the Quiet Day beforehand. "I can so clearly see him," wrote Margaret later, "standing in the great room at the big house (we had the services there) with his overcoat on because he still had a bit of cold and his back to the fireplace, just giving of his very best. I felt there was much power there that day."

Two days later the bishop sent him away from the church council to rest, and again his temperature soared. Right up to the last moment he was hoping to get to the ordination service on 9th February 1941 but to his intense disappointment he was not well enough. Margaret wrote,

I think it was the great disappointment of his life, he had longed for it so. In fact even in England ages ago he had said how he would love to be at the first ordination, and now he was counting on taking his part. However all he said with a smile to me was "Shall we receive good at the hand of the Lord, and shall we not receive evil?" I stayed with him and we read the service together. And the ordinands had tea with him and he was so patient and happy.

It was at that ordination service that Yosiya Kinuka was ordained, together with two other Africans, the first three Africans to come to faith and later be trained through the Ruanda Mission. Following his ordination Yosiya returned to his beloved Gahini. Yosiya was a tremendous influence on my life. He always seemed serene and had a cheerful word for us children, however busy he was. I remember him taking me for a ride on his new motor-cycle at Gahini, and how devastated he was when I fell off and cut my leg, but also how efficient he was in cleaning and tying up the deep cut.

Harold's illness

A week after the ordination, Harold was still not fit enough to accompany the bishop on his round of confirmations, and soon it was decided that he needed a nurse. After some discussion, to his great relief, it was decided that he would do better in his own home at Matana, so Peter drove him on a mattress in the back of his car, with Margaret driving Elisabeth and baby John. However a fortnight later, Dr Len Sharp, fearing that it was tuberculosis, felt that he would do better at a lower altitude and he was taken down to Rumonge, a small Arab village on the shores of Lake Tanganyika. Robert Serubibi went with them as he had been suffering from bad asthma and he was a great companion for Harold, whose dearest wish was that Robert could go to Mukono to train for ordination.

They had two weeks by the lakeside, a precious two weeks for Margaret as they talked over their lives together and their hopes for the future. Margaret and Robert were also able to visit a newly started church school where the teacher was one of those whom Harold had baptized in Bufumbira in 1926. After a week he took a turn for the worse and Margaret sent an SOS to

Matana which was answered by Harold Adeney, bringing fresh medicines and the unwelcome news that he might have to stay there for months. But within a week Dr Sharp visited and found him decidedly worse, and in need of better nursing, so he was taken back to Matana where he was put to bed in the house the Adeneys had just vacated for a bigger one. It was felt that he needed X-rays and hospitalization in Kampala, so Margaret and Lindesay stayed in their house packing. But then Harold developed pleurisy and Harold Adeney went to Buye to fetch back the Sharps who were just starting their holiday and warn Peter that Harold was unlikely to survive.

Peter drove to Kigeme to collect Rosemary who had just passed her language exam. He then picked up Elisabeth and John and drove to Bujumbura to find some oxygen which was needed by his father, all the time fearing the worst, but when they reached Matana he seemed to have come through the crisis and was making a good recovery. The next day, Sunday, they had a quiet communion service by his bedside with Kosiya officiating in English but otherwise just the family. "Oh, that has been nice," said Harold.

The doctors all agreed that he needed to go to Kampala as soon as he could manage the journey, and then he would probably need to go to South Africa to recuperate for months if not years, which meant that he was facing having to leave the work he had just taken up — a big blow for him — but in the meantime they had a pleasant family time with Harold delighting in his grandson, before Peter and Elisabeth returned to Buye.

Margaret asked the doctors and Kosiya to come and pray with him in a little service on Monday night 21st April. It was a wonderful time, with Harold claiming healing for the sake of the work which he believed that God had so clearly called him to do. They were all conscious of the Lord's presence but had no assurance about the outcome, as they had on a previous occasion in the family when they had prayed for a healing which was granted.

Next day Margaret read to him from Amy Carmichael's book *Gold by Moonlight* and he said, "Now I know what is the main key of this, it is that we should learn to accept things when we can't understand them. When God appears to lead us in wrong paths or we can't understand, we must accept. If I have to preach a farewell sermon here, now I have my message: we must accept his perfect will." Margaret wrote:

> That was his farewell message to us all. There was no further inti-
> mate talk. The family had just finished supper at the Adeneys
> when the boy left on guard called "arababara cyane" (he suffers
> much). I had a queer instinct and raced up the path without even
> waiting for a lamp. I was only just in time... I took off his glasses
> and he just turned his head slightly and rested it on my shoulder,
> and said faintly "I feel awfully bad", closed his eyes and nestled
> down, sighed just a few times and "fell asleep". I don't think it
> could have been more than five minutes from the beginning of the
> attack. I had just time to say, "Better soon — thine eyes shall see
> the King in his beauty", and then I sang to him "As the moun-
> tains", and I think that must have been the last earthly sound he
> could have heard. Dr Len came in just as he was actually going,
> and at once knelt down and committed him to the Lord, it was just
> lovely.

As they left him half an hour later, they found most of the peo
ple of the station waiting quietly outside so they all went to the
church to give thanks to the Lord for his life. At midnight
Margaret and Rosemary, with Harold Adeney for company,
drove off to Buye to tell Peter and the Stanley Smiths. "It's about
110 miles and bar a lot of fog on the low-lying part of the road,
it was a lovely drive. We saw a wonderful moon-rise and the
dawn — such a dawn. That drive was a great help as it gave me
time to think things out a bit and it was something to do."

The news came as a great shock, as the last any at Buye had
heard was that he was improving, but everyone piled into cars
to go to Matana for the funeral, where Harold was laid to rest in
a grave outside the church exactly a year after Peter and
Elisabeth had come out of it as man and wife.

Margaret sent a cable to her daughters in England: "STILL
ALL ONE FAMILY IN HEAVEN AND EARTH. DADDY IN HEAVEN
TUESDAY. HEART ATTACK, INSTANTANEOUS, PAINLESS."
Written on a plaque above his grave, are the words from
2 Timothy 2:15 (KJV): "A workman that needeth not to be
ashamed, rightly dividing the word of truth".

It is hard to understand why God gave such a clear call to
Harold and yet took him to himself so soon afterwards. The mis-

sion needed his abilities at that time, especially his clear under-standing of the Scriptures. They needed someone to guide them through the difficult times of excess in Revival with a scriptural understanding of what was happening. He was only 52 and could have been expected to give several years of godly leader-ship, and the work on both Bibles in Kirundi and Kinyarwanda was urgently needed. Yet God took him. Years later I had equal mystification as I watched a fellow mission partner die, exactly a week after she arrived in the country. I have found it helpful to read Harold's journals and to see his unwavering trust in the perfect will of God. It is indeed in acceptance that one can find peace.

Chapter 5

Growing Pains in the Revival

Reactions to Harold's death

Harold's death left everyone reeling. As the news came through to England the *Ruanda Notes* recorded the shock. "H.E. as we called him seemed so exactly the right man in the right place and it is difficult for us to see how he can be spared, but God knows how; He never makes mistakes so somehow or other it must be for the blessing of the land he loved and gave his life for. 'The Word of God abideth for ever' and H.E. more than anyone else has given that Word to Ruanda and Urundi." The tribute printed in the same issue of *Ruanda Notes* ended with these words: "He gave his all for Christ, money, intellect, family and home: he was consecrated to his high and holy calling. He loved Africa and there he rests, leaving behind in his wife and children a small army pledged to the salvation of Africa. There are saints and great souls in every age: here is one in the twentieth century."

Just after the funeral, Algie Stanley Smith asked Rosemary to consider taking on her father's translation work. She had just passed her first Kinyarwanda exam very well but she did not speak Kirundi and she felt totally inadequate to begin such a daunting task. Her mother was exhausted, and it was decided that they all needed a holiday before any decisions about the future were made.

Peter and Elisabeth experience Revival

At a hotel in Uganda, John was crying a lot and Elisabeth was not sleeping well. Peter was spending a lot of time supporting his mother and Elisabeth began to feel neglected. Then one

Growing Pains in the Revival 101

night Peter developed an acute pain in his back. Not wanting to disturb Elisabeth, he went to his mother who was so concerned that she arranged for the whole family to move to Kampala where Peter could see a doctor. It turned out that he had a kidney stone and was admitted to Mengo Hospital where he passed the stone without needing an operation. Although Elisabeth was pleased that Peter had been treated, she felt rejected because he had gone to his mother rather than her.

They had previously arranged to go to stay with Bill Butler for their holiday, so Peter took Elisabeth and John to Mukono, where Bill was chaplain at the theological college, so that he could recuperate. Margaret, Rosemary and Lindesay continued to stay with the bishop in Kampala.

At Mukono, Bill could see that all was not well with their marriage and talked with them both. Elisabeth admitted that she felt neglected. Harold's death had meant that Margaret had turned to her only son for comfort in a way that excluded Elisabeth. Bill said to Peter that according to Genesis 2:24 a man should leave his father and mother and cleave to his wife and that in marriage a man's first responsibility was to his wife. When Peter returned to Kampala, he tried to explain this to his mother but she did not understand and was bitterly hurt.

At Mukono, Peter and Elisabeth both attended the 4 a.m. prayer meeting which they did not enjoy. They felt, and showed, that it was too emotional and loud, and was probably just the way ignorant Africans could express their feelings, but that it was not for them. William Nagenda challenged them about their critical attitude towards those praying. At first Peter resented this rebuke, particularly as it came from an African, but as he allowed the Holy Spirit to speak to his heart he realized that it was mostly his pride that was reacting. Here he was, a trained teacher from England who had come to proclaim the gospel to the uneducated black men, and yet it was their love and knowledge of the Lord which was teaching him. That night he knelt and asked Jesus to deal with his critical spirit and fill him anew with the Holy Spirit. He often said in later years that God had to break his pride before he could heal his heart.

When they returned to Buye they were met by Gideon Kabano, who was helping Dr Stanley Smith as he took over the daunting task of Bible translation. Gideon took one look at their faces and gave them a great hug of welcome. No words needed to be said. He knew that they had had a new experience of the Lord. Later, Elisabeth was to say that that was the moment she felt accepted in the Revival movement. She had been inclined towards the Revival but had been held back by Peter's attitude. Once the Lord had dealt with their sin, the Africans could see a change in them and they were accepted without reservation.

They began to put into practice the lessons they were learning, and gradually developed the lifelong habit of discussing difficulties as they arose rather than leaving them to become real problems, so that, when one had offended the other in any way, they would bring it to the light of Jesus for cleansing and forgiveness. Soon Elisabeth realized that her resentment of Margaret had its roots in jealousy, and she wrote asking for her forgiveness for the way she had reacted in Uganda. She received a gracious letter in return, saying that her jealousy was perfectly understandable and asking forgiveness in return. When, two years later, I was born and named Margaret, my grandmother's delight was obvious.

Rosemary begins translation

Margaret, Lindesay and Rosemary returned to Matana and began the painful task of readjustment to life without Harold. Rosemary began working with his translation team and soon became immersed in the work. In October 1941 she wrote in the *Ruanda Notes*:

> Since my father's Home Call I have tried my hand, in a small way, at translation. I have wanted to do translation work since I was 15, though I had always imagined doing it with my father. But that was not to be. I have translated, with the aid of Stefano Ndimubandi, my father's chief translator, the first 12 chapters of Acts, and have gone through them with the Danish Baptist Mission at Musema and also two Methodist Stations. A good many alterations were, of course, necessary, but there were hopes of an agreed version arising from it. Do pray that if it be the Lord's will for me to take up this work He will make it plain. To me it would be an unspeakable privilege to be allowed to carry on the work my father loved so dearly.

Although she continued with the translation work, it took until March 1943 for her appointment to be approved by all the missions. She checked her work with the Danish Baptist Pastor, Hans Emming, at Musema, a hundred miles to the north. Unlike Rwanda, where the language is virtually the same throughout the country, in Burundi there are huge regional differences, so it was essential to try to find words that would be understood throughout the country. She gave the example of the sentence: "A night and a day I spent <u>in the deep</u>." "The Matana expression for <u>in the deep</u> is not known at Musema, while theirs means here <u>in the midst of a crowd</u> or <u>in the thick of battle</u>. We have so far failed to find a word common to both places!"

In 1988 she wrote describing the lengths she would go to find the right word.

I had any number of fascinating hunts for words, but perhaps the most intriguing was the search for the right word for "tongs" (Isaiah 6:6). With no dictionary all I could do was to try to describe tongs to Stefano, but he declared there was no such thing in Kirundi. I asked what the smiths used when holding hot metal, and he didn't know, so we set off to find out. We were on safari at the time, translating when we had a moment to spare between services or walking to the next place. We asked where there was a smithy and were given directions. Soon we could hear the sound of hammer blows. It was the time of millet harvesting and we were walking through a valley with very high millet both sides of the path, almost having to push our way through as it met over our heads. There were two or three of us and I suggested we just watch what the smith used, then in casual conversation ask what it was called, as the local people were not used to seeing Europeans and might be suspicious if asked outright. Then suddenly we came out of the millet and there in a clearing was a shack, with the smith and a little boy working his bellows over a glowing charcoal fire. The smith looked up as our shadows fell across his work, saw me and gave a yell of terror and dashed off into the millet, followed by the boy! The people with me shouted that I was quite safe, not a cannibal, only a woman, etc, etc, and we only wanted to greet him. Eventually he came back, very warily. I kept right behind the rest, at a distance, while the others talked and chatted and cajoled, till he and the child continued what they had been doing. To our disappointment, he was repairing a cracked hoe, which was of course still in its handle, so he was holding on to that. The blade was glowing red as the boy used the bellows. Eventually one of the men said, "That hoe is extremely hot. However would you hold it if it wasn't in its handle?" "Easy," said the smith, "I would use my *ikimano*." "What's that?" The man searched around in the grass floor covering and produced a piece of bark about 6" by 5" scored down the centre so that it would fold. "This is *ikimano*," he said. "When it burns through I cut another." So that is what, in Kirundi, the seraph used to take the burning coal from the altar to lay on Isaiah's lips.

During the war there were hazards in sending manuscripts to England, and indeed the manuscript of Daniel was lost when the ship it was in was sunk by enemy action, but at last, in September 1943, she wrote, "The Kirundi New Testament is finished! On 30th August at 12.15 p.m. I called mother for the last few words of Revelation, and then we had a time of prayer. How vividly we recalled my father coming to call us, on the morning of 13th February 1930, to hear those same verses put for the first time into Lunyaruanda."

There was still much revision to be done, and problems arose over orthography with the Tutsi of Matana refusing the spelling decided upon by the rest of the country. They persuaded Rosemary that it was a spiritual issue, and many months of unhappy altercations followed before she was able to persuade them to withdraw their objections and accept the majority view. Sam Sindamuka, one of her translators, later to become archbishop of Burundi, said, "I finally realized that the positioning of a 'y' was not important enough to lose my peace over."

It was November 1951 before the New Testament and Psalms were finally available. Margaret and Rosemary went to Bujumbura to collect as many parcels of books as their car could hold. On their return, as they neared Matana, they started hooting their horn. By the time they arrived, there was a huge crowd of dancing, singing people. Someone climbed the church tower and began drumming out the good news. The pastor cut the string of the first parcel and reverently took out the first book. They all went into the church, still singing. Ephesians 6:10-18 and Psalm 119:105 were read and then in prayer several people poured out their hearts in praise that at last they had God's word in their own language. Though it was getting dark, they went across to the bookshop where 58 copies were sold in half an hour. It was 20 years almost to the day since Rosemary had joined her father and mother on the trip to Gahini to sell the first Kinyarwanda Testaments on 8th November 1931. She wrote in *Ruanda Notes*: "I wish some of you could have been there to see the joy on the faces of the crowd round the bookshop and the delight as one after another got a copy."

One of her translators, Yosefu Sinkema, had died of cancer while Rosemary had been in England on furlough and his brother was also dying of the same disease. Rosemary took a copy to him in the hospital.

In spite of his pain and weakness, his whole face was alight with joy as he took it into his hands. He said, "If only one could take things to heaven, I would like to take this to show my brother how beautifully they have made it!" Two days later he died. We had several opportunities, during the times he was conscious, of reading him passages about Heaven. How he enjoyed being read to!

Margaret at Matana

During those years, Margaret did whatever she saw needed doing, teaching when she had the opportunity, and visiting in the villages. In 1942, she was able to start work on a small printing press in a tiny room at the end of the school, which soon absorbed much of her time. Peter had developed a scheme to teach reading, which she printed on sheets with accompanying cards of words, etc. In 1952, she supervised the building of a memorial bookshop and printing room as a more permanent memorial to Harold. At last there would be a lovely light and spacious room for printing with a separate one for book-selling.

She was also involved in the teacher training course where she did a weekly class on liturgy, and had a weekly Bible class with old women from the hills. In 1947 she wrote: "If it were only the light on the faces of some of the old women in the weekly Bible class, you would feel that all the Ruanda Mission stands for is well worthwhile. It is a wonderful thing to be allowed to be here." She also started a youth group, the first of its kind in the country, which she called *Intore za Yesu*, "Soldiers (or chosen) of Jesus". They all wore a simple uniform and would meet each week for games and basic Bible teaching.

In September 1949 she took 36 of the ... members to a camp near Rweza, about twelve miles from ... tana. They showed film-strips each evening to crowds of children and their parents from the neighbourhood, and during the day had games and Bible talks. On the Sunday there was a big children's service attended by many of the children in the area and some of the *intore* gave their testimonies. "One child from Rweza said he had never testified before but he wanted his schoolfellows to know that now they need never feel worried lest he should steal their pencils any more as he had given his heart to the Lord Jesus and if he found people's pencils he would always give them back."

Lindesay's schools

Lindesay started a kindergarten for the children of the Christian families who lived near Matana, but this was later extended to any who wanted to come. In November 1942 she wrote,

> We have about 90 three-to-ten year-olds who come every morning, bringing their "fees" in the form of cow-dung (for manure) or fire-wood. Their parents won't pay money for such tinies, so they practise self-help! They are of all sorts and conditions, from Kosiya's and Robert's children down to the scruffiest little Bahutu, but when they all get into their red "sunsuit" uniform, distinctions vanish, and the mixing of "rich" and "poor" is very good for them. Awful little snobs most of the Batutsi children are by nature!

She began training local girls, and later girls from other mission stations, to teach the children. They would watch while Lindesay taught in the mornings and then she would teach them in the afternoons until they were able to teach classes themselves. She also started a "brides' school", where young women who were about to get married would come for a month and be given teaching on Christian marriage, with cookery lessons, care of babies, right nutrition, etc. Many of them had never held a needle before they came, but by the end of the month were able to produce surprisingly beautiful pieces of embroidery or clothes to impress their young men! Later Lindesay also supervised all the schools in her area, which was no easy task.

In 1941, just after Harold's death, Robert Serubibi had been accepted for training at Mukono, so Rosemary spent time teaching him Greek which he picked up very quickly. He was ordained on 27th June 1945 and was posted to Rweza, some twelve miles from Matana, where Margaret had built a church totally in the Kirundi style, as a memorial to her husband. Robert and Eseri lived out the gospel there and were much loved. They had started a work among the despised pygmies, or Twa, sharing with them the love of Christ.

Margaret, Lindesay and Rosemary spent the Christmas of 1945 with them at Rweza, sleeping in tents near the church. Rosemary wrote:

> We had a good service in the morning, Robert and Mother both speaking. There were huge crowds, the church was packed and there were as many more outside. The chief from a neighbouring hill sat there with a number of his followers; he is a tough old heathen too. We were very encouraged. In the afternoon we went to the pygmies who live quite near. They are not so much pygmies as potters, but are called pygmies because of their trade, and are such social outcasts that if one enters a room everyone else gets up and goes out, and to visit them is considered quite impossible. We spoke and sang to them and they were very pleased. One of our teachers and his wife, in another place, have succeeded not only in getting four pygmy girls to come to church but also, far harder, getting the congregation to stay when they enter and sit with them.

Towards the end of December 1946, Robert developed meningitis. There was no doctor at Matana as the missionaries were beginning to return to Britain for leave, following the end of the war. Before they could fetch a doctor from Buye with the vital drugs he needed, Robert died, on 3rd January 1947, leaving Eseri with six young children to bring up. She moved back to Matana and soon took over the running of the brides' school from Lindesay.

As an example of the effect of Revival, Rosemary told the following story in *Ruanda Notes* in December 1947. The church teacher, mentioned earlier, had been interested for some time in a pygmy, or Twa, called Gasato, trying to tell him that the gospel was as much for him as for others in Burundi. The Twa are considered sub-human in Burundi, so Gasato was amazed when the teacher not only invited him to a meal but also placed the plate he had used with the others to be washed without breaking it as was usual. He soon became a Christian and joined the baptism classes, but then became withdrawn.

One day a team came from Matana to his church and preached on the power of the blood of Jesus to cleanse from all sin. Suddenly Gasato confessed that he had been holding himself back from true fellowship because he had murdered his mother-in-law many years before. He knew he had to confess this but he feared that he would be hanged. Now he decided that, at whatever cost, he had to repent.

> Radiant with joy at his new-found peace, he set off for the government post, and was given a hearing. The administrator questioned him closely, trying to find out whether he had come of his own accord, or whether the mission had told him to come. He witnessed boldly before the whole court, and said to them, "I would rather lose my life and gain my soul than keep my life and lose my soul." When the administrator had questioned the chief of his district and found that no suspicion had ever been entertained regarding the death and that it had happened 13 years previously, so that it could not have been fear of exposure that had prompted the confession, he let him go free. He was profoundly impressed by the incident, the more so as it came on top of the confession, with restitution, of two other Protestant Christians to cattle stealing in their unregenerate days.

Elisabeth's illness

Since his father's death, Peter had been teaching primary school teachers at Buye — the first such school. Early in 1942, Elisabeth fell ill and the doctors were baffled by her symptoms. She was sent with Peter and John to Dar-es-Salaam in Tanzania, where the war seemed very close. They woke up one morning to find the harbour filled with what seemed like the whole British navy!

Her symptoms continued and after about two months she was sent to Nairobi. Because of the war it was hard to find good accommodation and they were staying in an appalling hotel where Elisabeth began to feel worse and worse. Matters were not helped when she received a telegram saying that her father was unwell with neuritis. She was not too alarmed as it was not a fatal disease, though she wondered why they had sent a telegram. Then the next day she received another to say that he had died of a heart attack.

Mrs Rosalind Pitt-Pitts, widow of the archdeacon of Ruanda-Urundi, having heard that they were in Nairobi, tracked them down to the run-down little hotel where they were staying and swept them off to stay with her in her graceful home. She arranged for Elisabeth to see a doctor, who found that her spleen was four times the size it should be and that she was obviously suffering from malaria, although she had no other symptoms. Treatment soon set her to rights and they were able to return to Burundi.

While in Kenya, they were able to attend the Kenya Keswick Convention where they met a band of keen Christian soldiers mostly from South Africa. "They showed us by their example the blessing that results from effective witnessing, as they were weekly, almost daily, seeing some of their fellow-soldiers accepting Christ and being transformed by Him. We covenanted with God to speak to at least one person each day about Christ, trusting Him to arrange the contact. I can't say what a blessing this has been to us," Elisabeth wrote to her home church, replying to their letter of sympathy following her father's death.

She continued:

Many Africans who have been converted through the Revival have joined themselves into evangelistic teams and between each member there is a fearless honesty. Everything that would hinder the fellowship — jealousies, resentments, grudges — are all brought into the light where "the blood of Jesus Christ, God's Son, cleanses us from all unrighteousness." It is a costly business and there have been many mistakes, but it has brought an amazing fellowship which has spread also to include the Europeans. It is the way of victory over the barrier between black and white. I can truly say I have never had such fellowship in Christ as with my African brothers and sisters in Him. [...] They are fearless in telling us our faults as Europeans — our pride of race, position, possessions... As a result they help us to be more effective missionaries, as on the other hand they love us and they want us. They no longer accept what we say because we are Europeans, but only what is obviously revealed to us by God and lived out in our lives. So pray for us that we may stand the test.

Peter and Elisabeth at Buye

Back at Buye, Elisabeth had renewed vigour as she resumed teaching at the girls' school, and Peter returned to the teacher training school. Among those whom he was teaching were several who had been influenced by Revival at Gahini, including Eustace Kajuga. He was a first class athlete who had started to limp and been taken to Kampala for treatment, so he started his teacher training course with his leg in plaster.

One day, when the teachers in training were meant to be digging their field, there was such heavy rain that they could not go out. In their dormitory they were studying the Bible and praying when the Holy Spirit descended on them. They were filled with a sense of awe at the holiness of God and their need to repent of all sin. Some produced papers that they had received or written which were full of indecent writings, others confessed theft of blankets, etc. Peter had been repairing his car all morning, but was filled with joy when he went to the dormitory and heard what was happening. All that night and next morning the men continued to pray and to praise God. They started to compose a hymn based on *The Pilgrim's Progress* where three men give Christian a letter which will give him the right to enter the Celestial City, but one of his companions tries to enter without it. The hymn has the chorus, "I praise the cross, I praise the holy tomb; But above all else I praise our Lord Jesus." This hymn is still one of the best loved of Rwandan hymns.

The next day, after church, all the things connected with sin were taken outside and burnt, much to the consternation of some missionaries who considered it a waste to burn a perfectly good blanket. They were told it had been stolen from a lorry driver who could not be traced and the man who had stolen it wanted nothing contaminating in his room. Peter wrote: "Those of us who thought 'what a waste' were reproved by the next day's lesson in class from John 12:5-8. Everybody began to search their boxes for 'borrowed' property and we Europeans did not escape; it is amazing how we hang on to things — books, tools, chairs and so on and Satan dulls one's conscience (of course I'm going to give it back!)."

Shortly after this, the teachers took their final exams and sadly one failed. He was disappointed, of course, but he said,

"These exams would have given me a letter from the church enabling me to get a job but I have the more important letter which will enable me to enter heaven." Not long after this he fell ill with tuberculosis and died within a few weeks. At his funeral there was general rejoicing that he knew he had the letter which was more important than any church certificate.

Divisions through Revival

Difficulties were still apparent between those missionaries who had embraced the Revival and those who were deeply suspicious of the excesses. In 1939 Dr Algie Stanley Smith had been concerned about the developing division brought about by the Revival. He wrote in the *Ruanda Notes*,

> The two parties are the "Abaka" or keenites on the one hand, and the "orthodox" on the other. The one, fired with a great zeal for God born in the manifestations of his power in the revival, have no use for anything less than the really victorious life; while the others, seeing the dangers of extravagances, have felt that they had to be the custodians of sound doctrine. It should have been easy for the two to be complementary, but the devil has got them divided. The "Abaka" have been harsh in their dealings and their criticisms, and have tended towards the idea that only their party were real Christians; and the orthodox have been resentful of criticism, quick to see the inconsistencies of the "Abaka", sometimes only too obvious, and they have often sheltered behind their orthodoxy so as to go on comfortably at a low level of Christian living, and sometimes in secret sin. And both sides have indulged in definite misrepresentation of the other.

He asked people to pray. "Don't pray that things may settle down. We never want to go back to the old complacency. But pray that the fire doesn't go out."

Some five years later these same divisions were apparent among the missionaries. Peter, Joe Church and Godfrey Hindley, the doctor at Shyira, wanted to break away from the Anglican mould and have a united church of those who had accepted the Revival from all denominations, but this scandalized some of the other missionaries, especially Margaret. When they realized the division their proposal was bringing they backed away, but

Harold and Margaret Guillebaud in their Cambridge garden

Last photo of the family, May 1940 — Peter was already in Africa.
Front row: Veronica, Harold, Margaret, Mary. *Back row:* Lindesay, Rosemary, Philippa

Spreading the message of Revival. *Left to right:* Yosiya Kinuka, Lawrence Barham, William Nagenda, Joe Church

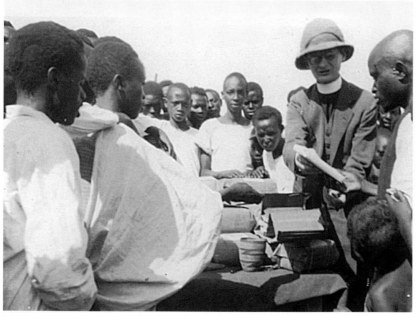

"Selling the Lord's own book on the Lord's own day!"

Batutsi high jump at the
king's court — Peter is the
small figure in the large
topee! (Note the small mound
which aided take-off)

On safari

The wedding — *left to right:* Canon Lawrence Barham, Miss Joy Sharp, John Sharp, Mrs Esther Sharp, Peter, Elisabeth, Miss Mary Sharp, Dr Len Sharp, Rev. Kosiya Shalita, Rev. Bill Butler

Guests at the wedding — Burundi chiefs

Peter and John, John and Peter, 1943 and 1970 (same tree). "A rabbit when it is grown, is suckled by its young!"

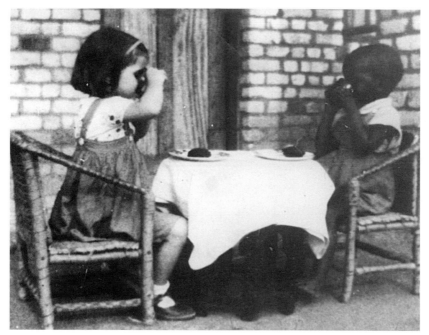

Meg's first boyfriend. Husi was killed in 1994.

"Sometimes Daddy lets me hold the string!"

Can't-sinki

Can-sinki

Shyogwe School showing the wall that nearly fell down

Marian and Eustace Kajuga with their family

in the end it was the Africans themselves, like William Nagenda and Yosiya Kinuka who loved the Anglican form of service, who would not agree to forming a new church. Often people ask why Europeans brought the divisions of the denominations to Africa. The answer is that the Africans themselves wanted to stay with them. Having seen the division their ideas would bring, Joe became committed to the idea of renewal from within the church structures.

Their efforts to break the mould of denominationalism brought down on them the wrath of church authorities. The bishop was beginning to see the missionaries who had been touched by Revival as rebels. He did not doubt their fervency for the Lord but he considered that they were trouble-makers and were teaching the Africans not to accept his authority as well.

In October 1941 there had been a problem at the theological college at Mukono where the principal objected to what he saw as the excesses of students who had been influenced by Revival. They met for prayer at 4 a.m., they challenged sin where they saw it and offended those who saw no harm in a little pilfering. The principal forbade this early morning prayer meeting, and the preaching to fellow students. After a time of heart-searching, 26 students, among whom was William Nagenda, decided that they must obey God rather than man. They refused to sign a paper saying that they would no longer get up early for prayer, and continued to challenge sin when they saw it. They were expelled from the college for insubordination, and the chaplain, Peter's friend Bill Butler, was transferred. Although the bishop accepted that they were the liveliest of the Christians in training at Mukono, he also considered them to be insubordinate and trouble-makers, and backed the principal in his actions. Although at first he saw this as a tragedy, William later saw the hand of God in it. He never was ordained but instead travelled the world as an evangelist.

The government was informed and, because there was a fear of insurrection, those expelled were classed as "a dangerous native movement in time of war". Bill Butler was called to see an official from the government to explain what had happened at the college. After a time the official said in a bemused way, "Now let me get this straight. Those who objected to stealing were expelled and those who did the stealing were allowed to stay. Is that really what happened?" Bill had to admit that it was.

Peter and Elisabeth were not alone in their initial suspicion of the Revival movement, nor in their gratitude to faithful African brethren who challenged missionaries to a deeper understanding of their faith. Dr Stanley Smith describes the effects of Revival in *Road to Revival* written in 1946, as follows:

> No one who understands spiritual warfare will be surprised to know that these five years have been troubled by profound disturbance and conflict. Among the Ruanda missionaries there was a great deal of distressing division. There seemed at one time to be three parties: those who threw themselves right into the Revival movement confident that the Holy Spirit would deal with difficulties; a central group, who while rejoicing in the movement as of God, were critical and apprehensive of some of its features and so felt excluded from real fellowship; thirdly, those who were so troubled at what they thought were dangerous and evil tendencies in practice and in doctrine as to feel that they must take strong measures of control.

He then listed the three main points of conflict. He used the name *Abaka* which was the name originally given to those changed by Revival. It meant "those on fire" but the name was found to be divisive and it was later dropped.

(1) "Wild singing and dancing often far into the night. Exaggerations of these did occur; but experience has shown that the African leaders, men of real spiritual insight, brought these things under control. On the positive side, it was clear that the African must express his joy in an African way, and the singing of our lovely hymns has been a constant spiritual inspiration." [Certainly it was preferable for hymns to be sung at night rather than the drunken spirit singing which was common among the pagans at that time.]

(2) "Wrong doctrine. Things have been said by the Abaka, mostly be it noted in the heat of controversy, which were wrong. But it was generally proved to be a matter of emphasis, not error. The overwhelming emphasis in the Revival was on the sins of the church, the need for repentance and

the efficacy of the blood of Christ for cleansing and life-giving power."

(3) "Exclusiveness. The most puzzling problem arose from the very nature of Revival as a revolt against low spirituality. This meant intolerance of any lowering of standards, and thereby the denial of fellowship to other Christians who were not heart and soul in the movement. It was labelled compromise to co-operate with them. There was no conscious spiritual pride in this. It sprang from jealousy for the truth and the fair name of Christ. But it perplexed and divided the mission."

In 1945 there was a significant gathering of missionaries of all denominations at Mutaho in Burundi. The speaker was J. W. Hayley of the Free Methodists, a real man of God who emphasized the need for the holiness of God to be reflected by holy living. He was concerned about the lack of unity among the Anglican missionaries and called them together to talk over their difficulties. At first the meeting was sticky but as they started to pray, gradually people began to repent of hardness of heart and judgemental attitudes, of lack of love and respect, and of anger and jealousy. They went to the ones they had found the hardest to relate to and asked them to pray for them. It was a very moving time and cleared the air. But that night in their room Peter and Elisabeth heard typewriters starting to tap. Letters were being written to the bishop saying that the Revival missionaries had repented, and were no longer rebelling.

The bishop used these letters to write to all the pastors in Uganda, particularly those who had been touched by Revival, saying the missionaries in Ruanda-Urundi had confessed to excesses and were no longer in rebellion. Shortly afterwards, Peter went to a large convention at Kabale, and was staggered when William Nagenda challenged him and Joe Church, asking them why they had compromised.

"How could you repent of what the Holy Spirit has been teaching you?" he asked. "Did you see those not supporting Revival repenting of their attitudes?"

Peter became very confused and depressed, saying later:

Many of us found this very hard. It had seemed so right at the time, how could we go back on it? The Ugandan leaders felt that we had joined up with those from whom we were divided by deep issues related to sin and repentance, had "papered over the cracks" and sought a fulness of the Spirit that by-passed true repentance. I went into deep spiritual darkness and was useless at the convention.

Joe said that there was no time to deal with this matter then. "Look at the crowds," he said. "They have come to hear the word of God. We must cater to their needs first and tackle our problems afterwards."

So they preached the Word of God and thousands responded in deep repentance. The theme of the convention was "Jesus Satisfies" and there were many testimonies to the way that Jesus satisfies: "I've got twelve children, I can't afford to educate them but Jesus satisfies." "My wife and I have been married for ten years without a child — but Jesus satisfies." A girl might say, "I'm getting on in years and have no husband but Jesus satisfies," and so on.

After it was over, the missionaries and the African brethren met and talked over what had happened. The missionaries could not deny what had seemed so right to them at Mutaho, but they made it clear that they had repented only of their own hard attitudes, not of what they had been learning through Revival, but it was a painful and confusing time.

Chapter 6

The Shyogwe Years (1944-1958)

Three volunteers for a new station

In 1944 Peter and Dr Algie Stanley Smith had been on the way to another convention at Shyira. They stopped at a site near Gitarama which was a possibility as a site for the new secondary school the mission had been asked to start in the area, as the Catholics had not at that time built any schools. They had with them a student from Buye, called Sira Kabirigi, who was nearly qualified. As he looked at the site, he felt a stirring in his heart.

Sira came from the north of Rwanda. As a young boy, herding his father's cows, he had been frightened when a white man, accompanied by some Ugandans, suddenly appeared at Gatsibo, in the north of Rwanda. He was fascinated by these strangers and listened, enthralled, as they told how he could get to know the remote Creator God, through his Son, Jesus Christ. He longed to go to learn in the small school which soon started, but his uncle (his father had died) refused to release him from his herding duties.

Whenever he heard the drums beating for school he would leave the cows and run to learn, hoping to gather them later before he had to return home, but often they had strayed and caused damage to fields whose owners complained to his uncle. However often he was beaten, he could not resist this learning. Then to his great joy his uncle, and later, his mother, became Christians and he was allowed to go to Gahini to learn. He was there when Revival started and was soon filled with the Spirit. He had been in the first class of those learning to be teachers at Buye.

At the Shyira convention in 1944, Peter spoke on 2 Kings 7:9. Samaria had been under siege and was starving. Four lepers decided that if they were going to die they might as well be killed by the Syrian army, as die of starvation in the city, so they went to the camp to find it deserted. During the night the Syrians had been scared away so the lepers started gorging on the food they found. But after a time they said to one another, "We do not well: this day is a day of good tidings, and we hold our peace" (2 Kings 7:9 KJV).

I have often heard my father speak on this story, which was one of his favourites. That time at Shyira was the first time he used it and he applied it to the situation in Bujumbura where he had been a few days before. Some American missionaries were desperate for helpers to develop their work and had appealed to the Anglican Church for help. One of those listening was Yohana Bunyenyezi. He had been Harold and Margaret's cook-boy at Kabale and was one of the two boys scared by a leopard when he accompanied Blasio Kigozi to Gahini. There he had accepted the Lord Jesus as his Saviour. He went to Mukono to be trained for ordination and had been one of the 25 students expelled. Now he received this challenge from the Lord and joyfully went to Bujumbura to help in this new work.

Yohana was not the only man there to know that God was calling him. Sira thought about the site he had seen, and the challenge of this new work, and knew that God was calling him. Back at Buye, Lawrence Barham received a communication from the government, saying that the Shyogwe site had been granted. He called all the students together, told them about the opportunity ahead and asked if anyone felt that God was calling them to respond to this need. Sira, and Eustace Kajuga also from Gahini, both responded but both had already been assigned somewhere else, so Peter went to Gahini to ask for their release in a year's time.

Eustace had left Buye to teach at Gahini in 1943 and there he had finally married Marian after four years of being engaged. Marian was the schoolgirl who had been so influenced by the early manifestations of the Holy Spirit at Gahini. Several men had asked to marry her but she had finally accepted Eustace in 1939. She had trained to be a nurse and was working at Kigeme Hospital. She had actually been with Rosemary when the news came through about Harold's illness and had been devastated by his death. After her marriage she continued nursing at Gahini until she had her first baby, and even then, she still helped out as a midwife when required. On one occasion a government official brought his wife in to give birth, and Marian was her nurse. Before she left, the Belgian offered her money, which she refused saying that she did it for love of the Lord. The Belgian was astounded. "It's the first time I've known an African refuse money," she said.

Another who felt God calling him to Shyogwe was Gideon Kabano who needed to ask Algie Stanley Smith to release him from the translation work at Buye. Gideon had been taught by Blasio Kigozi at Gahini, where he had professed faith. He had gone to Shyira to teach and had tried to live a holy life, but when he returned to Gahini in 1937 to teach in the primary school there, he realized that he did not know the joy of those who had been touched by Revival.

"I thought to be saved was to live a good life," he said, "but now I was hearing people repent and talk about the cross. I didn't understand what they meant."

He became aware of sins in his heart and wondered how he could become the new creation they were talking about. For three days he prayed and then he heard a voice in his heart saying, "Repent of your sins and know that Jesus died to take them away. There is nothing else. All you need to do is to accept that you are a sinner." As he accepted this and the fact that there was nothing that he could add to the finished work of Jesus, joy flooded his heart. He had twelve cows which had been given to him as a reward for things he had done that he now knew to be sinful, and he knew he had to return them. His family laughed at him and ostracized him but he returned what he could and gave the rest to the church. He had studied at Mukono for a year in 1938 to get his second letter enabling him to be a church teacher and evangelist, and then had gone to Buye where he helped Dr Algie Stanley Smith with translating the Old Testament. At Buye he met Peter and Elisabeth and joined with them regularly in prayer, so that when Peter was asked to start the new school, he knew he wanted Gideon to help.

Three grass huts

The site at Shyogwe was called, "Where the rabbits play". Little did they know at that stage that this was because no Rwandan was prepared to build there, fearing a site where evil spirits were said to dwell. It had a very bad reputation all over the country and Sira's mother was reluctant to let her son go there, fearing that he would be bound and possibly killed by evil spirits. Sira, however, was confident that where God had called, he would also protect. The history of Shyogwe shows a strong spiritual battle which, my parents were to say later, they were ill-equipped to tackle.

Gideon and Sira went to Shyogwe first and built three grass huts for them to live in. Then Peter left Elisabeth, who was expecting their third baby at Kigeme, and went to Gahini to collect Eustace, Marian and one-year-old Husi. Gideon's wife, Margaret, was expecting her third child and stayed at Gahini, and Sira was the only unmarried man on the team. It was some years before he met Geraldine, a nurse from Kigeme, at a convention at Shyogwe and later asked her to be his wife.

Marian's only experience was of established mission stations and nothing had prepared her for the desolate sight of a large grass field and three small grass houses, and nothing else anywhere. Peter pitched his tent nearby and they settled for the night. Next morning they were woken by Husi crying. Marian tried in vain to comfort him but when she took his clothing off she found that his little body was covered with grass ticks. She was horrified and wanted to take him straight back to Gahini, but Peter had left that morning for Kigeme and she just had to make the best of it.

Three weeks later Peter was back and again pitched his tent near the huts and ate with the team. This so impressed one young man called Daniel, who had expected him to stay with the Belgian planter a mile away, that he was wide open to hear their message, and in fact became the first to respond. Peter described that first visit in *Ruanda Notes*:

> At the morning service there were quite two hundred, including a number of Batutsi. Afterwards we went visiting. We first had an open-air meeting in the nearby market town and then went to see

the local big chief, an R.C. and decidedly on his guard; however we gave him our testimony and the Lord helped. Then we visited the Queen Mother who lives three miles away; we had a good time with her, and the dozen or so African nuns she was entertaining when we arrived. I think she rather enjoyed setting us off against one another! But here again the Lord blessed us and gave us liberty in testimony. In the evenings of the three days I was there we had grand times of fellowship and prayer together, the Lord binding us together as a team and giving us a vision of the opportunities of these days and the assurance that He will work in spite of our fewness and feebleness.

The queen mother referred to was not the notorious Kanjogera visited by Margaret at Nyanza, but the mother of King Rudahigwa who had been enthroned under the auspices of the Belgians in 1931.

The Belgian settler, M. Gengoux, invited Peter to stay with him but he refused, wanting to be near the team. He did not take offence but instead helped Peter to build his house which was completed early in 1946, when at last Elisabeth was able to join him at Shyogwe, together with five-year-old John, Margaret, aged three, and their new little baby, David.

Building Shyogwe School

Once they were settled in, Peter was able to concentrate on building permanent houses to replace the grass huts, and to start on building the school. On the hillside below Shyogwe, Peter marked out in white stone in Kinyarwanda the words from 1 John 5:12: "Who has the Son of God has life", and people were beginning to learn that at Shyogwe they could find new life.

Peter wrote about the start of Shyogwe School:

The Lord has given us a grand start from a spiritual point of view, better than my faith, for one, had thought possible. One day some of us went off to a convention for a week-end leaving a master in charge, and when we got back we found that Revival had broken out in the school during our absence. And ever since then there has been a growing group of saved boys going on with the Lord. It is a wonderful evangelistic opportunity to have all these lads from all over Ruanda and Urundi, from every one of our stations as well as two of the Belgian stations. How we praise God for the saved masters He has given us!

Out in the district too, the Lord is working. We now have eight out-schools and hope to start others shortly. Last week a team went out to tour the district to the east and there was great blessing and some turned to the Lord. At one place they burnt a bush which was held to be sacred, the abode of spirits. The local people told our people that they would be sure to die, but no one is the worse. Everywhere there is a great response to the gospel; even where people are not prepared for the cost, they are wistful and long to know the secret of this salvation.

Building continued for many years. I remember what fun it was to join the Africans in tramping the mud for bricks, and walking with my father down to the valley to see the hot fires as the bricks were fired in kilns. One day there was a tremendous rainstorm just before the roof was put on the dining hall. Peter went to the building site to see what damage had been done and to his dismay found one wall jutting out like the leaning tower of Pisa. He could not afford to pull it down and start again so he got several large tree trunks to prop it up. Every day he moved the props in a little so that the wall moved gradually closer and closer to the vertical. Once he was sure that it was truly vertical, he put the roof on quickly. Fifty years later my mother and I went to see round the school. That wall was still functioning beautifully!

Peter was in his element putting into practical effect the mathematics he had learned in theory. Once the school started on 28th June 1946 with unfinished buildings, he often had to be called down from the roof to teach a mathematics class! I gained my own love of mathematics as my father demonstrated how to solve problems in building. Often on our long journeys we would work out problems together. There were 75 boys, all boarders, in the first intake that June, but the buildings were very "rough and ready" with little equipment.

In the valley below Shyogwe, Peter had the schoolboys digging for their food. He dammed the stream and dug out a fishpond. He arrived home one day in a panic at some strange new disease he appeared to have caught. All over his body were small white dots. Eventually they realized that they were caused by splashes of mud shielding those patches from the sunburn else-where! There was great excitement when the first catch of fish was brought up to Shyogwe.

But my chief memories of that pond were when my father built a raft of two petrol drums connected with several planks. We all went down to watch as Peter and John braved the *Kontiki*, named from Thor Heyrdahl's book which had just been pub-lished, though Peter changed its name boastfully to the *Can't-sinki*. They had great difficulty in steering it and it was not very seaworthy. The final hilarious moment came when it turned turtle and Peter was dumped ignominiously into the water by the *Can-sinki*!

In 1999 the headmaster of Shyogwe asked me exactly where that fishpond was and whether there was any possibility of rebuilding it as a source of food. Two years later they were sell-ing fish from ponds further up the valley, although the original pond had defied efforts to restore it.

Holidays at Nabugabo

Life was not all hard work. Often Peter and Elizabeth would take their family to visit Bill Butler in Uganda. Roads had improved since the days Margaret and Harold travelled to Remera, but it still took a long time to get to one's destination. I have memo-ries of punctures and broken springs, landslides and trees across the road; all were hazards extending the journey. Near where Bill was working was a beautiful lake, called Nabugabo, where several round houses had been built as a holiday centre. A troop of vervet monkeys provided amusement, thousands of brilliant butterflies danced in the fields, and the swimming was safe from the hippos and crocodiles that made swimming in Lake Victoria out of the question.

One year Chrissie sent John a kite for a birthday present and he and Peter spent many happy hours on the hill above the campsite. John wrote to thank his grandmother: "Dear Granny, Thank you for the lovely kite you sent me for my birthday. Sometimes Daddy lets me hold the string. Love from John." Peter never really grew up!

Leave in England

In 1947, Dr Algie Stanley Smith came to look after the running of the school while Peter and Elisabeth took their family back to England on leave. This involved the long trip by train from Kampala to Mombasa and then by sea in a converted troopship. Storms in the Bay of Biscay added to the discomfort and they arrived at Tilbury at the start of the worst winter England had known for years. John was filled with questions about this strange new country, but the other two children were screaming in misery and Elisabeth wondered how she was going to face this new life.

It was wonderful to see her mother's smiling face but there were many adjustments to be made, particularly to life without her father. They stayed in Ealing with friends of the family, two elderly ladies who had a beautiful house. The first morning, John made an exciting discovery as he ran his battered dinky car without tyres over the highly polished furniture.

"Look, Mummy," he said. "It makes roads!"

Elisabeth was horrified and explained that in England polished wood was furniture which must not be scratched, unlike the plain wood home-made furniture at Shyogwe. Some months later Peter returned from a visit to Switzerland with a beautifully polished Swiss musical box.

"Oh, Mummy," said John. "Now we've got some furniture too!"

The family spent the spring and early summer at Margaret's house in Cambridge, where John went to the local school. Then they travelled up to Brora, Sutherland where George had inherited a small croft to which he had retired when he left the LNER during the war, and where he had died.

But Peter and Elisabeth were eager to share with others what God had been teaching them during their time in Africa. With Bill Butler and Joe Church, they travelled to many parts of Britain telling of their experiences. They tried to analyse what had led to Revival and developed what they called the five steps to Revival.

1 Prayer with a hunger
2 Repentance and cleansing

3   Brokenness and awareness of sin
4   Indwelling of the Holy Spirit
5   Fellowship and walking in the light

Soon William Nagenda and Yosiya Kinuka flew over to Britain to join the team there. They went straight to Joe's family home in Cambridge. In the car as they travelled to a meeting at the CICCU Joe turned to the team and asked, "What step are we speaking about tonight?"

"Step? What's this about steps?" asked William.

The missionaries began to explain. Yosiya and William looked at each other and began to laugh.

"You missionaries," they said, "you want to have everything tied down. We want to preach about Jesus. That's all."

Joe and Peter felt a bit foolish but realized that they had indeed been trying to proclaim a system rather than a Person. From then on they stopped preaching about Revival and instead preached about Jesus and what he had done for them.

Shyogwe grows

Next year, 1948, back at Shyogwe, Peter wrote,

> On our furlough we began to learn the lesson of resting. We saw that every need for every day had been met at Calvary: our part is to rest on His sufficiency. It has not been easy to go on learning this lesson amid all the little cares and problems of a missionary's day and there have been times of failure and falling into worry, but, as worry is confessed as sin and put under the blood, we marvel again at the experience of His Peace.

The school was growing and more staff joined them, among them Doreen Peck and Mabel Jones from England, and Yona Kanamuzeyi with his wife, Mary, who had come from Gahini as the evangelist and church teacher. There was still no church building so they met on Sundays in the primary school at the bottom of the hill. Building was still going on and Peter was very busy with school administration, supervising the building, and with less and less time for teaching.

Doreen remembered an occasion when Peter berated some

workmen for sloppy work and began to walk away. Suddenly he turned back and apologized to them for losing his temper. As he left she heard one turn to the other and say, "There must be something in this religion of theirs if a white man can say sorry to people like us."

Lindesay also wrote about the practical outworking of Revival as she described a particularly difficult church council meeting in 1950. She wrote that there came a sudden change:

> What happened? I believe it was only made possible because of a few simple words of apology. First a missionary expressed regret and accepted responsibility for an ambiguously-worded minute (it was not his wording), which had led to misunderstanding and so to wounded pride; then the whole council previously on the defensive about it, accepted responsibility corporately and apologized to the person concerned. Not only did his attitude immediately change, so that he repented of his fighting spirit and asked the council's forgiveness, but the Spirit of God came upon the whole gathering and turned it into a fellowship meeting.

She said it took some time to get back to the business in hand but when they did, it was despatched at record speed! She ended her letter with this challenge,

> Perhaps you at home sometimes ask yourselves, "How does it work?" when you hear of testimonies about "Walking in the Light" or "brokenness". Whatever you may call it doesn't matter, what matters is to be humble, not to wait for the other fellow to see his fault before confessing yours, to be nothing; and what happened here last Tuesday is just one example of "how it works". It works just the same way in all our dealings with those for whom we are here, for me with the house-girls, with school staff and with children. Something happens; one stands on one's rights (so-called) or position and everything goes wrong; or one is "broken", ready to be shown one's own mistakes or just to accept — and everything goes right. As simple as that! Have you tried it? Not "it" but "Him"; only He can break us.

In 1948, aged five, I had joined John at the Kabale Preparatory School in Uganda, a full day's drive from Shyogwe. I hated being so far from home and made life very difficult for my teachers, with many screaming temper tantrums. Yet my memories of the school are for the most part extremely happy ones, climbing the spreading pepper trees, the giant stride rope round a huge, straight tree, picnics in the swamps or on Sharp's Island in Lake Bunyoni. It was in the prayer room above the school dining room, when I was nine years old, that I knelt one night, thanked Jesus for dying for me and asked him into my life. I don't remember having another temper tantrum after that time. A particularly vivid memory comes from 1950, when I saw a car stop by the senior classroom and then John came running down to the junior classroom to tell me that we now had a new little sister, Christine. The news was brought by my aunt Veronica, who had come back to Rwanda for a time.

At home I have memories of playing with Husi Kajuga, my special friend, of climbing trees with John and David, although it was frowned upon for a girl, of long walks in the valleys with our house-girls while my parents were teaching, and of the special weekends when they were available to us. Sundays could be difficult as we were not allowed to read books or play with toys that we used during the week, but whenever possible my parents made it clear that Sundays, after church, were for us and we often went for long walks in the afternoon with a picnic tea by a waterfall. In the evening Dad would read to us from a book by Patricia St John or one of the Narnia tales by C. S. Lewis which we acquired as they were published. Other memories were of a large convention at Shyogwe when the place was crowded for days, and I gave up my bedroom to a visitor and had the fun of a tent in the garden. I remember a large bonfire on the football pitch when people burnt their pagan charms. I also remember a plague of locusts and the horrible feel of treading on them wherever you went, and the almost tangible fear of famine that came in their wake.

In 1952, Peter wrote to the *Ruanda Notes* of his vision for literature in Kinyarwanda, of which there was a desperate shortage, with the possibility of bookshops in the main towns.

We find ourselves picturing a travelling bookshop, housed in a lorry, based on the town depot and touring the hundreds of shopping and market centres in the country, with a little team on board and constantly linking up with the different missions. Perhaps this is just a dream, or is it really the Lord's voice? He will show us, we know. Anyway do pray about this great need of producing and supplying literature.

About 20 years later he fulfilled something of this dream as he and Elisabeth travelled the country for Scripture Union with a large box of literature for sale. And nearly 50 years later my vision is the same, as there is still an urgent need for Kinyarwanda literature in the land.

All this time the Protestant schools had been struggling to survive since the government policy was to Catholicize the country, and Protestants were there on sufferance. But in 1952, a more liberal government had come to power in Belgium, enabling Protestants to function more freely within the country, although there was still a strong bias towards the Roman Catholics. Grants were offered to enable Protestant schools to come up to the standard of the Catholic ones. To accept a grant meant accepting any teacher the government sent to the school.

Many of the missions hesitated long and hard about accepting these grants with the attendant regulations and reports that needed to be sent to Belgium. Peter also was hesitant, fearing the imposition of teachers who would have no clear Christian testimony.

While he was praying about the issue, Sira Kabirigi said, "If you can send away your own children to get a good education, you are morally obliged to let the children in Rwanda get the best education they can get."

Through the generosity of the Middlesex County Council, who gave him a grant for the education of his children, Peter could afford to send us to the best schools in Kenya; why then should he deprive Rwandan Christians of the chance of a good education for their children? From that moment it was no longer an issue for him, and he recommended that the mission accept the grants. As it turned out, those missions which accepted the government grants, despite all the attendant problems, were allowed to continue after Independence, whereas those who had refused to accept them were summarily expelled by the new government who declared that they only wanted to continue in a paternalistic role and had no interest in seeing Rwandans educated.

Government inspectors had arrived without warning one

day, and listened as both Peter and Elisabeth taught. They said that their French was so good that they only needed six months on the *cours colonial* in Belgium rather than the usual year.

Back to England

Early in 1953 we all set off for the big adventure. Peter and Elisabeth collected David and me from Kabale School, and in Kampala we met up with John who had travelled by train from Kenton College in Kenya. Early one morning we went out to Entebbe Airport where I remember almost being blown over as a Comet took off. Then we all climbed aboard a Viking aircraft for the long trip home. It was an unpressurized aeroplane and we were only able to travel for two hours without refuelling and could not fly at night, so we spent one night at Wadi Halfa in Sudan where I remember shivering in the early morning by the banks of the Nile.

The second night we had our first taste of European civilization as we stayed in a luxury hotel in Malta. David asked, "Will Granny have telephones by the bed?"

Our final day took us high over the Alps, and Elisabeth had severe heart palpitations which meant that she was ill for the first few days in England. Thick fog at the planned destination led to us being diverted to Heathrow Airport where Chrissie, Elisabeth's mother, was waiting for us, having chased around in a hired car. What bliss it was for us finally to be tucked into bed by our new Granny. She found it more disconcerting. The last time we had come home we had spent three weeks travelling by sea which gave us time to pick up English. The three days of this journey meant that Christine was still jabbering away in Kinyarwanda, and Chrissie was terrified to be left alone with her little granddaughter!

A doctor's examination revealed that Elisabeth was suffering from an over-active thyroid which necessitated an operation to remove a large goitre in her neck. We were all sent to different boarding schools in England, and, after the operation, Peter and Elisabeth took Christine with them as they joined about 80 missionaries from around the world who were heading for Ruanda-Urundi or Belgian Congo for the *cours colonial*.

Shyira and then back to Shyogwe

In January 1954, we returned to Rwanda, this time to Shyira, leaving John to be cared for by Chrissie in the holidays while he went to a boarding school in Kent.

After two years, John came out on a visit and there was a wonderful family holiday at Kumbya on Lake Kivu, the venue which had taken the place of Mutaho for the yearly missionary convention. Margaret, Lindesay and Rosemary joined Peter and Elisabeth with their family at this idyllic spot. To their great joy Philippa was able to join them from the Sudan where she was teaching in Yei near Juba.

After a year at Shyira where they were training primary school teachers, Peter and Elisabeth moved back to Shyogwe to find a strangely depleted station. The reason was that those who had only been taught by Peter at Buye needed to upgrade their qualifications to government standards, and had gone to Remera with most of the schoolboys so that they could continue teaching, while gaining their own qualification. Now, the teacher training school took their place as it moved from Shyira so that Elisabeth could continue teaching them.

In June 1955, they had the excitement of the visit of King Baudouin, when the school, smartly dressed in their uniforms, went to line the route near the turning to Shyogwe. Several boys carried a placard with a letter spelling out "Vive le roi" which was photographed and found its way into *Paris Match*. Peter wrote, "The King and the Governor-General and our own Governor (a Protestant) gave us a special wave as they went slowly by. It made us think of another King we shall meet one day, Who will not just pass us by like that, but will come and reign and Who knows us each by name if we are His."

Problems at Shyogwe were beginning to multiply. Two staff houses were mysteriously burnt down. Arson was suspected but no culprit was ever found. Problems in the country were also beginning to increase. Hutus were starting to feel restive under Tutsi and colonial rule. The king, Rudahigwa, had spent time in Belgium and was convinced that a minority could not keep ruling the majority so he was gradually trying to curb the power of the Tutsis, and encouraging Hutu education, but there was opposition not only from the Tutsi but also from educated Hutu who did not want to see their emancipation at the hands of a Tutsi king.

Peter had, meanwhile, been compiling a large hymn book on behalf of the Alliance of Protestant Missions of Rwanda. It contained 435 hymns, many translated by his father, but quite a number he translated himself. I well remember those days at Shyogwe as he hummed through the house trying to find the right Kinyarwanda word to fit the tune. About 30 of the hymns were written by Africans. "Many of these reflect with great vividness and freshness the sense of the sinfulness of sin, of the marvel of salvation, of the reality of heaven and hell and of the challenge of the gospel, which came out of Revival." He revised the hymn book with M. Durand, of the Belgian Protestant Mission, who had caused his father so much heartache when he resigned from the consultative sub-committee for the translation of the Kinyarwanda Bible so many years before. Although the largest printing press in that part of Africa was at Kabgayi, only two miles away, such was still the suspicion between Catholics and Protestants, that he had to send the precious manuscript to Leopoldville (Kinshasa) in the Congo, for it to be printed on a Protestant press!

Margaret and Lindesay go home

In August 1956, Margaret found that she was getting very breathless and the doctors considered that her heart was failing due to the high altitude at Matana. They advised her to return to England, where, at sea level, she should have no further worries. Lindesay was to return with her, leaving Rosemary to continue with the translation of the Old Testament.

After 31 years of service as an honorary missionary, Margaret finally prepared to leave Africa. She wrote to *Ruanda Notes* with some of her memories and the contrasts that she saw 30 years on.

> But great as are the physical changes that I have seen, they are nothing compared with the working of the Spirit of God in the hearts of men. I remember a time, walking over the hills in Bufumbira, when my husband wondered whether we should ever see truly "born again" Banyaruanda. I remember, too, the very

early days of Revival, when on our arrival at Gahini on one safari our African helper was kept up all night answering questions, and it was obvious that something great was beginning to happen. Now from that tiny spark, the fire of Revival has spread not only through East Africa but far beyond. "What hath God wrought!" How true it is that He chooses the weak things of the world.

For myself, though I have been a very slow learner, the Lord has taught me many things through Revival. I have many regrets, chiefly for my critical spirit and my lack of love and patience. But, praise the Lord, the precious blood of Jesus is always here for cleansing. I can only look back over the years with amazement and thankfulness and say, with Joshua, "I am going the way of all the earth... NOT ONE THING hath failed of all the good things... all are come to pass, and not one thing hath failed thereof" (Joshua 23:14 KJV).

Dr Algie Stanley Smith wrote an appreciation of her and all she had done with her family.

Now, only when compelled to follow medical advice for failing health, she leaves for home. She will be sadly missed in Urundi, where she is known far and wide as *Nyogokuru* (Granny). We all praise the Lord for her largeness of heart, her tireless energy and her utter devotion to His service. She has never been content with mere work; but her powerful mind has always been thinking deeply into the problems of the growing church and seeking how to build it on sound and abiding principles.

Lindesay also wrote,

It is a great wrench to me, as well as to my mother, to leave the place and the work we love so dearly, but in it all I have the assurance of being in the Lord's will which brings absolute peace. Were it not so, it would seem impossible to be going just at this moment of such desperate shortage of educationists; but I know that for me the call is now to England. Whose call is to Africa in my place?

She spoke of the schools she was leaving and then asked for prayer for the brides' school.

Wendy Moynagh will be mothering it as she did during my furlough, and Mrs Eseri Serubibi will, we trust, still be its mainspring. She has many problems connected with her family which sometimes make it hard for her to remain here at Matana, where she is as much a missionary as any of us, for her home is over the border near Kabale, but we believe God is still calling her to this great work. Please remember her especially in your prayers and ask that all difficulties may be overcome.

In fact Eseri stayed for another three years, finally retiring to Kabale in 1959. After her departure, sadly the brides' school came to an end.

I remember as a family travelling to Bujumbura to see Granny and Lindesay off on the plane. She did one final sketch from the top of the hill looking over the city. I remember there were tears in her eyes as she looked up to the hills of Burundi. It frightened me as I had never seen an adult cry before and I did not know how to handle the emotion. Margaret and Lindesay settled in their old home in Cambridge, and Rosemary continued to live at Matana.

Miracles, leave and holidays

A year later, Peter and Elisabeth went to Kabale where they collected Christine from school, and then all three got the train from Kampala to Nairobi. They took me from my school in Limuru, at the top of the Rift Valley, and collected David, who had followed John to Kenton, in Nairobi, intending to catch the train on to Mombasa, and there get a ship to England.

When they got out of the train in Nairobi, Peter could not find the railway tickets. They had been in a folder, together with the onward tickets to Mombasa. He had to pay for new ones which took most of his reserves of money. That night after praying about it, they went to bed in the Christian guest house in Nairobi. Peter could never say afterwards whether it was a vision, just as he was going to sleep, or whether it was a dream, but he saw the missing tickets.

In the compartments of the East African Railways, there were two long seats separated by a table. At night the seat backs were swung upwards to make upper bunks. The table top could be lifted, revealing a wash basin below. The windows had several screens, a glass one, a mosquito netting, a blind and a Venetian blind. What Peter saw was the folder of tickets on the table, which was then raised and the tickets posted through the gap between the screens towards the railway track below. He was quite certain that this was what had happened and that the tickets were lost.

A week later when we arrived at the station to travel on to Mombasa, my father suddenly seemed to go mad! He took one look at the notice board saying where our compartments were, shouted, "It's the same compartment!" and began running. When we finally reached the compartment, we found him peering down through the slats of the window. "There they are!" he cried and ran to an African policeman, begging for the loan of a stick he was carrying. The policeman followed him, protesting that it was needed in evidence. Breathless, we watched as Dad fished out the folder and found all the tickets intact. Restoring the stick to the policeman, he ran for the ticket office and claimed a refund. He was just in time to jump on the train before it moved off. We all sat in the compartment and sang the Revival chorus, "Tukutendereza Yesu" — "Glory, glory to the Lamb!"

The folder had snagged on a wire, inside out so the tickets could easily have fallen out, but in that condition they had travelled all the way to Mombasa, back to Kampala and on to Nairobi! David told this story at my parents' Golden Wedding celebration, and said that it was the knowledge that God had done a real miracle there, that kept him thinking that there must be a God somewhere, until at the age of 40 he finally accepted the truth, and made a commitment as a Christian.

That was a happy voyage home and I have a kaleidoscope of memories from it. We stopped at Aden where we visited an old friend of my father's, Dr Alan Fawdry. He was the only doctor still functioning in the government hospital which had been devastated by Asian flu. Though exhausted, he took time to take us swimming in a bay which had a shark boom across it. He assured us that it was quite safe, unlike the bay on the other side where, he said, a British woman had been swimming the week before and had been eaten by sharks. This captured my imagination and to this day I have been unable to see the film *Jaws*!

We were the first British ship to pass through the Suez Canal following the Suez crisis and we had to travel in convoy, with no possibility of stopping off to see the pyramids. I remember an Egyptian climbing to the top of the mast of his boat and, shaking his fist at us, he shouted, "This is our water!" I can still remember the heat of the Suez Canal. My father won the deck quoit competition, but he had taken off his shoes for a better grip and he burnt the soles of both feet in huge blisters!

Dad kept the children entertained for an hour each day as he read from *Treasures of the Snow* by Patricia St John. The stewardesses thanked him for doing their job for them. At Genoa we had two days to explore our first sight of Europe and then at Marseille we travelled out to the Château d'If where so many Huguenots were imprisoned. We had our photos taken in front of the memorial to them and Dad told us stories of his Protestant forebears in Catholic France. My chief interest was trying to find the tunnel the Count of Monte Cristo dug, to get out of his cell! At Gibraltar a Barbary ape climbed over my back. At last, the leisurely journey was over and we arrived at Tilbury, getting the train up to London where John met us.

I remember a very happy family Christmas with Margaret and Lindesay in Cambridge that year before we returned to Rwanda, this time by air with a night's stop at Khartoum on the way. I remember having a river trip by launch up to see some Egyptian temples that were about to be swamped by the Aswan Dam. I didn't appreciate it as much as I should, and wish I had the opportunity to do the same thing now! John had completed his "A" Levels and left school, so he travelled back with the family to spend a "gap year" at Kigeme where Peter was now inspector of schools for the Protestants.

In July 1958, there was another very happy holiday at Kumbya, this time with Elisabeth's cousin, Charles. He vividly remembered the end of the holiday when he and Peter waited for a bus, as there was no room in the small Volkswagen to take all the family as well as him. They did not arrive that night, so next morning Elisabeth drove back to look for them, wondering all the way what had happened. It was a horrendous drive through spectacular scenery but with terrifying bends in the road, and Peter was at first angry that she had attempted it on her own. For some reason the bus had never turned up and they were very relieved to see Elisabeth.

When they finally arrived at Kigeme, expecting to have another week there, they made the dreadful discovery that

David was still on Elisabeth's passport and they would need to travel early to Kampala to get a new passport because David was to go to school in England. John, too, was leaving Rwanda to study at Cambridge University. It was awful having to say good-bye to our two brothers, not knowing when we would next see them.

On her last night at Kumbya, Elisabeth had remembered her mother's favourite saying as happy times came to an end. She used to quote the apostle Peter on the Mount of Transfiguration, "Let us build three tabernacles here, one for you, one for Elijah and one for Moses" (Luke 9:33). Like the apostle, Elisabeth wanted to hold on to the good times, and dreaded the next phase when the family would be split up for ever. It really was the end of an era.

Chapter 7 # Revolution and Independence

Chrissie's death

In other ways, too, it was the end of an era. Life in Rwanda as we had known it was about to change for ever. John had been living with Chrissie during the holidays, but in the summer term of 1959 she suddenly had a heart attack, and died. Peter and Elisabeth arranged for their daughters to be collected off the school train by their close friends, the Moynaghs, who took them on a wonderful holiday in Uganda to the Murchison Falls and then to the holiday centre at Nabugabo.

They had meanwhile flown to London to sort out Chrissie's affairs and to find a home for her sister, Annie, who had lived with her until the day of her death. While they were in London, Peter read a small item in the newspaper, and turned white: "On 24th July the king of Ruanda, Rudahigwa, Mwami Mutara III, died in Usumbura under mysterious circumstances." No explanation of his death was given but Peter instantly knew that there would be trouble.

Soon after we arrived at Nabugabo, Ken Moynagh drove to Entebbe to collect Peter and Elisabeth. I remember my shock at seeing my father who was painfully thin and looked strained and worried. He had already had a difficult time with the schoolboys at Shyogwe before he left for England. They had gone on strike over food. Peter had bought a number of sacks of manioc flour but the schoolboys were refusing to eat it. One day they left the school and sat around on the hillside above. Peter's heart was wrung with compassion as he looked at them. "They are just like sheep without a shepherd," he said, and back he went to talk to the leaders, trying to understand their problems and talk them into returning, which involved getting rid of the manioc flour.

So he was tired even before they left for England, where they had had a busy time sorting Chrissie's affairs. They had also sold the croft in Brora in order to buy a flat in Edinburgh for George's sister, Katie, and had found an old people's home for retired missionaries in Tunbridge Wells, where they hoped that Annie would settle happily. Now they had come back to Africa but Peter was dreading returning to Shyogwe. What would the death of the king mean for his schoolboys?

Background to revolution

Rudahigwa had been placed on the throne by the Belgians in 1931 when they deposed the old pagan, Musinga. Rudahigwa was baptized as a Catholic and accepted most of the Belgian policies. He was educated in Belgium and for many years he was content with the status quo. He was the head of the country, ruling over chiefs, who in turn appointed sub-chiefs who reported to them. Any policy the Belgians wanted to implement went first to the king, who called his chiefs to a gathering at Nyanza and explained it to them. All the power was in the hands of the Tutsi.

In 1933 the Belgians had issued identity cards on which everyone had to state their tribe. The old system of changing tribes had gone. Even the poorest Tutsi felt superior to a Hutu. The Tutsi were keen to gain a good education to prepare for the time they would rule in independence. In 1946 the United Nations Trusteeship Council had ruled that Ruanda-Urundi were to be granted, by slow stages, limited self-rule leading eventually to independence. At that stage no one ever dreamed that any but the Tutsi would be the rulers in independence. The Hutu seemed more interested in digging their fields than in education and most of those in schools up and down the country were Tutsi. One of the reasons for starting Shyogwe was to provide accommodation for Protestants who came to do their feudal duties to the queen mother nearby.

The feudal system of Rwanda is hard to describe and to understand. As the kingdom had expanded to include the Hutu princedoms in the north and west of the country, with serious bloodshed in some cases, so the nature of society changed. At the head was the figure of the king, a semi-sacred person who held together all the different strands of his society. He would donate cattle to his chiefs together with land for grazing. They in turn would grant cattle and land to their clients or servants. Though the land granted was officially for grazing cattle, in practice it was often cultivated, with the client selling his labour, or skills such as music, to his patron in return. This was called *ubuhake*. The objective of a patron was to acquire many clients who would support him in disputes against other patrons. In turn they supported sub-chiefs who supported the chiefs and all was held in balance by the king. Resentment against *ubuhake* arose from the fact that, in order to become a chief, you had to be Tutsi, and many Hutu and indeed Twa, were "tutsified" in order to gain that power. The result was that there were no Hutu chiefs able to mediate between the king and the majority of peasants who were Hutu, although there were many peasant Tutsi. For most of them, their only means of survival was to sell their labour, and they had no rights in the land which was their livelihood. Their existence was at the whim of their *shebuja* or lord, to whom they were subservient, in the hope that he would support and protect them in times of difficulty.

As with the feudal system in Europe, if you had a good *shebuja* you were protected and reasonably content, but a bad overlord, of whom there were many, could make your life miserable in the extreme. Many would use force against their client who in turn developed extreme obsequiousness towards him in the hopes of avoiding trouble. Society began to be founded on deception, as in many ways it still is. It was fear of returning to a form of *ubuhake* which largely fuelled the rage behind the genocide of 1994 as many Hutu listened to the propaganda of Radio Mille Collines which spewed out hatred of Tutsi, saying that if they regained power they would subject all Hutu once more. In 1999, I met a Hutu who had been studying in Europe in 1994 and was not in any way involved in the genocide, but who was so convinced that the Tutsi would again subject the Hutu to servitude that he refused to contemplate returning to Rwanda under Tutsi rule.

Towards the end of the 1940s the king, Rudahigwa, began to see that it was dangerous to keep all the power in the hands of the Tutsi, and he gradually encouraged Hutu to gain an education. He considered that the British were preparing Uganda for independence better than the Belgians in Ruanda-Urundi. In

Uganda everyone was encouraged to go to school and to take an interest in government. He became more pro-Britain and the Belgians did not like it. Between 1954 and 1958, Rudahigwa decided that the inequitable distribution of land was wrong. He gave the land with its cattle to the people. He instructed the *shebuja* to give two-thirds of the cattle to the peasants since he had had the benefit of their labour over the years. Any disputes were to be settled in local courts.

But it was too little, too late. Suddenly the tide seemed to turn. The Belgians, who had always worked through the Tutsi, changed their policy and now began to work through Hutu. Talk of majority rule and democracy became commonplace. The uprising in Congo caused more fears. Political parties began to be formed. It was in this maelstrom of political change and fears that news of Rudahigwa's death spread. No post-mortem was performed and rumours abounded: he died of a heart attack; he was poisoned by Tutsi who objected to his giving up their traditional rights; he was poisoned by Hutu who wanted more power; he was poisoned by the Belgians who saw him as a threat to their new policy of favouring the Hutu.

As they had always done, the king's council met to appoint a new king and chose Rudahigwa's nephew, Jean-Baptist Ndahindurwa, who was given the name Kigeri V. The Belgians were not consulted in this traditional king-making, but they did not approve and never recognized the new king. At Rudahigwa's funeral at Nyanza, the new king had to be named. The Belgians accepted the nomination of Kigeri. They heard later that there were several Twa present, each with an arrow pointing at a Belgian. If Kigeri had not been named there would have been mass slaughter of the Belgians. However, although they had accepted his nomination, they would not allow him to be crowned. They were pressing for democracy, with a president, not realizing how intertwined with the life of the country the king was. He had to bless the crops and he was seen as the father of the nation, whether Hutu, Tutsi or Twa.

Revolution!

Over the next few months, several prominent Hutu were assassinated, with retaliations against Tutsi. The atmosphere was very tense, and finally in October 1959 it exploded into civil war. I was at school in Kenya at this time about to sit my school certificate exams (the equivalent of GCSE), and remember waking up one morning and seeing a banner headline in the East African Standard newspaper, REVOLUTION IN RUANDA — THOUSANDS FLEE TO MISSION STATIONS. There was no easy communication in those days and it seemed ages before the first reassuring letters came through.

The new political party, *Partie d'Emancipation des Hutu*, or PARMEHUTU, was formed by Gregoire Kayibanda who was secretary to the Roman Catholic archbishop at Kabgayi, and it was from there that the overthrow of Tutsi rule was organized. Kabgayi was only about five miles from Shyogwe, so violence came very close. Unlike the events in 1994, churches and hospitals were recognized as sanctuaries and were not violated for the most part. But all round Shyogwe, houses were burnt down, banana plantations destroyed and people were killed. Almost worse for the Tutsis was to see their cows butchered and often just left on the hillside, though sometimes they were eaten.

On one occasion Peter heard that a gang of Hutu brandishing spears and knives were going to cross Shyogwe to attack some Tutsi homes on the other side of the hill. At the boundary he faced them, told them that this place was a place where the love of Jesus was proclaimed and pleaded with them to return home. To his dismay they continued with their plans, but they did not cross the Shyogwe boundary.

On another occasion a man fleeing for his life was chased right up to the boundary. As he crossed, the killers yelled, "You are safe now — you have reached 'Praise the Lord'!" Many other frightened Tutsi fled to Shyogwe, and by the time I arrived home for the Christmas holidays there seemed to be refugee families in every room of the house. Situations like this resulted in missionaries, and indeed the whole Anglican Church, being labelled "pro-Tutsi" but how could they have done differently?

Peter wrote to Harold Adeney about one of these refugees, a schoolmaster who had come with his family to Shyogwe:

> After two nights here, however, he met the local bourgomaster who said to him, "I thought you were one who trusted in God. Now I see that you only trust in the missionaries." This schoolmaster

was challenged in his heart and he realized that he must only trust God. That night he and his family moved back to their own home and, although he has had many difficult times since , he is still there, a burning and shining light to Christians and pagans alike. (Quoted in *Only One Weapon*, p 40)

Another Christian suddenly found his house full of people. "Why have you come here?" he asked. "My house is thatched like yours, why do you think you are any safer here than in your own homes?" "It is because we know you have no enemies," they replied (*Breath of Life*, p 203). Peter wrote that he had often stood with this man, testifying to "off duty" gangsters!

On 5th November, Peter wrote to the family:

In the morning the grim, blood-curdling cries began about 9 a.m. Suddenly down the hill and across the site came pouring a motley host of hundreds of men and boys, shrieking and dancing, waving knives and spears, bashing in doors and pulling the tiles off the roofs of the houses in their way. They went on to the chief's house and the dispenser's house, destroying them both utterly. Bombs weren't in it! All we could do was go out in the evening and pick up their families and fix them up in our house.

Then the next day he added to the letter:

Rumours are rife that it is our turn to be attacked because we have sheltered the refugees. We went to rescue a judge's wife whose leg had been broken and on the way back we met a huge band (over 100) armed to the teeth. It was an alarming experience to pass between the divided ranks, glaring at us in silence. We now have to accommodate the judge's wife and children." (Quoted in *Breath of Life*, p 202)

Christine's distress

It was a strange Christmas that year. I don't remember understanding what was going on. I had not myself seen any violence and felt resentful of these people who had taken over my last few days at home. I was also packing for England. On New Year's Day 1960 I went for a last bicycle ride round my favourite spots before breakfast and then we left for Uganda. Poor Christine was bewildered by all that was happening. She had followed me to St Andrew's School, Turi, in Kenya. Going to school was always traumatic but at least I had travelled with her on the train as far as Nakuru before our two school parties had to separate, and I was in the same country even if we never met during term-time. Now I was going to England and she would be the only member of the family remaining in Africa. She clung to me at the airport and physically had to be pulled away from me. It was a terrible leave-taking.

This was followed by an even worse scene the next day at the Jinja Docks on Lake Victoria. Peter and Elisabeth had arranged for Christine to stay with Elisabeth's cousin for a few days in Kenya before going to school, believing that she would enjoy the trip across the lake and not realizing that the family of children who lived near Charles was not there. Meanwhile they were to return to the chaos and horror of Shyogwe. Christine felt totally abandoned by her family and made a deliberate decision at that point to turn away from God whom she blamed for the enormous sense of loss and betrayal she was experiencing. She was nine years old.

The following holidays, Christine spent at Butare (then called Astrida) where Peter had been asked to look after the Protestant students at the university in the Home Protestant for six months. That was a difficult time. One day Christine came in, white-faced, saying that she had seen a family friend, a Tutsi, being beaten up outside the house, and a few days later Elisabeth was in the street with Sira when she saw a Tutsi being beaten by soldiers. Instinctively she moved to intervene, but Sira held her back. "Don't," he said, "you'll be killed too." Shortly after that Sira was himself imprisoned. He was "beaten and left for dead under a pile of other bodies. Regaining consciousness, he crawled out in the night, and the guards had an awful fright in the morning to see him standing up reading the New Testament. They thought he'd risen from the dead and let him go! However, back home again, another group came along looking for cows to steal. 'You want my cows?' he said, 'Take them! When Jesus saved me I had no cows. He provided them for me, but they are not necessary for happiness, so you can take them.' 'Oh, let's go and get someone else's cows,' they said as they left!" (*God has Ears*, Doreen Peck, pp 168-169).

Somewhat unwisely, the film *King Solomon's Mines* was

shown at the school. It had been filmed in Rwanda the year before and contained the speech, in Kinyarwanda, "You are a bad king." There was a near riot in the school and it was with difficulty that Peter was able to get his students to calm down that night. A little later someone reported Peter for praying for the king. Puzzled, he denied this until he realized that in French he had prayed to God who heals our infirmities. "Qui guérit" could sound like Kigeri to someone not paying much attention! In the tensions of that time the most innocent phrases could sound inflammatory.

Christine returned to school in April, and soon Peter and Elisabeth received a letter from the headmistress reporting nightmares from a traumatized child. Her insecurity increased when she found that she was to return the following holidays to yet another home. Peter was back in his job as school's inspector and again based at Kigeme. They tried to shield her from the violence but inevitably she heard stories of what was going on without understanding much of it. At one stage Elisabeth took her to Uganda to stay with a schoolfriend and to have a break before she returned to school, but she was still conscious of the tensions.

Meanwhile the refugees had left Shyogwe, either fleeing to Uganda or Tanzania, or being transferred to a large displaced persons camp in the Bugesera, an arid, infertile area, infested by tse-tse fly which soon killed many of the Tutsi cattle.

Yona at Nyamata

Yona Kanamuzeyi had just been ordained deacon and when he was asked by the bishop to consider going to Nyamata in the Bugesera to help the refugees, he left his wife, Mary, and the children at Buye and went to live alone at Nyamata. Peter wrote, "God has given Yona great encouragement in his work there. Hundreds have come to our church from the Roman Catholics, and many have accepted the Lord Jesus as Saviour. Pray for him and for them: the future is very dark." Yona himself wrote a few months later: "We praise God that, during the past three months, twelve people amongst the refugees have been really saved and on Christmas Day, eight more were saved and it shows on their faces — they are filled with joy although they have lost everything." He went on to say that in the whole country about one third were either Roman Catholic or Protestant, with the remaining two-thirds still practising their heathen rites. In the refugee camps there were about 8,000 people living together at close quarters. Many were open to the gospel but there were many tensions.

In the *Ruanda Notes Review* for 1960-1961 there was this description:

> In the centre of a wide open space over-looking the encampment, where the Belgian camp commandant (who has been most helpful) has his post, is a large forest tree. Almost certainly this was one of the old "Imana" trees where witchcraft and heathen gatherings took place. With the commandant's permission, we beat a drum and call people together these days to hear of the One Who said "Come unto Me all ye that are weary and heavy laden... Pray for the Rev. Yona Kanamuzeyi, a man sent from God to these people. His wife has joined him now; the people look to him like a father and he is surrounded by a crowd of children wherever he goes.

Rev. Geoffrey Kinyanza came to Shyogwe to take Yona's place. Geoffrey had been born at Gatsibo where Geoffrey Holmes had set up a small centre, and was named after him. As a schoolboy at Gahini he had been much impressed by Blasio Kigozi's peaceful response to persecution. At home, during the holidays, he began to read his New Testament carefully. When he came to the account of the death of Jesus, he began to weep. His pagan mother was alarmed. "What has made you cry, my son?" she asked. He replied that Jesus was on the cross because of his sins. There and then he asked Jesus to take control of his life. His wife, Chloë, was one of the girls at Gahini school when the Holy Spirit descended on it in 1936. They soon became much-loved members of the team at Shyogwe.

Refugees at Hanika

By August 1961, the sporadic violence against Tutsi had spread to the royalist stronghold of Nyanza. The pastor of the nearby Anglican church at Hanika, was Misaki, that little boy who had travelled to Gahini with Blasio Kigozi and Yohana Bunyenyezi, and had been so impressed by Blasio's faith in the protection of

Jesus even from leopards. Here he had to trust that protection through the fierce times ahead as many Tutsi fled to his parish. They were able to accommodate most of the women and children in the church, but the men had to remain outside with their cattle. With his wife, Dorothy, and the headmaster of the school, Gershom, they cared for the bewildered refugees. Peter came to visit them and wrote, "We cannot thank God enough for these three and their testimony of quiet peace and patience and love. They were a team prepared by God for what was to come. We never saw them angry or seriously disturbed and their spirit of calmness pervaded the whole place."

As the numbers of refugees mounted, the missionaries from all over Rwanda took it in turns to spend a day and a night at the church centre, collecting supplies of food from the Belgian administrator's office and seeing it distributed at the church. Dorothy would check the sleeping women at night and surreptitiously cover with one of her few blankets those who had none.

Peter wrote:

When school started at the beginning of October, it became a routine matter to evacuate all buildings by 7.30 in the morning so that the school children could occupy their classrooms. In consequence, no school day was lost. We never cease to wonder at this daily take-over in spite of burning houses and chaos all round, and a milling crowd of over five thousand on the site! Three "shanty towns" of grass huts sprang up on the fringe of the concession; one or two thousand must have been accommodated in these leaky hovels. Every night hours were spent packing women, children and old men like sardines into the church and schools. At the peak period, they just could not be fitted in. Many slept sitting up. Hundreds lay bundled together outside in the mud, many without even a blanket. (We needed three on our beds in the tent to keep warm.) (Quoted in *Only One Weapon*, p 36)

One letter Peter wrote to the family says more about the conditions:

In spite of hopeless sanitation we have had no typhoid and very little dysentery. All the way through we have been marvellously protected from attack. Again and again police come to arrest people on dubious charges, but they never seem able to find the people they were after. Above all we praise God for the high morale and cheerfulness of the refugees. They seem to understand that they are on God's hill. At night we hear groups singing hymns out in the cold mud, and if someone starts a quarrel or uses abusive language, others at once reprove him, saying, "You must not talk like that on God's hill." Spiritually it is a wonderful opportunity and we have had wonderful times telling about the Saviour who forgives and sets free from the curse of sin and hatred, showing us our own sin and not other people's. [...] To most the Gospel is utterly new. (Quoted in *Breath of Life*, p 216)

Once, after they had shared several meals with the refugees, Peter and Elisabeth decided that they would get their own simple supper that night.

"I have decided to give up being a missionary," Peter announced.

Elisabeth's heart sank — was all the horror they were witnessing finally getting to him?

"I'm going to set up as a barrage balloon instead," said Peter, "as a result of all the beans we have eaten!"

When they were not at Hanika, Peter would often set off in his Beetle Volkswagen to find those who were in danger, and take them to join the thousands of refugees at Hanika. One day Christine asked her mother, "How do you know that you love God before everything? Don't you love Dad best?"

"Every time Dad leaves here, I have to give him to the Lord," replied Elisabeth. "I love Dad, yes, but I have to let him go, knowing that he might die, but knowing that God comes first both for him and for me."

In September they took Christine to catch the train to school in Kenya, managing a few days holiday with her at a tea-farm near Kampala. On their way home they heard that more violence had broken out near Gahini. When they got there, they found that all those with cars had gone to rescue threatened people. Peter and Elisabeth each drove a car taking people to Kabale. Once Peter saw a family and offered to take them to safety. "We must go home and collect our belongings," they insisted and he arranged to meet them the next day. To his horror, when he got there, they had all been killed.

Elisabeth wrote to the family, "We saw Nsibambi just before we left Kampala. He said when the enemy comes in like a flood then the Spirit of the Lord lifts up a standard against him. He said that our job must be to uplift that standard continually so that many can rally to it. He also said that we must be very forgiving and have much love."

In 2000, I visited a church not far from Gahini with my mother. We were greeted with great joy by an elderly woman who said that she was one of those whom Dad had taken to safety that dreadful time, and she had recently returned to Rwanda for the first time since those dark days.

The bloodshed also spread to the Byumba area where about 2,000 Tutsi were believed to have been killed. Elisabeth wrote in a family letter following a visit to Byumba, "You seem to see the evil and hardness in the faces of practically everyone you meet, the exception was a dear brother called Shem, a Hutu [...] His happy smiling face seemed to shine in that darkness! He has been looking after a healed but maimed Tutsi leper who had been terribly cruelly treated by the population." Some years later Elisabeth had the joy of meeting Pastor Shem, by then retired, and I was able to go to his funeral in 1999.

In October 1961 a Republican government was declared, with Gregoire Kayibanda as prime minister, and a few months later he became president. All refugees were encouraged to return home, but frequently those who did, had returned to Hanika a few days later, bleeding from being beaten up. The majority of refugees continued to camp out at Hanika.

One night early in 1962, Elisabeth was sleeping in the tent alone at Hanika, when the tensions in the area erupted once more into violence. Houses were burning all round the site but no gang appeared near the church. Despite the horror nearby, she finally managed to get to sleep but in the early hours of the morning was woken by a tremendous cracking noise. She shot out of the tent but the fires had died down and all seemed peaceful. When she went back, she discovered that the canvas of her camp bed had split and this was what had woken her! She wrapped herself around in her blanket and managed to get to sleep again on the groundsheet. Meanwhile, Peter at Kigeme had seen the fires coming from Nyanza and was fearful at what he would find when the curfew ended and he was finally able to get there. He was very relieved to find all was peaceful at the camp.

Peter felt that it was time to take decisive action. Numbers in the camp had risen to about 6,000. Pastor Misaki was accused of harbouring undesirables and protecting those responsible for violence and it was feared that his life was in danger. Peter wrote to some friends in Burundi asking them to send transport to drive the refugees to safety in Burundi. About a week later, three lorries arrived and that night they tried to load them quietly with as many as possible from the camp. Suddenly, their hearts stood still as a shot rang out. One of the leaders of the Hutu gangs had arrived and shot in the air, but the noise terrified everyone and they fled back to Hanika, scattering their belongings as they fled. Peter and Elisabeth, having heard the noise, came from Hanika to see what was happening. The Hutu leader was furious with them and refused to let them return to the camp. He drew a line in the dust across the road. "If you take one step across this line," he said, waving his gun at them, "you will be out of the country tonight. Go back to Kigeme. Go away." But, although they did not cross the line, they were fearful for the people at Hanika, worried that there might be mass murder planned. They were determined to be obvious witnesses to anything that happened, so they stayed where they were. Soon a Belgian official arrived. He too was very angry. "You are bad people," he yelled at them. "You are trying to send Rwandans out of the country. You ought to have sent them back to their communes where they belong."

Peter tried to explain that they had done just that, but that those who had returned home were attacked again and arrived back at the camp bleeding, which effectively discouraged others from leaving. Finally Peter and Elisabeth were permitted to go to the camp, on condition that they reported to the Belgian administrator the next day. To their amazement they found that the incident with the lorries had acted like a catalyst. In the morning the site was deserted. All the refugees had fled, most slipping over the border to Burundi on foot. Misaki and Dorothy soon fled to Tanzania where they continued to serve the Lord until, in 1995, they were able to return to Gahini. Peter and Elisabeth reported to the administrator as he had promised and had to endure another harangue. "You are not fit to inspect the schools," the official said, but eventually they were allowed to return to Kigeme.

A week later, Godfrey Hindley came to see them. He was the

mission field secretary and had received a warning from the Belgian administration that Peter and Elisabeth should leave the country or they ran the risk of being deported. Godfrey said that for their own sake, they were relocated to Burundi where Peter would be schools inspector in the south. Elisabeth was almost in tears as they left Rwanda. Would they ever return? What would happen to all their friends? How would their beloved country survive the horror of that time? They were accused of being pro-Tutsi in Rwanda but in Burundi they became pro-Hutu almost overnight as they saw how often the Tutsi disparaged the Hutu. The Tutsi of Burundi had learned from what was happening in Rwanda. They closed ranks against the Hutu, and were determined not to allow divisions among themselves if they wanted to maintain power.

Peter wrote in the *Ruanda Notes Review* of 1962-63:

> Although we have been spared the literal fires of Rwanda, the fires of politics and racialism have been testing the church and burning up a good deal that has proved wood, hay and stubble. Especially this is so at Matana. We have been finding in these days that even simple church matters requiring a decision, tend to provoke an immediate and almost inevitable alignment into opposing racial factions.

Independence for Rwanda and Burundi

Shortly after their arrival at Matana, on 1st July 1962, the former country of Ruanda-Urundi became two independent countries: the Republic of Rwanda under its Hutu president, Gregoire Kayibanda, and the Kingdom of Burundi with its Tutsi king, Mwambutsa. Dr Harold Adeney wrote in the *Ruanda Notes* on 5th July 1962:

> Last Sunday independence was granted to Rwanda and Burundi, with their teeming multitudes. Though small, they are two of the most densely populated lands of Africa. [...] How our hearts rejoice to see Africans taking control of their own countries! For too long we have been identified, in the minds of many, with white domination. Some have even thought of us as agents of colonialism! But now we can live among them just as their servants for Christ's sake; and what greater joy and privilege can we desire?

Chapter *8* ## *Burundi and England (1960-1969)*

Adjustment to England

Back in England, it was hard to receive letters and not really understand what was going on. I was staying with Veronica who had herself come out to Rwanda for two years to help Mrs Stanley Smith run the Home Protestant in Butare (then called Astrida). This was a residence for Protestant students studying at the university, still necessary in those days of hostility between Catholics and Protestants. She had also helped Dr Algie by typing up the manuscript of the Kinyarwanda Bible which had finally been completed in 1952. She had then returned to England where she married Dick Madeley in 1953. By the time I arrived they were living near Reigate and had three small children.

Although they welcomed me very lovingly, I found the transition to life in England traumatic. Worry for my family and friends in Rwanda and starting a new school meant that I lost my voice for most of one term. Christmas 1960 had been spent in Cambridge with Margaret and Lindesay. Uncle Tom Stockley, Mary's husband, arranged for me to see a specialist, and I remember his kindness as we walked home from the consultant's office. He explained that there was nothing physically wrong and that I needed to relearn how to talk.

Margaret dies

In June 1961, I heard that my grandmother, now in Cambridge with Lindesay, was very ill. Rosemary got the news in Burundi just as she was finishing the translation of the Old Testament into Kirundi. She flew home and was able to place the completed manuscript into her mother's hands just before she died. "Lord, now lettest thou thy servant depart in peace," she whispered, "for mine eyes have seen..." Shortly afterwards she slipped into a coma, and died three days later. I was able to leave school to get to the funeral in Cambridge, representing the grandchildren. On the front of the service sheet, words taken from *The Pilgrim's Progress* were printed: "And the trumpets sounded for her on the other side."

Life in Matana

At the time of his mother's death, Peter and Elisabeth were helping refugees and could not come back to England. Later that year they were transferred to Matana where Margaret had spent so much of her life. Once again Christine found she was coming back from school to a new home. She had had a miserable time at her new school and at last was able to talk freely to her parents. "I don't want to go back," she cried and was amazed to hear them say, "You don't have to." At last they had the time to give to the emotional needs of their youngest child.

She was due to follow me to Clarendon School in the following September, so arrangements were made for her to stay with American friends in Bujumbura and attend the Belgian school as a day pupil for the remaining six months. Peter had to visit Bujumbura frequently, because he was once again schools inspector but Elisabeth stayed in Matana where she was trying to start a secondary school for Protestant boys who could no longer travel freely to Shyogwe. Obviously this involved much separation, and they longed for Elisabeth to be able to hand over the work to Paul Bell who had just arrived from England.

David and I flew out to join them at Matana for the summer holidays before I started at Edinburgh University. We had a happy holiday, with my mother teaching both of us to drive round the hills of Matana, followed by a wonderful fortnight at Nabugabo in Uganda, before we returned to England.

Problems for Philippa in Sudan

On 18th November 1962 my father wrote to us:

We were very distressed to hear this week that Auntie Philippa has been given a month to leave the Sudan. The reason being given that she is "redundant". We know how she must feel. After furlough we hope that she will be able to continue her translation work over the border in Uganda so that the Word of God can get there when missionaries cannot.

Philippa was one of 300 missionaries expelled from the Sudan at the start of the long and bloody civil war because the government saw no need for Bible translation. She settled in the north of Uganda where she was able to continue to translate the Bible into Bari, a language of Southern Sudan.

Life in England

I was by this time at Edinburgh University where I lodged with my great-aunt Katie, George's sister. She had some wonderful stories to tell of the old days in Edinburgh. She remembered the first car in Edinburgh, driven by Edward VII, halfway up Arthur's Seat.

On one occasion she was enthusing about King Olaf of Norway who was over on a state visit to Edinburgh.

"He will be visiting Prince's Street Gardens this afternoon," I said one day. "Would you like me to take you down to see him?"

"Oh no, my dear," she replied, "I haven't been in a crowd since the Relief of Mafeking!"

It was rather astounding to realize that she spanned such a long history, the Relief of Mafeking having happened at the end of the Boer War in 1902! I was 19 at the time and she was 82, but despite this difference in age we got on very well together, and I was very happy to have a good home as I struggled with the alien culture of university.

One of the difficulties we were experiencing in England was that all of us had different guardians, and although we made strong efforts to meet for at least a week every holiday, it was not easy being separated and we desperately wanted a home where we could be together as a family once more. So our parents had promised us that they would have an extended leave of at least 18 months to make a home for us in England.

My father soon wrote about the shortage of staff in education in Burundi and his unease at leaving when other teachers would also be on leave. He had been asked to consider staying on for another year but felt it vital that they should come on leave as planned. However, he wrote to ask how we would feel if they returned for another year before taking their promised extended leave. Very reluctantly I wrote back that if they really thought it God's will then they should do so, but I was upset because I was so looking forward to a home of our own.

That summer, 1963, my parents came home with Christine. At a holiday conference at Abergele, in North Wales, my father drew me to one side. He explained that the problem over teachers in Burundi had been solved but that he had been asked to remain as schools inspector for one more year, training his replacement, and also to fulfill a long-held desire to work in the shanty town of Bujumbura. My mother had finally handed over Matana School to Paul Bell, and would be free to help him. I remember walking up and down the beach as he explained that he had sounded out the other members of the family, and wanted to know what I thought. In my heart I was angry and upset, but again all I said was that if this was what he felt the Lord was asking him to do I would not object.

Bujumbura

In October 1962 Peter had written of the needs of Bujumbura: "There are hundreds of Matana folk, chiefly youngsters, milling about the town without anyone to care for their souls because they are not known to the other Missions. We feel how good it would be if one of our people could be a real Pastor to these folk and follow them up and seek them out." Their good friends, Pawulo and Dorotiya Rutwe, had responded to this call, but Peter longed to be able to join them and work together with them as a team. So, in October 1963, they returned to Burundi, leaving the four of us in England, all with different homes.

The following January Peter wrote describing their situation:

There is a thrill in being in Bujumbura after years on mission centres where people are used to the Gospel. People here come off the streets for a chat or to ask for a tract. A few Protestant schoolboys in government schools come in just to be "at home", but there is much more that could be done on this line. We are welcomed into houses to speak of the Lord; everywhere there is interest and, of course, desperate need. Sin of every kind is rife and poverty such as one does not meet "up-country" where everyone has a garden and a few crops. Then there are the hundreds of Rwanda refugees who live in odd out-houses and eke out a miserable existence on one knows not what. Some cases of near starvation come into church on Sundays; one young widow was too weak to stand for the hymns. I know of two tiny hovels which contain fifteen souls at night. I marvel that they do not suffocate in the heat of Bujumbura. Sometimes we all feel overwhelmed by the depth of human need and suffering and sorrow, but we know that we come to them with a Christ Who is able to meet that need.

However, even as he wrote this, life was going to change again.

That Christmas, the four of us children had met up in Cambridge at Uncle Tom and Auntie Mary Stockley's home. It was wonderful to be together, but as we chatted I sensed that all was not well with either David or Christine who seemed very unhappy at school.

One night I was talking to Uncle Tom and Auntie Mary. "How I wish we had a home together!" I cried.

"Write and tell them how you feel," they advised.

That night I sat down and poured my heart out on paper to my parents. I told them of my resentment that they had gone back, despite the fact that I had said it was all right, and I told them of my fears for David and Christine. I filled three air letter forms, carefully labelled them one to three, and posted them before I could change my mind.

Having written them it was as if I had unloaded a huge burden and I returned to Edinburgh with a light heart. I do not know what I expected them to do, but at least they now knew exactly how I felt. I was totally unprepared for the telegram a fortnight later saying that my mother was arriving in England in the middle of January.

It was wonderful to have her home. She came up to stay with Auntie Katie and me in Edinburgh and we enjoyed exploring Edinburgh together. Shortly after her arrival we heard the devastating news that Yona Kanamuzeyi was dead, but we had to wait some time before a letter from Dad gave us the details.

Yona's death

Yona had refused to leave his flock at the Anglican Centre near Nyamata, despite several warnings that his life was in danger. He was a true pastor who spent his days visiting and encouraging his people. On several occasions, bands of Tutsi, known as *inyenzi* or "cockroaches" had begun raiding over the border from Burundi to try to regain a foothold in their home. These raids fostered unrest, and reprisals were often taken against Tutsi who had accepted the new regime and were rebuilding their lives near Nyamata.

On 1st December 1963, Peter wrote to the family describing how Godfrey Hindley had been asked by the UNHCR to use his influence to try to dissuade a band of refugees from attempting to invade Rwanda. Godfrey had taken Peter with him, and they had travelled through the night, arriving at 6 a.m., to find what the UN officials described as "straggling bands of men armed with bows and arrows and spears, who would not be deflected by any argument from their purposes". Peter and Godfrey spent time talking with them and eventually persuaded them to return to their camps.

They then wired to UNO authorities in Bujumbura for help with transport to get them back. Peter wrote:

> The Lord worked a series of near miracles, and next day about 10 lorries were sent through, and one of food. We trust that by now most are back at their camps and that none have died of starvation, exposure and sheer sorrow! You never saw such distress. [...] We feared at first that we would not be able to stop them getting into Rwanda to be massacred (2-3,000 of them), and that this would provoke liquidation of Tutsi at Nyamata and elsewhere in Rwanda itself.

Peter and Godfrey may have been able to avert trouble on that occasion, but a few weeks later another, larger, invading force of Tutsi refugees in Burundi had gone through the Bugesera on the way to Kigali, where they were defeated by the government army. Suspected Tutsi sympathizers were searched out and arbitrarily executed. Soon the reprisals spread to any Tutsi, and in some areas wholesale slaughter took place.

Like many in Rwanda, Yona was of mixed descent, but he

looked like a Tutsi, and because he was helping displaced Tutsi at Nyamata, he was seen as a Tutsi sympathizer. On the evening of 23rd January 1964 a jeep containing five soldiers drew up outside the pastor's home and took Yona away for questioning.

He was given time to comfort Mary and the children and left, assuring them that he would be back in the morning, though both he and Mary knew that very few returned from these night-time visits. The headmaster of the primary school, Andrew, was taken with him. As they travelled, Yona, knowing what was likely to happen, said, "Let us surrender our lives into God's hands."

At the river the jeep stopped and they were ordered out. Yona asked permission to write in his diary. "We are going to heaven," he wrote and then wrote a careful account of the church money. He gave a soldier the few francs he had with him and asked him to give the diary, with the key to the church cupboard, to his wife.

One man said, "You had better pray to your God."

Yona prayed, "Lord God, You know that we have not sinned against the government, and now I pray You, in Your mercy, accept our lives. We pray You to look upon our innocent blood and help these men who do not know what they are doing. In the name of Jesus Christ our Lord, Amen."

Then they sang the hymn: "There is a happy land... where saints in glory stand... "

Yona turned to Andrew, "Do you believe this?"

"Yes, I believe," he replied, "and whoever believes will be saved."

Andrew and another prisoner were left by the jeep with their hands bound, while Yona was taken to the river. They heard a shot and then silence.

The soldiers returned amazed. "They had never seen anyone go singing to his death or walking, as he did, like a man just taking a stroll," wrote Andrew later. He was the next to be taken to the river.

They ordered me to sit again and asked if anyone had an axe or a knife, and I knew that perhaps they were going to cut me up as they had done to many others. They asked me my name, and then they returned my watch to me; I asked them to keep it to send to my wife, but they ordered me to put it on. They then put me in the jeep again and, leaving the third prisoner on the road with some of the men, we returned and they told me to go home.

This account of Yona's death was sent from Burundi where Andrew fled during the night. He added,

> The death of this man of God amazed those men who saw him die because he truly died as a man of God, praying for his enemies, and for himself. He did not fear death because for him, as for all saved people, death is the door to heaven. As for me, who has been saved from this bodily death, it has taught me again that God wants to save me from the second death which is the final judgement, saved through faith in Jesus Christ Who died for us, and I before Him repent of my sins.

Mary wrote a letter to a friend a few weeks later:

> For my part, I want you to know that Jesus is very near to me. At first after Yona had gone, I fell into days of despair. But then the Lord Jesus gave me this word from Mark 9:8, "And suddenly, when they had looked about, they saw no man any more, save Jesus only." And he reminded me of the hymn "Jesus is mine". It is true that Jesus is mine even though I have lost the friend whose life I shared and with whom I used to talk everything over; yet Jesus is mine!

Mary soon fled the country to Uganda where she found refuge for herself and her young family at Namutamba, a tea farm near Kampala run by Christians who had been much influenced by Revival. The account of his death so moved the dean and chapter of St Paul's Cathedral that they added his name to the list of modern martyrs in the Memorial Chapel of St Paul's Cathedral.

As my mother and I read Andrew's description of Yona's death, we wept. Yona was the first of the group of people who symbolized my childhood to die. But what a wonderful testimony to God's grace even at the moment of death!

We were still coming to terms with his death, when we received another blow. Late one evening, in May 1964, the telephone rang, and we heard that my Uncle Tom, who had been such a tower of strength to me as I struggled to adjust to life in

England, had died that afternoon from a heart attack. My mother immediately left to help Mary in whatever way was possible, and I was left struggling to understand what God was doing.

Yona's replacement

Eustace Kajuga and Marian had been in training at Buye with Yona and when he left for the Bugesera, they had stayed at Buye to help with the students, and had soon found themselves inundated with refugees fleeing the violence in Rwanda. They had done what they could to help, but were horrified by what was happening in their own country. When the bishop asked them to consider going to replace Yona, their initial reaction was fear for their children, but as they prayed about it, they felt that God was indeed calling them to go. Although there was no guarantee of safety in this life, there was the security they had in Jesus for all eternity.

Doreen Peck, a missionary who had worked closely with Yona, first at Shyogwe and then later at Nyamata, wrote to the *Ruanda Notes*:

> Eustace was one of Yona's oldest and closest friends and it seemed to us who know the opportunities of Nyamata that no one could be better suited to follow Yona. It was a great joy to me to take him there and introduce him to some of his parishioners (there are several thousand still) early in July. How the hymns of praise rang out again and again that day! Now he is well settled in and is already greatly beloved. Some of his friends were alarmed at his going, and indeed wrote many letters begging him not to risk his life as Yona had done, but he resolutely turned a deaf ear to these suggestions. "What more wonderful work is there," he said to me recently, "than to tell these needy people of a Saviour whom I know saves and satisfies?" And Marian added: "We know that the Lord Jesus alone holds the keys of the future and we're not afraid of going through any door which He opens; if He opens the door of death, we'll go to Him rejoicing."

Peter and Rosemary together

Peter wrote in the *Review* that spring:

The Lord had called Elisabeth and me to go and settle in a little home on the edge of the Belge [a suburb of Bujumbura], at the beginning of November. He gave us two and a half most happy months setting up the Alliance educational office and making contacts with our neighbours, Congolese, Barundi and Rwandan refugees. I was tied up with work, but Elisabeth was free and she had wonderful opportunities among these needy people. Then the Lord allowed this arrangement to break up, for she had suddenly to go home to supply a base for our family in England. Rosemary, my sister, came and helped out very kindly to keep house for me, but she is not as free as Elisabeth was, for she has the urgent job of preparing the Kirundi Bible for the press.

Neither Rosemary nor Peter was good at housekeeping, both being very absent-minded like their father. On one occasion Rosemary wrote that Peter had been deep in papers over breakfast when he suddenly said, "Was your egg bad? Mine was!" She smelled the empty shell and was horrified that he could have eaten it without being aware!

She was also getting involved in another project. She had met a young shoemaker, called Joel Abekyamwale, from the Bembe tribe in Congo, who showed her a translation of Mark's gospel which he had made from Swahili so that his people could read it in their own language. As soon as the Kirundi Bible was in the hands of the Bible Society for publishing, she set about learning Bembe and revising Joel's translation with him.

Peter and Elisabeth had not been apart for more than a fortnight since they got married and this six months' separation was very hard on them. We used to tease Elisabeth as she eagerly watched for the post and grabbed her fat letter of about 50 pages as soon as it appeared, but it was so good to have a home, in Chrissie's old house, where we could bring friends unexpectedly and know that she would welcome them.

To Elisabeth's horror, now that she was back in England and able to provide a home for the children, Haringay Council said they would no longer provide funds for Christine's education. Elisabeth pleaded with them at least to let her complete her "O" levels to which they finally agreed.

So Christine was able to have two years at Clarendon and then followed in her mother's footsteps to the North London Collegiate School. David had spent a year seeking to improve his

"A" level results, without success, and finally started at the North London Polytechnic where he soon became very friendly with a fellow student called Peta Steele.

Work with overseas students in Britain

At last, in the summer, Peter handed over his work to an African, and came home. He spent the first year in England speaking on behalf of the Mission, but then he resigned. He soon found work with the Inter-Varsity Fellowship (IVF), later called Universities and Colleges Christian Fellowship, working with overseas students.

In October 1965 he wrote for the last time for several years in *Ruanda Notes* about "A do-it-yourself Mission Field".

> In September we gained valuable experience in the International Friendship Campaign organized by the IVF to contact new student arrivals to this country from overseas. Well over one thousand contacts were made. Since then we have started keeping open house for overseas students at our home each Sunday afternoon and we have had some good times with them.

At the office he was involved in arranging hospitality for those requesting it and he got involved in missions at universities, discussions on Saturday afternoons, and so on. I shall never forget the first evening as he arrived home after struggling with London rush hour.

"I'm going to get a motor-bike" he announced.

"I thought you were finally going to settle down and become respectable!" exclaimed Elisabeth.

But he bought a Honda 50cc, and a moped for Christine, and every morning they set out together for their different destinations, threading their way through the traffic.

That summer they attended the first Fountain Trust meeting at High Leigh. There was teaching on forgiving people for what had happened in the past — even though those people might have died and one was unable to say it to their face. Peter spent much of that conference working through the pain of being abandoned by his parents in 1925.

After the conference they came on to Cambridge where I

was staying with Mary, having helped her move to a smaller house. I remember my mother asking me to go for a walk round the football pitch nearby, as she described the conference.

"Is there anything you need to forgive us for?" she asked.

For the first time I felt I had the freedom to talk about some of the difficulties I had experienced as a missionary's child. I date my adult relationship with my parents from that conversation. Many of my friends never got through to the sort of relationship that I had with my parents as adults, and I am so grateful that from then on we were able to be completely honest with each other, respecting one another's point of view, even when we disagreed.

Peter worked for two years with the IVF and then took a secular job, teaching mathematics and religious instruction at the Haberdasher Askes School in Elstree, while Elisabeth also taught religious instruction at the Henrietta Barnet School in Hampstead. Despite this, they continued their contacts with overseas students.

For several years they took a group of overseas students to "Casa Moschia" on Lake Maggiore in Switzerland where they had good times of fellowship and made several lasting friendships. On one occasion the lady of the house took Elisabeth aside and questioned her about the Revival in Rwanda. Then she asked about her own family.

Elisabeth's face must have fallen for she instantly exclaimed, "I do not want to criticize. I have a real burden for the children of Christian workers and I want to know so that I can pray for you."

So Elisabeth told her about how hard it was to welcome the overseas students in one room and yet all the family remained in another room watching TV.

"Never mind, my dear," was her reply. "You have a big heart. Rejoice that you have one family in one room and another family in the other."

She also said that she wished that some of her church members would rebel rather than continue with a second-hand faith, since in her experience the further teenagers went from the Lord, when they came back, the more they were on fire. This was such an encouragement for Elisabeth since at that time John, David and Christine were all rebelling against anything Christian.

Problems with my faith

Outwardly I was still a practising Christian but was going through real difficulties at university. I was studying mathematics and science and my fellow students could not see how this could be compatible with a belief in God. Some of the lecturers were also scathing about Christianity. As I had never before had to question any of my beliefs I did not know how to cope. I became more and more unhappy, but I did not want to add to the problems my parents were experiencing with the others.

Things came to a head in my third year at university when I decided that God did not exist. I became very depressed and spent my time wondering how best to kill myself, and on one occasion took a train to the Forth intending to throw myself from the Forth Bridge. When it came to it, I was not absolutely certain that God did not exist, and I did not want to meet him after killing myself!

Soon after this I was talking to my father on the phone and blurted out my unhappiness. I could only cry down the phone. Next morning my mother was in Edinburgh, having dropped all her commitments in London and caught the night train. She brought with her a letter from my father, that I kept for many years, though I lost it somewhere along the lines. He advised me to read Isaiah 41, and then said, "You say you cannot believe in God, but I do, and you can believe in me — just hold on to that." This letter and the practical demonstration of my mother's love kept me through that difficult time.

That summer I had promised to help my parents cook at the Keswick camp for male students at the Keswick Convention. I went reluctantly, determined to cook but not attend any meetings, but on the Thursday I went to the youth meeting. As the text was announced, I very nearly walked out. It was 1 John 1:7. "If we walk in the light, as he is in the light, we have fellowship with one another, and the blood of Jesus his Son cleanses from all sin" (RSV). How often had I heard those words in my childhood. I really did not want to hear another sermon on walking in the light! However, the speaker was more concerned with that word "fellowship". He said that there was a difference between fellowship and relationship and he illustrated it from his life as a sailor.

"A ship coming to harbour often needs a tug to manoeuvre it to its berth," he said. "Connecting the ship and the tug are two cables — a huge thick anchor cable, and a thin communication cable. Sometimes in a storm the communication cable is broken, but the anchor chain of relationship remains firm."

I don't remember anything else from that sermon. It was as if my whole world had suddenly righted itself as I realized that my relationship with Jesus Christ had been established way back at Kabale when, as a girl of nine, I had invited him to take over my life. All that had happened in the last few months was that my communication cable had been broken and I had lost touch with my base. I cannot describe the sense of relief I felt. I do not think I ever again doubted my relationship with God, though I doubted most other things to do with my faith, as I grew in it.

I still did not find my last year at Edinburgh easy, but I somehow got a degree, and the following summer I set off for Malawi with Voluntary Service Overseas (VSO). It seemed strange that I was the one to fly off to Africa leaving the family in England.

During my time there I was able to travel back to Burundi to spend Christmas with Rosemary, visiting Philippa in Uganda on the way. She had been expelled from the Sudan, had settled in Gulu, Uganda, and was now working on the Bari Bible with some Sudanese refugees. When I saw her, she had just fallen and broken her hip and was in hospital in Kampala. I spent a few days with her and then flew to Bujumbura. It was lovely to renew my contact with the country of my birth.

The family settles down

At the end of my time with VSO, I returned to England by sea from Cape Town, arriving in Southampton on Boxing Day 1967. Early in the New Year we went to the annual Ruanda Mission party where we renewed contact with so many friends, collecting Christine on the way. As my father was negotiating the traffic at Elephant and Castle, Christine suddenly spoke from the back of the car.

"I just wanted to tell you," she said, "that I have become a Christian."

I felt the car swerve as Dad took in the statement. He then

drove round and round the roundabout trying to compose himself before continuing through the traffic. I had been in Africa through the worst of Christine's rebellion but from letters had gathered that all was not well with her. She had spent the New Year with a friend and had talked out all her doubts with the Christian faith, finally accepting its truth around midnight. Though I was delighted, my parents were even more so, walking on air as they went to the party.

Soon afterwards both she and Dad got flu and spent hours talking together in a way they had not been able to do for years. She finished at school that summer and started at York University the next autumn.

In March, David married Peta Steele, with John as best man, sporting a large beard. He arrived back just in time from the Brazilian jungle where he had been medical officer for a Royal Society/Royal Geographical Society expedition for the past six months. I joined the Metropolitan Police that summer and spent four stressful months at training school in Hendon before being posted to the West End as a constable.

While I was at the training school, I heard that my mother had been taken into Bart's Hospital with a lump on her breast. They discovered that it was cancer and she had a mastectomy while still under the anaesthetic. She and my father had been considering the possibility of returning to Africa in the near future, now that most of the family had left home, and Christine was due to spend a year in Germany as part of her degree course. Now, however, it appeared that their hopes were to be dashed. But she made an excellent recovery and her surgeon had no qualms about her returning to Africa, provided that she had regular check-ups.

A new opportunity

They wrote to the field representative of the Ruanda Mission, Rev. Albert Brown in Kigali, asking him to sound out the bishop of Kigali to see whether, after all this time, they would be able to return to Rwanda. That summer, they visited the Schaeffers at L'Abri, in Switzerland. While there, their great friends, the de Benoit sisters, came over to visit them. They were heavily involved in the work of Scripture Union in Switzerland.

At one point, as they were sharing their hopes of returning to Rwanda, together with their doubts that they would be acceptable, Elisabeth de Benoit suddenly said, "Why not go to Burundi with Scripture Union? I know they are wanting to appoint a new agent there."

Peter's eyes lit up. This would be the sort of work he had longed to do. But then his face fell. "The Mission would never release us from education," he said. "There is such a need for teachers."

"Try them out and see," persisted Elisabeth. "You are just the sort of person Scripture Union is crying out for."

On the principle of "nothing ventured, nothing gained", they did indeed approach Scripture Union, but the church leaders in Burundi did not want an Anglican in charge of their affairs, and in fact soon appointed Dorothee de Benoit, Elisabeth's younger sister who was already teaching in Burundi, as their first staff worker. However, to Peter's amazement, not only had the bishop of Rwanda successfully negotiated with the government that they could return, but he agreed to release them from education so that they could start the work of Scripture Union in Rwanda. In fact, the bishop was labouring under a misapprehension. His only experience of Scripture Union was in Uganda where most of the active members were Anglicans and he thought that it would be another branch of the Anglican Church under his control.

Peter and Elisabeth, however, had spent time with the General International Council of Scripture Union, and were told that they had to be careful to appoint their first committee with no reference to outside bodies. They must be elected for one reason only — their quality as Christians, irrespective of church affiliation. That requirement, though obviously right, was to cause many problems in the years ahead.

In July 1969, Peter wrote of his joy as they prepared to return to Rwanda and then said:

We came home from Burundi in 1964, Elisabeth in January and I in July, after nearly 25 years in Rwanda and Burundi. We came because of the need of the family for a home in England. Since then much has happened. Our three eldest, John, Margaret and David, are of age and in jobs. John is a surgeon at Luton, Margaret is in the Metropolitan Police, and David is married and working for Esso. Christine is 19 and is at the end of her first year at York University where she is studying German and Swahili. She has to spend all next year at Cologne and we are trusting that she will be able to find Christian fellowship there and, if possible, Christians to live with; otherwise it will not be easy for her. We hope she will spend next summer with us in Rwanda.

After a paragraph describing what they had been doing during those five years in Britain, he added:

We thank God for all the fresh insights and experiences He has given us during these years at home, especially among students of many nations and with young people. The time with IVF brought us into contact with people from the East, and this has given us a burden for the Asians in Rwanda. Previously we had tended to look upon the Indian traders or lorry drivers as "not our parish". We feel rather afraid of making a fresh start at our age and in the present circumstances. We shall be cast on the Lord completely. We need Him to equip and empower us, but He is faithful. Please pray for us and our family.

Chapter 9　　　　　　　　　# A Second Wave
# of Revival
(1969-1973)

Welcome to Kigali

So, in October 1969, Peter and Elisabeth returned to a very warm welcome in Rwanda. Initially based in the Anglican Centre in Kigali, eventually they moved into a temporary house, built in the traditional style of mud but with iron girders replacing the wattle sticks. Peter promptly christened it "Meccano Villas". It was a semi-detached house and soon they were joined by Rev. Eric Townson with his wife, Ruth, who had been appointed to start Boys' Brigade, and who soon became invaluable colleagues in youth work.

One thing that thrilled them about their location was that, as in Bujumbura, they were surrounded by African neighbours and were very close to an extremely poor suburb. Elisabeth soon got involved in Sunday School work at the cathedral and many of the children would come in during the evenings to sing with them, learn Bible stories and chat. They were unintimidated by their surroundings and felt free to wander in and out as they would in any African house.

Peter's first priority was to see how the vernacular Scripture Union notes could be improved. He was concerned that there was so little Christian literature in the vernacular and was determined that the SU notes would really help in interpreting the Scriptures. This was a vast task and needed competent helpers, so his next job, with Elisabeth, was to visit as many schools as they could and identify committed Christians who might be able to help in this process. It was also a chance to encourage Bible reading in the various schools.

Peter wrote at the end of that year: "Everywhere we went we found a spiritual hunger which was certainly not there seven years ago. We came back to Kigali with a sense of expectancy that God was going to pour out Revival blessing again." And indeed he did.

Another Revival

For some years there had been racial tension at Kigeme Girls' School, culminating in an incident at the end of term prize-giving in July 1969. It had been a generally disappointing day with none of the exuberance usually displayed on such occasions. The girls had seemed dull and flat and, although the parents had seemed satisfied, Mabel Jones, the headmistress, felt uneasy. That evening she was called to the dining hall where she found all the girls milling around outside. They were demanding separate dining facilities for the Hutu and Tutsi as they would not tolerate eating together. Angrily she ordered them into the dining hall and harangued them for some minutes on the evil of tribalism.

Later she went to the classroom where they were all congregated. She asked them to forgive her for her anger and the way she had spoken to them. "If we repent, God will forgive all of us," she said. For the next two hours they prayed, and some did indeed ask for God's forgiveness. After a peaceful night they all went home.

The following term there was a different atmosphere, and more girls began attending the voluntary school prayer meeting. There was a desire to read the Bible. Some of those girls had been present the year before when Mabel and a volunteer from Ireland, Holly Moore, had been called to deal with a demonized girl in one of the dormitories. Mabel described this incident:

> At first they had been very afraid, but then they began to see that using the Word of God was effective, and as we quoted powerful verses, they appreciated that the Sword of the Spirit caused quite a reaction among the demons. The girls sang with us hymns praising the sacrifice of Jesus and the power of His blood. Sometimes it was quite late when we felt we could go home. Often outside the school we looked to the hills where the mother of one student

lived. She was a sorceress and her brother a witchdoctor. How wonderful it was to take authority over the work of Satan in the Name of Jesus and pray that God would pour out His blessing over the area.

When Holly returned to Ireland in 1968, she took with her a list of every girl she had taught during the year. Daily she prayed for each girl by name. But while she and Mabel prayed, racial tension in the school was being stirred up by local leaders, and sometimes Mabel felt quite despondent, but God began giving her words of encouragement.

"Fear not. I will come in the dark places and these little ones I will deliver from deceit, from the spirit of lying. You cannot organize this. Let Me take over." These words were a great encouragement as there was a real problem with cheating. It seemed very difficult to prevent this because some of the brightest girls seemed to think it was the generous thing to write their answers very clearly and in such a way that the others could copy them.

During the time of Revival, small prayer huts or *kazu* had been built on every station run by the mission, and at Kigeme local Christians would meet every Tuesday at 4.30 p.m. to pray together and share God's word. That term, some of the girls from the school began to join the local Christians each week. On 13th January 1970 Mabel was startled to see the *kazu* full, with several students standing outside. About 80 girls from the school were there. She gave out a hymn, suggesting that they sing it prayerfully, asking the Holy Spirit to come to their hearts, revealing their sin, and also to show them their Saviour.

As they sang, the Holy Spirit came. They read a passage from the book of Joshua and then first one and then another came under conviction of the sin of racial hatred. Hutu girls repented of hating Tutsi girls, Tutsi of hating Hutu. Some confessed to keeping sticks hidden in their beds for protection and attack. Soon, all over the hut, Tutsi and Hutu were hugging each other as their hatred was replaced by the love of Jesus. As they returned to the school singing, their faces transformed, other students came out to find out what had been happening. Soon they were sharing what Jesus had done for them.

Later when Mabel went to supervise "prep", one of the girls

offered her a Bible and a hymn book. "Please can we continue to share what God has done for us," she begged. Many more repented that night and asked Jesus to forgive them for their sins, particularly of racial hatred.

Next day they wrote to the nurses at the nearby hospital asking them to come to the school that evening and hear what was happening. Mabel wrote:

> They came and soon the Holy Spirit was showing them what they needed to bring to Jesus. During the following days the hospital sister, Maureen New, received cotton wool, dressings, medicines, that had been stolen, and the nurses repented of hatred of patients and colleagues, and some of neglecting their work. The whole atmosphere changed and soon there was an evening meeting in the outpatients' department and many patients came including the children suffering from malnutrition.

Maureen New wrote of changed lives: "One of the hardest nurses had a vision of Jesus on the cross when she went to bed and she sobbed as she saw large nails in his hands and feet and the blood running down his brow. She came to hospital the next morning, 'a new creature in Christ'. Others quickly followed her."

Elspeth Cole, another missionary nurse, told of a child who had been unconscious for twelve weeks for no medical reason that the doctors could find. His father was influenced by what was happening in the hospital and was transformed as he put his trust in Jesus. As Elspeth was praying for the child one morning, she felt that there was witchcraft behind his illness so she asked the father if any among his family had been involved in witchcraft.

"Yes," he answered, "I was. But I have given it all up now."

Elspeth, the father and an African nurse, went to pray for the child. "We prayed that all the satanic work be undone in the Name of Jesus, then again in Jesus' Name that this child be healed completely and saved to bring glory to him alone. A short, simple prayer, that was all." Next morning the child began to move, and within four days was walking and eating normal food! (Quoted in *Fire in the Hills*, pp 195-6)

The school electrician, son of one of those who had been saved during the Revival, who had rebelled against it, was also convicted by the Holy Spirit. He developed a gift of hymn-writing. The hymns were copied and distributed among the students and soon they were all singing them. Every Sunday afternoon, teams of students, nurses and local people went off up nearby hills to share the good news of love instead of hate.

Having dealt with the main problem of tribalism, God went on to convict the girls about cheating in exams. Before the state exam, God gave encouragement from 2 Chronicles 20. Mabel, together with some of the girls, made a large poster with the words, "We have no strength. We don't know what to do, but our eyes are on YOU." This was placed in the front of the classroom.

When Mabel went to see that all was well with the official invigilator, he said, "But all the girls have different answers."

"That's wonderful," she replied. "If you had been here some months ago, you would have found that they all had the same answers!"

To everyone's joy, all the girls passed and were able to continue their studies.

On 28th January 1970, every secondary school had to send a small group of students to Gitarama for the *Fête de la Démocratie*, where they paraded a school banner in front of President Kayibanda. The banner Kigeme School paraded depicted two flaming torches with a dove hovering over them, and the words, "LOVE AND TRUTH. KIGEME". After the parade, the Kigeme girls stayed at the nearby school of Shyogwe for the night.

They asked if they could share what God had been doing at Kigeme during the school assembly next morning. One girl was allowed to speak, the first time a Rwandese girl had addressed boys in this way. They were astounded at her authority and wanted to learn more.

The following May, student delegates attended a meeting of MEPRA (*Mouvement des Etudiants Protestants du Rwanda*). Jacqueline Lugtenborg, a teacher at Remera, who had been praying daily for a breakthrough of the Holy Spirit, wrote to a friend:

Two of our students, Thamar and Ruth, came back completely changed and began to witness to other students. Then in September, five girls from Kigeme School came to follow the two-year course for *Monitrices Techniques*. They were fully convinced about what happened at Kigeme — how hatred and disharmony had been repented of, and how the love of Jesus had taken over. They wanted to give testimony to the whole school. I said, "Show it by your lives."

Girls from Kigeme School began travelling to other schools to tell what God had done for them. It was at one such meeting at Gahini, that Emmanuel Kayijuka, who later became general secretary of Scripture Union in Rwanda during the time of the genocide and in the years afterwards, gave his life to the Lord Jesus, having seen the changed lives of those schoolgirls.

Scripture Union camp at Shyogwe

Over Easter 1970, Peter and Elisabeth held a Scripture Union camp at Shyogwe, having invited several students to come so that they could discuss how to write the Scripture Union notes. Many came who were still bound by tribal hatred, and many came through to a new experience of the Holy Spirit. As they gave their testimonies there would be an exuberant outpouring of praise, with the person surrounded and hugged and often thrown into the air. Jacqueline commented to Elisabeth: "This appears to be a new form of Christian confirmation!"

Jacqueline later wrote to her supporting church about the camp, which seven delegates from Remera School had attended:

> It was very well organized and we saw God working. On returning to Remera the girls shared everything at the Saturday school prayer meeting. The whole school attended, with the exception of one girl. The meeting lasted two hours and several girls stood up and said they wanted to go the way of Jesus. One girl who had been unable to speak for some months, stood and spoke. It was a miracle! The following day, Sunday, Peter and Elisabeth brought some boys to share their testimonies.

Peter wrote in the *Ruanda Notes*:

> How can we possibly describe the Shyogwe camp? It was an experience we shall never forget. It was the first time the recently saved boys and girls had been able to get together, and their joy had to be seen to be believed. With so much praise and love for the Lord, the camp just ran itself like a well-oiled machine — just as

well since the two of us are hopeless organizers. One boy said, "I suppose heaven will be even better than this!"

In the same issue Peter wrote:

> Our work is now clear: to encourage all these embryo Christian Unions. We are planning camps for training and teaching leaders. We have also been visiting most of the parishes in Rwanda encouraging Bible reading and distributing Scripture Union notes. The circulation of these notes is increasing, but its future production is a problem.

At the Shyogwe camp they chose their first committee for Scripture Union. The president, Aaron, was a Methodist, the vice-president, Simeon, was a Presbyterian, and several committee members were Anglican. This committee did not meet with the Anglican bishop's approval, and relationships became very strained between him and Peter.

Years afterwards, the bishop spoke at Peter's memorial service. "We often had severe disagreements," he said, "but because Peter was able to walk in the light and repent of anger, we were able to continue working together."

The SU committee chose their first agent to work with Peter. He was a Methodist called Nathan, an *assistant médical*, working in a government post near Gisenyi, who was prepared to lose his status and salary in order to do this work. He had to work a year's notice before he was free to join them, but he was such an outstandingly good candidate that everyone, including the bishop, agreed to wait for him.

Family visits

That summer Christine went out to visit them as planned. She flew to Nairobi where she met John, who had bought a rather battered Ford Escort estate car from a friend, and drove through Kenya and Tanzania to Bujumbura where they stayed with the Johnsons, with whom Christine had stayed for six months when she was at school in Bujumbura. The car John had bought had various problems, one of which was that its brakes failed. He had to negotiate the hills of Burundi using only the handbrake which he managed very successfully. Unfortunately in the relief of arrival he forgot and drove, fortunately quite gently, into the back of the Johnsons' car!

I had also managed to get a few weeks' leave and had spent a few days with my parents in Kigali, and then we drove to Bujumbura where there was a convention, with their close friend, the evangelist and later bishop, Festo Kivengere, as the main speaker. It was good to meet up with John and Christine again. We drove in convoy (John's brakes now fixed) back to Kigali, stopping for a night in Buye on the way.

We had a photo of John, aged about three, sitting on his father's shoulders beside a very spindly jacaranda tree which Peter had planted a few years before. To our amazement we discovered that this was now a giant of a tree, so we took another photo, this time of John with his father sitting on his shoulders! The Rwandans have a proverb, "A rabbit when it is grown, is suckled by its young", and they produce it whenever they see these two photos together. Sadly, since the genocide, they have changed the proverb to say, "A rabbit when it is old ought to die", or even worse, "A rabbit when it is old is eaten", and that indeed is what we have seen recently. It seems that the genocide had a profound effect on the traditional morality of the country and several times we have found widows who have been thrown out of their homes and left destitute by their own children — something that would have been unheard of years ago.

After a night in Kigali, John had to leave us. He drove the car back to Kampala where he was able to sell it for almost exactly what he had paid, which meant that his East African travels had only cost the petrol!

Christine and I spent a few days in Meccano Villas, seeing the busy life our parents lived, with the many visitors who dropped in to see them, interrupting the time-consuming work of preparing Scripture Union notes.

One of those who came to see them was a young trainee *assistant médical* called John Gakwandi. He had recently come to the Lord at Kigeme. As a five-year-old, in 1959, he and his family were forced out of their home which was burnt down and their cattle killed. They lived where they could, often sleeping in the open air, or taking shelter in school buildings, until his father eventually managed to build a small house, and life began to settle down. Then when he was ten, at Christmas 1963, violence erupted again and he saw several of his friends and neighbours being killed. His aunt, Julienne, and most of her family, were burnt to death in their house. His father kept their family together, reading to them from the Psalms and praying with them. Somehow they survived, but the next few years were hard, as he struggled to be accepted at school, despite his tribe. Now he had found a new identity in the Lord Jesus.

Other visitors came for money, or food, or simply to chat. As we left for a fortnight's holiday at Nabugabo, in Uganda, my father remarked, "Just think. Two whole weeks, with nothing to do but work!" Although I protested at the time that we were going on holiday, I now realize what he meant, since I too have to leave home in order to find time to do preparation work, and for the same reason.

School visits

In August 1970 the government decided that there should be no more segregation between Catholic and Protestant schools, so many Protestant pupils went to join formerly Catholic schools up and down the country. Peter and Elisabeth were able to visit them and often were given permission to take meetings in these schools, with the result that more and more young people came into an experience of the Holy Spirit and were freed from tribal hatred. Peter and Elisabeth used to travel with a number of young people who gave their testimonies in the different schools as to what God had done in their lives.

One of those who travelled with them was a girl called Jennifer. She had been a very shy girl until a meeting in 1969 when the evangelist, Festo Kivengere from Uganda, had visited Shyogwe school. She had been certain that God was speaking to her and, when an appeal was made, she found herself on her feet. "I thank God that he has enabled me to stand up," she said and sat down again. She used to say that she had experienced no conviction of sin, no repentance, but she had made a commitment, and later, at the Shyogwe camp, she was able to sort out some of the things that the Holy Spirit had been bringing to her mind.

Following the genocide, her husband, Emmanuel, a

Pentecostal pastor, was falsely accused of involvement in the genocide and imprisoned in 1998. It was a time of great hardship for Jennifer who was looking after several orphans and hardly ever sat down to eat with fewer than 20 people to feed, but whenever my mother and I visited her, she was always cheerful. One day she took us to see her husband who was excited by what the Lord was doing in prison.

"I am baptizing new Christians every day," he said. "The Anglicans also baptized 60 new Christians the other day. There is great fellowship between denominations and many, many of the prisoners are coming to the Lord. Only last week the man who accused me became a believer, and he is going to the government to withdraw his accusation."

Although the accusation was withdrawn, because of the chaos in the legal system following the genocide, he had to wait for his case to be heard, and at the time of writing, a year after the allegation was withdrawn, he is still in prison, still writing letters rejoicing at what the Lord is doing there. (Sadly, just as this book was going to press, we heard that Emmanuel had been taken to Kigeme hospital in a coma from meningitis. The next day he died, and my mother and I travelled across the country to his funeral. Jennifer was devastated but was still able to testify to her husband's faith and trust in the Lord. Several of her friends had had assurance from the Lord that he was going to be released. "He was," she said, "even though not in the way we expected!")

In 1971 Peter heard the news that his sister, Lindesay, who had been ill off and on for several months, had died of heart failure. A year after her mother's death, Lindesay had got the job of candidate secretary with CMS. She was responsible for interviewing all new applicants to work with CMS overseas, and also for supervising their training before they went. She was extremely happy in this work. She bought a small flat in London near Waterloo, and would go home to Cambridge most weekends. After a few years, the new general secretary of CMS, John V. Taylor, later to become the bishop of Winchester, asked her to become his personal assistant, which she considered a real privilege. She was still doing this when she died, and John Taylor preached at her funeral at Holy Trinity Church in Cambridge.

Christine visits again

In the summer of 1971, Christine was again able to visit her parents. She had recently returned to Germany on a summer scholarship to do a course in Marburg, on the border with East Germany. Most of those doing her course were extremely left-wing in their politics and were offended by her Christianity and seemed determined to convert her to communism. She said later that two things kept her from joining them. One was that they seemed to have no interest in the beauty of the world around them.

"One evening," she said, "we were having a particularly intense discussion, when I looked up and gasped. The sunset was simply magnificent. I said, 'Look at the sky', but only a few glanced round, and then returned to the discussion." This lack of interest in the beauty of the world kept her interested in the Creator.

Another aspect of their belief system also distressed her. This was that change had to be on the mass scale — one should care for the "proletariat" as a whole, not for the individual peasant. As they were discussing how the world revolution could be brought about, she cried out, "But what about the poor people with no power, who will starve if you do that?" She was informed that there would be necessary casualties so that a more equitable world could be produced. This left her in emotional and ideological turmoil as she left for Africa: was Christianity or communism the real answer to the world's problems?

She was thus very shaken in many aspects of her faith as she arrived, and her time in Rwanda was very timely. She was able to share her confusion with her parents, who listened sympathetically and gave her time to talk it through. Peter had also toyed with communism during his time at Cambridge and he had insights to share, arising out of his own struggles from that time. "What helped me," he told her, "was to realize that God cares for each individual, and that lasting change in the world can only happen as an individual truly receives new life in Christ and walks in his ways." Seeing the reality of what the Lord was doing in the lives of young people in Rwanda also helped. The unity she saw seemed to embody the principles of communism at its best.

Peter and Elisabeth felt very lonely after she had gone but were soon cheered by a letter from John. He had become active in the environment movement and some of their literature painted a bleak picture of environmental scenarios that could lead to the end of the world.

"But the Bible told me that years ago," thought John. He decided that if the Bible could be right about that, then it might also be right about others things, so he returned to it with new eyes.

Later he wrote about the way he had come back to Christian faith:

I have come to see humanity's persistent failure, through pollution, consumption and violence, to preserve on the planet a habitable environment for all God's creatures, humans included, as caused principally by sin: chiefly the sins of human pride and greed. The solution can be found in two commandments of Jesus (Mark 12:29-31):

- LOVE GOD: If we truly love God would we not wish to protect all that he has made, ie steward and look after his creation rather than permit the extinction of so many species?
- LOVE YOUR NEIGHBOUR AS YOURSELF: If we truly love our neighbour then would we not more sacrificially
  a   love our OVERSEAS neighbour, and
  b   love our FUTURE neighbour, ensuring that he or she does not live on an overcrowded, resource-depleted and ultimately uninhabitable planet?

It was because he had discovered that Christian love was the primary solution to both poverty and the environmental crisis that John's faith had been renewed.

Scripture Union fostered Christian unity

Delighted with this news, Peter and Elisabeth returned to their work with renewed vigour. Peter wrote in the *Ruanda Notes Review* of 1971-72:

The joy of Scripture Union work is that it brings us into partnership with all branches of the African church in Rwanda including the Roman Catholic Church. At the theological college at Butare for the Presbyterian and Baptist Churches one of the students came out with this in an open discussion. "People talk about ecumenism but where it really works is at an SU camp when the Holy Spirit is working."

In those days following Vatican II, the old antagonisms and suspicions between Catholics and Protestants had largely disappeared. Peter and Elisabeth, with a few Protestant girls and Suzanne Furst, from Switzerland, who was lecturing at Butare Theological College, decided to go to a Catholic retreat led by Père Philippe, the chaplain to King Baudouin of the Belgians. At the last moment, Peter heard that Brother Andrew of Open Doors was coming on a visit, so he returned to Kigali to meet him with Nathan.

Elisabeth and Suzanne had a wonderful time at the retreat despite certain difficulties. On the first evening, the Protestants with them said, "What do we do about Mass?" They went to ask Père Philippe. He said, "If you are willing to join us, we are happy to have you. You will be remembering the Lord's death in your way. We will remember his death in our way. When we get to heaven, we will probably find that we are both wrong!" What a far cry from the struggles experienced by the early missionaries!

Peter arrived back in Kigali to find that Brother Andrew had been given their only spare bed in the room that doubled as the SU office. They had received a consignment of Bibles just before leaving for the retreat, and had rapidly pulled out some to take with them, flinging wrapping paper and parcels into the office. Brother Andrew, who had studied time and motion, gently commented, "I wish I had more time here so that I could help you organize your office better!"

Once, Peter and Elisabeth were travelling to Burundi for a Scripture Union camp. They had been told of a Roman Catholic centre which was doing some beautiful handcraft and took time to go and see it. After showing them round, the sister said, "I have a very sore back which is the cross I have to bear." Peter had recently read a book on healing by Francis McNutt in which he said that sickness should not necessarily be considered a cross, since Jesus could heal, so he offered to pray for her. They prayed briefly by their car and went on their way, thinking no more about it. A few months later they were again in Burundi and were told that this sister particularly wanted to see them, so once again they made the detour.

"Thank you for praying for me," she said. "The Lord healed me that very day and I have had no more pain. I went to Bujumbura the next day, something I always dreaded since the heat brought on the pain, but at the end of the day I realized that I had no more pain."

They became lifelong friends, and until she retired she had no further trouble from her back. Then she wrote to Elisabeth, saying that the trouble had returned, but praising God that he had kept her fit throughout her active life of service.

The Scripture Union camps were tremendous times when young people from all the schools met together. There was a free mix of denominations, which was remarkable for those who were used to the rigid denominationalism of the country. These camps were largely evangelistic in nature. But this was not the only type of camp that Peter and Elisabeth organized.

They also run one for committed, educated Christians who would be able to help them with the Scripture Union notes. Groups of young Christians would study the passages which would be used for daily Bible readings during the coming year. They were asked to write their own comments on the passages. Peter would then read these and use the best of them as a basis for the notes, even though in those early days the largest proportion of the notes were written by Peter and Elisabeth. He was still writing some of the notes until just before his death and Elisabeth is doing them even as I write! Each year a huge amount of time and energy was spent in getting the notes ready for printing and distributing, particularly in the days before word processors and computers. The notes were collected into a booklet which would last the whole year. From those early students they gradually formed a pool of keen Christians who had the ability to write pertinent comments on the Bible readings. Many of them are still writing these notes today.

In the camps, during school visits, in churches or just out on the hillside, Peter would play his accordion and gather crowds to hear him teach them songs. He was unable to read music but had an exceptional ear for a tune and could play almost any hymn on his beloved accordion. He would often go out in the hills and start playing. A crowd soon gathered and he would then speak to them of the love of God in sending his Son to die for them. I am constantly meeting people who describe my father with the accordion. Many can remember choruses that he taught them. As children, it was a particular treat to be allowed to play the notes of his *inanga* and he used to produce it to keep us occupied while jiggers were being taken from our toes. During those years with Scripture Union, his accordion was never far from his side.

Political tensions

Those were good years for Peter and Elisabeth, but the country as a whole was experiencing increasing tension. Although it was now a republic, President Kayibanda had taken over the culture and ethos of the old kings. He was responsible for all appointments down to the lowest level of administration. He ruled, as the king had done, through a small group of rulers, who passed on power to favoured subordinates, just as the old *ubuhake* system had worked in the past. He emphasized the importance of democracy. Because the Hutu were the majority tribe, they had a right to rule.

According to Gerard Prunier in *The Rwanda Crisis*, Tutsi were 9% of the population and so were permitted to hold 9% of jobs and places in schools. In practice, since Tutsi had received more education under the old regime, they were the best qualified to do most of the clerical jobs and so they exceeded this quota, especially in the civil service.

The people were urged to live moral Christian lives and not to get involved in politics, but to leave all that to their leaders who would see what was good for them. There was no way that they could express any dissatisfaction with the regime, and the people felt stifled. Already poor, the fighting of the previous years had led to Rwanda becoming one of the poorest nations in the world.

Then in 1972 there was an attempted coup in Burundi. Unlike Rwanda, Burundi still had a Tutsi regime, although they had overthrown the king in 1968. In April 1972, some Hutu from the predominantly Hutu area in the south of the country, had attempted to follow Rwanda's example and overthrow the

Tutsi government. In the process, they had slaughtered as many Tutsi as they could. They were soon suppressed by the Burundi army, and the government then systematically arrested all the educated Hutu in the country. They were accused of involvement in the plot and killed, often horribly. It is estimated that between 80,000 and 120,000 educated Hutu, including schoolboys, died in a few weeks. Many thousands more fled to the surrounding countries, including Rwanda, as refugees.

By June, the Anglican Church had lost about a third of their pastors, and as many of their teachers, nurses and office staff. One of their missionaries, Canon Ian Leakey, was imprisoned and expelled from the country. Yet through it all came many testimonies to the peace, and even joy, that Jesus gave in prison and in bereavement.

The effect on Rwanda was predictable. President Kayibanda was already feeling insecure, with opposition beginning to materialize among the Hutu of the north. He felt that the one sure way that he could regain his ascendancy was to unite the country in hatred against the Tutsi. He organized vigilante committees to check whether Tutsi had exceeded their quotas in schools, university, the civil service and even private businesses. The most vigilant on these committees were the educated Hutu who could expect to get the jobs left vacant by the Tutsi. Many Tutsi were purged from the civil service, school and the university, often with violence which sometimes led to death.

Increasing tribal tensions

It was a time of terror for Tutsi, many of whom changed their identity cards in an effort to find security in schools or at work. Christian Hutu were also in a dilemma. One Christian boy at a school near Kigali heard that certain Hutu were planning to kill all the Tutsi in his school. He telephoned the army for help, naming the Hutu concerned. Soldiers came to arrest the Hutu, but also supervised the expulsion of all the Tutsi, as well as the Hutu boy who had telephoned them.

One who lost his job was John Gakwandi. He had finished his training and was an *assistant médical* in Kigeme. One evening, while scrubbing up to assist with an operation, his chief doctor told him that he no longer had a job and must leave immediately. He said, "I had to leave not knowing what was waiting for me outside. It is wonderful to have Jesus in your life."

His home had been a centre for Christians to meet in for prayer and Bible study most evenings, but now few dared to visit him, though not everyone ignored him. One evening a military car approached his house. A young girl grabbed his hand and pulled him into a field of sorghum where they hid until the car left. John wrote, "While we were still there, it occurred to us that it was not necessary to hide any more because we knew that our lives were in the hands of the Lord. We came back into the house and the Lord honoured his promise and protected us."

Peter and Elisabeth continued to visit schools during this difficult time. One Roman Catholic school near Ruhengeri had a group of 25 Protestant girls whom they had frequently visited. On one visit they asked the headmistress for a meeting of anyone who wanted to know the relevance of the Bible in today's world.

"What's the use of talking about that to barbarians like these girls?" she said, describing some of the atrocities that had been committed against the Tutsi girls in the school. "We are not proud of our Christian education — indeed our chaplain has given up teaching them religion. There is no point!"

Peter said that it was as bad in some Protestant schools and the only hope was that hearts could be changed through Jesus Christ. The headmistress agreed to a meeting, although she said gloomily, "You won't get much of a hearing from that lot!"

Despite her expectations, many more girls came than were expected and they listened in rapt attention. But then Peter got cold feet. "What would happen if there were a mass movement of the Holy Spirit here as there was at Kigeme? How would the staff react? Would we be able to cope?" Out of fear, he did not ask for a response to what he had been teaching. They left feeling that an opportunity had been missed.

Two weeks later, they were in the vicinity of the school and, on impulse, drove in. They were greeted warmly by the headmistress who had been so despondent on their previous visit. "Something has changed," she said. "There is a different atmosphere now." Despite the short notice, a meeting was hastily arranged and most of the school crowded in to hear what it was that had changed the lives of some of the girls who had come to the previous meeting. There was some mockery at first from some of the older girls, but as Peter spoke of the Saviour who prayed for his enemies, and who gives power to love, a strange hush came over the room. Then Peter handed over to William, the young lad who had accompanied him, and they listened avidly as he told his story. That day, many lives were permanently changed as girls received the transforming love of their Saviour.

William was a Hutu from Burundi whose mother had married a Rwandan Hutu at Matana, the week before Peter and Elisabeth's wedding. His father had been killed by Tutsi in Burundi the previous year and he had fled with his mother to Rwanda. He had been distressed to find the same tribal hatred in Rwanda. A gang of Hutu had invited him to join them to kill Tutsi in vengeance for his father's death. He had not had the courage to withstand them and that night he took his *muhoro* (sickle) and went with them.

To his relief, he had not had occasion to use it, but as he told the girls, "How ashamed I would have been if Jesus had come back that night." Never again would he seek to kill anyone. Instead he was able to rescue some Tutsi and get them to safety. Later, during the genocide, he was able to rescue some Tutsi, hiding them in his house. Despite this, he was accused of involvement in the genocide and removed from his job as lay preacher. He went to Uganda in 1999 to look for work and there he disappeared, presumably killed by robbers, although nothing further was heard of him.

As Peter had said, things were bad in Protestant schools, and nowhere as bad as at Shyogwe. Although missionaries still taught in the school, the headmaster by now was an African. A gang of Hutu ruled the school in a reign of terror. A minister from the government was sent to enquire into their grievances. One lad, called Edison, accused the pastor, Geoffrey, of preaching sedition. Despite the fact that the others all declared this to be a lie, Edison insisted that it was the truth. President Kayibanda himself sent for the bishop and told him that although he, personally, had nothing against Geoffrey except that he was Tutsi, he must be moved from the school. He was transferred to help in the parish of Kigali.

A few weeks later the gang went on the rampage. They beat up one teacher, Andrew, who managed to escape and went to a Christian for help. Some Christian students rushed him and his wife to the main road. It was late afternoon and unlikely that a car would come by at that stage, but they stood there praying. Within a few minutes a car arrived and they forced it to stop by standing in the road, waving. The car was full, but they persuaded some to stay the night so that Andrew and his wife could be taken to safety in Kigali. "It's a matter of life and death," they kept insisting.

Meanwhile, Andrew's daughter had heard that her parents had been killed. In despair, she felt there was nothing left to live for and headed off to Burundi, with other Tutsi students who had been thrown out of their schools. At a parish south of Shyogwe she heard that her parents were still alive and managed to get a message to them. Peter drove down from Kigali to take her back to a very joyful reunion with her parents.

The Christians used to meet for a time of prayer after supper before doing their homework. One evening there was a noise outside where about ten of them were praying. The gang of students were clamouring for them to join them as they went to nearby Kabgayi to clear it of Tutsi. The Christians flatly refused to go with them whereupon the gang attacked them, severely beating each of them in an effort to get them to change their minds, but all stood firm, asserting that their faith would not allow them to become involved with violence. The ten included Onesphore Rwaje, who was later to become bishop of Byumba, and Israel Havugimana, later head of African Enterprise in Rwanda (where it still retains its old title of Africa Evangelistic Enterprise or AEE).

A few nights later, they were again praying when they saw the house of the *assistant médical* in flames. Hurrying to see what they could do to help, they met his wife, Helene, with her baby in her arms. "They have killed my husband," she cried. They helped her to get to a place where she could hide, although she said she did not think she was in any danger now. Apparently Edison had prevented them from killing her, saying that it was against Rwandan culture to kill a mother with a suckling child. This did not prevent the mass slaughter of mothers and babies during the genocide some 20 years later.

Next day, once again, the Christian boys heard a noise outside the room where they were praying. Going to investigate they found some of the gang beating up a fellow Tutsi student. They rushed to protect him with their own bodies, taking the beating instead of him until they could get him to a place of safety.

Helene, meanwhile, had got to the Roman Catholic hospital at Kabgayi with her baby, where Peter and Elisabeth found her. To their amazement she was completely peaceful.

"I know my husband is in heaven with the Lord he loved," she said. "Jesus protected me and I know he will continue to do so. But I have such sorrow for the boys who did this terrible thing. I wish I could find them and tell them that I forgive them."

As soon as she was fit to travel, Peter and Elisabeth arranged for her to get to Burundi, where the Lord indeed cared for her. After the genocide she returned to Kigali, where she did finally meet one of the killers of her husband.

Edison had listened to many talks at Scripture Union camps, and testimonies from some of his school friends. Although he had rejected them, he could not stifle his conscience. He might have saved Helene and her baby, but he was one of those who killed her husband. Some ten years later at a Scripture Union meeting in Kigali, he listened once more to the truths he knew so well. This time he did not resist what the Holy Spirit was saying to him. He stood and, in tears, began to confess what he had done. Soon there was a hubbub all round him. Geoffrey and Chloe had their arms round him, dancing round the church with him. Peter and Elisabeth looked on in amazement until someone whispered to them, telling them who this boy was.

More than 20 years after that killing, Edison proved how completely his life had changed. During the genocide, several Tutsi fled to his house for protection. The Hutu gangs suspected they were there and came to him. He stood at the door with his wife.

"Yes," he said, "they are here, but to kill them you must first kill me and my wife."

Amazed at his boldness they backed away and never came back. Later, hearing that Helene had returned to Kigali, he sought her out to beg her forgiveness.

"I forgave you the day it happened," she said.

Two years later, they stood together in the Amahoro stadium in Kigali, testifying to what Christ had done in their lives. Many people thought she was mad to forgive the killer of her husband, but Helene asserted that there was no other way to bring peace to her own heart, or to this troubled nation.

In 1972, Shyogwe had gained a reputation throughout the country for violence and murder. Eric Townson felt that God was telling him to go there with a team from Youth with a Mission. He wrote in the *Ruanda Notes* how frightened he had been of those boys, but that he had to go.

> The hall began to fill. We sang praises and prayed for forgiveness. There was silence as nearly the whole school listened to two young boys from Youth with a Mission, both with brand new challenging testimonies of how the Lord had met them and delivered them from drugs and other evils of this present time. Then came the challenge. Suddenly a gang of thugs came into the room brandishing all kinds of weapons, waving them at us. How we prayed! Suddenly one of the team leapt to his feet and in the loudest voice I have ever heard, cast Satan out in the name of Jesus. Before this could even be interpreted, the gang shot out of the door like an arrow from a bow! Praise the Lord!

Despite the violence in schools elsewhere, Kigeme School had a different reputation. Although some of the girls were forced out of the school when they were visited by about 50 students from another school, there was no violence. The staff explained why.

> Three years ago, the community at Kigeme was divided by intertribal hatred and jealousy. In answer to many prayers, the Lord poured his Holy Spirit into the hearts of many girls. The blessing spread to quite a large number of other young people in this region. Since then the Christian girls have been witnessing with assurance to each new group of pupils and every year other girls have accepted Christ as their personal Saviour and have been transformed by his love. The strongest influence in the school is that of these young Christians. It is surely God's doing — to Him be all the glory (*Ruanda Notes Review*, 1972-73).

Coup d'Etat

Soon, the killings of Tutsi and general violence began to change in nature. What had started as a move against Tutsi to unite Hutu, began to turn into a means of resolving personal animosities, and once again the Hutu from north and south began to turn on each other. Enough was enough, decided Major General Juvenal Habyarimana. He was a northern Hutu who had long despised the southern President Kayibanda. On 5th July 1973, he took over the government in a bloodless coup. Next morning he announced over the radio that the killing must stop.

"From now on," he said, "there are no more Tutsi, no more Hutu, we are all Banyarwanda and must work together."

Overnight the killing stopped. Tutsi friends said that those who had been avoiding them the day before were all smiles. The new regime had started well.

Chapter 10

The Calm Before the Storm (1973-1980)

Habyarimana's early days

The early years of the Habyarimana regime were relatively peaceful and were characterized by a dedication to improving the economic situation of the country. At the time of independence there were only two countries with a lower per capita income than Rwanda — Burundi and Bangladesh! Until Habyarimana took over, together with Haiti, these four countries remained the four poorest countries in the world. But things began to change with the energy of President Habyarimana, until by 1990 Rwanda had risen to 19th from the bottom. Tanzania in those same years had fallen from 25th from bottom to second poorest, and Uganda during the Amin years from 33rd to 13th from the bottom.

I remember visiting my parents in 1976. My father was praising the president's efforts. "This is one of the few countries in Africa where money given by the world community goes into the project for which it was given, rather than into the president's pocket," he said. "Indeed my fear is that he will be assassinated by someone close to him, who wants the easy pickings of foreign aid which he will not allow them to keep." Little did he know how he had prophesied future events. The infrastructure of the country improved until the road system was one of the best in Africa, and the water supply was also excellent. The proportion of children in school had grown to about 62% in 1986 and health care had improved so that fewer children were dying in infancy and people were living longer (Prunier, p 78).

This brought its own problems from the increased population in the country. By the mid-1980s 50% of the population was under 20, and these young people were moving into the towns in increasing numbers, forsaking the land where their parents were finding more and more difficulty in supporting them, and seeking their fortunes in the towns, with limited success. A sub-culture of bandits and beggars was growing in all the main towns.

During those early years, the Tutsi, while no longer actively persecuted, were still marginalized politically. Indeed, according to Gerard Prunier, "The unspoken understanding was, 'Do not mess around with politics, this is a Hutu preserve'. As long as Tutsi stuck to that principle, they were generally left in peace" (p 76). Politics as a rule were so corrupt that Peter, among several church leaders, felt that it was safer for Christians not to get involved.

After the genocide, I remember a conversation with Antoine Rutayisire, the new general secretary of African Evangelistic Enterprise, when he challenged Peter about this attitude. "Because of it," he said, "we left politics to the bad men. No Christians would soil their hands in politics and the result was that the devil had it all his own way."

But not all church leaders left politics alone. In 1974 President Habyarimana created a single party system, the *Mouvement Révolutionnaire National pour le Développement* (MRND).

This was a truly totalitarian party: every single Rwandese citizen had to be a member, including babies and old people. All bourgmestres and préfets were chosen from among party cadres. The party was everywhere; every hill had its cell, and party faithfuls, hoping for promotion and a professional boost, willingly spied on anybody they were told to spy on and on a few others as well (Prunier, p 76).

In the climate of opinion at that time, the Anglican bishop in Kigali thought nothing of wearing an MRND shirt and the Roman Catholic archbishop was on the MRND ruling council. The old system of *shebuja* and client which had flourished under the monarchy was still present, with every leader seeking a group of clients to support him. Flattery and hypocrisy flourished and no one could be certain who was supporting whom.

Any opposition was quickly stamped out, with several unexplained deaths occurring, particularly towards the end of the 1980s.

The economy, which had been steadily improving, suffered a severe set-back in 1986 with the collapse of world coffee prices, and soon afterwards the failure of the world tin trade, two of the main exports of Rwanda — the third was tea. The political élite of the country found it more and more difficult to sustain their standard of living, and the strain on the subsistence level agriculture led to real hardship for the vast majority of the people. It was at this time that the Tutsi refugees from the 1959-73 years, mainly those living in Uganda, asked to be allowed back into Rwanda. President Habyarimana, with some justification, said that the country was already overpopulated and there was no room.

The situation of those Rwandan refugees in Uganda had varied over the years. Many of those who had been born in exile had put all thought of returning to Rwanda out of their minds, considering it a pipe dream of their nostalgic parents. They had no status or land and many, like young David Ndaruhutse, whose father, Isaac, had been killed before his eyes at Gahini, had been taught to read and write in refugee camps, using his skin as paper and a sharpened stick as pen. He had been bright enough to get to a good secondary school and later the University of Makerere in Uganda. His story is told in the book *An African Apostle*, by Penny Relph, and is typical of many of those living in Uganda at that time.

In 1981, Yoweri Museveni and 26 companions, including two Rwandan refugees, Fred Rwigyema and Paul Kagame, attempted a coup against President Obote of Uganda. Obote then accused Museveni of being a Rwandan, since his grandmother is indeed a Rwandan Tutsi, and he comes from a tribe related in many ways to the Tutsi. This led to a backlash of government wrath against the Rwandans living in Uganda. They had never been allowed Ugandan nationality and now found themselves attacked, raped and murdered at will. Many fled to the Rwandan border but were not admitted, being kept in camps in the no man's land between the two countries, where thousands died of malnutrition and disease. Those who had regarded themselves as Ugandan now suddenly found themselves without a homeland, and their thoughts seriously turned to the possibility of returning to Rwanda. Many thousands of Rwandan Tutsi swelled the growing guerilla army of Museveni, and about 3,000 of them were among the 14,000 who stormed Kampala on 26th January 1986. Fred Rwigyema was soon made the commander-in-chief of the Ugandan army and minister of defence in the new government.

Seeing their success, Rwanda refugees flooded Uganda and soon became a serious threat to the Baganda business class. Museveni could not afford to offend the Baganda and began to cool off towards his Rwandan supporters. They had been promised Ugandan nationality but this was not forthcoming, and in November 1989, Fred Rwigyema was sacked, first as minister of defence and then as commander-in-chief of the army. To the Rwandans, this appeared to be a replay of the persecutions under Obote, and many more joined what now became known as the Rwandan Patriotic Front (RPF), which was seriously committed to a return to Rwanda, by force if necessary.

The need for Christian homes

All of this was in the future. During those early days of Habyarimana's regime there was no hint of the bloody end to come. Peter and Elisabeth were still working with Scripture Union and there was still a massive work of the Holy Spirit in the land. They continued to travel, visiting all the schools in Rwanda, and even some in Zaire, near Bukavu and Goma. They held Scripture Union camps and worked with Nathan, training him to take over from them.

One of the burdens they had was that Christian girls should marry Christian men and set up Christian homes which would be a witness to the neighbourhood. It was hard for girls to resist their parents, who saw no reason why the traditional way of finding husbands for their daughters, where the parents looked for a man from a compatible family who would increase their status, should be changed. The girls themselves often saw no real reason to stand against their parents, until at one camp Dorotiya and Pawulo Rutwe from Burundi spoke. She was a Rwandan, from Kigeme, who had been trying to resist family pressure to marry a pagan man. Peter had taken her to Shyogwe to teach there, and so she was still unmarried when Pawulo, who had spent several years recovering from tuberculosis, came to visit them.

Pawulo told the young people that he had been so determined to find a saved wife that he crossed the Kanyaru (the river separating Burundi from Rwanda) to find one! He told of one Christian in Uganda who was pressed to get engaged before he went to Europe to study, because by the time he returned all the nice girls would have been taken. "Oh no," he said, "God has a cupboard full of nice Christian girls and when I get home, He will open the door and out will come mine!" Then Pawulo held Dorotiya's hand and said, "Thank you, Lord, for keeping this girl in your cupboard just for me." Turning to Peter and Elisabeth, he added, "And thank you for putting her in the cupboard!" The obvious affection between them and the respect which Pawulo had for his wife spoke louder than all the words that Peter and Elisabeth had said.

Suddenly the young people saw the point of a Christian home and there was a spate of Christian weddings. Nathan married a Christian girl called Helene, and Israel Havugimana, later head of AEE in Rwanda, who was killed on the first day of the genocide, married Jacqueline, and Onesphore Rwaje, later my bishop in Byumba, married Josephine, a Presbyterian from Kirinda. Differences of tribe and denomination were less important than the fact that both were committed Christians with a testimony to the power of the Holy Spirit in their lives.

Another Christian wedding was that of John Gakwandi who married a girl who had been converted on 13th January 1970, the night the Holy Spirit began moving in power at Kigeme. Viviane had been orphaned in 1963 when she was eight years old and was brought up by her sister, then aged eleven! There were also two younger members of the family. Somehow they kept together and managed to survive, but she had been severely traumatized and could not believe in a God of love. The night at Kigeme when she saw her own sins, she experienced his overwhelming love and found her security in him. In 1972 she had been obliged to flee to Burundi as a refugee, but never lost the sense that God was protecting her. John had met her in SU camps in Rwanda, and when he heard that she was a refugee in Burundi, he sought her out, asking her to marry him. Following

Habyarimana's coup, they felt that they could return to Kigeme, where they got married in 1977, and their home became a centre for Christians to meet and pray together.

Israel Havugimana was another who was a leading influence among young Christians at this time. Soon after his conversion at a Scripture Union camp, he had gone to Butare University where the initiation rites for new students were particularly severe. Among other things, they were forced to say many shameful things, and to deny the existence of God. Many Roman Catholics submitted to these rites, receiving absolution from their priests because what was done was under duress, and therefore was not considered a serious sin. Israel, however, flatly refused to submit, saying it would be a denial of his Lord. He was ostracized and persecuted in many different and difficult ways. He would have been turned out of the university but he was too good at football, so he was told he could not attend class for three weeks and he had to find his own lodgings in town. At one point, Peter and Elisabeth went to visit him and encouraged him with words they had read that morning in their *Daily Light*: "Israel hath not been forsaken of his God" (Jeremiah 57:5 KJV). Ten years later the initiation rites were abolished by law.

Problems over baptism

If there was much good which came from these camps, seeds of disunity were also sown. During the early years of Scripture Union, Peter and Elisabeth, with Nathan (SU agent-in-training) and Jennifer (not Nathan's wife, but a friend of the Guillebauds), had visited a large Pentecostal station where they had ministered at a camp, with many being truly blessed. They decided to stay on for the Sunday service and sat at the front as honoured visitors. Just before the communion, the pastor came and asked each in turn how they had been baptized. Peter had been baptized in the Anglican Church, Elisabeth in the Presbyterian and Nathan in the Methodist, all as infants, but Jennifer as a believer had been baptized in the Anglican Church. None of them had been baptized by immersion and so all were refused communion, to their great embarrassment. Elisabeth had faced this question early on in her Christian life when her closest friend asked her to join her in baptism by immersion. After a lot of thought, she said that she had been given the sign of baptism as a baby but now she had the reality of the Lord. To be re-baptized would simply mean that she would be going back to the sign, and it was therefore not essential.

Some years later, a Pentecostal prophetess came to one of the SU camps saying that unless people were baptized according to the Lord's command by immersion they could not be true Christians. When they realized what she was teaching, Peter and Nathan tried to stop her, but the damage had been done. Several committed Christians, including Jennifer, mostly from the Kigeme area, were strongly influenced by this woman, and after a few weeks, they took themselves to that same Pentecostal station, where they were all baptized by immersion. They had not consulted their pastors beforehand, not considering it to be anything more than a private act of obedience to the Lord.

Their return to Kigeme was stormy. The pastor took it very seriously, considering that they had repudiated Anglican baptism and, by extension, Anglicanism. They were all excommunicated until a church council could be held to decide what should be done. Peter was particularly distressed by all this, considering that focussing on external signs was taking away from the reality of what the Holy Spirit was doing. He was horrified to see some of the keenest Christians sitting at the back of the church while those with no clear testimony were received at the Lord's table. Eventually the bishop called them to the church council, where they apologized and pleaded for mercy. The bishop said that the water of baptism could not be removed and formally expelled them from the church. They had no choice but to join the Pentecostal church, which was a sad loss to the Anglicans. This controversy severely weakened the church and witness at Kigeme. It is still an issue in the country at large, preventing genuine fellowship between the two largest Protestant churches in the country.

John and Christine married

During one of their leaves in this period, Peter and Elisabeth sold the house in Muswell Hill and bought a flat in Ealing which I was able to rent from them. In 1972, John married Gwyn Jones and moved to Oxford. Christine was now happily working with UCCF as a travelling secretary based in York, and in 1975 she married Ross Paterson, whom she had first met when he was working with David Watson at St Cuthbert's Church in York. He had been sent out by them as a missionary to Taiwan, where, after a period of intensive language study, he was involved in student evangelism and discipleship. Theirs had been an off/on relationship for several years, but in 1975 he arrived on leave and within a few days they were engaged, and married eight weeks later. Ross returned to Taiwan, leaving Christine to work out her contract and follow him later.

Peter and Elisabeth had flown home for the wedding and spent time with us as a family. Just before they were due to return, they went to a prayer meeting at St Michael-le-Belfrey, in York, where they were prayed for. One person there had a prophecy for them: "The Lord will open doors before you that no man will be able to close," she said. Shortly after their return, they were due to visit a school in Zaire. There had been trouble in the area and, as they approached the border, they met some missionaries who had been refused entry into Zaire. "Go home," they said. "You will never get in today." As they were wondering what to do, Elisabeth suddenly remembered that prophecy. "I believe that the Lord will open the doors before us," she said. "Let's at least try to get through." At the border-post, the Rwandan officials were not encouraging. "We can let you through," they said, "and you might even be able to get into Zaire, but I doubt whether you will get out again!" They decided to take that risk as at least they would reach their camp. As they reached the Zairean side of the border there was a sudden downpour. A Christian soldier recognized the Scripture Union badge on the car and was extremely helpful. His colleagues didn't want to get wet and simply waved them through! When they reached the school, there was utter amazement! Theirs was the only car to get through the border all week. They spent two weeks at the school and, by the time they were ready to return, the difficulty had been sorted out.

From police to Bible college

Meanwhile, back in England, I had been promoted sergeant in 1973, the first woman to be promoted after the amalgamation of the men's and women's forces. I found myself in charge of men, and less and less involved in the welfare work which I had so enjoyed. I was injured in a struggle which brought to a head a congenital weakness in my back, which had been causing problems off and on for several years. An operation on my back coincided with a time of home leave for my parents, and I was able to recuperate with them. But once I got back to work, life was a continual struggle. I wanted to return to the work I had enjoyed, but was told that I should be showing the men that I could do the same work as them. After four years I felt that I had sufficiently demonstrated this and became increasingly unhappy in my work, but was fearful about leaving, since I had no training in anything else. I approached Tear Fund for possible work abroad doing handiwork, perhaps with Tear Craft. At this point I went on an extended holiday to visit my parents in Rwanda in 1976.

While there I received a letter from Tear Fund giving the possibility of a job in Ethiopia, but it said that whoever took this job would need to be prepared to learn the language and culture. There I was in Rwanda where I already knew the language and culture. As we talked and prayed, it seemed that the Lord was saying, "Here is where I want you to work." On my return to England I approached the Ruanda Mission general secretary about the possibility of returning to Rwanda. I could hardly believe that things had turned full-circle and that I was after all "going to be a missionary like your grandparents and parents"!

I finally resigned from the police in September 1977 and that autumn I went to All Nations Christian College, initially for one year. At the end of the first term, I attended a CMS selection conference. While they were happy to accept me as a candidate, they insisted that I had to do two years at All Nations, studying theology. I was horrified by the prospect since I had done no studying for ten years, but I am so grateful for their insistence since it changed the whole course of my life.

I had also suggested to my sister that I use the cash I had remaining, to visit her in Taiwan during the summer before I went to Rwanda. My letter had come as an answer to prayer for her, since she had just discovered that she was pregnant, with the baby due in the summer, at Ross's busiest time with students, and he would be absent for most of the summer. My presence would be so welcome to help with this first baby. Yet the CMS decision meant that I would not after all have spare money.

That Christmas, I went to stay with David who was working for a large management consultancy firm in Algiers. As I read some books lent to me, and discussed with David the possibilities, I began praying that if the Lord did indeed want me to go to Taiwan, I would be provided with at least my first term's fees in the bank after I had paid for my ticket to Taiwan. To my amazement, David gave me a cheque for £600 for the trip, and when I made enquiries I found a travel agent which could give me the fare for £240 — leaving me with the term's fees as I had asked. Confident that this was all part of God's plan for me, I went ahead and booked — only to hear from the travel agency, three weeks before I was meant to go, that the airline I was to travel by had been refused landing rights in Hong Kong and my flight was cancelled. The next cheapest they could find was for £600 which would wipe out all my reserves!

I spent a day tramping the streets of London searching for a cheaper flight to no avail. Should I cancel? If I did, how would Christine cope? What was I to do? I remember John saying on the telephone, "Meg, what are you worrying about? Can't you trust God to find your next year's fees?" To my shame I replied, "John, I need over £1,000 and, no, I'm afraid I don't trust him enough for that!" I decided that I would have to go, and by the time I had paid for the tickets on the Friday before I flew on Tuesday, I had £10 remaining in my bank account. Next morning the post brought my bank statement reminding me of £50 in the deposit account, and a cheque from John for £50. On Sunday morning the church treasurer handed me a cheque for £100 and at the evening service a man came up to me. He was someone I had only met once in my life but he said, "I have a substantial sum of money in my account which the Lord is telling me to give to you. Please give me your bank account number so that I can transfer it to you while you are away." I thought, "I don't know what a substantial amount is, but if it is £100 or even £50, then I now have the term's fees I originally requested!" I flew to Taiwan on Tuesday with a light heart knowing that this was right. On my return two months later, my bank statement recorded, not £100, but the whole £1,000 that I had not trusted the Lord to provide! This was the first, but by no means the last, time that I was humbled by the way the Lord looked after me — and yet whenever I get into financial difficulties, I still find it hard to trust the Lord to care for me in that practical way!

As I went back to college, I was no longer sure that it was right to go to Rwanda. I was frightened of being seen as my parents' daughter rather than a person in my own right. I remember talking to one person who said, "Meg, unless you are certain that you want above all else to tell the Rwandans about the love God has for them in Jesus, don't go." I was not at all certain that this was what I wanted. I was prepared to go to relieve poverty and to help materially, but proclaiming the gospel hadn't really entered my thinking. I went to see the general secretary to ask for time to rethink what God was really asking of me. For the next two months I felt I was in a vacuum, continuing to study but with no idea what it was leading to.

At that point a friend from church told me that he was considering training for the Anglican ministry. The thought flashed through my mind that this could be something I could do, but I pushed the thought away. Later I jokingly said to some friends at All Nations that I could always be a parish worker. "The very thing!" said one friend. "I was joking," I said. "But I'm not," she replied, "I can just see you doing that." Once the thought had taken root, it refused to leave me. I explored what was involved and kept on thinking, "Yes, it is an interesting job, but not really me." However, I eventually spoke to my vicar, and we considered that at least I ought to explore further. I have never known the Church of England act so quickly. It was as if the Lord knew that I needed a dramatic answer to prayer to convince me that I was doing the right thing. I applied to my bishop in April and by the end of June, I had not only been accepted by ACCM (the church's selection procedure) but I had a place at Durham Theological College for that autumn. I still felt that Africa was somewhere in the future, but I knew that this was the next step.

From Scripture Union to Bible Society

Meanwhile, Peter and Elisabeth were preparing to hand over the Scripture Union work to Nathan, and to retire. To Peter's amazement, however, the bishop called him in one morning. "I have just been on a conference dealing with ecumenical things and it was decided that we need a new version of the Bible in Rwanda and we would like you to come back to supervise an ecumenical translation team." Peter's relationship with this bishop had been decidedly stormy during the years that he had worked for Scripture Union, and he was astounded to receive this invitation. He had always envied his two sisters who were involved in Bible translation — Rosemary, who had just retired after 39 years in Burundi, and Philippa in southern Sudan — and he was excited at the possibility that at this late stage he, too, might be involved in Bible translation.

They arrived in England in 1980 for what should have been their retirement leave, breaking their journey in France where David and Peta were now living. The day after their arrival, Peta took Elisabeth shopping. On the way, she told her that she had accepted the Lord Jesus the day before. Peta says that it was Elisabeth's life and witness that had spoken to her over the years, and finally she felt that she needed to surrender her life to him. That night as they praised God for this news, Peter remembered a verse they read the day that David was born. "This people have I formed for myself. They shall bring forth my praise." From his birth they felt sure that God was going to call David but now they realized that this verse was in the plural, and included his wife. With renewed hope they continued praying for David, though they had to wait another ten years for him to make the same commitment.

Soon after their arrival in England they were preparing to return to Rwanda. Peter described his new role as co-ordinator of the team of translators who consisted of pastors from the Presbyterian and Adventist churches and a Roman Catholic priest, all of whom had been trained in theology and knew Greek and Hebrew. Peter's knowledge of schoolboy Greek had to be rapidly improved and his knowledge of Hebrew was non-existent, but he saw his role as co-ordinator as making sure that the new translation would be true to the original. He wrote in the *Ruanda Notes* (now changed in name to *Partners Together*) of the need for a new translation rather than a revision of the old.

> There are three main reasons for this.
> 1 The old translation is already dated — the language is changing fast.
> 2 The Bible Society now only backs translations that give what they call "dynamic equivalence" of the original: this in general gives results that are more meaningful and faithful to the original than a rigid word-for-word rendering, which can be stilted and hard to understand.
> 3 The Romans Catholics — 80% or more of our population — are now beginning to thirst for the Word of God. But they find our version particularly hard to understand, because traditionally many important doctrinal terms have been differently translated by Protestants and Catholics (cf in English "repentance" and "penitence").

They came to my ordination service at Southwark Cathedral in July 1980 and helped me settle into my new home in the parish of Christ Church, New Malden, before returning that winter to Kigali.

Chapter *11*

The Violence
Begins (1980-1994)

Life in Kigali

For the next six years, Peter and Elisabeth lived in Kigali, where Peter set up an office for Bible translation in their house. They had moved to a larger house, one end of which became a guest house. Elisabeth ran this, and also taught Kinyarwanda to new missionaries.

A large cathedral had been built at the diocesan centre in Kigali. Eustace Kajuga had been the first pastor there in 1968 when he left Nyamata. He had built up the diocesan centre until he was sent to train deacons at Gahini a year later. During that year in Kigali, the Kajugas had experienced the sadness of losing their fourth son, Richard, a keen Christian, in a motor-cycle accident. During the years before President Habyarimana took over, their children had experienced many problems. Two other children, Wycliffe and Wilberforce, were thrown out of school and joined their older brother, Husi, trading in Cyangugu. Husi had been working with the water company but he, too, lost his job because he was a Tutsi. He wanted to leave the country, but his Belgian wife, Annie, refused to let him. She had just had her first child and wanted him to be brought up in his own land. Billy Graham came to take a rally in Bujumbura and Husi made a commitment to Christ at that time. The Kajugas' youngest son, Robert, was at the Methodist school in Kibogora, where he made a definite commitment to Christ, and became a leader among the Christian schoolboys.

Those were happy days for the Guillebauds. Peter was doing work he loved, although he found it very challenging. The Catholics and Protestants had developed so separately during those early days of hostility that he found there were over 50 key terms for which they had different Kinyarwanda words. They called God, Jesus, the Holy Spirit all by different names. Their words for the church and repentance and many others were all different. Each term had to be discussed and a consensus reached as to which word to use. Sometimes they decided that neither conveyed the exact meaning of the Greek, so they chose a third! All of this took time but, as his father had before him, he found it all-absorbing.

On leave in 1982, Peter was asked by the Bible Society whether he would be willing to pioneer the use of a word processor, to enable corrections to be made quickly. The electricity supply was erratic in Kigali and he had many problems, but he persevered, often getting up at 3 a.m. in order to take advantage of a steady electricity supply. There were times when Elisabeth threatened to throw the computer down the longdrop (pit latrine), but gradually the difficulties were ironed out and, as the hardware improved rapidly, so the advantages of using a computer far outweighed the disadvantages.

Retirement

By 1986, the New Testament was complete. Peter knew no Hebrew so he handed over his role to Rev. Giles Williams, and finally he and Elisabeth retired, first to a flat in London's Dockland and then to a village near Reading. Peter remained on the council of the Mission for three years and then became a senior adviser until finally retiring in 1990. But he never lost touch with the country he loved so much. As a Golden Wedding anniversary treat, in 1990, he and Elisabeth returned, and travelled round the country, visiting old friends, and making new ones. Although they were thrilled to meet up with many who had not lost their vital witness as Christians, they were also distressed by much that was happening in the country; they felt that the church was no longer making a vital impact on the country.

On one occasion, they had gone to a soldier's camp near Gisenyi to look for their friend, Ephraim. He had come to faith following a talk by Peter in 1973 and was a keen member of Scripture Union. In 1976 he had had a dream in which he saw himself standing on a road, dressed in a soldier's uniform, with his right arm raised, holding a Bible. When he woke up, he felt that the Lord was telling him to become a soldier. At first he had rejected this as not something he felt he could do as a Christian, but the thought continued, and he realized that it was an open mission field where he could tell people about Jesus Christ. When Peter and Elisabeth arrived, they asked for him by name but no one knew whom they meant, until eventually someone said, "Oh, you mean the pastor!" His wife, Francine, had just had their first baby, and they were thrilled with what the Lord was doing in the camp. In 1980 Peter had given him his small accordion when he, himself, had been given a larger one, and Ephraim was in the music division of the army, rather than a regular soldier. They had had to get special permission for Peter and Elisabeth to come into the camp and have a meal with them, as security was tight.

Poverty and violence

Tensions were obvious in the country. The population of this small, landlocked country now had about eight times as many people as there had been when the Europeans had first entered the country back in 1897. This led to enormous social pressures. Traditionally, a man divided his land between all his children on his death, which meant that the size of fields had got smaller and smaller. The Pentecostals, as well as the Roman Catholics, were opposed to birth control, so families were huge, on ever-decreasing fields, and people became land-hungry, and more than ever dependent on the weather. Towards the end of the 1980s, several bad harvests had led to a famine, and several thousands had fled to Tanzania in search of food.

At about the same time, the fall in world coffee prices, followed closely by a collapse in the world tin market, had severely affected the Rwandan economy. This seriously affected the élite around President Habyarimana, many of whom, it is believed, had been taking their cuts of the lucrative trade. They had to find some other means of feathering their nests and turned to the foreign aid which was still flooding the country, as to Western eyes, Rwanda was one of the most stable and forward-looking of all African countries.

By this time, Habyarimana had been in power for nearly 20 years and was getting tired and less able to control the machinations of his wife. Habyarimana himself was a Hutu from the Gisenyi area, a self-made man with no traditional clan supporting him. His wife, on the other hand, was from one of the princely clans which had been forced by the Germans to accept the Tutsi monarchy around 1912. She deeply despised the Hutu of the south who had accepted the king voluntarily, regarding them as slave material. She had a large entourage of supporters and rewarded them with jobs and money. The president himself may not have wanted to enrich himself at the expense of his people, but his wife and her cronies, known in the country as the *kazu* (or little house), had no such inhibitions. Anyone who appeared to be a threat to them was quietly arrested, often tortured and sometimes killed. More and more it seemed that it was the *kazu* that was running the country. In fact, Madame Habyarimana was nicknamed Kanjogera, after the notorious queen mother visited by my grandparents back in 1928.

In April 1988, a close friend of the president, Colonel Mayuya, was murdered, apparently by a member of the *kazu*, although it was never proved, because the man who actually pulled the trigger was murdered in jail. It appeared that Habyarimana had been grooming Mayuya to take over as president when he gave up power. He was the president's man and the *kazu* had no influence over him. He was thus a grave threat to their power and had to be disposed of. This was perhaps the best known, but by no means the only, unexplained death of a prominent person. As well, there were many abuses of human rights which went largely unprotested by church leaders.

The start of the *interahamwe*

One of those caught up in the spiral of violence was Robert Kajuga, the youngest son of Eustace and Marian. He was an extremely good footballer, and when he left Kibogora School, he was invited to join the presidential football club. Flattered and enthusiastic, he had no hesitation in joining the club and soon immersed himself in football, teaching different tactics. There was a closeness between the members of the club which led to them being called the *interahamwe*, or "those who act together", or, perhaps, "the party of unity". Soon he was the acknowledged leader of the club, becoming friendly with the president, who enjoyed discussing tactics with him. But gradually during 1990 and 1991 the footballers were becoming mixed up in politics. Rumours were spreading that they were behind the unexplained killings which were increasing in number.

Eustace and Marian were concerned and had several discussions with Robert, who always denied the violence. Although he agreed that they had been politicized, he did not see how he could get out. "The president relies on me," he said. Later, when his brothers tried to persuade him to get out, he admitted to fears. "Some of them do not want me to lead them because they say I am Tutsi," he said. "If I try to leave, they would probably kill me. Unless I leave the country, and then, probably, the Tutsi would kill me!" He assured them that he was still reading his Bible daily and would never do anything against his faith.

In July 1990 President Habyarimana went to Paris to visit his friend, President Mitterrand, who advised him that it would be prudent to set up a multiparty system in Rwanda, and, indeed, that there would be no more French money until he did. On his return to Rwanda, Habyarimana made a speech which paved the way for the existence of opposition parties, but before they could come into being, the situation changed. In October 1990, the RPF invaded the country from the north.

The RPF attacks

The Rwandan refugees in Uganda, as we have seen, felt there was no future for them in Uganda, and had formed the Rwandan Patriotic Front (RPF). They had secretly gathered near the border, Major-General Rwigyema telling everyone that he had been put in charge of organizing the military parade to celebrate Ugandan independence on 9th October. Instead, on 1st October they crossed the border at Kakitumba and rapidly advanced about 60 kilometres south. The government army (FAR), although well trained and equipped, was taken by surprise and could not initially stop them. However, on the second day of the attack, Fred Rwigyema was killed, throwing the leadership of the RPF into confusion, and the French forces came to the aid of FAR, saying that a friendly power was being attacked by a hostile force. On 7th October, they counter-attacked and within a month the RPF had been routed.

Paul Kagame, who had been in America for some months, flew back when he heard of the death of his friend, Rwigyema, and he took command of the disheartened soldiers who managed to straggle out of Rwanda. He marched them by night along the border until they reached the forests round the Virunga mountains. There in the cold heights he regrouped and began training his troops in guerilla warfare and, within a short time, on 23rd January 1991, he attacked Ruhengeri. They attacked the prison, releasing 1,000 people, most of whom were political prisoners, mainly Tutsi, and gaining a fair amount of military equipment, before retreating to the mountains.

Peter's friend, Ephraim, was on duty about 20 kilometres outside Ruhengeri, but his wife, Francine, was in their house in the camp with their nine-month-old baby. She heard the shooting start, and, praying for protection and that the baby would keep quiet, she locked herself into the bedroom. She heard shooting going on outside and she could see the tops of soldiers' heads. She heard them smashing up her house, but no one attempted to enter her hideaway. After a time the noise died away but she was too frightened to come out. Then the baby started crying. She heard someone say, "There is a baby still alive." She still refused to open the door until she heard the voice of one of Ephraim's friends and realized that she was truly safe. Once she got outside she found herself surrounded by the corpses of friends, and was amazed that she had survived. She was taken to Kigali for safety. Ephraim, meanwhile, could not find out for certain what had happened to her. He telephoned the camp but was told by one person that she was dead, while another said she might have survived, but he did not know where she was. It was nearly two months before Ephraim was able finally to get to Kigali where they had a joyful reunion.

Attacks on Tutsi unite the Hutu

Although Kagame did not hold Ruhengeri, this attack panicked the Rwandan government, which then conducted a series of massacres of Tutsi, with local leaders instructing the peasants to kill all Tutsi in their area, describing it as their accustomed work (*umuganda*) for the government. In retaliation, the RPF conducted a series of guerilla attacks mainly in the Byumba prefecture, which became more vicious as extremists on both sides sought to wipe out the other tribe. They had expected that the Hutu peasants, as well as Tutsi, would welcome being freed from the oppression of the *kazu*, but far from this being the case, the Hutu were terrified of the RPF and fled *en masse*. By 1992, Byumba prefecture was virtually deserted, with some 300,000 people being in displaced persons camps.

The reason for this fear was that President Habyarimana, seeing a way to unite the increasingly divided Hutu, many of whom had set up parties in opposition to him, allowed a blatant anti-Tutsi campaign to spring up again — and found that he had unleashed a tiger.

The divisions among the Hutu had become more obvious as different political parties were formed from March 1991. One attracted southern Hutu, another educated people of both tribes, another was largely composed of business men and so on. There were dozens of such parties, each with its own slant. In March 1992 the president's own party (the MRND) split, with hardliners forming their own party in opposition to what they saw as the soft line the president was taking against the Tutsi invaders. They took over the independent radio, *Radio Libre des Mille Collines* (to be known as *Radio Mille Collines*), and started broadcasting attacks on all opposition members and particularly began to demonize the Tutsi who had invaded their peaceful land and who were causing such havoc in the north.

In a country where about 60% are illiterate, it is hard to underestimate the impact of radio broadcasts. Every peasant has access to radio and listens regularly for notice time before the news. The radio announces the names of those who have died, giving the times of funerals, or coming government or church meetings. Sadly, the church did not avail itself of radio to counter the pernicious hate messages of Radio Mille Collines, preferring to rely on the written word. This meant that they reached the educated people rather than the peasants. The RPF had set up their own Radio Muhabura, which broadcast from the Virunga mountains, trying to get over their message that they were no threat to the ordinary people of Rwanda, but were seeking peace and a multi-ethnic society. Unfortunately, the radical demonization of the Tutsi by Radio Mille Collines was more effective.

In June 1992 members of the RPF agreed to meet some of the opposition parties to talk about peace, and on 14th July they signed a cease-fire in Arusha, Tanzania, and began discussing terms for a lasting peace. The news was greeted with a sigh of relief by the general population, but with consternation by the extremist Hutu nationalists within the ruling MRND party, and eventually led to many leaving MRND and joining the hard-line CDR (*Coalition pour la Défense de la République*). The president attempted to justify the need for a breathing-space, but the hard-liners became increasingly unhappy and, when he eventually signed the Arusha peace accords in August 1993, it was tantamount to signing his own death warrant.

These peace accords contained provisions for power-sharing in a broad-based transitional government, power-sharing within the army, and also provision for the repatriation of refugees, most of whom were Tutsi who had fled in the 1960s and 1970s. All of this was anathema to the hard-core Hutu nationalists who wanted at least to see the Tutsi marginalized, or even exterminated. It is likely that the plans for a full-scale genocide began to be formulated at this time.

Problems within the church

When Peter and Elisabeth returned to England in May 1990, they were uneasy at much of what they had seen, but were particularly distressed by what was happening in the Anglican Church. With some wonderful exceptions, the leadership seemed more concerned to exercise power than to speak out against evil, and there seemed to be an unhealthy acceptance of the government which Peter in particular found difficult. While most church leaders tended to keep themselves aloof from all political manoeuvring, they were involved in machinations of their own which would have been laughable if it were not so tragic.

The Anglican Church at that time was part of the Province of Rwanda, Burundi and Zaire, but there were moves afoot to split into separate provinces for each country. This could only be so if there were at least four dioceses in each country. At that time Rwanda had three: Kigali, Butare and Shyira. Plans were made to make Byumba the fourth on 24th November 1991.

A power struggle had developed between the bishop of

Kigali in the north and the bishop of Butare in the south. When the bishop of Butare realized that his would be the only diocese in the south he decided to pre-empt the creation of Byumba diocese by unilaterally creating three more dioceses out of his diocese and by consecrating four new bishops just a week before Onesphore Rwaje was consecrated bishop of Byumba. By the mercy of God, these new bishops were truly men of God who wanted to see their church involved in evangelism and cleansed of the horrible wrangling which had brought it into disrepute.

Onesphore Rwaje had been one of those who became a Christian at Shyogwe during the 1970s, and who had stood out against Hutu violence at that time, to his own cost. He was doing a course at New College, Edinburgh, in 1991, when he received a fax telling him that he had been elected bishop of the new diocese of Byumba. He had known of the plans to create the diocese before he left for Britain, but when he heard of the fighting going on in Byumba, he had assumed that these plans would be postponed. The thought of becoming bishop when there was fighting in his diocese, as well as fighting in the church, daunted him. He took the fax to the bishop of Edinburgh who encouraged him to accept this appointment without reserve. "Who knows whether God has called you to the church for such a time as this," he said.

For the first time a diocese was set up where there had been no previous mission work. Byumba had been an out-school, which I remember visiting with my father when I was a child, but there were no buildings left by missionaries. The house rented for the new bishop near the church was unfinished, with no floors or ceilings. The church was tiny, although a new, larger one was being built. There was a church primary school on the diocesan site and a house for the pastor, but nothing else.

Bishop Rwaje's first priority was to see how the mess within the church could be sorted out. He met with two of the new bishops to pray and see how God could turn things around. After much prayer and discussion, it was agreed to re-consecrate all those who had been illegally made bishop, and to confirm the creation of the new dioceses. The date was set for the re-consecration on 5th June 1992, the day before the bishop of Shyira was to be enthroned as archbishop of the new Province of Rwanda.

Attack on Byumba

On Friday 4th June, Bishop Rwaje had been at a meeting in Kigali when he heard that Byumba town had been attacked by the RPF and that there was serious fighting going on round it. He tried to ring his wife, Josephine, but there was no reply. Nor could he find the archdeacon. He decided to forget about the re-consecration ceremony and return early next morning to his diocese and family. When he arrived, he found the government troops in control, the RPF having retired to the border. His house and that of the archdeacon were both empty and no one was around except soldiers who were looting and pillaging everywhere.

Meanwhile Josephine had been feeding her children before they went to school when she heard the noise of shooting coming from the town. She decided to keep the children with her until she had heard what was happening. The fighting became worse, and she tried to telephone her husband in Kigali, but no one seemed to know where he was. She spoke to Israel Havugimana who gave her the good news that an agreement had been reached, the problems within the church were resolved and that the bishops were to be re-consecrated the following day. During the next anxious days, she kept on saying to herself, "God has been able to bring peace in the church, He is in control and can bring peace within the country." Although worried about her family, she had an assurance of God's protection.

At about 10 a.m. she received a phone call from a total stranger, advising her to leave the house. He said that she would stand a better chance outside if a mortar shell hit the house. Strapping her youngest child to her back, she set off with the family, not knowing where to go, except that they headed away from the town. After walking for about two hours she came to a large group of displaced people where there was water, but no food provided. After a rest and a drink she decided that she would do better to try to make for a neighbouring parish where her husband would be likely to find her. As they walked, they met a group of government soldiers who shouted out, "Here come some of those who are causing us problems!" and started shooting at them. She said, "It was just as well that they were all drunk because they missed us!" The family scattered and hid behind houses until the soldiers had gone. Josephine waited a bit until it was safe, and then tried to find everyone. "By the mercy of God, we were all there and no one was hurt."

By this time it was getting dark and she realized it was too dangerous to keep on walking. She saw a house down in the valley and determined to ask for shelter. To her joy the owner turned out to be a widow from her church who recognized her. The widow had been intending to hide in the bush, but Josephine said, "God has led me to your house. He will protect us here." They spent the night in the house and early next morning they all walked to Kavumu where they found the church packed with refugees. As they approached the parish, they had been met by the diocesan accountant who took them to his father's house and that was where Bishop Rwaje found them that evening. He left them there and spent the night alone in his house at Byumba. He found that the archdeacon, who had fled to the bushes with his wife, had also returned as soon as the fighting had died down. Early next morning, he took Josephine to Kigali for the enthronement of the archbishop.

They took their children to their uncle in Kigali for safety and then returned to the diocese where they found 12,000 displaced people camping in the primary school, church and open air all round. They did what they could to find food and shelter for them, until two months later an official camp was set up for them. In February 1993, Bishop Rwaje was sent to Nairobi on a course for newly consecrated bishops, so Josephine was again alone when fighting resumed around Byumba. This time she managed to get to Kigali, and when Bishop Rwaje returned, they decided to work from Kigali since the diocese was now deserted and all their people were in large displacement camps.

After the signing of the peace accords

In August 1993, when the Arusha peace accords were signed, there was a period of calm in the country and people gradually began to return home, though Bishop Rwaje still had his diocesan offices in Kigali. The archdeacon, Muzungu, returned to his home in Byumba and began distributing agricultural equipment and seeds, as a gift from Christian Aid, to help people get back to producing food as soon as possible. Life seemed to be returning to normal. Commenting on the situation he faced when he became bishop, Rwaje said, "The situation in the country was horrible and worrying, but what really hurt me was the situation in our church."

Roger Bowen, the general secretary of Mid-Africa Ministry (formerly Ruanda Mission), was asked why a country which had experienced Revival could have had a genocide. He commented on the church situation in the years before the genocide. He said,

> Prior to the genocide, some of the Anglican leadership had brought public shame and disgrace on the church, to the despair of the laity, through an open and public conflict between two bishops which nearly led to schism within the church. Anglican leadership was exclusively Hutu, and the major characteristic of Revival times that had done away with ethnic divisions was conspicuously lacking within the hierarchy of the church. Anglicans were not alone in seeing church leadership as a means of advancing and gaining in wealth and power. A Catholic laywoman wrote an impassioned appeal to the Catholic bishops at this time: "Your very affluent style of life (luxury cars, fashionable clothes, expensive houses) increases the gap between you and us ordinary people, and this adds to our lack of confidence in you. The Christians feel abandoned, whereas you and your priests ought to be the voice of the voiceless, the outcasts and serve the common people."

One Christian who was doing what he could to bring reconciliation between the different factions and tribes in the country was Israel Havugimana, himself a Hutu. He had already shown his fearlessness when he stood out against the evil initiation rites at Butare University. Now, as head of AEE in Rwanda, he worked tirelessly to bring about peace and reconciliation. His wife, Jacqueline, had tragically died shortly after the birth of their third child, leaving him desolate. He knew he could never replace her so, unusually in Rwanda, he was rearing his children alone. His elderly father was also part of his household. He and his entire household were all shot on the first day of the genocide. One daughter was wounded but survived.

Although there was officially peace in Rwanda following the signing of the peace accords in Arusha, the killings continued, sometimes of Tutsi by the hard-core CDR, sometimes of Hutu by extremist RPF in revenge for massacres. The atmosphere in the country was extremely tense and was exacerbated by news of the murder of President Ndadaye of Burundi on 21st October 1993.

Assassination of the Burundi president

President Ndadaye had been the first Hutu president Burundi had ever had, being elected freely in June that year. His predecessor, President Buyoya, had resigned graciously and it really seemed that some of the difficulties Burundi had been experiencing with a minority Tutsi government were going to be solved. But that was to reckon without the Hutu radicals, who expected instant Hutu power in every area of life, and the Tutsi extremists, who hated the thought of losing power. When the president was murdered by Tutsi extremists, Hutu rage erupted, and several hundred Tutsi were killed. Then Tutsi began revenge killing, and the situation was only calmed down when there was a military coup and the Tutsi once more seized power. Within a few days, some 50,000 people had been killed, almost equally Tutsi and Hutu. About 150,000 Tutsi fled to internal camps, and some 300,000 Hutu fled over the border to Rwanda.

Many of the Hutu of Rwanda saw these events as exemplifying the way Tutsi had to be in power at whatever cost. The murder of the Hutu president of Burundi strengthened their resolve to have a final solution in Rwanda and remove all Tutsi for ever. Radio Mille Collines increased the vitriolic hate broadcasts, representing the Arusha peace accords as untenable, since Tutsi could not be trusted. If the Tutsi began sharing power, they said, they would seize it all. Hutu would lose all they had gained over the past 40 years and would go back to being the slaves of the Tutsi, digging their fields for them and rearing their cattle. Tutsi would also probably kill many Hutu as they were doing in Burundi. The option of "Kill first or you will be killed" was proclaimed daily and worked on the fears of the largely uneducated Hutu peasantry. Hutu refugees from Burundi spread further fear in the minds of the Hutu populace.

Meanwhile, the United Nations had finally put together a force to supervise the transfer of power to a broad-based government. Despite sporadic killings and the tension in the country, the UNAMIR (United Nations Assistance Mission to Rwanda) felt there was nothing to prevent the transfer of power. President Habyarimana did not agree. Time and again the deadline was cancelled and delaying tactics were employed for two months. Finally, on 4th April, UN Secretary General Butros Butros Ghali threatened to withdraw the UN presence in Rwanda if the Arusha agreement was not realized. Two days later the president flew to Dar-es-Salaam where several of his peers, notably President Museveni of Uganda, President Ali Hassan Mwinyi of Tanzania and President-elect Ntaryamira of Burundi urged him to implement the peace accords without delay. That evening he flew back to Rwanda, having offered a lift to President-elect Ntaryamira, whose plane was nowhere near as comfortable as the Rwanda one. They were to fly first to Kigali and then on to Bujumbura. At about 8.30 p.m., as they came in to land at Kigali Airport, two missiles were fired and the plane dropped into the president's own gardens, where it burst into flames, killing all on board. Time had run out for a peaceful settlement in Rwanda.

Listening to the news in England

Back in England, Peter and Elisabeth heard with concern of the murder of the Burundi president in October 1993. They worried about what was happening to the country and people they loved so much. Over the next few weeks, as news came in about the death of friends and the miraculous escapes of others, it seemed as if nothing would ever settle down. Then a new president was elected and Burundi began to fade from the news.

In April, after the first shock of hearing that for the second time in six months Burundi had lost a president, just as Rwanda had lost its president, the first news of the killings began to come through. We were shattered to hear within a few days that Eustace and Marian had both been killed, together with their eldest son, Husi, my childhood friend. Then came news that Geoffrey and Chloe had also been killed, and Israel Havugimana, together with his father and children. I began to dread the ringing of the telephone.

As the days went by, we watched in horrified fascination as

the brutal killings went on. Often I could barely see the television for tears. How could anyone escape the holocaust? Yet amazingly they did. One day I heard the wonderful news that Marian was still alive and then that Chloe too had survived, but news was so unreliable that nothing was certain.

One evening Peter and Elisabeth were watching the news with another Rwandan friend, when the general of the *interahamwe* began to speak. To their horror they recognized Robert, the youngest son of Eustace Kajuga — how could he condone this bloodshed? Then Peter heard on the World News that another friend, Archdeacon Muzungu of Byumba, had been seen giving out the machetes that were being used for the killing. Who could be trusted now? We did not hear, at that stage, that the machetes he had given out were part of a Christian Aid consignment and were given out with hoes and seed corn long before the genocide began.

I was ordained that summer, and still the bloodshed continued. Finally, on 19th July, the RPF, having managed to capture Kigali, was sworn in as an interim government. Now it was the Hutu who fled in terror of the reprisals that were likely to happen. Pursued by the RPF, they fled south to Cyangugu, or followed the Tutsi refugees over the border at Goma, where they stayed in enormous camps, stretching the care agencies to their limit. But, gradually the situation inside Rwanda began to display a semblance of order.

Should we return?

I felt that, with my knowledge of the language and the country, there must be something that I could do, either in Rwanda or among the refugees. But every non-governmental agency that I contacted refused my help, saying it was not the sort of situation where they were prepared to use amateurs. I understood that, and yet I felt frustrated as I longed to go out. I met Lesley Bilinda whose husband was missing, believed killed. She wanted to return to Rwanda to search for her husband, and it was possible that I could have accompanied her. But in the end the way opened up naturally, without further efforts on my part. Lesley has told her story in *The Colour of Darkness* (Hodder & Stoughton, 1996).

I had spent part of the Christmas holiday with my parents and they, too, were longing to be back. Despite their age, and my father's weakness following a stroke four years earlier, they felt that they should be there, mainly as a listening ear, but also to show their love and, more importantly, the love of Christ. A few days earlier, the general secretary for Scripture Union in Africa, Dr Mutombo, had visited them and told them about Emmanuel Kayijuka. When he left Rwanda, with Dr Mutombo's backing, he had organized the work of Scripture Union in the camps. But this was a temporary measure, and it was impossible to run Scripture Union in Rwanda itself from outside the country.

"It cannot go on," said Dr Mutombo. "It is against policy for SU to be run from outside the country. Either he must go back, which he is afraid to do, or we must appoint someone new from inside Rwanda."

Peter said, "We are considering returning ourselves. Would it help Emmanuel to go back with us?"

Dr Mutombo jumped at the idea, and from then on it began to seem a real possibility. I was unhappy at them travelling alone and was amazingly granted compassionate leave from my work so that I could accompany them. And so, in February 1995, we set out on the next phase of my family's long involvement with Rwanda.

Chapter *12* # The Aftermath of Genocide — 1995

On Sunday night, 19th February 1995, we flew from Heathrow. Despite my father's protests, we arranged for a wheelchair to meet him at each stop. He was frightened of appearing decrepit so that those we were going to help would rather view him as a liability, but when he saw how helpful it was in getting us from plane to plane, he soon changed his mind. However, when we arrived at Nairobi Airport and had collected the luggage, he insisted on getting out of the chair and walking to the entrance. There we were met by Dr Mutombo and several friends from Rwanda. As we loaded our cases into the car, there was a spontaneous outburst of the old Revival praise song, "Tukutendereza", and someone prayed and praised God for our safe arrival.

We were driven to the Province of Kenya guest house, where over the next few days, we had a succession of visitors, each with a story to tell, more harrowing than the last. Much of what I write here, was taken from the diary I wrote at the time. These are the stories I was told, which give a flavour of the sort of thing that had happened during the dreadful months of slaughter.

We met a pastor and his wife from Butare. Her home was in the Gitarama area where her whole family — parents, brothers and sisters — were all killed. But her face shone as she described the time in Butare. She said that, as soon as the news came about the president's death, they knew there would be trouble, so they called the Christians together to pray. Daily they met in their home. Soon others came. Many became Christians at this time. As refugees fled from the Kigali area, they were able to shelter some and help them out of Rwanda. They prayed that no one would die who was not ready for heaven. As the killing came closer to home, so their prayers intensified. Several of those they hid for a short time became Christians — then they had to move elsewhere for safety reasons. Often they were killed elsewhere. Once, one man became a Christian and, as he left the home, he was killed — they found his body outside. Eventually they were warned that the killers were coming for the pastor, even though he was Hutu, because he had saved so many Tutsi, and that they should flee. They said that they were prepared to die, but someone said she had had a vision of them in a blue lorry driving away. They telephoned a friend who sent a blue Daihatsu and they managed to escape to Bukavu, and then eventually to Kenya. When we saw him, he was studying at the Christian college there.

I commented in my diary, "One of the things that has impressed me has been the way that, time and again, when we are told a sad story, there is a pause and then the comment, 'But God is good,' and the talk goes on to concentrate on how he has saved or helped in difficult circumstances."

Yvonne came to visit us and told of the time she had spent with her husband, Fidele, in Kigali. When the *interahamwe* came, they hid in their house with their two small children. They were both Hutu. After the gangs had gone, they went out and found several badly wounded people among the dead. At the risk of their own lives, since to be found helping Tutsi meant death, they took them in and hid them in their roof. Neither had medical training and the wounds were horrific. At night, Fidele would go to the nearby Red Cross post for medicine and medical advice. Several times the gangs came by. Each time they rescued the survivors. Once, a woman and her baby were thrown in the longdrop latrine. They could hear her calling for two days. Eventually Fidele could no longer bear it. He went to the soldiers and borrowed a rope, telling them an animal had fallen down the latrine. He then pulled her out. She had been up to her armpits in ordure and the acid had bleached her skin white. She was in a terrible state, but so grateful. Her baby had died soon after being thrown in. They took her to the Red Cross and, the last they heard, she was doing well. It was hard keeping their children quiet when the gangs came, so Yvonne took them towards Gitarama. When she got there she found the killers had been at work and all her family had been killed. She managed to go on to Bukavu and eventually reached Nairobi. Meanwhile the RPF took Kigali. They searched all the houses for weapons, but when they came to Fidele's house he showed them fifteen Tutsi refugees hidden in his roof. They were so impressed that they loaded all of them, together with Fidele, on to a lorry and drove them towards Byumba, but he never arrived, and nothing more was heard of him. He simply disappeared.

On the Sunday we were taken to a large church in Nairobi which the Rwandan refugees had taken over. Peter was asked to preach, taking his message from 1 Peter 4:17: "For it is time for judgement to begin with the family of God." He spoke of the need for true believers to show the way to bring healing to the land, in forgiveness and in demonstrating that in Christ there is neither Tutsi nor Hutu, but a new tribe of the people of God. There were about a thousand people in that church, and we saw several old friends, including the former bishop of Kigali, but sadly most, if not all, were Hutu. The Tutsi generally met elsewhere. One friend told me that although she had forgiven her husband's killers, she found it hard to meet with others of the same tribe.

It was good to meet up with Emmanuel Kayijuka who had a committee meeting of SU while we were there. But most of the members were themselves refugees, and plans were to help the work of SU in the various camps rather than in the country itself. He took us to meet his wife, Julienne, and their family, giving us a lovely meal and then taking us to meet neighbours who were also refugees from Rwanda. Hearing that we were coming had given Emmanuel the necessary courage to return to Rwanda and he had already gone with another SU member, Niyi Daramola from Nigeria, a few weeks before we arrived. He had only spent a few days there but he had seen the conditions and now knew the ropes, so there was no difficulty in arranging our transport there. We had to wait until he was ready to go, which meant that we waited ten days in Nairobi. Our days were full as more and more people came and told their stories.

Then finally we were off. We were driven out to a small airport where we boarded a UN transport plane, as regular flights had not yet started. It was very noisy and uncomfortable, but at last we were on the last leg of our journey. Soon we were looking down at the green hills and blue lakes and rivers of Rwanda. What misery were we going to meet under all that beauty? I am sure that I was not alone in fearing the next few days.

I bought a visa without any problem, and the immigration officials honoured my parent's permanent visas, even though they had been given by the previous government. They were delighted to hear *bazungu*, or white people, speaking Kinyarwanda fluently. Sylvester, Emmanuel's second-in-command at SU, was there to meet us and he drove us to the Presbyterian guest house which showed signs of the past few months. The plumbing was not working too well, and the roof of the church next door had obviously had grenades exploding in it, but the beds were reasonably comfortable, and they were able to give us a cooked meal every night. Tired, but happy to be back, we slept well that night.

One of my mother's chief fears before we left England was of water pollution. She had heard that thousands of bodies had been buried in shallow graves, and she feared the contamination of the water supply. My chief fear was of bedbugs! In the event, neither fear materialized. Just before we left England, my mother had been reading in Deuteronomy and came across this promise in Deuteronomy 8:7: "For the Lord your God is bringing you into a good land — a land with streams and pools of water, with springs flowing in the valleys and hills", which she took as reassurance from the Lord. Certainly, we had no real problems with the water, though we used water purifiers and took sensible precautions.

However, during those weeks that we were in Kigali, they were digging up the bodies which were causing drainage problems near the hospital. One of the infamous barriers had been just below the hospital, as well as a military camp nearby. They counted over 7,000 skulls in that small area. It was horrible driving anywhere near the hospital at that time because of the sickly smell over the whole area.

For the next few days we tried to find somewhere to stay on a more permanent basis. But as we looked, the message soon got out that the Guillebauds were back, and soon the visitors came. Again, we spent time listening to their harrowing stories. One of the first to visit was Denis, whose family had all been killed in the previous troubles in the 1960s. My father had written to me about him when I was working in a parish outside Lowestoft. He had been struggling to look after his orphaned niece who had no other relative to care for her. Our parish had adopted her and provided money for her schooling even after Denis had married and been ordained as a Baptist pastor.

Denis' story

Denis told us his dramatic story. When they heard of the president's death, they stayed at home on the outskirts of Kigali. Then some of the *interahamwe* came to his house. Two of them grabbed him by his throat while others held his wife at the other side of the room. They said they would kill her first, and then him. Francine, his niece, and the children were in the inner room. The man had a machete raised to kill his wife. Denis cried out, "In the name of Jesus do not harm that woman!" He saw the machete begin to tremble and cried out again, "In the name of Jesus I forbid you to kill her." Then a young man jumped over the fence into his garden, and the gang chased after him. They came back accusing Denis of hiding "enemies of the state". Denis said, "I am a pastor and not *inyenzi*. As a pastor I am not involved in politics." One of them said, "My uncle was a pastor — I can't kill a pastor." They searched the house, but they did not open the door to the bedroom in which was hidden a pastor and his wife — then they left! Denis managed to get his family to the Amahoro stadium where they stayed for some weeks with very little food or water, and in constant danger from mortar bombs and so forth. Then, when the RPF took the city, they were all transferred to Byumba. They made Denis *conseilleur* for the camp — he said because of his grey hairs above his ears! This meant that he was responsible for meeting all the refugees who came to the camp and hearing their stories. He confirmed that many Tutsi owe their lives to Fidele, but said that he never got to the camp.

There had been a mass killing of Hutu men who had been called to a meeting in the Byumba stadium about that time and it is assumed that Fidele was one of them. The Human Rights Watch book, *Leave None to Tell the Story*, comments:

> In some places RPF forces killed civilians at meetings organized soon after their arrival in the community, a practice which gave rise to the bitter joke that *kwitaba Imana* meaning to die, had come to mean the same as *kwitaba inama*, to attend a meeting (p 708).

Antoine Rutayisire

At the camp were several pastors and church leaders of all denominations. Antoine Rutayisire of AEE was helping organize interdenominational meetings, and Denis was able to get a room for them to meet in. They had all things in common, sharing what little money they had in order to buy bread and sodas, so that they could break bread together in the Lord's Supper, making no distinctions between denominations. They had tremendous times of blessing as they prayed for their land, with many becoming Christians in the camp, showing great unity among all Christians. It was hard sometimes to know how to advise the hundreds of new believers how to be baptized and which church to join. Sadly, that visible unity has largely been lost.

We visited Antoine Rutayisire in the AEE office and heard some of his story which he has told in his book *Faith under Fire*, a collection of stories in which he describes how a number of Christians transcended tribalism during the genocide. He also described how he himself had to face death when the killers came to his house in Kigali. "Am I going to let them rape my wife, kill my child and all these young women and men in my home under my very eyes without even some attempt to protect them?... Why don't you grab a stick or any other weapon at hand and go out and fight them? Can't you die like a man?" As he thought this, many other incidents, when he had been subjected to abuse because of his tribe, flashed through his mind, and the desire to take vengeance was almost overwhelming. "Then I felt my spirit grow calmer and I heard a quiet voice inside, telling me: 'You have been preaching sermons on loving and praying for your enemies, and now you want to die shedding blood. Instead of trying to die like a man, why don't you just die like a Christian?'" He then made a short prayer of confession: "Lord, forgive me for thinking of making my own defence and give me grace to obey you even unto death. I ask for your blessing on these people, and if it is your will that we die, have them give me time to die praying for them as you did on the cross."

All this took only a few moments, but he felt that it had lasted a lifetime, and the peace that he felt then had lasted throughout the following horror-filled days. Just as he finished praying, a detachment of RPF came near and his would-be killers left to fight them and he and his wife were preserved to do all they could to bring reconciliation between the tribes in the years after the genocide. They managed to escape with their baby to the Amahoro stadium where they stayed for a week. Then they were evacuated and sent north. They stayed for three days in a shelter halfway to Byumba, and then walked to Byumba where they stayed in a camp for the next three months. They joined Denis in organizing interdenominational worship. Antoine has been such a help to me as I wrote this book, particularly in checking the Afterthoughts for me.

Marian Kajuga, Wilberforce and Frederick

It was a tremendous joy to see Marian Kajuga and her son, Wilberforce. She told us details of Eustace's death. She and Wilberforce had gone to Zaire for the funeral of her son-in-law, Janine's husband, who had just died of cancer. Eustace had malaria and she had not been happy to leave him alone in Gahini, so had brought him to stay with their eldest son, Husi. In fact, the whole family had been together that evening, including Robert. She said that she had a presentiment that she would not see them again. She read a passage of Scripture and said to them, "When we say goodbye we don't know what the future holds." She and Wilberforce drove to Ruhengeri the day before the president's plane was shot down. They spent the night at Gisenyi intending to fly from Goma. The next morning, they left not having heard the news, and were stopped at a barrier where a great fuss was made of her papers — her maiden name was on one piece of paper and Kajuga on another. They tried to detain them, but eventually they let them go. A Rwandan soldier, whom she knew, followed them on to the tarmac at the airport at Goma, to their great puzzlement, until they heard the news, when they realized that he had been trying to prevent them from leaving, either because of their name or because they appeared to be Tutsi.

That morning, fairly early, a troop of soldiers came to Husi's house and shot the whole family. Annie, Husi's Belgian wife, fell back on to Frederick (aged fifteen), who lay pretending to be dead until the soldiers left. Then he managed to get up. Husi and Annie were both dead, but Eustace was still alive. He told

Frederick to ring a friend to tell him what had happened, and also to ring Wilberforce in Zaire. Instead of sending help, the friend sent the soldiers back, which Marian said was the hardest to forgive. Frederick heard the soldiers come back, but Eustace had told him to hide in the roof. He had had a bullet through his arm and apparently left bloodstains on the wall showing where he had gone. He heard the soldiers say, "The old man is still alive", before they shot him again. They searched the house for him, knowing that he was still alive. How they missed the bloodstains, Marian could not understand, because they were very obvious when she saw them later. She said that the Lord must have blinded them. Later Frederick managed to telephone another Belgian friend of his mother, who came to find him, and he was evacuated to Belgium, where his brother and sister already were. But Frederick found it hard to concentrate on anything and eventually returned to Rwanda for a few weeks. Just before I left to return to England, Marian took me to see Eustace's grave in their garden where the whole family were buried. I saw the bloodstains which were still prominent on the wall. It was indeed a miracle that Frederick was not killed.

That same day, Wilberforce took me to see the mass grave of 93 people, including his wife, Nora, and three of their children. She had apparently taken her four children to the nearest Roman Catholic convent for safety. There the killers came, rounded everyone up, separated out the small children, who included his youngest daughter, Celine, aged eight, and then killed all the adults and older children. The nuns in charge of the younger children went to the government soldiers, saying they had no food to care for all those orphans. So the soldiers drove them to an orphanage at Gitarama. When the fighting drew nearer Gitarama, they were forced to walk to another centre about fifteen miles south. There Celine managed to send off a letter to her father. Then they had to walk through the Bugesera, round Kigali and then on to Byumba, a total of about 200 miles, walking all the way. Meanwhile Wilberforce had managed to get his mother to Nairobi where his eldest son, John, was studying. He thought that his whole family had been killed, until he received that note from Celine and realized she was still alive. Through the telephone he traced her to Byumba, so he drove through Uganda to Byumba, only to be told that his sister-in-law had driven her to Kabale the day before to try to find him! He drove straight back to Kabale where he had a joyful reunion with his little daughter.

Harriet

Marian's niece, Harriet, told how she and her husband, Silas, had sheltered in his office, with their entire family. Silas was the rural development officer working for Tear Fund, with responsibility for co-ordinating rural development work in the three southern dioceses. They had already heard that Marian and Eustace and their whole family had been killed on the first day of the bloodshed, and Silas's brother had had his head cut off outside his home. His daughter, Hope, was sheltering with them. When the killers came to the front door the two younger boys, Harriet's brother and Silas's younger brother, jumped out of the window at the back. She told her husband to follow them while she hid in a cupboard with the three girls, aged between eleven and thirteen. Somehow the Lord prevented them from being seen, but she heard someone call out, "Look, there are some Tutsi escaping!" She then heard some shots and knew that her family had probably been killed. When it was dark and all was quiet, she left with the three girls, but as they crawled through the bushes, they got separated. Suddenly they heard shots, and her daughter, who was still with her, panicked and ran. Harriet saw her shot down in front of her. She stayed where she was until all was quiet again, and then made her way to a Hutu friend where she heard that the other two girls had also been killed. In despair she told her Hutu friend to help himself, and her, by killing her or giving her up, as she had nothing to live for. Instead, he dressed her up as an *interahamwe*, paid an enormous sum (500,000 francs, the equivalent of over £1,000) for a Hutu ID card, and set off with her and a band of Hutu now fleeing the RPF. They managed to get to Burundi where she heard that her aunt, Marian, and Wilberforce were still alive and that she was not totally alone in the world, as she had thought. Once it was safe, she returned to Butare where she heard the details of her husband's death. He had indeed been shot as he fled the house but not killed. The killers had then stabbed and mutilated him but he took three days to die. Better news came when she found that one of the girls, her niece, Hope, had somehow survived. She got a temporary job with the Red Cross and later adopted two orphans, who knew nothing about who they were or what had happened to their family. By the time we saw her she had no job and no home, but she said that the only possible thing was to trust Jesus. Later, she became a member of parliament and was doing all she could to rebuild the country.

Robert Kajuga, *interahamwe* General

Marian also told me about her youngest son, Robert, who had become the general of the *interahamwe*. He had not known that his family had been killed by soldiers on that first day, and so had not been able to help them. Towards the end of the war, as they fled before the victorious RPF, one of his own men had shot and wounded him as a Tutsi. Once they got to Cyangugu, his men again tried to kill him, but he was rescued by friends who helped him into Zaire, and finally to Kinshasa where his sister lived. He was not sure how she would receive him, so he stayed with friends, but his wound was festering. Marian was visiting her daughter and heard that he was there. She and Janine went to visit him, although his brothers would have nothing to do with him. She said, "He was my son, what could I do? When he saw me, he just cried. He assured me that he had not killed anyone and, in fact, had used his position to save as many as he could. But he knew that he had much to be forgiven. I visited him three times before I returned to Rwanda in November." Later that month she heard that he had died from his wounds soon after she left. She also heard, and took comfort, that before he died he had asked for God's forgiveness.

Pierre Gakwandi and Rosa

Also staying at the guest house with us was Pierre Gakwandi (no relation to John), a Presbyterian pastor who had been one of the team of translators of the Bible working with my father ten years before, although he had returned to Butare in 1991 to pastor a church. The translation team had been killed, or fled, during the genocide, and Giles Williams had recommended that

Pierre be asked to assist with the new ecumenical team he was trying to get together to provide experience and continuity.

We had heard that Pierre had been killed, so it was a great joy to meet him. He had been at a church conference at Kirinda when he heard the plane was shot down. His one thought was to get home to his wife and children at Butare, knowing that, as Tutsi, they would all be in real danger. He got a lift part of the way and then managed to find a cycle for the rest — about 50 miles. He was nervous as he approached a large barrier outside Butare, but at that stage there was a *préfet* in Butare who refused to allow any killing, and the soldiers were quite friendly, greeting him as pastor. Later, that *préfet* was killed by the *interahamwe* and the killing got really bad. Pierre had found his wife, Rosa, quite peaceful, and was convicted of the sin of panicking rather than trusting the Lord. They read the story of Noah and felt that God was saying to them, "Your house will be like Noah's ark and I will shut you in and will send angels around the house to guard you." Several times over the next few weeks the *interahamwe* came to the door, but something always distracted them. They left saying they would return but never did. Their seven children were with them, learning about God's protection. Their house-boy and another friend, both Hutu and Christian, got them food and water and, provided they stayed in the house, they felt quite safe, even when things got really bad in Butare. Then the French arrived and wanted to evacuate them but they said, "These are not our promised angels — we will stay in our ark where we are safe in God's protection." When the war came to Butare they were in the firing line but the bullets all went over the house! And because they stayed in the house it wasn't looted. When the RPF finally got there they asked who had protected them. They said, "God did." "Well, you must have a very strong God," was the reply! They had been in their house for three months without ever going outside.

Later, Rosa started an organization to help orphans who had no one to care for them, many of whom were, themselves, caring for younger brothers and sisters. She wanted to show them the love of Jesus and tell them that God would care for them in the way he had protected her family during those dreadful months. Initially they worked in Butare, then started another in Kigali, but then she felt the Lord telling her to start another in Kirinda where there had been a terrible massacre and hardly any Tutsi survived. Both she and Pierre came from that area and had lost their entire family. She found it hard to face going back, and was faced with complete disbelief by the authorities when they realized that she would be caring for Hutu children, but she persisted, and now cares for over 200 children in that area. She said that the Lord had given her such a love for these children and such peace as she faced her fears about returning. God had used this organization to heal her bereaved heart.

Master disk of the new Bible

While in England, we had been praying so much for the new translation of the Bible. We had heard that Giles Williams had taken the master disks to the office to transfer the latest work on to them. There had been a power cut and he had left the disks there, intending to work on them next day — but that night the president's plane was shot down and he could not return to the office. We knew that Giles had returned soon after the killing had stopped and had found the precious disks, representing several years of work, intact. But we also knew that computers had been destroyed in mindless anger all over the city, and so we were interested to find out what had happened. Apparently soldiers had made their headquarters in the rooms at the front of the house and had never entered the inner room where all the translation equipment was kept. Because of their presence no one else had looted the office and all the precious documents and equipment were untouched!

John Gakwandi and Viviane

It was wonderful to meet John Gakwandi who came to see us one evening with his wife, Viviane. On the evening of 6th April they had read in *Daily Light* two verses which became a lifeline in the days ahead: Deuteronomy 33:27, "The eternal God is your refuge, and underneath are the everlasting arms. He will drive out your enemy before you", and Proverbs 18:10, "The name of the Lord is a strong tower; the righteous run to it and are safe." At 6 a.m. the next morning the killers came. They had already heard that their neighbour had been killed, and they felt the Lord tell them not to open the door. Instead all seven of them hid in the tiny storeroom of their kitchen, praying that the Lord would blind their eyes. They stayed there for 37 hours, hardly daring to move. During the night John had pulled a telephone into his hiding place and so heard what had been happening.

Two days later the killers came back and searched the house. They heard them climb up to the tiny window of their store and prepared for a grenade to be thrown, but somehow the killers' eyes were blinded and they did not see the terrified family. John managed to contact a German friend, Marianne Schmeling, who lived next door to the Swiss ambassador. A short time later the ambassador arrived in her official car and took the whole family to the Schmelings' home where they found other refugees. Eventually there were 21 refugees in the home, trying to pretend that it was only the German family of three who were there.

Then, two days later, the Germans were pressurized into being evacuated, leaving them to their own devices. The night guard, a Christian, would warn them of danger and tell them not to make any noise. Under cover of noisy rainstorms they were able to get the water they needed. Outside was a barrier where people were being killed every day. They could hear the killers boasting of how many they had killed. One day John had his four-year-old daughter with him in a cupboard. She was so thin that he feared that she would die if they did not find food soon. At that moment a bar of chocolate fell from a shelf above him! As he felt about in the darkness, he discovered a whole hoard of chocolates and sweets which kept them going for the next few days.

After five days of hiding like this, they were discovered and ordered outside. But the man in charge turned out to be one of his patients. John presented the other refugees as members of his family, even though he didn't know all their names. Their identity cards were collected and taken away, but they were allowed to stay, being told that their case would be dealt with later. That evening one of the refugees was taken outside and shot, but the rest stayed, praying that the Lord would soften the hearts of the killers and that they would forget that they were there. They never returned!

Although they were still careful not to draw attention to themselves, they no longer felt that they had to hide. One night, as they were reading the Psalms for comfort, just as John's father had done so many years before under similar circumstances, they claimed as a promise Psalm 118:17: "I will not die but live and will proclaim what the Lord has done!" It was not always easy to hold on to this promise, but God was faithful. By now the RPF was fighting round Kigali and bombs were falling near the house. One day a bomb hit an avocado tree covered with ripe pears. Several were thrown into their house which provided nourishment for a number of days. Also mushrooms suddenly sprouted on the cement floors all over the house. They were delicious. Like manna they had to be picked daily. They went bad if kept overnight. During those long days they learned to trust the Lord for all their needs.

At last the RPF won the battle for Kigali and it was safe to come out after 89 days in hiding. Gradually they discovered that most of their families had been killed. John had lost 99 members of his family on his father's side alone. The emotional cost was severe, but they had proved the protection of the Lord. John has now started a ministry to care for the thousands of bereaved people in Rwanda, called Solace Ministries, to help them in their physical needs, but mainly to provide trauma counselling to enable them to face their emotional needs, and to share with them the love of Jesus Christ. Their theme is taken from Isaiah 40:1, "Comfort, comfort my people, says your God."

Christians who failed, others stood firm

Another Presbyterian pastor and his wife came to see us, together with a Pentecostal pastor. They told us about some of the chaos of those days. The wife told us that you did not know who to trust. Even some of the Christians they had worshipped with and known for years got involved in the killing. "Yes," said the Pentecostal pastor, "when the Holy Spirit left a man, he became worse than the worst of the killers." Those words were to haunt me for many months. But they also gave more encouraging news of two churches, one Anglican at Ruhanga, and the other Pentecostal in Kigali, where the Christians showed a united front. In both cases, when the killers demanded that the

Tutsi be sent out of the church, they had replied that they were neither Tutsi nor Hutu but just people of God. In both cases, grenades were thrown into the churches, and everyone, both Hutu and Tutsi, were killed. The church at Ruhanga has since become a memorial to the genocide and its witness has gone round the world that not all Christians joined in the killing.

Edith

One of my sister's childhood friends came to visit. Edith had been a founder member of Scripture Union and was a close friend. Her husband, the aunt who had raised her and her five children had stayed in their home until the killers came, when they scattered. She took her youngest son, aged four, with her, and with two young Tutsi men headed towards Shyogwe. They came to a barrier where she recognized one of her neighbours. He said he was going to kill her.

She said, "I'll be all right for I will go straight to heaven, but what about you? How will you feel when you meet God with my blood on your hands?"

He laughed. "Don't you know? God is dead — we can do anything we like now."

She was horrified. If God was dead then she could not die. She must go on living if this life was all there was. She prayed quickly, " Lord, I don't want to die unless I get to heaven — show me that you are still alive."

They were stripping her and at that point they found her money which she had hidden in her clothing. The one who found it ran off into the bush, chased by all the rest who realized he was making off with something valuable. She and the two young men quickly dressed. An elderly Hutu, a stranger to her, then accompanied them to the next barrier, where he said, "These are very important people whose deaths are to be a showpiece. They mustn't be killed here." So they got through to Shyogwe. When asked why this man protected her, she replied, "I don't know — it was just Jesus." She knew God was still alive and protecting her!

At Shyogwe she got the news that her eleven-year-old daughter had escaped the killers and was back home, being cared for by a Hutu neighbour. All the rest had been killed. Her oldest daughter had been visiting a friend in Kigali and tried to get home when the killing started. At one barrier she had been put into a pit and stoned and left for dead. After they had gone she managed to climb out and went back to Kigali where she was one of the Tutsi rescued by Fidele, whom I had met in Nairobi.

Edith also gave us the sad news that just after she left Shyogwe for Goma, the killers arrived and Geraldine Kabirigi, Sira's widow, had been thrown alive into a longdrop latrine where she died. Some years later, my mother and I visited Shyogwe and were comforted by the way they had covered over the latrine with a tasteful tombstone.

Later, she heard that the man who had killed her husband had been arrested and was in prison in Butare. Although a local pastor, she described him as being without any knowledge of Jesus and his love. She got permission to visit him. He was brought into the compound where she said, "Many people have been saying that God is dead. I want to tell you that He is alive. He saved me from you. But Jesus had already saved me from worse than death, when he took my sins away. He can do the same for you. He told me to forgive my enemies and to feed them, so if there is anything I can do for you, please tell me."

About six years later, in March 2001, when I took my manuscript round to Edith for her to check its accuracy, she told me that she had something else to add to this story. When she started rebuilding her life back in her old home, her neighbours told her who it was who had killed her aunt. She refused to believe it, as he was one who often spoke of the Lord in church. He had been taught by her aunt and, in fact, had become a Christian through her teaching.

Late in 1999 he came to her and confessed that he was indeed the person who had killed her aunt. He said that he had been terrified for his own life if he had refused to kill, but that he could no longer live with what he had done. For six years he had had no peace, and now he had come to ask for her forgiveness, but also to say that he was ready to go to prison to expiate his crime. Edith had told him that she was not able to forgive him just then. It took her a whole year, but in the New Year of 2001, she felt before God that she could forgive. She realized that he had been imprisoned by his own guilt for six long years, and that she could not send him to prison on top of that. It had taken time but she was finally able to forgive from her heart. (On Pentecost Sunday 2001 he stood up in church and confessed what he had done. Then he looked at the congregation. "I know that some of you have similar things to confess," he said. "You will never have peace unless you acknowledge what you have done before God and man." It is now feared that he might be killed by those who fear that he will betray them.)

Scripture Union base

Several times we went out to the Scripture Union headquarters where we met other friends. Our search for somewhere to live was getting nowhere, and Emmanuel suggested that it might be possible to make comfortable quarters in the Scripture Union dormitories. There was running water, showers and toilets at one end of the block, and plenty of beds, though many mattresses had been looted. In one dormitory we put a bed each for my parents, with a double bunk as storage space, a wardrobe and a small table and chair for Dad's computer. Next door we put a bed for me by the window, curtained off, and a dining table and two benches in the middle of the room, with a cooking area for two paraffin stoves near the door. There was a plentiful supply of water across the passage in the washing area. I was so relieved to see them settled in relative comfort, for my time in Rwanda was rapidly coming to an end.

Geoffrey and Chloe

There was still one important visit we had to make. Wilberforce's son, John, who was visiting from Nairobi, was able to drive us to see Geoffrey and Chloe. It was a delight to see them — both looking older, but just as full of the Lord as ever. Their story was that soon after the troubles started they were reading the Scripture Union passage with their two sons, Samuel and Yohana. Yohana took his Bible and went off alone to pray, coming back saying he had given his life back to the Lord. Then a gang of *interahamwe* came towards them. They were in the house praying. Samuel said, "You can stay and pray if you wish — I'm going to hide among the corn." But when he got there, he found they had already chopped it all down and so he was found and hacked to death. When the gang arrived at the house, they all scattered.

Their house help wanted to stay with Geoffrey and Chloe, but they told him to hide himself. He was Hutu and they didn't know what happened to him. Yohana was caught and killed. Geoffrey and Chloe stayed in the house. The gang told them to come with them, but Geoffrey refused, saying he was old and ill, and they could do with him what they will, but he wasn't leaving. They took Chloe off and beat up Geoffrey, cutting the back of his head open, both calves, one elbow and a hand. Leaving him for dead, they locked the door.

Meanwhile Chloe was taken to the communal centre with a good crowd of other Tutsi. Someone came up to her and told her to go home. She was an old woman and could harm no one. She went home to find the door locked and blood coming underneath it. Assuming Geoffrey was dead, she went to a neighbour where she stayed several hours. One of the neighbours suggested they ought to bury Geoffrey rather than leaving him for the gangs, so they got help in breaking the door open. To their amazement he was still alive, though seriously injured. One of the neighbours was a nurse who said that his injuries were beyond her, and he needed hospitalization. But when they rang for an ambulance they were told the medical facilities were already overstretched and there was no way they could help him. So the nurse said she would bandage him up, though he needed stitches, and then see what God could do. Chloe cared for him, with the nurse coming in daily to change the dressings — and he made a remarkable recovery. One finger was cut in his left hand and that finger is now stiff, but apart from that he seemed better than ever, though with little strength.

While Geoffrey was recovering, the *interahamwe* kept coming back. They wanted to kill Geoffrey but one of the soldiers said, "You have tried already. If you kill him, I will kill you!" But they still searched for Chloe, coming back day after day. Once she hid behind the longdrop. They looked in it but didn't think of looking behind it. Another day she was warned they were coming and went to a neighbour until she was told it was safe to return. Somehow they never found her. Every time they came they took things from the home — the mobile phone, electric kettle, all his medical dressings, etc.

Despite all that had happened, Chloe was full of joy at the goodness of God. She said that she had been kept going by two passages from the Bible. Isaiah 40:28-31, which speaks of the everlasting God who gives power to the faint and strength to those who have none. The other passage was Isaiah 41:9-10, "Fear not for I am with you... I will strengthen you... I will uphold you with my victorious right hand." She said that she had found that whenever they needed help, it would come. Once they had no water or charcoal. Two little children, both under ten, came and collected water and fuel for them, making several trips. This was one of the impressive things about their home — the number of young people who came in and obviously felt at home. Geoffrey and Chloe had been offered a house at the diocese, but they chose to stay where they were because they felt that the people around needed a pastor, and God still had work for them, having spared their lives. About a year later, as they became increasingly frail, they did move into a house in the diocesan centre, where Geoffrey died in February 1997, and Chloe followed him in October 2000.

They heard later that, the same day that the gang had come to them, their older son, Emmanuel, and his whole family, were killed. But then it transpired that a soldier had taken the two children, Diane (seven) and Fiona (five) to Kibuye, some 150 miles away, and dumped them by the side of the road. A Roman Catholic brother found them and took them to an orphanage where they were put under the charge of a lady who fed her own children, but not them. Another lady then took pity on them and fed them. She discovered they came from Kigali and arranged for them to come back. Chloe was too frail to care for them, so they were initially taken in by one of Marian's sons, Wesley, but now are being fostered by Helene, whose husband had been killed in the troubles at Shyogwe just before Habyarimana came to power in 1973. Helene had returned from Burundi and was now living in Israel Havugimana's house as there were no known relatives who could take it over.

Squatter houses

This was one of the features of life in Kigali after the genocide. Returning refugees from Burundi, Uganda or Tanzania, with nowhere to live, just found an empty house and moved in. Even as early as that, the government was trying to restore order and decreed that if the rightful owner returned and could prove his claim, then the squatter had to move out, but it was fatally easy to accuse the rightful owner, especially if he was Hutu, of involvement in the genocide, and imprison him. We also heard of those who simply disappeared and were presumed dead. The Scripture Union houses had been taken over in this way and, although the government served eviction orders on the squatters, they refused to leave. Emmanuel was understandably afraid to press too hard, and my father did all he could to persuade them to go, but it was over a year after my parents left, before Emmanuel was finally able to return to his home. Meanwhile, he stayed in a small room at the SU Centre and had his meals with us.

Emmanuel had a real burden for the thousands of widows in Rwanda. On the Sunday before I left, he called together all the members of Scripture Union who had been widowed and asked me to address them. Having heard some of their stories I was very diffident, but I spoke about the stages of bereavement, as spelt out by Colin Murray Parkes. When I spoke of anger, indeed of being angry with the one who had left them with the problems they were facing, I saw several weep, and one woman walked out of the room in tears. It had obviously struck a deep chord.

Gideon and Margaret Kabano

On my last full day in Rwanda, Marian and Wilberforce drove me to Gahini where I was delighted to meet up with Gideon and Margaret Kabano, who had walked back from Tanzania with their cattle. They had found that it was unsafe for Tutsi to be anywhere near the large refugee camps where several of the Hutu killers were still continuing their bloody work. They were delighted to be back in Gahini, having left in the 1960s. Initially, Gideon had not been classed as a refugee, having been asked by the church to minister to the refugees in Tanzania. But as the years went by he found that he could not return and so had eventually retired in Tanzania. He said, "I never dreamed that I would ever see my home again. God is so good to us."

In the years ahead, we found that many of those like Gideon, who had left in the 1960s, wanted to go back to what life was like then. They were sad that so few missionaries were there, and they could not see that the church had moved on. Yet their true hunger was that God would move again in Revival and I could not but agree; even though I did not expect the same manifestations, I longed for the unity that only the Holy Spirit can bring. In October 2000, Gideon finally succumbed to the cancer which had been eating him for two years. As he died, Margaret said that he appeared to be conducting a heavenly choir, as he had so often conducted choirs in the church!

We left Marian at Gahini, and Wilberforce drove me home, taking me first to see his parents' house by the lake. I was chilled at the sight of the horrific violence and hatred which had destroyed the building even though there had been no one there. On the way home he said to me, "I know that, as a Christian, I am expected to forgive my enemies, but how do I forgive those who killed my wife and family? They are not repentant at all. And if I forgive, it simply sets them free to do it again." His son had said that the hardest thing for him was that it was friends who had killed his brothers. How can one forgive injuries such as these? Yet, as I said to Wilberforce, for his own sake he needed to give up the bitterness which could destroy him. Somehow the country needed to address the roots of hatred which had led to these waves of killing over the years, each feeding on the bitterness left by the last.

Healing and forgiveness only found at the cross

Everywhere that my father was asked to preach, this was his theme. It was only at the cross that the burden of anger and hatred and bitterness could be dealt with. It was only as Christians demonstrated a practical love for their enemies, and showed that in Christ there was no tribalism, that they would have the right to be heard.

Dad had been horrified by a young 16-year-old soldier who visited him with another friend. "I have lost all my family," he said. "Now my only family is this," and he patted his gun. Philip Gourevitch tells the stories of two RPF soldiers, quoting Paul Kagame. One wrote a letter "telling me how he was left alone in his family, and how he knew that some people killed his family during the genocide and how he has chosen not to hold anybody else responsible for that. Instead, he has decided to take his own life because he doesn't see what his life means anymore." The other was of a soldier who suddenly started shooting in a bar and killed three people and wounded two more. His reason was that he was seeing killers wandering around Kigali with impunity and he could not take any more. (*We Wish to Inform You That Tomorrow We Will Be Killed with Our Families*, p 312.) Earlier, Gourevitch writes, "Nobody in Rwanda escaped direct physical or psychic damage. The terror was designed to be total and enduring, a legacy to leave Rwandans spinning and disorientated in the slipstream of their memories for a very long time to come, and in that it was successful" (p 224). As I was struggling to understand the after-effects of the war and the genocide, I realized that almost everyone in Rwanda had lost members of their family or close friends. All were in bereavement, you could say that the whole country was in bereavement, and this helped me to see that one had to allow the government time to work through the difficulties of bereavement. Indeed, I am amazed at how much has been achieved in so short a time as, on the surface at least, Rwanda now seems to be a stable, prosperous country once more.

Yet the traumas and loss still need to be faced and dealt with. Like my father, I believe that it is only at the cross that these deep psychic wounds can be healed. Yet the church, too, needed healing. Someone had described the church in Rwanda as "a shallow lake — very wide but with no depth to it". The bishop of Kigeme had said to me that what the church needed more than anything else was solid Bible teaching. "Even if you could come for three months, it would help," he said.

Feeling that I had done all I could to settle my parents, I finally left for Nairobi, my head filled with the stories I had heard and my heart aching for my beloved land. I was also wondering how the church in Britain could help the hurting church in Rwanda, and what the future held for me.

Margaret visiting a
friend — sitting on a
stick to avoid the mud
(1954) (MAM Collection)

Geoffrey and Chloe Kinyanza

Sergeant Meg (c 1973)

Pastor Meg

Mary Kanamuzeyi looking at a photo of her husband after he had been killed in 1964

Peter and Elisabeth receiving a present from Shyogwe School as they were about to retire in 1986. "You built Shyogwe — we will never forget you"

Golden Wedding, 1990. *Left to right:* John, Christine, Elisabeth, Peter, Meg, David

Peter and Elisabeth with their grandchildren on his 80th birthday in 1994

Skulls at Nyamata Genocide Memorial (Bill Hawes / CMS)

Spots of light from bullet holes in the roof of Ruhanga Church where Hutu and Tutsi died together (MAM Collection)

Elisabeth at Geoff Holmes' hut at Gatsibo (MAM Collection)

Elisabeth with Simon and Deborah outside Meccano Villas

Edith and Simon at Hanika where his grandparents had looked after refugees some 40 years earlier

Bishop Onesphore and Josephine Rwaje in their garden (MAM Collection)

Elisabeth dancing with the widows — the day before she had her stroke

Chapter 13   A Missionary After All! (1995-1997)

Back in England, for a number of reasons I felt, as I prayed, that it was time to leave my parish. I started to look for other parishes, but at the same time I approached Mid-Africa Ministry to go as a volunteer to Rwanda for three to four months. The general secretary, Roger Bowen, commented, "It is not often that we have a volunteer who is not only trained in theology, but also speaks Kinyarwanda!" My Kinyarwanda was not that good since I had only really spoken it as a child, and had no theological vocabulary, but we were confident that I would soon pick it up. Plans were made to send me to Byumba in September, where they had suffered from four years of war and had lost many of their pastors and catechists, who had either been killed or fled as refugees.

Over the next few months I was asked to speak at several churches about my experience in Rwanda, and so had a chance to reflect on what I had heard. I also read a number of books to try to make some sort of sense of the sequence of events which led up to the genocide and what actually happened on a wider scale within the country. Particularly helpful were two books, *Rwanda: Death, Despair, Defiance* by African Rights, and *The Rwanda Crisis: History of a Genocide* by Gerard Prunier, which I have quoted extensively in this book. Other helpful books which were published later and chronicle the aftermath of the genocide as well as its background are *We Wish to Inform You That Tomorrow We Will Be Killed with Our Families* by Philip Gourevitch, and the Human Rights Watch book *Leave None to Tell the Story*.

The progress of the war

When the president's plane was shot down on 6th April at about 8.30 p.m., the *interahamwe* almost immediately set up road-blocks; houses were searched by the presidential guard for those they classified as "enemies", who were then shot. By the following morning, the prime minister, Mme. Agathe Uwilingiyimana, and the ten Belgian UN troopers guarding her, had all been shot, as had the foreign minister who negotiated the Arusha peace accords, and the information minister. Also among the first to be killed were the leaders of all the opposition parties, journalists who had been critical of Habyarimana's party, Catholic priests who had supported the peace accords, human rights activists and Israel Havugimana who had worked so hard for reconciliation between tribes.

The commander-in-chief of the army had been killed, along with the president, and his successor, who was not involved in the conspiracy, tried to keep the army from joining in the killing. There were clashes between those obedient to his orders who tried to stop the slaughter, and those involved in the killing, although it was not long before he was replaced and the army became active supporters of the killers.

Although the reason why the plane was shot down, and who actually did it, is still a mystery, with all sorts of theories being put forward, the fact that the first roadblocks appeared within an hour, and the first killings started soon afterwards, argues a well-laid plot. I cannot conceive that the plane could have been shot down by anyone other than those who immediately started the killing.

On Friday 8th April, the RPF, which had kept a small force near Kigali since the signing of the peace accords the previous year, again went on the offensive and moved south from the Byumba area where their main army had stayed. On the 10th, Belgian paratroopers arrived, and over the next few days almost all the *bazungu*, or expatriates in the country, were evacuated, and the United Nations troops were withdrawn, in effect leaving the Rwandans to get on with the killing.

The RPF reached Kigali on the 11th and, for the next three months, while the work of slaughter continued elsewhere, there was a fierce battle between the FAR troops and the RPF for control of the capital. At the same time the RPF steadily gained control of much of the country north of Kigali. When they seemed about to gain control of Kigali, towards the end of June, there began another mass exodus of refugees, this time of hard-core Hutu killers who fled their feared retribution, but the demonization of Tutsi was so complete that almost the entire Hutu population fled with them, whether or not they had been involved in any killing.

Reasons for the genocide

But what caused the killings? After the first deaths, which were mainly of selected targets who were shot by the presidential guard, the *interahamwe* largely took over. They killed by hacking people to death with machetes or sickles. When I arrived in Byumba and saw these instruments being used for their intended purpose, I would feel sick, imagining how they had been used a few months before. The victims were for the most part Tutsi, or Hutu who, through intermarriage, looked like Tutsi, but also Hutu who attempted to hide or help Tutsi, and human rights defenders who were regarded as sympathizers of the RPF.

It is hard to understand how this killing mania took over. During those days in Kigali, I heard several people say, "I don't understand it. We were at peace with our neighbours and had nothing against them, and then suddenly we were killing each other." There are some elements which are possible to identify which go towards a partial explanation:

1 The ingrained culture of obedience to those in authority in the country. It is a fact that where the *préfet* in Butare refused to allow his people to kill, they didn't, until he himself was killed and replaced by an extremist. In only one commune, Giti in Byumba préfecture, the *bourgmestre* was a committed Roman Catholic who forbade the killing. It was the only commune in the country where no one was killed.

2 Radio Mille Collines was pouring out a constant stream of horrendous instructions, scaring the population about what the Tutsi would do to them if they gained control, and pre-

senting the extermination of the Tutsi as an act of self-defence. The logic was also presented that the RPF were the descendants of Tutsi women and children who had fled in 1959. If they had been killed then, there would be no RPF invaders. It was therefore a matter of survival to spare no one: old people, women, children and babies were all slaughtered without mercy.

3   The language used of the Tutsi served to dehumanize them. They were "cockroaches" to be stamped out, or "weeds" to be pulled out and burned. Loyal members of the government were called "to clear the bush" as part of their accustomed work for the government.

4   Land-hunger in the countryside, and envy in the towns, also played its part. Some killed and looted in the hope that when all had settled down they might claim the fields of the victims. Others were street-children and unemployed who saw the killings as an opportunity to steal, rape and get drunk with impunity. As Prunier says (p 232), "Social envy came together with political hatred to fire the Interahamwe bloodlust."

5   Prunier identifies all of the above as elements in the tragedy. I would add satanic and demonic activity, as I will discuss further in the Afterthoughts. Prunier summarizes these elements on p 248. "But greed was not the main motivation. It was belief and obedience — belief in a deeply-imbibed ideology, which justified in advance what you were about to do, and obedience to the political authority of the state and to the social authority of the group." It was that ideology that Hutu had a right to the country, and that Tutsi were invading intruders, that was fuelled by demonic powers in an almost irresistible bloodlust.

Sadly, many church leaders, while not actively involved in the killing , did nothing to prevent it or even to condemn it. Indeed, Prunier quotes a letter by 29 Roman Catholic priests to the pope on 2nd August 1994 "in which they denied any Hutu responsibility for the Genocide and attributed it to the RPF, denouncing the idea of an international tribunal to investigate crimes against humanity and defending the FAR." And Roger Bowen of Mid-Africa Ministry said, "Anglican Church leaders were too closely aligned with the Habyarimana government. The Archbishop spoke openly in support of the President and his party" (quoted by Prunier, p 252). Yet, as we have seen, and as Prunier confirms, "It was a time of undisputed heroism by people who expected no reward but the satisfaction of a clear conscience. Many of these unsung heroes were Christians who believed deeply in their religion and whose charity and courage made up for the compromises of their church hierarchies" (p 259).

It was some of the stories of those unsung heroes that I told as I travelled round churches during the early months of 1995. Meanwhile, though I was short-listed several times, I did not find the sort of parish I was looking for, and began to wonder what the Lord was saying to me. When the last one turned me down just before I was due to leave, I did not feel distress but rather an enormous sense of release. Now I would be free to extend my time in Africa if that were right, rather than rushing back to start a new job. I made arrangements for my cat and dog to be cared for, and for my furniture to be placed in store, and faced my final service with excitement, but also some distress, as I had grown to love the people I was leaving behind, though I knew that most understood what I was doing and would be praying for me. That afternoon, I stubbed my toe very badly on an armchair and spent the afternoon in hospital where I found I had broken my big toe. I had to use a stick for my final communion service, and the journey back to Rwanda a few days later was very painful!

Peter and Elisabeth in Kigali

During those final six months, I had telephoned my parents frequently, and received several letters from them. I had heard how they had started travelling to various churches, Dad still playing his accordion. On one occasion they had had a horrendous journey to a parish miles from anywhere with a terrible road. They were told of another way home and felt it could not be as bad — but, if anything, it was worse! My mother and Sylvester, from Scripture Union, said that they had walked most of the way as they checked to see whether the dozens of bridges would hold. Most had only two planks across a stream, and the wheels had to be guided so that they hit the planks right. It didn't seem as if much had changed since my grandmother's day! However, they had found a crowd of about 3,000 people waiting for them who had spent the previous two days in Bible study and prayer for the land. They felt that the trip had been worth it, although everyone said that they must not again try to go so far off the main road.

They preached at Butare Presbyterian Church where they met a lady called Marie who gave her testimony in church. She, a Hutu, had had a regular prayer time with a Tutsi lady. Before the war, the Tutsi lady had a dream; she saw herself and her elder child going away on a journey, leaving the younger child, Rosine, behind. She was distressed about this but then she saw Rosine being hugged by Marie, and knew she would be all right. In the morning she told Marie her dream. She had laughed at the thought that her friend could go on a journey without Rosine, but she promised that if it ever happened, then, of course, she would look after her. During the dreadful fighting in Butare, all Tutsi were commanded to go to the commune, where grenades were thrown and all were killed. When she heard the news two days later, Marie remembered her promise. She went and looked under a pile of corpses and found Rosine still alive. She had slashes on her head and neck, which Marie treated as best she could since it would not be safe for her to seek medical help, but she said, "Jesus alone healed her." Rosine is now her child, along with two other orphans she has taken in. After the war, Marie began working with Rosa Gakwandi, caring for orphans who are themselves looking after younger siblings.

Peter and Elisabeth were told many stories of dreams and visions that came out of those times. Apparently someone had a vision at the Scripture Union camp just before the genocide. They saw rivers of blood and several people, some of whom they knew, going to heaven in clouds of glory. At the time, they interpreted it as the river of blood flowing from Jesus' side, but later they realized that the Holy Spirit had been preparing them for what lay ahead. It encouraged them to know that God was in control, even in such distressing events as those which took place in 1994.

Peter and Elisabeth had also travelled to Uganda for the

Kabale convention which had been held every ten years since that first one in 1945. They were distressed to see how dominated by bishops it had become, rather than giving space to ordinary Christians as had been the case in the early days. However, it was a joy to see so many old friends from the past, and the teaching was excellent.

Another large meeting they attended at the Amahoro stadium in Kigali was arranged by African Enterprise, who had been so successful in bringing together opposing parties in South Africa before their historic elections. The main speaker was Archbishop Desmond Tutu, who had a wonderfully light touch as he asked how people could decide a man's character, or integrity, or whether he should die, by the length of his nose!

Another meeting was with the archbishop of Canterbury and his wife, who greeted them as old friends. He had been generous in supporting me as I prepared to come out again. I remember a picture of the archbishop at the genocide site of the Anglican Church of Ruhanga, where both tribes had been killed, since the Hutu refused to separate themselves from their fellow believers. The picture showed him surrounded by skulls, as he tried to take in the scale of the massacres.

Meg returns to Rwanda

It was wonderful to see my parents again and to settle down in the Scripture Union dormitories as if nothing had changed. But this was an illusion. Scripture Union was beginning to get back to normal, and the other dormitories were now being used for conferences so that they were sharing the washing facilities with up to 100 people! The two dormitories at the other end of the block had been made into quarters for two other families: Michel and Immaculée were feeding themselves, but Jacqueline and her two little daughters ate with us.

Michel and Immaculée

During the war, Michel and Immaculée had been sheltered by Hutu, at first by a pastor, but as things got more difficult he feared for his life and that of his family and asked them to leave because he feared that their presence was known. That night they managed to get to Kigeme and stayed for a week in the house of the bishop there, who was also hiding other Tutsi. While there they heard of a massacre of about 40,000 Tutsi who had fled for shelter to a camp organized by the leaders of the commune. Later they heard that all Michel's family had been killed in that slaughter. After a week, the bishop feared for their safety and arranged that a young Christian man care for them. He had his own house and hid them in his inner room. His sister, the only other member of his family to know about them, fed them. For three weeks they hid — the children kept quiet for all that time, until the sister could not face the strain any longer and threatened to tell their parents about their visitors. The young man dared not take them to anyone in the neighbourhood because he feared that they would kill them, so he got a message to the bishop. That night he and his wife arrived with his car and made two trips, taking the parents and youngest child, hidden in the boot, and then coming back for the older children. They were terrified as they approached barriers manned by *interahamwe* but the bishop bluffed his way through both times without the car being searched. The bishop took the two older children, and said he would care for them, and then took Michel and Immaculée, and the three younger ones, to the house of an old woman, who welcomed them with open arms. At one point they feared that their presence was known and said they should leave, but she would not hear of it. She said that they could all go to heaven together. After about five weeks with her, they escaped to a camp the French had set up in the area. They stayed there for three days and were then flown by helicopter to Bukavu where they stayed for three months in the same camp as some of the killers. Michel said, "The Lord taught us patience during that time and also how to forgive." In October that year, Michel came back to Kigali where he started a society called Moucecore whose main aim is to preach the gospel as a means of bringing reconciliation between the tribes. Although both he and Immaculée had lost almost all of their extended family, Michel was praising God for the way he had protected them and their five children. Michel had the courage to speak at the Amahoro stadium meeting organized by AEE, telling how he owed his life to Hutu — but this was a message that the majority of people at that stage did not want to hear.

Jacqueline

Jacqueline was the widow of the Scripture Union schools worker. She was great fun to be with, sharing many jokes with us. She often travelled with us to churches at the weekends, giving her testimony while my father preached. She became a Christian at a Scripture Union camp during the 1980s. She realized the importance of a Christian home and told the Lord that she was willing to remain single rather than marry a non-Christian. However, after a time, she met a young man at the Christian Union in the university and they both realized that they should marry. They were both studying at the time and they knew it meant a bit of a wait, but they were content. However, their parents were not. The problem was that she was Hutu and Simon-Pierre was Tutsi! It took three years of prayer before they reluctantly agreed. They had a very happy marriage with two little girls born in quick succession. However, the younger was only two months old when the president's plane was shot down. All Scripture Union staff took refuge on the site, together with dozens of others. One day, the man who had gone to dig sweet potatoes to feed them all, was killed and his body left in the field. Emmanuel went to negotiate with the soldiers so that they could bury him. In his absence the killers came and herded them all down to a barrier where they had to produce their identity cards. Jacqueline was sent home with most of the others, but Simon-Pierre was taken away and presumably killed, although they never saw his body. Emmanuel realized that it was time that they tried to leave. The Tutsi among them made their way behind the RPF line, whilst the Hutu fled to Bukavu and thence to Nairobi.

Jacqueline used to say that she spent several days arguing with God. Then she said she heard the Lord reply, "Simon-Pierre's work is done and I have taken him home. But I still have work for you to do." She said that she had thought that she would never laugh again, but gradually God had restored her healing sense of humour. She always finished her testimony in the same way: "Jesus satisfied me as a single girl. He satisfied me in an extremely happy marriage. And now he satisfies me as a widow." Her words were such a help to my mother when my father died and she realized that his work was done, but that there was still work for her to do among the widows of Byumba.

Meg starts work in Byumba

A week after my return I received two visitors from Byumba. "We are ready for you," they said. "When can you come?" "When do you want me?" I asked. "Next week?" I simply could not start that soon. Once I had got back and realized how inadequate my Kinyarwanda was, I was terrified at the thought of teaching, but these men wanted me — and soon. Finally, we settled on my doing a two-week course, starting in three weeks' time. That night I was sleepless as I tried to think how I should teach. Eventually the thought came that I could write out my lessons in English and get my parents to translate them. Then I could get enough pages printed so that each student could have one and that would deal with the difficulty of the lack of language.

The next week was a flurry of activity as I wrote out what I had taught as a basic confirmation course in England. I also tackled a series of Bible studies on the book of Nehemiah as we faced the need to rebuild the nation. A series of ten lessons on preaching, a few basic ones on pastoralia and another series of studies on 1 Peter, the letter written to suffering people, completed my lessons for that first course, but I had only prepared enough for the first week when I found myself in Byumba. All these lessons were in the form of questions which the students were expected to answer from the Bible, with a little information and explanation from me. Out of my need, I had discovered a method of teaching that I have continued ever since.

There had been so much destruction during the years of war, that very few houses remained intact. The bishop was living with the archdeacon while his house was being repaired. At first I had to commute daily from Kigali, about an hour's drive away. I would write up a lesson when I got home; Dad would translate it the next day while I was teaching! I taught in the church with repairs going on all round me. By the time my second course started, I was able to sleep in what was to be the bishop's bedroom, while my students slept in other rooms in the house, again with builders still working on the house. Conditions were far from ideal. I had never felt so inadequate for any job that I had ever tackled, but I was amazed that somehow we seemed able to communicate. I was so conscious of people praying for me and felt that I had received the same gift the

apostles received on the day of Pentecost. We seemed to understand each other's language even though I knew I was not speaking it well.

Gradually we developed a routine as I spent Monday to
Friday in Byumba and returned to Kigali every weekend.
Saturday morning I would usually spend teaching the SU cook
how to make marmalade or different kinds of jam. On Sunday,
Dad would drive us out to a different church near Kigali where
we would preach, have a meal with the church leaders, and then
return for a good night's sleep before leaving early next morning for Byumba.

Onesphore Rwaje and Josephine

It was good to see Bishop Rwaje again and get to know him. I
had met him in Nairobi, little dreaming that I would eventually
find myself working for him. He was on crutches at that time,
having been involved in a serious accident. Now he was back in
Byumba, although Josephine was studying in Nairobi and the
children were all with her. He told how, following a wonderful
Easter service of hope in Byumba church in 1994, Josephine had
left for a Mothers' Union conference in Zambia on 5th April.
They were planning to move back to Byumba when she
returned, but on April 6th the president's plane was shot down.
Bishop Rwaje had received a phone call from Israel
Havugimana, warning him that soldiers were on the rampage
and advising him to stay indoors. Later he heard that Israel
must himself have been killed shortly afterwards. A neighbour
had come to his door, bleeding and telling of members of his
family who had been killed. He took him in and patched him up
and he joined their household. Bishop Rwaje was living in an
area where there were few Tutsi, and he wasn't well known, so
although he was aware of killings going on elsewhere in Kigali,
he and his household stayed indoors until the RPF attacked the
city and they felt it was time to leave. He fled to Shyogwe. His
youngest son was ill and needed hospital care so he went on to
Rubengera where his wife managed to find him. Eventually they
got to Bukavu where some CMS (Australia) missionaries helped
them to get to Nairobi. After two weeks there, he went to
Tanzania where he had heard that many of his clergy had fled as

refugees. By the end of August, as soon as he could, he returned to Rwanda and to his diocese, which was in a mess with soldiers billeted in the small church and using the larger one as a canteen. In the middle of September they left the church and he was able to re-consecrate it. He had heard that people were saying that there was no church left in Rwanda, so in October 1994 he went, with Bishop Alexis, to a conference in Botswana to assure people that the church was still functioning despite difficulties. On his way back, in Nairobi, he was knocked down by a bus and had severe injuries, from which he was recovering when I met him in Nairobi in 1995.

Over the next three months, I taught three courses at Byumba, and a similar one to deacons in training at Kigeme. As Christmas approached, Emmanuel said that the message of Revival needed to be spelt out for younger Christians. It was suggested SU members should seek out all those who had become Christians in the 1930s and 1940s, and invite them to a camp in January. How glad I was that I was free to extend my time in Rwanda by another month and was not rushing back to another parish. I also arranged for a final course to start in Byumba during the first two weeks of January.

On Boxing Day, we drove to Kisiizi, in Uganda, for a much-needed break and to visit some friends from our parish in England. On the way there we visited Eseri Serubibi, my grandparents' old friend, who had been a missionary in Matana for so many years. She was still very spritely and when she heard about the gathering of old people, she insisted on coming as well. She had often travelled with my parents when they visited schools in the Scripture Union days and was well loved in Rwanda as well as Uganda. So we collected her on our way back from Kisiizi. After the camp I had to take her home as she was very ill with malaria. Julienne came with me and I was very relieved to have her along as a nurse. Another friend came to help with the border crossing. As we passed one of the barriers, he said, "I hate this place. Thirty-six members of my family were killed here and their bodies thrown into that swamp."

Sylvester

Statements like that brought home the horror of what this nation has been through. Another incident which brought it home to me, was when I went with Sylvester to his home to collect a couple of suitcases that he had kept safe for Emmanuel. Coming away from the house he casually kicked a bone from the path, saying, "This is the bone of a child." From the brief glimpse I had of it, it appeared to be a tibia broken raggedly at one end — somehow it summarized for me all the horror of these stories. I gathered that the *interahamwe* came to his house to kill the family and several neighbours who were sheltering there. Somehow they heard a rumour that he had a large gun in his house so they said they would come back with some soldiers. Three truckloads of soldiers arrived some time later but just as they drew near, the RPF approached from the other side of the valley. Fierce fighting took place round their house and everyone fled — except his mother who took refuge in a cot behind his armchair! He and his wife and children fled to her parents through the bullets. They stayed there some days at the top of the hill, but when the fighting came towards the hill, they went back to their own house. Unfortunately her parents and brothers were all killed. Over 300 people in that community were killed, but somehow Sylvester, his wife, children and mother all survived and praised the Lord for his protection.

Camp to relive the message of Revival

The camp for the "oldies" was a wonderful time. Mabel Jones came out from England as one of the main speakers. It was great to hear some of those old people telling what God had done for them over the years. Gideon Kabano stood and told how the Holy Spirit had prompted him to return stolen cows in restitution. Marian told how God had enabled her to forgive the killers of her husband and sons. But my main memory was of two people who told of struggles they were still having.

A Tutsi man spoke of how his wife and family had been killed. "I have forgiven," he said, " but then something happens, and I miss her all over again. The anger comes back and I have to forgive all over again. I can only do it by the help of the Holy Spirit."

A Hutu then spoke about his fears as he returned to the country. He came from the Byumba area where the fighting had been most prolonged and he had a picture in his mind of the RPF soldier as a killing machine. He had been frightened to return to a country controlled by them. Then he heard God telling him to return. "Whether I live or die," he said, "I know I am where God has put me — and at least I would die in my own land." But his fear of soldiers was still there, until at one of the many barriers, he really looked at one of the soldiers examining his papers. "He was just a young lad," he said, "and then he asked me for a Bible. I realized that he, too, had needs like any other person, and I lost my fear of the RPF at last."

How important it was for those there to hear how both tribes were struggling with fear and anger, and together to ask the Holy Spirit to heal their wounds, as they recognized that they were one tribe in Christ Jesus. This was what Dr Rhiannon Lloyd had been doing in various seminars, one of which my parents had attended during the months when I was in England.

Rhiannon is a medical doctor who is also qualified in psychiatry. For the last few years she has been working in countries where there is ethnic conflict, trying to help people recover from their mental scars. She had first come to Kigali while I was in England and met my parents at one of the big rallies in Kigali. Then she started seminars to help traumatized people find healing. At a seminar in Kigali, she told of her own tribalism as a Welsh child who was brought up to hate the English for what they had done in her country. She had been saved from this ongoing hatred by Christians she met in medical school in England. They apologized to her on behalf of the English and this released her to let go of her hatred. While she was telling her story, my parents entered the seminar late. "Oh," said Rhiannon, "I am so glad that some English people have arrived to hear my story." Mum bridled. She hated being called English when she was Scottish. As she listened to Rhiannon she realized that she, too, had tribalism in her heart!

Initially these seminars were on trauma healing but soon the emphasis changed to helping church leaders find "the role of the church in healing, forgiveness and reconciliation". These are still being held at different locations throughout the country, now run by people she has trained.

Rhiannon had come out at the request of AEE and the main focus in her seminars is a workshop on the cross. First, she asks people to write out the worst things they have suffered. Then they get into groups to share their stories and listen to each other's pain.

> We always try to get an ethnic mix in the groups if possible, so this is a major step in choosing to trust. Then the most important part is pouring out their pain to the Crucified Lord, believing that He carried their pain as well as their sin on the Cross (Isaiah 53:4). Often there is much emotion expressed during this time, even from Rwandese men!! By faith they transfer their load of pain to Jesus. This is what has proved to be life transforming. Then, as a visual representation of what they have done, they nail their stories to a large wooden cross. Incidentally, the testimony we have heard over and over is that transferring their pain to Jesus is what freed up their hearts to be able to truly forgive.

Then she asked them to talk about good things that had happened to them. It was amazing how often, once the consuming hurt had been exposed, they were able to recognize some of the acts of kindness they had received from the other tribe, and they could at last begin to see them as human beings.

Initially, Rhiannon found no difficulty in getting people to talk about their experiences, but as time went on, it became harder. People started to say, We have forgotten, and We now want to carry on with life. But unless these fears and hurts are truly faced, Rwanda could so easily do what it has done before and the whole cycle of killing could start again.

Return to England

Early on Sunday morning we were driven to the airport. So many wanted to see us off that we had to make two trips, one for my parents and their friends, and then I returned for the luggage. When I got there for the second time it was to be greeted by long faces. The flight to Nairobi had been cancelled. I began to think that I would have to drive the whole way to Nairobi. It would be an exhausting trip but if we left immediately we should just make it. Then I realized there was a flight to Entebbe which would connect to Nairobi. I waited in a queue but the flight was filled just before I got to the head of the queue.

As I returned to our group, Wilberforce turned up with another man. "This friend of mine has just started an airline," he said. "The first flight today was to Dubai, but tomorrow he will fly to Nairobi. Do you want seats?" Not only was it cheaper, but we were allowed more luggage which meant that Dad could take his prized accordion with him. He was intending to give it to someone in Nairobi who could pass it on to his friend Ephraim, who had written from a refugee camp in Bukavu, lamenting that in the confusion of war, he had lost the accordion that Dad had given him some years before.

We spent that night with friends in Kigali as we had said all our goodbyes and did not want to return to Scripture Union. Next morning I got our money back from the cancelled flight and bought fresh tickets. We got to the airport that evening to see the ominous notice that the flight had been delayed. However, to my relief it arrived and we left within half an hour, just as the sun was setting. We learned later that the airline failed three weeks later, sad for the owners, but it had been such a provision for our need! At Nairobi a taxi was waiting to take us to the guest house where we were too late for the evening meal and had to make do with some dried prunes that my father found in his pocket.

Plans for my future

Next morning I woke early, relieved to have got that far. I started to face what lay ahead. I had no job so would need to sign on at the job centre. I had no home and would need to do something about all my furniture. I must collect my cat and dog from the people who were caring for them. I suddenly shook myself. What was the use of lying there worrying? I took out my Bible for the morning reading. The Kinyarwanda version of Scripture Union notes sent me to read Jeremiah 29:11: "I know the plans I have for you, declares the Lord, plans to prosper you and not to harm you, plans to give you hope and a future." I felt that the Lord was speaking directly to me. I went on reading in that chapter and the next and the last five words at the bottom of the page leapt out at me. "I will bring you back." It was as if the Lord was shouting at me. "My plan for you is to bring you back to Rwanda."

Just before I left Byumba, I had told the bishop that I would probably be asked to speak to several churches when I got back to England. "What do you want me to tell them?" I asked. "What is your greatest need?" He had thought for a moment and then said, "My greatest need is for Bible teachers." I had been surprised in view of the huge material needs of his diocese but he explained, "Unless their spiritual needs are met, there is no point meeting the physical needs of the people. I need to train my catechists and clergy so that they can meet the spiritual needs of this diocese." Now I felt that the Lord was telling me that I would be part of the answer to that need.

As soon as we had got settled, I went to Mid-Africa Ministry for a debriefing on the situation that I had left, and told them that I believed that the Lord was calling me back to Rwanda on a more permanent basis. Interviews and a selection panel followed. It was while I was waiting for the result of the interviews that I remembered thinking, 20 years before, that Africa was still somewhere in the future but that I needed to train as a deaconess first. Now was the time the Lord had been preparing me for. I was delighted when the CMS Panel announced their decision. I was accepted and, in view of the urgent need, I would not have to undergo any further training but could prepare to go straight back.

Plans were made for me to return at the end of July. I sold all my furniture, gave my dog to the vicar in our village, who had always wanted a sheltie, and prepared to go. My commissioning service was at the annual MAM rally in Liverpool where my father was asked to preach. It was the last time he ever preached and it was very powerful. My one big concern was at his frailty. I knew that it was unlikely that I would ever see him again but he did not want me to delay my going for his sake. Indeed there was no knowing how long he would linger. But he was ready to go. I remember him reading a passage from 2 Corinthians 4:16 – 5:8, just before I left. "My tent is wearing out," he said. "There are patches all over it and the zip is stuck. I can't wait to get a new one in heaven."

We had one last week together on the Isle of Wight, staying in a Christian guest house. His appetite had picked up and he was able to go for short walks in a place he had not visited since he was a boy. Then finally the whole family came to the airport to see me off.

Back to Byumba

I had a warm welcome at Byumba, despite the chill in the air. I was to stay in the guest house the bishop had built on to his house. It was small but ideal for me. A widow, whose husband had died just before the war, came three mornings a week to help with the washing and ironing and to do bargaining for me at the market — something I hate! This released me to prepare my lessons. Patricia was a dear, and we had many discussions over lunch before she returned home to care for her three children.

I found that I was expected to teach ten men who had been trained as third letter catechists. I was to give them a crash course in theology and they would be ordained as deacons at the end of the year, as the need for more pastors was so great. I insisted that although I could teach the Bible and church history, others would need to teach Prayer Book, preaching and pastoralia.

The next few months were extremely hard work, but so fulfilling. I would work out my lessons and then fax them to my father who would translate them and fax them back. There was also another pastor in Byumba who spoke English and he helped with translation. I grew to love those ten men, and as my language improved we had very stimulating discussions. I listened to their stories of what had happened to them in the war. One had taken his entire church congregation to the refugee camp in Tanzania and had continued to care for them there. Another had hidden his very pregnant wife in a water butt and was distressed because he had lied to the killers when they came looking for her. She had given birth to their first child that evening! One came from a totally pagan background and told of his fears as he broke oaths he had sworn to Nyabingi, yet nothing had happened to him. "I have proved that the power of Jesus is greater than these spirits," he said. One was a returnee from Uganda, and because he spoke English, he was a great help to me when I could not think of the right word in Kinyarwanda.

Peter dies

Every week my parents would telephone me and we would chat over what we were doing. Then one Thursday in November my father telephoned. I had another whole batch of lessons prepared for translation and asked if he would he be able to do them. There was a pause at the other end. "I have just finished my work for Bible Society," he said. "If you are not in any hurry I could do it, but I am now very slow." That day I prepared what I wanted to fax home but there was a power failure and I was unable to send it off. Next morning I was called out of staff prayers to speak to my mother.

"I'm sorry to tell you," she said, "that Dad went to heaven last night." There was a crackle on the line just as she reached the vital word and I could not tell whether it was heaven or hospital, but eventually the truth sank in. I had been expecting it but I found it so hard to believe. I had to let Marian Kajuga and Emmanuel Kayijuka know the news. The Rwandans use the term, "So and so has responded to the call of God" when they say that someone has died. It used to jar me when they used it of people murdered in the genocide, but it was the only way I could talk of Dad's death as I spoke to those who had known him so well.

I tried to carry on as normal, and went up to teach my first lesson, but the men stopped me. "We have also lost a father," they said. "We cannot take in what you are trying to teach." An hour or so later, Emmanuel was there with me. Over the day, as the news got out, more and more people came to see me, sit with me and share their memories of my father. Emmanuel wanted to come to England with me for the funeral, but could not get a visa. Instead, plans were made to hold a memorial service for him in Kigali to be held at the same time as the funeral in England. I could not decide which to go to, until Bishop Rwaje came back from a conference. "The Rwandans would never understand if you don't go to England," he said. "You must go."

So the following Wednesday I flew back to England to be met by my mother and sister and to hear the full story of Dad's last days. Christine had been over from Singapore and had been able to stay with my parents for a few days, taking them over to Cheltenham, where her children were in school, for a weekend.

Dad had completed the notes he was writing for Scripture Union for the following year. He had just finished the batch of work sent by the Bible Society for him to read and correct. He had completed all the lessons I had sent him. It was as if he waited until all that he had on hand was complete. After he had spoken to me on the telephone, he had told my mother that he was very tired and had spent the day in bed. She had been speaking on the telephone to David's wife, Peta, when she heard him call for her. She went upstairs to him and he collapsed in her arms, dying a few minutes later.

She phoned her doctor who lived nearby and he and his wife both came and did all that was necessary. A neighbour came to sit with her until Peta and then Christine were able to get there. Friends from the church came and they had a very peaceful time by the body, praying together. As one person commented, "It took away my fear of death, to see his obvious joy."

Ross, Christine's husband, flew back from Singapore to speak at the funeral on the following Friday. He asked who would take up the baton that Peter had laid down and "stand in the gap" for an unbelieving world. Mabel Jones gave some memories of Peter as she knew him in the Shyogwe days, and I spoke on behalf of those in Rwanda now. At the graveside, Mum spoke as any widow in Rwanda would, speaking of their life together and the love of the Lord which had kept them for 56 years. She shared, too, some of what she had learned all those years before of the need to walk in the light together. After the service we went back for tea in the village hall and continued with reminiscences for hours. A local clergyman, who had only known Dad as an old man, commented after the funeral, "I never realized what a giant of a man Peter was."

The refugees return

That night we turned on the television for the news and saw the refugees returning to Rwanda in a massive wave of humanity. How my father must have rejoiced in heaven to see it! At last there was a hope for Rwandans to start to live together.

My mother said that she did not want to remain in their house alone but rather to come out to Byumba with me. As a widow she felt that she might be able to help the 30,000 widows in the diocese. I was delighted at the thought of having company, and arrangements were made for us to return just after her 82nd birthday in January. Before that, we wanted to have a memorial service in All Souls, Langham Place, so that some of those who had not had the opportunity to get to Dad's funeral might be there. A friend wrote later that the two most memorable services that she had attended that year were Dad's funeral and memorial service.

My brother, David, spoke on behalf of the family, describing Dad as a truly humble man; Harold Adeney spoke of the years they had shared, as schoolboys and then as missionaries; Emmanuel Oladipo, international secretary for Scripture Union, spoke of his work in Scripture Union; Julienne Munyaneza spoke on behalf of all those who had made Christian marriages because of what Peter had taught; and Rev. Jim Graham spoke of the confidence that Dad had in eternal life. But the highlight of the evening was when my cousin, Jane Goddard, Mary's daughter, sang "I know that my Redeemer liveth" from *The Messiah*. At the end of the service we asked all who were intending to go abroad for the Lord, for however short a time, to come up to the front to be prayed for. Mum and I were going to Rwanda; Christine and Ross and family were going back to Singapore; their eldest daughter, Deborah, was joining her cousin, Simon, on a trip with World Horizons; Harold and Isobel Adeney were going back for a visit to Burundi, to be joined by my mother; others who were going with Tear Fund, Christian Aid, MAM and other societies flocked to the front where the rector, Richard Bewes, prayed for us all.

Just before we left we had a birthday party for Mum at our house with our home group from the church. It ended with them praying for us as we prepared to leave. I shared the sense of reluctance I felt at returning, because the Sunday before I left I had been speaking at a church and after the service someone waved her stump of an arm in my face as she spoke of the problems she was facing. I felt at that point that I could not face going back to such need. A friend, who was staying with us, said that she felt the Lord was saying to me the word "Comfort", not in the sense of feather-bedding but in the sense of the Bayeux Tapestry which pictures Bishop Odo comforting his troops by prodding them forward with a spear!

Promises for Rwanda

A few days later the same friend rang to say that she felt the Lord wanted to speak to me from Isaiah 40:1-5 which starts, "Comfort, comfort my people, says your God. Speak tenderly to Jerusalem and cry to her that her warfare is ended, that her iniquity is pardoned" (RSV), and ends with these words, "The glory of the Lord shall be revealed and all flesh shall see it together" (RSV). I felt that the Lord was saying to me that just as the whole world had seen the shame of Rwanda as they watched the slaughter on television, so the whole world would see the new thing that the Lord would do in Rwanda and would give glory to the Lord.

Buoyed with a sense that God was going to do a new thing in Rwanda, Mum and I set off a few days later for Nairobi, where we saw several friends, although many had returned to Rwanda. In fact, so many came to see us that Niyi Daramola remarked as he was taking us to the airport, "In Africa if you are loved, people exhaust you with their loving!" It was good to have a few days to rest in Kigali before we went to Byumba. We stayed with Emmanuel and Julienne in the house my father had done so much to try to get returned to Scripture Union, which had finally been given back to them about a month before he died.

Emmanuel asked us to go to the widows' meeting which I had spoken at the year before. Antoine Rutayisire was speaking on the passage from Isaiah 40:1-5! He said that they felt that this was the message that the Lord had given to AEE for Rwanda for the coming year. Our first Sunday in Byumba, we heard a man speaking from Zechariah 3:6 – 4:10. Two verses in particular stood out to me, continuing the theme of what I believed that the Lord had already been saying. In 3:9 it says, "I will remove the guilt from this land in a single day" (RSV), and in 4:6 it says, "Not by might, nor by power, but by my spirit, says the Lord of hosts" (RSV). The pastor of Byumba then took us to chapter 8:12-17. He looked at verse 13, "As you have been a byword of cursing among nations... so will I save you and you shall be a blessing" (RSV), but he said there were conditions in verses 16 and 17: "Speak the truth to one another... render true judgements... and do not devise evil in your hearts against one another" (RSV). This was still in the early days following the return of thousands of Hutu and there was an uneasy truce in the land. I felt that this was a true word from the Lord, and wrote to my supporters asking them to pray along these lines for the nation.

Problems with the returning refugees

My mother remarked on how strange it was to go to church in Rwanda where she did not recognize anyone. She had never worked with my father in Byumba and so it did not hold as many memories for her as other places would have done. There were many faces that I did not recognize either, as so many had returned from Zaire in my absence. I gathered from the bishop that it had been quite an exercise when they arrived. The *préfet* and all the churches had co-operated, with all available vehicles taking the returning refugees back to their own home area. Each was provided with appropriate cooking equipment and blankets but as soon as possible everyone was back in their own home. Often the houses had been destroyed but at least the fields were there and as soon as a rough shelter had been built the many widows began to dig their fields for food. Often there were disputes over the fields, and the widows frequently found themselves disadvantaged, and forced to find another home. But if they had the courage to go to the authorities, on the whole the system began to work again and disputes over ownership were fairly heard. The trouble often was that other members of the family, hearing that a brother had died, took over the field and worked it for the two years before the refugees returned, and they were not willing to give up fields that they had begun to regard as their own.

On the whole Byumba did not have as many of these disputes as some other areas which had been predominantly Tutsi areas in the past. There the Tutsi returnees from Uganda, Tanzania or Burundi who had arrived immediately after the genocide, had taken over empty houses. Sometimes these were their family homes from the 1960s which had since been taken over by Hutu families; more often they were simply empty houses, abandoned when their owners were killed or had fled. Now the returning refugees wanted their houses and fields back.

My students had been ordained deacons in December but

were expected to come back for a month at a time, three times before they were made pastors a year later. As I met them again, I asked how they had fared since they had been ordained. All said how different it was to be the one in charge rather than the catechist. Theirs was the responsibility for all that happened and they found it awesome but very fulfilling. One of them told of bitter disputes in his parish, with people claiming the same piece of land sitting on opposite sides of the same church. "How am I ever going to get them to agree?" he asked. "We are all members of the family of Christ but this is tearing us apart."

Another spoke of a spiritual battle going on in a new daughter church he had just started near a centre of influence of Nyabingi. A curse had been put on the church and anyone entering it was possessed by an evil spirit. He had had a message to say that if he went there he would die. "I was afraid," he said, "but I knew that if I did not go to baptize those waiting for me the next day, I would never function again as a pastor." After a day and night of fasting and praying, he climbed the hill to the church next day. He found a scene of utter chaos, as anyone entering the church was possessed, many screaming, others dancing and still others stripping off their clothes. Those awaiting baptism had feared to enter. He decided that they would follow Joshua's example outside Jericho. He led his group of Christians in a hymn as they marched round the church seven times, claiming victory over the powers of darkness, in the name of Jesus. By the time they had finished, all was quiet in the church and he was able to conduct the baptism service. "Many others in the neighbourhood have become believers," he said, "because they saw how much stronger Jesus is than Nyabingi."

Patricia

A day after we arrived, the new curate, one of my students, came to tell me the distressing news that Patricia had been taken ill the day after I had left for England and was dying but wanted to see me. Mum and I walked to her home to visit her and found her lying on a mattress on the floor, with her sister supporting her so that she could speak to us. She was obviously very weak, but still praising the Lord and so happy to see us. We read a passage of the Bible and she asked us to sing a hymn with her. Next day she was taken into hospital and two days later I had an early morning call to say that she had just died. I was expected to go to the hospital to view the body and help prepare her for the funeral which was to be that same day. Surprisingly this was the first funeral I had attended in Rwanda. I was asked to give a few words and said that Patricia had been more than a worker, she had become my friend. After the service in church we drove miles into the hills and then walked, following the coffin, to a beautiful spot on her husband's fields where she was buried in a banana plantation. Soon after this, I heard that her youngest child had also become ill and within a few weeks had died. As so often happens, AIDS had claimed almost the whole family.

Start of widows' work

Soon, Mum, with the pastor's permission, had called together the widows. At the first meeting there were 30, the following meeting 90, and soon afterwards over 400 were meeting regularly for prayer and Bible teaching. They knew that their problems were different from other women and were so grateful to have this opportunity to share and pray together. One blind lady had come to the hospital nearby. It was raining, so hearing singing coming from the church she entered, and never missed a meeting after that.

One Monday I was teaching in the classroom near the church when I heard tremendous sounds of rejoicing coming from the widows' meeting in the church. At lunch Mum told me that one of the women had told how she had gone home the previous week, feeling there was something she still needed to do in her life. "When I became a Christian," she said, "I put right as much as I could before God, but there was one thing I was too frightened to do. Suddenly I knew I had to break the oath which my parents had sworn when they dedicated me to Nyabingi. So when I got home I told my family that I was renouncing Nyabingi. They looked at me expecting me to drop dead. That was a week ago and I tell you today that I am free!" The widows erupted in joy, hugging her and praising God. Then one of the ladies, who only had one leg, jumped up. "I did that ten years ago," she cried. "Am I dead?" and she bounced up and down on her one leg in joy.

If I was not teaching, I would drive my mother and her two helpers, Jeanne and Juliette, out to a place where we could leave the car, and then we would walk along the hillside to visit the ladies in their homes and pray with them. It was heart-rending to see their situations but they were always so pleased to see us and give what hospitality they could. A friend came out to visit and we took her to see some of these widows. She described what she had seen in her home church and suddenly we found that we had money to help some of them put roofs on their houses.

In a meeting, one lady told how her house had been washed away in heavy rains, and the men of her area had refused to help her because she no longer slept with them or got drunk with them, since she had become a Christian. The widows said, "Let us help you." The following Monday, instead of meeting in church, they met at her house. Some cut down trees, others carried water to make mud, others stripped the bark to make thongs to tie the tree trunks together. Once they had the frame, they pressed mud into the gaps and by evening had a rough house. The people around were staggered at this practical example of Christian love. Only two men had turned up — the curate and the diocesan building supervisor. People were amazed that women could build. The diocese provided iron sheets for the roof and by the end of the week the house was complete.

The women had decided to put a small amount of money in a common account each week and a committee decided how it should be used. Some was used to help members who were ill but after a while they decided that what they really wanted was a recognizable uniform. Juliette, Jeanne and I went to Kigali to choose the pattern so that all the women could wear the same clothes. By buying full rolls of the material they were able to save on the cost as it was cheaper than if they had bought it in the market. One Sunday they all came to the cathedral in their new clothes, and led the service. Mum preached and the widows' choir sang. The service was followed by the local non-alcoholic drink which they had prepared from sorghum, and a good time was had by all.

Ephraim

One evening, a few weeks after we had arrived in Byumba, there was a knock at the door and Ephraim walked in. He had come back from Zaire with the others but he said that when he heard that Dad had died, he simply had not been able to face coming to see us. He told us that for the second time he had been separated from Francine and had not known whether she was alive or dead. When the president's plane was brought down, he was very sick with malaria and did not know what was happening. For a month he could hardly move, hidden in what he described as his cave, in Kigali. When the fighting became severe around Kigali, the army evacuated Francine and the children to a town near Kigeme, which was her home area. He was still too sick to move and stayed where he was. Eventually he fled with the other Hutu to Bukavu where he miraculously found Francine! While he was in the camp there, he had received a letter from Dad saying that when he finally returned to England, he would send his accordion to Ephraim. He had been delighted since, during the confusion of the war, he had lost Dad's original gift. He missed it terribly when meetings got going in the camp. He praised God at this news, and vowed that when he had the accordion in hand, he would spend four days fasting and praising God.

Weeks went by and he heard nothing further until one night he heard a voice telling him, "The time has come for you to fulfil your vow." It took a bit of thought to recall the vow and then he said, "But Lord, I promised I would fast when I actually had the accordion." The voice said again, "The time is right for you to fulfil your vow." He woke Francine and told her, and Francine said, "You had better do it then." For the next three days he continued his normal activities while fasting and at night he went to the local Baptist church where they were based and prayed all night. By the third day he was weak and disheartened. "Lord," he said, "is this really you telling me to do this? I have no sign that the accordion is coming. What is this all about?" As he prayed, he was suddenly filled with a sense of joy. A short time afterwards, while he was still praying in the darkened church, he heard footsteps and the door opened. He heard his name called, but in the uncertainties of those days, he feared to answer. Then at last he heard that voice again, "Go on, answer. It is quite safe." He came out of his dark corner and saw a Christian friend. "Ephraim," he said, "your accordion has arrived! Go to Bukavu, to the pastor's house and you will find it." Ephraim's final day of prayer and fasting was filled with joy as he praised the Lord and played his accordion in the church. How he used it over the next few months, in various meetings in the camp. He wrote to thank my father who replied in what must have been one of the last letters he wrote. In fact Ephraim received this letter in January 1997, after he had heard the news of Dad's death and felt that it was a voice from the grave.

In November, when the RPF took over the camp, he and his family were heading deeper into Zaire, when he again heard the voice. "Go back to Rwanda," it said. He was very fearful, because, although he had not been involved in any killing, he had been a soldier of the previous regime. When he got to the border, there was no problem about letting him in and he was soon given new papers allowing him to travel to his home area of Byumba. However, shortly before he reached the border there was a skirmish and the family was caught in the cross-fire. They had to run for safety and Ephraim had to make the hard decision to leave the accordion behind. "It was either that or a child," he said, "but I felt as if it were a child I had left behind!" As soon as the firing stopped he went back to look for the accordion, even though he had heard the voice telling him, "Be comforted, you will receive another accordion." When he got to the area where he had left it, he saw that it was not safe to spend time searching for it, so reluctantly he had to return to his family. We told this story to Containers of Hope and a few months later we were able to present Ephraim with another accordion, to his great delight. The next Sunday he dedicated it to the Lord in the cathedral. He had become a driver for the diocese and the choir leader for the cathedral.

Archdeacon Muzungu

Another welcome visitor was Archdeacon Samson Muzungu. He had been the archdeacon of Byumba when it first became a diocese, and helped the bishop, visiting the camps and doing what he could to encourage and help the people. He had also supervised the building of the larger church to be the new cathedral, which was all paid for by members of the diocese with no out-side help. In the days following the signing of the Arusha peace accords, he had returned to the parish and had distributed a large consignment of aid to help the people restart their disrupted lives. In that consignment from Christian Aid were machetes, hoes, strings of sweet potato plants, seed potatoes and such like. When the RPF soldiers again approached Byumba two Sundays after the president's death, he was leading a service in church. His wife was frightened that the fighting was so near and wanted to flee but he felt he had to lead the service and distribute beans that were being stored. "They will only be taken by the soldiers if our people don't take them," he said. He told his wife to go and he would catch up with her and their small children. When he saw the soldiers approach the bishop's house, he fled from his own across the road. When he got to the valley, he found that there was a large column of soldiers between him and where he had told his wife that he would meet her. He turned the other way and by slow degrees made his way to Shyogwe. His wife, meanwhile, had heard that all the men in Byumba had been killed by the advancing soldiers, and mourned her husband as dead for three long years.

Muzungu fled to Zaire where he was teaching a Bible class one day when he was called out to listen to the radio. To his horror he heard that he was accused, as a senior churchman, of distributing the machetes which had been used in the genocide. No one explained that it was a gift from Christian Aid. This was the broadcast which had so distressed my father when he heard it in England. He was so glad to tell us what had really happened.

Over the next few weeks we heard many stories of the Lord's protection during the war years, as we gradually settled into a routine in our little house. Mum was fully involved with the widows, but she was able to take over Dad's role as translator for my lessons. It was not until 2001 that I felt confident enough in Kinyarwanda to write my lessons directly in the language. I do thank God for all my parents did for me in those early days of teaching. I could not have managed without their help and encouragement.

Chapter 14

Passing On the Baton (1997-2001)

Visit of Deborah and Simon

On what would have been my father's birthday in April 1997, we had a very welcome phone call from my nephew, Simon, David's son. With his cousin, Deborah, he had been with a team from World Horizons, travelling through Europe, the Middle East and Africa, to deliver a van to a mission group in Kenya. They had left the others there and were heading by bus across Kenya and Uganda, and hoped to be with us in a few days' time.

I was in a meeting, struggling to understand what was going on, when I suddenly saw Deborah standing in the door of the church. They had tried to cross the border the night before but found that the Rwanda side had closed, so they pitched their tent in no man's land. That morning they had met a pastor who spoke English and was coming to the meeting in Byumba. He had helped them get a minibus, called a taxi in Rwanda, and had shown them where to get off. They had left Simon with the luggage, and Deborah had hitched a lift with the pastor. I borrowed a car and drove down to collect Simon, who was entertaining the local children with his guitar. I was reminded of my father playing his accordion wherever he had an audience!

It was wonderful to hear the story of their adventures and to listen to them as they preached at every opportunity. It was so encouraging to see the younger generation also filled with a zeal for Jesus Christ. Every time I looked at Simon I would have a sense of *déjà vu*, because he reminded me so of my father, not so much physically, as in his passion for preaching the gospel. Deborah was only able to stay a short time but Simon wanted to stay for two months. We arranged for them to spend a week with the schools worker at Scripture Union, while I finished teaching my course. Then we set off for a tour of Rwanda and Burundi.

My mother had had a wonderful two weeks in Burundi earlier in the year, with her old friends Harold and Isobel Adeney, but she was looking forward to a return trip. John Riches, who was working with African Revival Ministries, had arranged to collect us when he was next up on one of his regular trips to Rwanda. We had a good trip down and stayed in his lovely house in Bujumbura, with a beautiful view out over the lake. Burundi was going through a period of relative calm, although there were still signs of the war they had been experiencing in recent years.

We went to visit Carl and Eleanor Johnson, who had looked after my sister, Christine, when she went to school in Bujumbura. They had moved from their beautiful old house up on the hill above the city, and were now in the suburb, which had been hardest hit in recent months. Over 20,000 displaced persons had descended on them, and Eleanor took us round, showing us how they had set up feeding centres and medical facilities in the canvas city of UN sheeting huts all in straight lines. Carl and Eleanor were of my parents' generation and had spent a lifetime in Burundi. At one stage the government had told Carl, along with other missionaries, that he had to leave the country. Carl had replied, "I'm sorry, but God has not told me to go, so I'm staying!" They threatened to remove his passport and force him out. He smiled and said, "Until God tells me to go, I'm staying." After a time they stopped trying to make him leave, and for many years he and Eleanor were the only missionaries in the country.

A few weeks before I started writing this chapter, I heard that Carl had gone to be with the Lord he had served so faithfully, dying in the night. Over 2,000 turned up at his funeral next day, a witness to the love and respect the Burundians felt for him. Barely two weeks later, violence erupted again in Burundi and, once more, Eleanor found herself caring for 6,000 displaced persons.

Back in 1997, Simon and Deborah went to a Scripture Union camp up country, while my mother and I took it easy in Bujumbura. In fact, I had the pleasure of a sail in Harry Johnson's sailing boat and a swim in the middle of the lake where I could be sure no crocodiles could get me!

John Riches kindly drove us up to Matana where many memories were brought back. We stood by Harold's grave and read the inscription, "A workman that needeth not to be ashamed, rightly dividing the word of truth" (2 Timothy 2:15 KJV). In the church vestry we saw a photograph of Harold and gasped. It could have been Simon! We visited Margaret's old home and I pictured Christmases there. It came to me, very strongly, how wonderfully Simon would fit into the life in Burundi with his fluent French. I was very careful, however, not to say this, having suffered in my youth from those who asked me if I would be a missionary like my parents and grandparents! Finally we had to leave to return to Bujumbura and then back to Rwanda, so that Deborah could fly home. Simon stayed on for a few more weeks before leaving to go on the Cornhill training course in London.

Installation of new bishops

Life seemed very empty once they left, but I had to make a round of various dioceses where new bishops were to be installed. Following all the problems of the Anglican Church, just before the genocide, the government had accused some bishops, and the archbishop, of involvement in the genocide, not in the sense of actually killing, but because they had not opposed it. Bishop Rwaje of Byumba was the dean of the province and acting primate. The situation was complicated because three of the bishops refused to resign; there were endless talks with leaders of the Anglican communion worldwide, so that the situation could be sorted out and new bishops legally installed. Without Bishop Rwaje's wisdom and patience during this difficult time, I believe the Anglican Church would never have recovered in this country. Finally all was resolved and new bishops were installed in every diocese, with a new one being created out of Byumba and Kibungo, so that the dioceses could follow the boundaries of the préfectures. Once there was a legally constituted house of bishops they could elect a new archbishop. I shall never forget seeing Bishop Rwaje the day after Archbishop Kolini had been installed in Kigali. He looked ten years younger. "At last," he said, "I have time to devote to my own diocese."

Bible training

A priority for him was training and development, and he has built a large training centre in which I have a classroom. The problem is that it is so well used that I frequently have to be moved into a small room in the diocesan offices! I thoroughly enjoy my role of teaching and am mainly teaching catechists. These are men and women who have been put in charge of daughter churches in each parish. They love the Lord and know their Bibles well but have had little or no education, many only just finishing primary school. They have had no Bible training of any sort but are in charge of churches whose number varies from 60 to 500! My task is to teach them to understand the basics of the Christian faith. I have discovered that most of them know their Bibles as well if not better than I do, but that they do not know how to evaluate the text, or even to put it together. It is great fun teaching the minor prophets and putting them into their context of 1 and 2 Kings, for example!

With a plethora of new churches and sects coming into Rwanda since the genocide, it seems to me a priority to help people to think about their faith, and to give them the tools so that they can sort out truth from error. The education system of Rwanda is against this. They are so used to someone standing at the front and telling them what they need to know, then writing that information on the blackboard. The students then write it in a book, learn it by heart and reproduce it in exams. This might help them to pass exams, but it is not teaching them to evaluate information.

I teach by asking questions. I say, Find the answer in such and such a verse. They look it up and have to analyse the verse to get the answer. At first they found this stressful. Why was I not giving them the answers? But as discussions got going about the true meaning of a particular passage, so they began to appreciate what I was trying to do. They still find it hard that I give them several pages of notes about church history, for example, or the background information on the Assyrians or Babylonians. "What are we to learn for the exams?" is a constant cry. They have not been taught, as we have in the West, how to read a page of writing and take out key sentences to summarize it. This is hardly surprising since there is so little literature in their own language and most of my students speak no other. My desire, like my father's before me, is to get books written in their language — but even when they are available they are so expensive that they are beyond the reach of most of my students!

Another problem I face is the literalistic interpretation of the Scriptures, which leads to a very legalistic form of Christianity. How can I show that there might be other ways of interpreting a passage, without at the same time destroying their belief in the Bible as God's word? With a strong Seventh Day Adventist Church in the country, a frequently asked question is: "Why do we worship on Sundays rather than Saturdays?" The Pentecostals often teach that you cannot be a Christian unless you have been baptized by full immersion, a problem for us Anglicans! Others teach that it is a sin to eat rabbit or pork, because of the Levitical food laws. Problems are also brought regarding polygamy, which is totally accepted by non-Christians. How should this matter be dealt with by the church? There are also some hair-raising stories of people claiming gifts of the Spirit but using them in destructive ways. It is important to teach about the person and work of the Holy Spirit and how to use his gifts to build up the church rather than an individual.

I have found it a challenge to evaluate these questions myself, and more important, to give them the biblical tools so that they can evaluate them for themselves. This has been my work for the past five years and I love it! Yet I am aware that I constantly need to be on the alert, not to give quick and facile answers to their questions. I thank God for the many people praying for me, particularly in Britain. I also thank God for my mother, with whom I could discuss thorny issues, and for the freedom I have to talk things through with Bishop Rwaje who has been a tower of strength, supporting me in so many different ways.

Our new home

It was wonderful to live in the guest end of the bishop's house for the first couple of years we were in Byumba, but once Josephine and the family returned from Kenya where she had been studying, it was obvious that we needed to move on, since there was now nowhere that he could accommodate his many visitors. He offered us a large house up the hill from the diocese, but we were very nervous of that road. It would also have meant a longer walk than Mum felt she could do on her own, which she felt would seriously hamper her usefulness in the church. Finally we were able to move into a small house right next to the church, which has been ideal, and has become a real home.

The reason we were so nervous of the road to the first house was because of what had happened one evening when we had walked up the hill to visit our neighbours, a pastor and his wife. As the custom is in Rwanda, they were walking part of the way home with us in the half-light of late evening. We heard a car coming down the hill behind us and moved on to the verge of the road. Next moment I felt myself hurled across the ditch. In the uneasy peace of that time, my first thought was that I had been shot in the back. Then as I looked round and saw that all four of us were lying in various attitudes round the road, I thought that a grenade had been thrown at us. Perhaps I may be excused these thoughts for there were a number of soldiers around. Only then did I see that a blue lorry was stopped in front of an army car, and realized that we had been knocked over by it. My mother was lying in the ditch, and I thought she was dead. "Are you all right, Mum?" I cried. "No," she said. I was just relieved to hear her talk at all! Once we got her upright, we found that she had a nasty gash on her leg and she was taken to the nearby hospital in the soldiers' car, where we found our pastor already waiting for us. His four-year-old son had seen the accident and had told his father that the *umukecuru* or "old lady" was dead! Indeed she had lost so much blood in the road that many others thought the same. In fact she was the only one of us to be injured, and after several weeks incapacitated with a severely sprained ankle, she made a good recovery and was back at work with the widows, saying, "God still has work for me to do."

Another brides' school

Life was very full in Byumba. I was busy teaching catechists, and Mum had been asked to start a new venture. The widows had said how helpful they had found their meeting, and were wondering what could be done for their daughters, who had finished primary school, but could not afford secondary school. They were very vulnerable to unscrupulous men, who feared AIDS and felt that a young girl was the answer to their sexual needs.

After a lot of thought and prayer, Mum decided, with the pastor, that the answer would be a similar meeting to the widows, with prayer and Bible teaching, but that they would also try to teach them a skill such as sewing and embroidery so that they would have some means of earning a living and of helping their widowed mothers.

My sister, Christine, had come out for a fortnight to be with Mum on the anniversary of Dad's death, and to join in a memorial service for him arranged by Scripture Union a year after his funeral. The cathedral was packed with many of his old friends wanting to share their memories of him. Mum was to write later that the Lord had helped by providing special things on each of the potentially painful anniversaries of that first year of her bereavement. Simon and Deborah had telephoned on Dad's birthday and were with us for their wedding anniversary. Now Christine was here for the time of remembering his death.

Christine was at the second meeting for the girls. A week earlier they had arrived in a rainstorm, but despite the weather 30 girls had turned up, and the following week there were over 50. She helped distribute lengths of material and needles and showed some of them how to hold needles, as it was the first time many had tried to sew. After learning a few basic stitches which they sewed on ruled lines to enable them to sew in a straight line, the girls were to embroider their names on a length of material which would be formed into a bag in which they could keep future work.

A few days after she had returned to England, Christine was at a Bible study with her brother, David, and his wife, Peta. She was asked to tell them about her time in Rwanda and mentioned the need for hand sewing-machines. One of those present was an airline pilot who rarely attended the group. His jaw dropped as she was speaking. "I don't believe this," he said. "Just today I have been shown round a warehouse filled with hand and treadle sewing-machines which no one knows how to use!" "My mother does!" replied Christine. Although these particular machines were not used, this conversation led to a regular supply of sewing-machines being sent to Byumba by container through Faith in Action, a Christian organization which sends supplies to needy people in Africa. This was the start of a very helpful partnership between that church and our girls' meeting as they began sending out all sorts of sewing materials and clothes. Recently, similar meetings have been started in several other parishes to which we have also been able to give sewing-machines.

Later, this girls' meeting developed into a sort of brides' school similar to that started by Lindesay and Eseri back in the early days of Matana, with some of the brighter girls learning to use the machines, embroider and cook. The Tuesday meeting, however, continued for Bible teaching and prayer as well as sewing. Mum discovered that, because their schooling had been so disrupted through years of war, some of the girls did not know how to read. On Thursday mornings she started reading classes, using reading books written by Dad years back. She was helped by the parish cleaner, Julienne, who eventually became so enthusiastic that she took over the teaching. Whenever a girl was able to demonstrate that she could read a passage of the Bible, Mum would give her a Bible, provided by a friend who gave us a regular donation to enable the poor to have their own Bibles.

Protection in danger

I had started by visiting all my students in their parishes and ended up visiting every parish in the diocese, which meant that most weekends we travelled, often considerable distances, to preach at the Sunday services. Inevitably a large meal was provided and it was rare that we were able to get back before dark. The roads were atrocious and in my letters home I wrote of several instances where the angels had worked hard to protect us. One friend wrote back that she thought I needed a whole battalion of angels just for us! Another friend commented after a visit, "I noticed that you started every journey with prayer and it wasn't very long before I realized why!"

We were very conscious of God's protection in all our travelling, and also in the house, which was several times struck by lightning. Eventually we discovered that the electricity had not been earthed and we put in a lightning conductor as well. In the early days of recovery in Byumba, most of the skilled workers had been killed or were refugees, and so some of the buildings left much to be desired!

One student I visited was very distressed because one of his catechists, also a student of mine, had been killed by guerillas who were raiding from the Virunga mountains, as Paul Kagame and the RPF had done before them. The parish had a wonderful view across a swampy valley to Muhabura beyond. As I looked out over the swamp I could see columns of smoke rising from the reeds. "The soldiers are searching for guerilla fighters," I was told. "They make a shelter among the reeds, above the level of the water. When the soldiers find one they set fire to it." As I watched, another column of smoke rose and I saw a line of soldiers beating the swamp, for all the world like a line of beaters at a pheasant hunt. It was horrible to watch this manhunt, but the people I spoke to said that it was the only way to get rid of the remaining *interahamwe* whose only aim was to destabilize the government and who did not care how many people were killed in the process. I have recently visited again and worshipped in the church built by the Christians right through those troubled years as a symbol of their hope for the future. They told me that finally there is peace in the area and they can start rebuilding their lives.

Simon takes up the baton

While we were busy in Byumba, we had occasional news of Simon. At Easter 1998, he spent a month in Cambodia, wondering if this might be where God wanted him to work, but he became very ill there. Although he had a burden for the country, he realized that he could not work in that climate. That summer we had a letter saying that he simply did not know what God wanted him to do when he finished his course a month or so later. There were several possibilities, one of which was Burundi. Had we any advice? I wrote back very tentatively that I could see him working in Burundi, but I think even before he received my letter a series of remarkable events had taken place. Robert de Berry, then general secretary of Mid-Africa Ministry, had sought him out on the second last day at the Bible course.

Simon still did not know what the Lord wanted him to do and was stubbornly praying, "Lord, I'll go anywhere and do anything so long as you make it clear what you want of me." Robert and Simon were both members of the same church, although they went to different services and so did not normally meet. Robert spoke passionately about the needs in Burundi and the opportunities for the gospel. Simon listened excitedly, wondering whether this might be what the Lord wanted for him. A few days later, he returned to his marketing job in Woking. There he prayed, "Lord, today, as I sit in front of this computer, I want you to give me a sign about Burundi." Shortly afterwards, the phone rang and he heard a voice say, "Do you know anyone who wants to work in Burundi?" That extraordinary "coincidence" was all he needed as very specific confirmation to a very specific prayer. The friend who rang had no idea that Simon was even considering going to Burundi!

A few days later he rang us up to say that he had just had a meeting with the personnel secretary of MAM, Chris Hindley, son of Godfrey who had worked for so many years at Shyira. Simon was coming out as a volunteer and would spend three months in Byumba, learning Kinyarwanda, which is so similar to Kirundi that he would have no difficulty in changing over.

Madeleine

In October 1998 I went to the airport to meet him. I had just come back from Kigeme, where I had taken a friend to see a different part of the country, and had found that Bishop Norman, though welcoming, was not his usual ebullient self. A few days later, we were getting ready to leave for an MAM conference in Uganda when we heard the shocking news that Madeleine, Bishop Norman's wife, had died in Kenya. Instead of going to Uganda we went to the airport where the body had been flown in, and then joined the long cortège back to Kigeme for the funeral.

Madeleine and Norman had both come to faith early in 1970 and he was one of the new bishops who had to be re-consecrated the day the war reached Byumba. My mother remembered going to a Roman Catholic school where Madeleine had been transferred from Kigeme School, and asking if the Protestant girls could come to church with them. They were told that, provided Madeleine was with them, there would be no problem as she was the most trustworthy girl in the school. She had a passion for sharing with anyone she met what Jesus had done for her.

She had recently been ordained as a pastor in Kigeme and had a real burden for the young people of Rwanda who had been through such traumatic times. She also had a gift for writing and had already published a book in Kinyarwanda, and was writing another. At the funeral we were told that, a few weeks earlier, she had heard the Lord tell her that he was going to take her home. She had argued with him that her family needed her, that she had an unfinished book and that the young people of Kigeme also needed her. She heard the Lord say, "I can take care of all that." She had shared all this with her husband, which explains why he was so subdued when I saw him. She went to see a friend to explain what she was trying to write in her book and to ask her to complete it for her. The friend had said that she must have heard the Lord wrongly, but Madeleine replied, "I know my Lord's voice by now, and that is what he said." She had then flown to Kenya to see her children who were all in school there, and was preparing to go to speak at an evangelistic meeting when she was electrocuted by a faulty bathroom heater and died before she could reach hospital.

The church was packed at Kigeme and the service went on until sunset when we had to leave if we were to go to Uganda the next day. We arrived in time for the final communion service and then Mum and I stayed on for a rest while Simon took my car to Entebbe to meet his parents, who were coming for a brief visit. We had a happy week with David and Peta, visiting Shyogwe where he had grown up, and travelling on to Kigeme to spend a little time with Bishop Norman. Madeleine had stayed with David and Peta in England a few months before, and they had been in Kenya when she died and had joined others for a memorial service there.

The fourth generation

For the next three months Simon stayed with a Rwandan pastor and his wife, doing language study, and coming out at the weekends to visit different parishes with us. He was feeling very unsettled because he had heard from MAM that the bishop of Bujumbura had said that he did not need another evangelist, since he had several, but that he wanted Simon to be an administrator. "I am not an administrator," said Simon, "I am an evangelist — and I only joined MAM because they said they needed evangelists in Burundi."

Robert de Berry was to come out in January 1999 and travel down to Burundi with him to try to sort out his future. In November, Mum had gone to a Scripture Union meeting in Kigali, where she had met Safari, the SU general secretary in Burundi. She had told him that her grandson was going to Burundi, and he had said, "How we need someone like Simon." Simon, too, felt that working with Scripture Union would be ideal. Working with SU meant that he would not be attached to any one church, but would have a brief to preach in all of them, and also their work was concentrated on youth for whom he had a real burden. He began praying that the Lord would open up the way for him to work with Scripture Union in Burundi.

On Simon's last night in Byumba, Mum prayed that the Lord would overrule so that he could work at SU in Burundi. Simon packed, said goodbyes and headed off for Kigali for his last night in Rwanda. In Kigali, he went to the SU guest house where he met Robert de Berry to talk things over. Just then, the head of Scripture Union, Burundi, stopped off on his way to Tanzania. He was delighted to meet Simon. "Ever since your grandmother told me about you," he said, "we have been praying that you could join us in Scripture Union." None of them could get over the way they had come together. Here they were, three men from three different countries, on their way to two different countries, praying the same agenda, meeting in the same guest house in the capital city for just ten minutes! That was all the time it took. Each of them saw the Lord's hand in it and they prayed together before they went their separate ways.

Next day, having seen the SU buildings in Bujumbura, he sent out an SOS email to his praying friends: "Pray that I can work for SU. They are in a terrible state and don't even have a computer!" That very morning, a friend in London woke up and prayed, "Lord, whom do you want me to give this computer to?" He then logged on to email and read that message from Simon!

After all these coincidences, the bishop of Burundi, recognizing the Lord's hand in it, graciously seconded Simon to Scripture Union. "After all," he said, "if you work for Scripture Union, you work for us all."

So, nearly 75 years after his great-grandparents left England for Uganda, Simon Guillebaud started work in Bujumbura, the fourth generation of our family to work for the Lord in these two little countries in the heart of Africa. How faithful the Lord has been to us over these years!

Postscript

On Sunday 9th September 2001, Elisabeth preached to a full church on a special day for the widows. The pastor, Samuel Kayitare, had said that he wanted it to be a special day to show all people that, contrary to custom, widows are valued as members of the body of Christ. Elisabeth began by giving her testimony, adding that she was getting old and weak and unable to see who had come to visit her, but quoting 2 Corinthians 4:16, she said, "Though my outer nature is wasting away, yet my inner nature is being renewed every day." She went on to preach from Jonah chapter 4, speaking about the reluctant prophet who had been successful in his own land but who, rather than preach to his enemies, had fled to the other end of the known world. Even when he eventually obeyed God and preached judgement on Nineveh, he was horrified when they repented and God withheld his judgement. Elisabeth challenged the church: "Are we willing to receive God's forgiveness or are we, like Jonah, still holding on to our anger and refusing to accept that God could possibly bless our enemies?" She ended her sermon with these words: "We do not know at what time death will take us, and then it will be too late to accept the mercy God is holding out to you. I pray that we will not hear the men of Nineveh reproach us (Matthew 12:38-41) because we refused to accept God's mercy to us."

As I listened to my mother I suddenly felt that this was the last time I would hear her preach, and afterwards many were amazed at her strength in giving a full sermon, saying that they had expected only ten minutes or so from her in her frailty. But there was nothing frail in what she said. Following the sermon, the widows began dancing and Elisabeth joined them. After the service there was a meal in the church which went on until about 4 p.m.

Then we went to visit a couple whose wedding we had attended the previous day. It was down a steep slope and I suggested that she stayed in the car while I went down for a few minutes, but she insisted on coming with me. After about half an hour the bridegroom and a friend helped her up the hill, with me pushing behind. "They are more out of breath than I am," said my mother at the top! After telephoning John in England, we had supper, played Scrabble, prayed and went to bed.

Next morning I found that she had had a stroke in the night. I called for the doctor and she was transferred to a hospital in Kigali where she lingered for two days without regaining consciousness, and finally, at 6.30 a.m. on 12th September 2001, she passed quietly into the presence of the Lord she had served so long. I was holding her hand and saying the *nunc dimittis* as she went.

A week later, my brother David and his wife Peta having flown out to join me, we had a triumphant funeral service in Byumba Cathedral with about 1,200 people present, who had travelled from all over the country and Uganda, to pay their last tribute to their dearly loved *mukecuru*. A tropical downpour meant that the committal was disrupted, although this was interpreted as God's blessing being sent from the *mukecuru*! Her final resting place is a beautiful spot overlooking the hills of the country she loved so much.

Afterthoughts

When I returned to Rwanda with my parents in 1995, I was asked, and was myself asking, a lot of questions. I have continued to wrestle with many of them and what I present here does not pretend to be a definitive answer, but these are some of the conclusions that I have come to as a result of struggling with these questions before the Lord.

I   Why did Christian Rwanda experience genocide?

The first question to ask is, "How Christian was Rwanda?" In the 1991 census 90% of Rwandans called themselves Christians — 62% Roman Catholic, 18% Protestant, 8% Adventist; the rest were Muslim or had traditional African religions — but as one Roman Catholic priest said, "We baptized many people but we did not disciple them as Christians." Another, in the Burundi context, said, "We have sacramentalized the Barundi, we have not evangelized them" (quoted in Roger Bowen's J. C. Jones lecture).

Despite the two Revivals I have described, there needs to be a fresh movement of the Holy Spirit in every generation for the effects to live on. I was brought up on the saying, "God has no grandchildren." In other words, everyone needs to have a personal encounter with God and cannot rely on what their parents know of him. Both in 1959 and again in 1994, it was apparent that many church people were going through the ritual without having a dynamic personal faith in the Lord Jesus.

David Ndaruhutse of African Revival Ministries was asked this question. He said that in his opinion there were only about 8% of Rwandans who were true, Bible-believing, Spirit-filled Christians in the country — and he added that they did not get involved in the killing. Indeed, as I hope I have shown, they were willing to risk all to save others, and several of them were themselves killed.

Antoine Rutayisire, of African Evangelistic Enterprises, was quoted in a book, *The Peacemaking Power of Prayer* by John D. Robb and James A. Hill: "Before the Genocide up to 90% of the people were merely nominal Christians due to the failure of the church to do the work of discipling these multitudes." Robb adds, quoting Rutayisire, "In his opinion only 10% were 'real Christians' that is, committed to the lordship of Jesus Christ over their lives. He and others I spoke with said it was the nominal or cultural 'Christians' who did the killing, not the minority of true believers" (pp 178-9).

Even during the first Revival which had such an impact worldwide, it was not the numbers that made the difference but the quality of their lives. As one person said to me, "For the first time the devious Rwandans were seeing truly transparent lives and they were bowled over by it." This was why the message spread so far and so quickly. But a Kenyan observer said at the time, "This has come at a time before the effects of civilization have really made an impact on this country. I wonder how long it will last as they are drawn into the modern world." Sadly many did indeed compromise their faith as more and more material wealth came into the country, but then the apostle Paul also had found one of his converts backsliding when he wrote that "Demas, because he loved this world, has deserted me and gone to Thessalonica" (2 Timothy 4:10). It is not a new phenomenon!

Second, the church was not in good heart at the time of the genocide. I have described some of the difficulties within the Anglican Church but it was not the only church with problems. Many church leaders were living sinful lives, the teaching in the churches was often shallow and, as a result, Christians were not being discipled. There was a longing to be filled with the Holy Spirit but often from selfish motives. They wanted the power of the Holy Spirit for their own manipulative purposes and for self-fulfilment. I have heard it said that God allowed the genocide in order to cleanse his church, and there may be some truth in this, difficult though it may be to comprehend. There is no denying that sometimes God allows his people to experience difficulties in the hope that this will turn them back to himself (see for example Amos 4:6-13; Haggai 2:17 and Romans 1:18-32).

Many Christians said that before the war they were believers in name only, but the hardships they experienced threw them on the Lord and they proved him in a way that they had only dreamed about before.

Another reason for the lack of dynamism within the church was the practice of syncretism. Particularly in the Roman Catholic Church, which is far and away the biggest church in Rwanda, the early missionaries dismissed the cultural beliefs in ancestral spirits and their powers over the lives of the living as "nonsense". Traditionally Rwandans believed that there was a Creator God but he was remote and far from the lives of people, who had no way of contacting him. Instead, their lives were dominated by fear of *abazimu*, or spirits of all who died. I remember one of my students saying, "You are so lucky if you were brought up in a Christian home and were not taught to fear the spirits. I loved my mother, but when she died I suddenly had to fear her and the way her spirit tormented me." In order to control these spirits, many Rwandans would practise *kubandwa*, which meant identifying themselves with a small group of controlling spirits, or *imandwa*, which meant that they no longer feared their ancestral spirits.

Antoine Rutayisire says that the early missionaries missed an opportunity. Instead of showing that God is even stronger than these controlling spirits and, that if you approached him through Jesus Christ, there was no longer any need to fear the *imandwa*, they said this was all nonsense. As a result, although many had a real belief in Jesus Christ and were happy that they could pray to their remote God, it was an intellectual belief and they were still left with the very real fear of the spirits. They would go to church to pray to God, and then return home to make offerings, propitiating the spirits. Antoine quotes his mother, a devout Roman Catholic, who would take him to traditional ceremonies. When he asked her why, she replied, "There are some things which the white man's God can help with, and other things which need to be dealt with by Rwandan methods."

My grandfather carefully examined the traditional beliefs about their God and came to the conclusion that there was nothing in them that was against the biblical view of God, although the Bible taught more than these beliefs. He therefore chose their name for God, *Imana*, for use in the Bible, but the Roman

Catholics had used the Swahili name *Mungu*, which meant that this new religion was alien in its language, and was indeed the "white man's God". Despite the fact that Protestants did not feel this same alienation from God, they too, practised traditional beliefs, because the early missionaries had not taught them how to deal with their fear of spirits. I will be discussing all this again later in a question about Satan, but I believe that even though so many Christians believed in Jesus Christ, the fact that at the same time they practised the traditional religion meant that they allowed Satan to have control of their lives, through the controlling spirits, and that there was a spiritual dimension to the genocide, which is not always recognized.

When I was in Kigali in 1995 listening to so many stories of those who had stood firm, as well as those who had failed, I prayed, "What was it, Lord, that made the difference?" That Sunday I was reading the passage set for the first Sunday in Lent, Hebrews 2:14-18, and I think I saw one answer. Jesus, in his death, destroyed the power of the devil who had kept people in lifelong bondage *through fear of death*. Those who genuinely did not fear death because they knew it was a gateway to the presence of the Lord they had served in life, were able to stand firm and face death despite their fear. But those who did not have that confidence, feared that this life was all there was and compromised on their Christian faith.

Having said that, I doubt if any one of us has had to face the pressure that many Rwandans faced in that dreadful time. How would you or I react if we were told to kill a neighbour or have our children killed? This was no idle threat as many found out when their babies were indeed slaughtered before their eyes. Also, although some might not have feared death itself, they did fear the manner of dying. Many were prepared to pay the killers so that they could be shot rather than hacked to death.

II How do I forgive the killing of my wife? Doesn't that set them free to kill again?

Wilberforce said this to me as I travelled back to Kigali from Gahini with him in 1995. As far as I remember, I replied something like this, "However hard, you need to be willing to forgive for your own sake, since lack of forgiveness leads to bitterness and hardness of spirit. God freely holds out forgiveness to us all but we cannot receive that forgiveness unless we acknowledge our sin and seek his forgiveness. In the same way, though you might have forgiven, the killers will not be able to receive your forgiveness unless they acknowledge their sin and ask you for it."

I think I would still say something similar, but over the past few years of teaching, I have come to realize something about the Kinyarwanda word for forgiveness. In their thinking, to forgive means that there will be no consequences as a result of sin. A widow whom I had helped lied to me in order to get more. I told her that I had forgiven her but that she would not receive one franc more from me and that she needed to learn that sin brought its own consequences. Her reaction was, "That means that you have not forgiven me."

On one occasion I was discussing with a class of deacons the incident in Numbers 13 and 14 when Moses sent the spies into the Promised Land. Ten of them returned saying that it was indeed a wonderful land but that the inhabitants were too strong for them to tackle. Caleb and Joshua said, "Yes, the inhabitants are strong, but we have the Lord with us and he is stronger!" They pleaded with the people not to rebel against the Lord, but their reaction was to try to stone them! God told Moses that he would destroy the people and make a new nation from Moses, but Moses was anguished on behalf of his people and also he feared for the good name of the Lord, because the Egyptians would say that God was not strong enough to do what he promised. So he pleaded with God on behalf of his people. "In accordance with your great love, forgive the sin of this people, just as you have pardoned them from the time they left Egypt until now. Then the Lord replied, 'I have forgiven them, as you asked. Nevertheless, as surely as I live and as surely as the glory of the Lord fills the whole earth, not one of the men who saw my glory and the miraculous signs I performed in Egypt and in the desert but who disobeyed me and tested me ten times — not one of them will ever see the land I promised on oath to their forefathers. No one who has treated me with contempt will ever see it'" (Numbers 14:19-23).

As I reached this point in the story, all the men protested. "How can God say he forgives them and yet still punish them?" We had a long discussion about the nature of forgiveness and how the consequences of sin are not automatically done away with. AIDS is very common in the country and they could see that someone who had committed adultery and contracted AIDS could confess his sin and be received back into fellowship and yet still die of AIDS. Yet the Kinyarwanda word for forgiveness involves forgetting the consequences, and they find it hard to think differently.

They consider that a person who forgives someone for the murder of a loved one must inevitably tell the courts that they want the murderer set free. No wonder there are few people prepared to do this, and that bitterness continues to fester in their hearts. How can forgiveness and the desire for justice go together? I recently read an article by Alan Harbinson, which compared the very different reactions to appalling things which two people had suffered. The mother of Lesley-Ann Downes who was tortured to death by Myra Hindley and Ian Brady in the Moors murders, said that she could never forgive Hindley for what she had done. Even after death she would return to haunt her. While such statements are understandable, the hatred and bitterness has taken its toll. Her face shows how much it consumes her. By contrast, Jill Saward, who was raped and beaten up in the so-called vicarage rape, said how hard it was to forgive the men who had violated her. But then she saw that failure to forgive would keep her enthralled to them. "I did not want them to have such power over me," she said, and forgave them. Her face shows the peace that God has given her as a result, despite the fact that the men concerned showed no signs of repentance.

Much has been said in recent years about forgiveness, since Gordon Wilson publicly forgave those who killed his daughter at the Enniskillen bombing. This did not mean that he considered that the bombers should be allowed to escape justice. Since then, I have noticed a tendency for journalists to ask people who have just suffered appalling loss whether they forgive the killers. It strikes me as a crass and irrelevant question. Despite the grace given to Gordon Wilson, forgiveness is not a facile emotion but is often a hard-won battle, as my friend Edith found when it took a whole year for her to be able to forgive the killer of her beloved aunt.

David Pawson, in his book *Once Saved, Always Saved?*, points out that there are two conditions for forgiveness. In Luke 17:3-4

Jesus says, "If your brother sins, rebuke him; and if he repents, forgive him. If he sins against you seven times in a day, and seven times comes back to you saying 'I repent,' forgive him." In other words, our forgiveness should be unlimited, *provided he repents*. The other precondition for forgiveness is brought out well in the parable of the unforgiving servant in Matthew 18:21-35. Having been forgiven, the servant was not prepared to show mercy to another servant, and his Lord then revoked his forgiveness and flung him out. These are sobering words, but I think it is clear that we must at least be prepared to forgive if we want to receive the forgiveness of God.

Charles Colson, who founded the organization Prison Fellowship, came to realize that there is also a need to help the victims of crime, so he started an organization called Neighbours who Care. In 1999, following a symposium of many victims of crime and those trying to help them, a book of essays was produced called *God and the Victim — Theological Reflections on Evil, Victimization and Forgiveness*.

One chapter was called "Forgive and forget and other myths of forgiveness" by Dr Dan B. Allender. He describes what he terms the myths of forgiveness, such as "forgetting the harm". He describes one man

> who seemed enormously proud that he had forgiven his alcoholic father and promiscuous mother. I asked him if he ever felt overwhelmed by the sadness of his personal history. He responded "I've forgiven them. I don't look behind me. I just press on like Paul to the goal of godliness." For him forgiveness meant cutting losses, ignoring the pain of the past and keeping busy enough to outpace the sadness.

I have met many in Rwanda who would say the same. When I first went back to Rwanda in 1995 people wanted to pour out their stories as soon as they met us, but over the past few years no one speaks about it. I thank God for the work of Dr Rhiannon Lloyd who has spent many visits doing seminars on trauma counselling in Rwanda. Like Dr Allender, she has frequently found that people do not want to face the pain of the past. She says that as they talk about their pain and then transfer it on to Jesus on the cross, they find that their hearts are set free to be able to truly forgive. Then she asks them to remember the good things they saw during the horror. Many are set free to remember those who helped them, something they had blacked out as they tried to forget the pain. Yet it is important to let people move at their own pace. A forced discussion of the past may re-open wounds that were beginning to heal. A wise lecturer of mine at All Nations used to say that in counselling, "one should never go ahead of the Holy Spirit."

Another myth Dr Allender deals with is the myth of released anger. He says that often Christians believe that handing our anger to God means the end of it and they are surprised when another incident triggers anger again. "Forgiving another is an on-going process," he says, "rather than a once-and-for-all event." He asks whether hurt and anger are contrary to forgiveness and replies by quoting Jeremiah 31:20 where God speaks of his own hurt and anger in the face of Israel's (or Ephraim's) rebellion against him. "'Is not Ephraim my dear son, the child in whom I delight? Though I often speak against him, I still remember him. Therefore, my heart yearns for him; I have great compassion for him,' declares the Lord." But if there is no freedom to talk about your feelings, how can you face this on-going need for forgiveness? Rwanda is a society where feelings are not often discussed. Tears are more frequent now than in the past, but on the whole people do not know how to deal with them

A third myth that Dr Allender mentions is that Christians should not desire vengeance. "Revenge involves a desire for justice. It is the intense wish to see ugliness destroyed, wrongs righted and God's glory restored," he says, but this, too, as I have shown, is alien to Rwandan thought.

Gerald Sittser, associate professor of religion at Whitworth College in Spokane, Washington, was travelling home one night when a drunken driver crashed into his car, killing Gerald's wife, his mother, and his four-year-old daughter, leaving him and his three other children, who somehow all survived the accident. He wrote a book called *A Grace Disguised — How the Soul Grows through Loss*. Eight months after the tragedy, the driver was acquitted of all counts of vehicular manslaughter. Sittser wrote, "I was enraged after the trial, which in my mind turned out to be as unjust as the accident itself. The driver did not get what he deserved any more than the victims, whether living or dead, had gotten what they deserved." One whole chapter of his book describes how he wrestled with this question of forgiveness and justice.

> Most victims of wrongdoing want justice to prevail after their loss, and for good reason. They know intuitively that there is a moral order in the universe. The violation of that moral order demands justice. Without it, the moral order itself is undermined, simple rights and wrongs are made irrelevant, and people are given license to do whatever they want. Anything becomes possible and permissible. People who have suffered loss recoil before such an idea.

Following the trial, Sittser fantasized about the driver, picturing him in all sorts of horrible situations where he was suffering as Sittser was suffering.

> It eventually occurred to me that this preoccupation was poisoning me. It signalled that I wanted more than justice. I wanted revenge. I was beginning to harbour hatred in my heart. I was edging toward becoming an unforgiving person and using what appeared to be the failure of the judicial system to justify my unforgiveness. I wanted to punish the wrongdoer and get even. The very thought of forgiveness seemed abhorrent to me. I realized at that moment that I had to forgive. If not, I would be consumed by my own unforgiveness.

He realized that unforgiveness wants more than justice. It wants the wrongdoer to suffer as much as the victim is suffering — but that is not possible. Anger in the face of loss is a healthy response, as is grief and the desire for justice, but unforgiveness is different.

> It is as ruinous as a plague. More destruction has been done from unforgiveness than from all the wrongdoing in the world that created the conditions for it. This destruction can occur on a large scale, as we see in Northern Ireland or in the Middle East. It can also occur on a small scale, as we observe in gang warfare, family feuds and conflicts between former friends. In the name of unforgiveness people can do terrible things.

As Sittser was struggling with his own loss, the genocide was occurring in Rwanda. To a large extent it occurred as a result of unforgiveness. Generations of Hutu have suffered injustice and loss at the hands of Tutsi; they feared the returning Tutsi army — with some justification as there was large-scale killing of Hutu men in the north of Rwanda, justified by the army as an act of war. But Tutsi have also suffered at the hands of Hutu. That very invading army was largely composed of the children of refugees from the killings in the 1960s and 1970s, many of whom had suffered the loss of parents or family members and had seen unspeakable things as children.

Roger Bowen, who was general secretary of Mid-Africa Ministry at the time of the genocide, wrote in 1995,

> In Rwanda the lesson had not been learned that an unresolved injustice in one generation will return to haunt the next. [...] The history of Rwanda and Burundi is scarred by outbreaks of appalling ethnic conflict of an horrific nature. In all cases there has never been a bringing to justice of the major perpetrators. A climate of impunity has been created which gives the impression that people can get away with such behaviour without fear of being brought to trial. There is little doubt that the assassination of President Ndadaye of Burundi in October 1993, and the fact that no one had been brought to justice for that event, gave the green light to the Rwandan Government that they too could get away with their genocidal plans without fear of arrest and trial.

In the South African context, Desmond Tutu made a similar point when he said, "We must deal effectively, penitently, with our past or it will return to haunt our present and we won't have a future to speak of" (p 23 of *Struggling to Forgive* by Brian Frost). The unresolved injustice about which Bowen wrote gives rise to the unforgiveness which Tutu feared and which worried Gerald Sittser. Tutu describes his visit to Rwanda in 1995 in his book, *No Future Without Forgiveness*, in which he describes his experiences in the Truth and Reconciliation Commission in South Africa. He says that at the stadium,

> I told them that the cycle of reprisal and counter-reprisal that had characterized their national history had to be broken, and that the only way to do this was to go beyond retributive justice to restora-

tive justice, to move on to forgiveness, because without it there was no future (p 209).

Sittser wrote,

> But forgiveness is costly. Forgiving people must give up the right to get even, a right that is not easy to relinquish. They must show mercy when their human sensibilities tell them to punish. Not that a desire for justice is wrong. A person can forgive and strive for justice. Wrong that is forgiven is still wrong done and must be punished. Mercy does not abrogate justice; it transcends it.

But it is just this concept that is totally alien in Rwanda. Their word for forgiveness means that justice cannot prevail. A Christian in Rwanda believes that if he forgives he must also let him off the consequences of his actions. My friend Wilberforce was called before the courts in January 1996 to identify the murderer of his wife and family. He refused to charge them saying they will face the judgement of God. Was his action right? I don't know. What I do know was that it cost him very dearly as he struggled with his grief at his loss once more.

Gerald Sittser said,

> I think that I was spared excessive preoccupation with revenge because I believe that God is just, even though the judicial system is not. Ultimately every human being will have to stand before God, and God will judge every person with wisdom and impartiality. Human systems may fail; God's justice does not. I also believe that God is merciful, in ways that far exceed what we could imagine or muster ourselves. It is the tension between God's justice and mercy that makes God so capable of dealing with wrongdoers. God is able to punish people without destroying them, and to forgive people without indulging them.

Yet God's justice ultimately depends on acceptance of his mercy. Psalm 73 shows the psalmist frustrated, as we so often are, at the way villains seem to slide through life without any problems, but when he went into God's sanctuary and contemplated their end, then he lost his envy of them! The soldier who killed randomly because he saw killers, as he thought, getting away with their crime, must have felt the frustration of the psalmist, without the same solution. In Romans 3:23 we read that all have sinned and come short of the glory of God. In other words, we all deserve the end described in Psalm 73. But on the cross Jesus took upon himself the punishment that we all deserve as sinners, and fulfilled God's just requirements so that we can receive his mercy, not through our own righteousness, but because we accept his righteousness. One of my favourite verses in the New Testament is 2 Corinthians 5:21 where Paul says that Jesus, "who knew no sin became sin for us, so that in him we might become the righteousness of God" (RSV). At the cross we see how God's justice and mercy finally meet, as his forgiveness is freely held out to us — but we need to accept it.

Up to now I have been dealing with the nature of forgiveness, but one part of Wilberforce's question was, "How can I forgive?" Mary White was another member of Charles Colson's symposium of victims of crime and those trying to help them, referred to above. She wrote an essay called, "Every knee shall bow".

She said, "An unwillingness to forgive can lock victims in the past and enslave them to the offender", and she outlines ten things that can be done to help victims forgive their offenders:

(a) Help the victim face what has happened.
(b) Help the victim acknowledge the severity of the hurt.
(c) Help the victim see that God's personal forgiveness is available for every human being.
(d) Help the victim seek God's strength so that he can obey God's command to forgive.
(e) Do not make the victim feel guilty if he/she has a struggle to forgive.
(f) Help them see that forgiveness is an ongoing process which needs to be practised on and on — 70 times seven says Jesus.
(g) Help the victim face the future.
(h) Give ongoing prayer support.
(i) Form a support group of people willing to stay with the victim in the struggle.
(j) Avoid pushing the victim into reconciliation with the offender too quickly.

I have said that receiving the forgiveness offered depends on our willingness to repent, and it is to the nature of true repentance that I now turn.

III It doesn't matter what we do today — we can repent tomorrow and God will forgive us.

Many people during the genocide said something like that. What does this say about presumptuous sin? Is there forgiveness for it? Jesus said that the only unforgivable sin is blasphemy against the Holy Spirit. What does this mean? And what does it mean to repent?

As I have been teaching the Jewish system of worship, and seeing how so much was fulfilled in Jesus, I was struck by the fact that the sacrificial system appears to be for inadvertent sin. Those who deliberately offended against God or their neighbour were either stoned or cast out of the assembly. They had no place in the tribe thereafter, for they had deliberately broken the fellowship. True, there was provision made for restitution for theft in the guilt offering — another concept that my students have found difficulty in coming to terms with — but for deliberate, high-handed sin there was no coming back.

The reason my students have found the concept of restitution so hard is that the concept of repentance has been largely debased. To so many people in Rwanda, repentance means standing up in church and confessing your sin and that is all. This is a practice that developed during the Revival. Then it was impelled by the Holy Spirit and often involved costly acts of restitution as I have shown, but now it has often become a mere matter of ritual. Frequently, there is no thought of restitution nor of being willing to face the consequences of sin as we have already discussed in the previous question. Neither is there any real understanding that true repentance must involve a change of lifestyle. So often, repentance to them is purely a matter of words, and much teaching needs to be done on the nature of true repentance.

In the New Testament, Paul addresses the problem of deliberate sin in Romans 6. He has been talking about how the grace of God is sufficient to deal with all sin in a way that the Levitical law could not. He says in Romans 5:20, "Where sin increased, grace increased all the more". Then it is as if he caught up on himself. Is that really true? Can I really sin as much as I like so that God's grace will have the opportunity to flow the more? In the first verse of the next chapter he asks just that: "Shall we go on sinning so grace may increase? By no means! [In the KJV this is translated as God forbid!] We died to sin, how can we live in it any longer?"

And there you have the answer. Those who have truly faced the awfulness of sin and the consequences of it, the separation from God that results, cannot contemplate deliberately sinning. How can they? Their sin, yours and mine, sent Jesus to the cross. He bore my sin, was separated from God, was accursed by God, so that I might draw near to God and have new life in him. How can I then contemplate sacrificing all that? It is unthinkable!

Does this mean, then, that those who made the sort of statement we are now discussing, could not have been Christians in the first place? If they are truly penitent now, would God forgive them? I don't know the answers. Only God can know the hearts of men. What I do know is that many who went into the killing gave every appearance of being truly converted beforehand, even though they may not have experienced the fulness of the Holy Spirit in the way that those involved in Revival did.

Jesus said there was only one sin which cannot be forgiven and that is the sin of speaking against the Holy Spirit (Matthew 12:22-32). But what does this mean? There are several answers given to this question. David Pawson, for instance, says that if you consider it in the context, it must mean saying that the work of the Holy Spirit is really the work of the devil as the Pharisees had just done. Others would say that it means denying the Lordship of Christ. As far as I can see, the unforgivable sin is refusing to listen to the Holy Spirit. One of the works of the Holy Spirit is to convict us of sin (John 16.8). If, then, we refuse to listen to him, how can we be forgiven? My aunt Veronica remembers that this was one of the last questions she discussed with her father before he left for Burundi in 1940. His understanding of the unforgivable sin was, "It is sin with the deliberate knowledge of what you are doing, when you understand what you are doing." In other words, having faced the implications of what the Holy Spirit is saying, and knowing the consequences, if you then deliberately refuse to accept the redeeming love of Jesus Christ, this is the sin against the Holy Spirit for which there is no forgiveness.

I had reached this point in my conclusions when I read Philip Yancey's book *Finding God in Unexpected Places*. He talks about the scandal of grace. In chapter 34 he discusses his friend, Daniel, who announced that he was leaving his wife of fifteen years for a younger woman, despite the pain he knew it would inflict on his wife and daughters. "Do you think God can forgive something as awful as what I am about to do?" he asked Yancey. Yancey replied:

Can God forgive you? Of course. Read your Bible. David, Peter, Paul — God builds his church on the backs of people who murder, commit adultery, deny him and persecute his followers. But because of Christ, forgiveness is now our problem, not God's. What we have to go through to commit sin distances us from God — we change in the very act of rebellion — and there is no guarantee we will come back. You ask me about forgiveness now, but will you ever want it later, especially if it involves repentance?

Yancey quoted a story told by Robert Hughes, a convict sentenced to life imprisonment in a maximum security island off the coast of Australia. One day he murdered a fellow convict and was shipped to the mainland to stand trial. There he calmly described what he had done. "Why did you do it?" asked the judge. The convict replied that he was sick of the island and saw no reason to keep living. "But why not commit suicide?" asked the judge. "Well, it's like this," said the prisoner. "I'm a Catholic. If I commit suicide I'll go straight to hell. But if I murder I can come here and confess to a priest before my execution. That way, God will forgive me." It seems to me that many of those involved in the genocide were like that prisoner, believing they could do what they liked and come to God for forgiveness later.

Yancey ends his chapter with these words: "God took a great risk by announcing forgiveness in advance. It occurs to me though, that the scandal of grace involves a transfer of that risk to us. As George MacDonald put it, we are condemned not for the wicked things we've done, but for not leaving them." In the next chapter he says this: "More and more, I have begun to see that Paul's explosive response 'God forbid!' is the only appropriate response to human questions about exploiting God's grace. If you're the kind of person who seizes upon God's grace just for the chance to push it to the limits, why, you probably haven't understood that grace at all."

IV When the Holy Spirit left a man, he became worse than the worst of the killers.

This statement was made soon after we arrived in Kigali in 1995 by a Pentecostal pastor. It was a statement that was to haunt me for several months. Even raising it with fellow clergy aroused strong reactions. "Of course the Holy Spirit cannot leave a man," they said. "If they got involved in the killing, it meant they were not saved in the first place," but to me that was to beg the question. Some of those involved in the killing had indeed presented every appearance that they were truly saved — so how can you tell who is saved or not? One friend described how he saw a man standing with a bloody machete in his hand, and recognized him as a man he had himself led to Christ. Had his profession of faith been a sham?

Another friend pointed out the truth of the statement. "Look at Stalin," she said. "He was a trainee monk, but when he turned his back on the Christian faith he became the worst killer the world has known." I realized that it is indeed a matter of fact that some who have turned away from faith become worse than the worst of the killers. But is this the same as saying that the Holy Spirit has left a man? Is it possible to lose one's salvation? Many evangelicals in the West are indoctrinated with the view, made popular by Calvin who built on the writings of Augustine of Hippo, that once a person has made a commitment to Christ, then he/she is saved and can have assurance that he/she is going to heaven since no one can snatch them out of the Father's hand (John 10:29).

Christians in Rwanda have no such assurance. My mother was teaching on the death of Ananias and Sapphira in Acts 5. She said that although they were killed as an example to the early church that holiness of life was essential, they would probably not have lost their salvation. This was met with adamant denial: they both died with unconfessed sin in their lives and therefore must have gone to hell.

Judas was chosen by Jesus as one of his close friends. He obviously appeared trustworthy enough to be entrusted with the common purse, though John seems to imply that the temptation proved too much for him and he started stealing. Who knows exactly what it was that eventually led to the statement that Satan entered him as he went out in the night to betray his friend and Lord. Could one say that the Holy Spirit had left him?

There are several examples in the Old Testament where it specifically says that the Holy Spirit left individuals. King Saul presumed to take upon himself the role of priest, rather than trusting God and waiting for Samuel. It is said that the Spirit left him. Samson, too, lost his special abilities when the Spirit left him. I think one of the saddest verses in the Bible comes in Judges 16:20: "But he did not know that the Lord had left him." Solomon was a king who had been tremendously blessed by the Lord in wisdom, wealth and ability, but he died a disillusioned old man if the book of Ecclesiastes is anything to go by. Why? Because through disobedience to God's laws, he had contracted many foreign alliances, and those foreign wives had allowed idol worship into Israel. Uzziah, too, started as a great king but became presumptuous and insisted on sacrificing as a priest — he ended his life as a leper, an outcast from his people. But all these examples are from the Old Testament. In the New Covenant, when Jesus sent his Holy Spirit on all who believe, is it possible for the Holy Spirit to leave a person once he has come into his life?

Although this question was a real problem to me, I could find no one prepared even to discuss the issue, and it was with some relief that I found a book by David Pawson called *Once Saved, Always Saved?* where the whole issue is discussed.

Pawson points out something that I have often taught, that salvation has three tenses, with, if anything, the emphasis on the future tenses (eg Matthew 24:13; Romans 5:10; 1 Corinthians 5:5; 1 Timothy 4:16; Hebrews 9:28). We were saved in the past from the penalty of sin; we are being saved in the present from the power of sin; and we will finally be saved in the future when the Lord Jesus takes us to be with him and there will not even be the presence of sin. All three aspects of salvation need to be complete before we can truly say that we are "saved". In other words, the Christian life is a journey and it is the one who completes that journey who will "receive the crown of life" (Revelation 2:10). Pawson says:

> What do we conclude from this? That salvation is a process which takes time rather than an instant happening. The gospel is about "the Way" of salvation along which we need to travel to reach our destination. In other words, salvation is not yet complete in any of us. The most appropriate description of our present state is that "we are being saved" (p 16).

His conclusion is that salvation covers two aspects. "Negatively we need to be saved <u>from</u> our sins, both their subjective and objective consequences. Positively, we need to be fully restored <u>to</u> that original image of God in which we were created and which is perfectly seen in the character of Christ." This process is the work of the Holy Spirit and will only be complete when we see Jesus Christ as he really is and are finally changed into his likeness (1 John 3:2).

Pawson also points out that many verses are written in the present continuous tense in Greek, a tense we do not have in English, and our simple present often obscures the meaning. So that, for example, John 3:16 would be better translated, "For God so loved the world that he gave his only beloved Son so that whoever goes on believing shall not perish but goes on having eternal life." Faith, too, is an ongoing process, as Jesus makes clear in his discourse on the vine in John 15. It is those who abide in him, that is, who continue to abide in him, that bear fruit, and he makes it clear that a branch which does not continue to abide in him will be cast out to be burned — which certainly sounds as if the Holy Spirit could leave a man. There are also several wonderful promises that are conditional, often connected by that little word "if", all saying that we must hold fast to our faith if we are to inherit the promises (eg Romans 8:13, 8:17, 11:22; Hebrews 3:6, 3:14, 12:25).

There are two parables that Jesus taught which have obvious bearing on this question. The first is the parable of the sower (Luke 8:4-5). The first soil did not receive the seed because the path was hard, and the birds of the air snatched it away. Jesus says this was satanic action preventing the Word of God being received. The next two soils received with joy, but afterwards fell away, either because there was no depth or because "the cares and riches and pleasures of life" choked the seed, and fruit did not mature. Only those who heard the Word and let it develop in their lives brought forth fruit. I am aware that some would say that the middle two soils speak about those who were not fully converted, but they gave every appearance of it. Others would say that all they lost was their eternal reward. Yet Jesus says that "they fell away", which seems to imply that they were lost.

The other parable is in Matthew 18:21-35, the sombre parable of the unforgiving servant. The Lord, having pardoned the enormous debt of his servant, hears that the same servant had refused to show mercy to another who owed him a trifling amount. The Lord rescinds his pardon and orders the servant to be imprisoned until he repays the whole amount. Jesus concludes, "This is how my heavenly Father will treat each of you unless you forgive your brother from your heart" (18:35). In a previous question I discussed how lack of forgiveness can lead to bitterness. This in turn can destroy our relationship with God — and may indeed end with the Holy Spirit leaving us.

The only book in the New Testament which specifically addresses the question of backsliding is the letter to the Hebrews which was almost certainly written to Jewish believers, possibly priests, who were being tempted to renounce their faith because of the persecution they were experiencing (Hebrews 10:32-34, 12:4). They were considering returning to the synagogue where they would be welcomed, provided they publicly denied their Lord. I have always had difficulty with three passages which seemed to deny that aspect of assurance that I had accepted.

Hebrews 2:1-4 speaks of the danger of drifting away from the truth we have heard (2:1) and contains a strong warning. If every violation of the law of Moses (the message given through the angels) received its just retribution, how shall we escape if we neglect so great a salvation — especially if we have seen signs and wonders, miracles and the various gifts of the Holy Spirit.

Stronger is the passage in 6:1-8. The first thing to note is that this, as indeed the whole letter, is addressed to Christians, to those who have been enlightened, who have tasted the heavenly gift and have been partakers of the Holy Spirit (6:4-5). In the previous chapter the writer complains that they have become dull of hearing (5:11) and are stuck in a childish faith, still drinking milk when they ought to be on solid food (5:13-14) and that they are unskilled in the word of righteousness and unable to distinguish good from evil because they are stuck in the elementary doctrines of Christ and have not had their faculties trained in the Scriptures (5:12 – 6:2).

In many ways this is a good description of the majority of church-going Rwandans before the genocide. Almost all the bishops I met the year after the genocide said that what they needed beyond anything else was someone to train their church leaders in discipleship, which had been so lacking before, so that they could then train others. I thank God that I have been privileged to be involved, with others, in this vital task.

Hebrews 6 goes on to say that if these people fall away, how can they possibly be restored since what they have done is equivalent to crucifying Christ afresh. What is probably being talked about here is the sin of apostasy, that is, the deliberate denial of Christ. Those who went out with machetes in 1994 may not have been denying Christ by word, but they certainly were in their actions, and I do not find it surprising that a pastor could say that the Holy Spirit had left them.

The final passage I would like to look at is Hebrews 10:26-31 which contains the awesome words, "If we deliberately keep on sinning after we have received the knowledge of the truth, no sacrifice for sins is left, but only a fearful expectation of judgement and of raging fire that will consume the enemies of God" (10:26-27). To live, and continue to live, a life in direct contradiction to the life of holiness to which we have been called is akin to spurning the Son of God, to cursing his saving blood which he sacrificed and to outraging the Spirit of grace. There are several warnings in Scripture that God will confirm us in the choices that we make and the time may well come when the Spirit will leave us to continue in the life we have chosen to live.

Sadly, in many cases, the Rwandan church had preached, and still does preach, a gospel of conversion with no emphasis on discipleship and training in the holiness of a Spirit-filled life rather than following a set of rules, with the result that when the test came, many failed. The New Testament makes it clear that it is not the starting, but the finishing of the race that counts. Those "who stand firm to the end will be saved" (Matthew 24:13; see also Revelation 2:10). I believe that we in Britain also need to take heed from these verses.

Yet several passages promise that God will keep us for himself once we have believed, notably John 10:29 (no one is able to snatch from the Father's hand the sheep who hear Jesus' voice and follow him), and Romans 8:38-39 (nothing is able to separate us from the love of God in Christ Jesus our Lord), but we need to note that they are addressed to those who are following Jesus, who acknowledge him as Lord. If we, of our own volition, deliberately choose to live a life of sin, or to go on the rampage of murder that some Rwandan Christians did, God will not force us to remain in his will. Reluctantly, I come to the conclusion that, in such circumstances, the Holy Spirit of God can indeed leave a person and that his state is then worse than if he had never believed.

However, we need to keep the balance found in Scripture. My own experience is that the fact that I was a child of God was very important. My communication with him had broken down while I was at university, but the relationship was secure. However bad a human child is, nothing ever breaks a blood relationship, and if we have been called a child of God, it is a blood relationship since we are washed in the blood of Jesus, and sealed by the Holy Spirit. How can we say then that we can possibly lose our salvation? As with many other thorny problems, I believe that Scripture teaches both that we can lose our salvation and that God keeps us so that we will find our inheritance in the end (1 Peter 1:3-5). One verse in the chapter I have quoted above (Hebrews 10:14) brings out this dilemma. It says that, by his sacrifice once offered, Christ "has made perfect for all time those who are being made holy." How can someone who has been made perfect lose his salvation? Yet we are only being made holy! I do not know how God can be both transcendent and immanent; how Jesus can be both God and Man; how God is One yet Three; how there can be predestination and free will at the same time. Yet all these truths are taught in Scripture and all need to be kept in balance. Putting too much emphasis on one aspect at the expense of its counter-balancing truth inevitably leads to error.

I also know that God's grace is such that he will forgive even the foulest of sins. Paul described himself as the chief of sinners and rejoiced that God's grace had been sufficient to cover all his sin. As we have already seen in the previous discussion, there is only one unforgivable sin and that is deliberately with full knowledge of the consequences to refuse the forgiveness that God offers. Yes, I believe as I have shown above, that it is possible deliberately to forsake God's grace and for the Holy Spirit to leave such a person, but we are also told not to judge lest we ourselves be judged. We do not know the state of mind of those who joined in the rampage of killing. Only God knows that. Our task is to preach the all-encompassing grace of God to all who will receive it — even those who were involved in genocide!

V Satan was to blame.

This was probably the thing most commonly said, following the genocide. I think I have made it clear that Rwanda is a country where the spiritual world is very real and no one doubts either the existence of God the Creator, or Satan and evil spirits. In traditional Rwandan religion, the Creator God is totally remote and, although he is just, there is no way of relating to him. Instead, Rwandans' lives are ruled by fear of the *abazimu* or spirits of the dead. Every day, they offer libations to these spirits. If something bad happens, or if they fall ill, they ask a diviner why this has happened. Often they are told they must propitiate the spirit of a particular ancestor. Frequently the reply is that a neighbour has poisoned them using another spirit, and they need to appeal to a more powerful spirit to break the spell.

These powerful spirits, called *imandwa*, are few in number. The most powerful is a cruel and bloodthirsty spirit called Binego. Binego's father is Ryangombe who owns the whole land of Rwanda. Ryangombe was a chief in the 17th century who was killed by a buffalo. Antoine Rutayisire went through an initiation when he was 21 when he identified with Binego. This initiation ceremony is called *kubandwa* and means that you have the strength of Binego to defeat the *abazimu*. He learned to sing a song in praise of Binego which went like this: "I am the slaughterer, the son of the angry one. I am the one who washes his hands in blood. I am the spy, the son of the warrior. I spy to attack, to loot and enrich myself. I killed the bride and the dowry had to be paid back..." It continues through a whole list of people he has killed and stolen from. (Quoted in *The Peacemaking Power of Prayer*, chapter 9, by John D. Robb and James A. Hill.)

To refuse initiation to the cult of Ryangombe, *kubandwa*, means that you will be tormented by *abazimu* throughout your life. But to break the secret of *kubandwa* involves terrible penalties, including death. When a man died, they planted the sacred red flowering tree known as the *umurinzi* [watchman] because they believed that Ryangombe would encourage the spirit of their ancestor to watch over the *rugo*, or household, and keep it safe.

It is hard for us in the West who have largely lost our concept of the spiritual world to understand the fear that rules the lives of most Rwandans. My mother says that when she came out, she dismissed much of this traditional teaching as "nonsense" and it was only during the 1970s when, for instance, she saw the power that curses had over some of those who had turned to the Lord Jesus in the second wave of Revival, that she came to understand the reality of the evil spirits being worshipped. When you read the sort of hymn sung to Binego you can begin to understand the frenzy of bloodletting that took place in 1994.

In the north of Rwanda, the cult of Ryangombe is mixed up with another cult, that of Nyabingi. In 1912, when the northern Hutu were forced to accept Tutsi rule, it was a medium who inspired much of the bloodshed. This medium claimed to be possessed by the spirit of Nyabingi, a relative of the 17th century king, Ruganzu Ndori. Nyabingi lived near the Virunga mountains and the king swore never to attack her home, provided she remained north of the Nyabarongo river, with the result that the people of the area began to see her as their saviour. People began asking her for children and sent girls to her as servants. Antoine wrote in 1998 that the northern region of Rwanda is plagued by demons of rebellion in links with Nyabingi the female demon. [...] The northern range of volcanoes/mountains called Virunga has been given to the spirits as their abode, and even now when Christians cast out a demon they still send it to the Virunga which shows that even now we recognize the covenant that was made with the evil spirits to live on our highest points." (Quoted in *The Peacemaking Power of Prayer*, chapter 9, by John D. Robb and James A. Hill.)

Girls are dedicated to Nyabingi at puberty, and to break the oath sworn to her is believed to bring death. Hers is a cult of fear and deception, but many of her prophetesses also diagnose the causes of disease, often casting suspicion on someone who has caused the disease by witchcraft. Charms, potions and curses are all sold in the name of Nyabingi. These, almost certainly, were the charms that my grandfather's translator, Samsoni, renounced during the Revival.

During the Revival, and since, whenever men and women were sincere in their whole-hearted acceptance of the Lordship of Christ, they have totally rejected any involvement in pagan beliefs and practices. Charms were often burnt publicly and the watchman trees were cut down. Sadly, however, today many church-goers, and even some pastors, see such rejection as the rejection of their traditions and, while accepting the Christian faith, they see no reason to renounce their heritage as Rwandans, and so they still continue with the rituals of Nyabingi and Ryangombe. Indeed, a pastor of one of the many denominations which has sprung up since the genocide has written to the president and to the minister of cultural affairs, as well as many church leaders, asking for help in building a shrine to Nyabingi, saying, "The only hope for peace in Rwanda is to return to the cult of Nyabingi!"

Where God has been working in spectacular ways as he did in Revival, and again in 1973, it is not surprising that Satan would want to counter-attack. When a stick is floating downstream there is little disturbance to the water, but when it is caught on a rock the water does all it can to dislodge it. In the same way, when individuals, or a church, are complying with Satan's desires, there is no need to attack them, but when they are standing firm on the Rock of Christ, Satan does all he can to dislodge them. I believe a large part of the explanation for the genocide of 1994 lies in the spiritual battle that is going on in heavenly places for the soul of this land.

While not denying that there is a very real spiritual warfare going on, I feel that many people consider that the statement, "Satan is to blame", is sufficient explanation for their actions, and that, therefore, there is no need to take personal responsibility. For example, a few months ago I discovered a friend of mine stealing from my purse. Her explanation was that Satan had tempted her. She still has not really faced up to the reality of her sin.

One of the questions I like to ask when teaching from Genesis 3, the account of Adam and Eve's fall into sin, is "Who was to blame? Was it Satan as Eve said, or Eve as Adam accused, or even God for making her in the first place?" More often than not, I get the answer, "Satan". When I follow up with a question about Eve's responsibility, there is a blank silence, until I point out that Eve chose to listen to Satan's voice. She had the option of obeying God, and chose to rebel. Similarly, Adam could have refused Eve, but chose to go along with her sin.

Another example comes in John 13:27, where it says that "Satan entered Judas" and he went out to betray Jesus. Did he have the choice, since it was foretold that Jesus would be betrayed by one of his friends? Could he have repented, as Peter did, rather than go out and commit suicide? I remember several talks during Revival days, giving the contrast between Peter, who went out and wept bitterly, and Judas, who went out and hanged himself, but my students do not see that it was possible for Judas to repent. Satan had entered him, they say, as God foretold, and he had no personal responsibility for what happened.

I do not believe it is possible for true healing and reconciliation to happen in this country unless people face up to their personal responsibility for what they did and stop hiding behind the statement, "It was Satan to blame."

VI If God is all-powerful, why did he allow the genocide to happen?

This question of the sovereignty of God has been one of my biggest problems. I remember a journalist questioning a

Christian aid worker in a refugee camp, "How can you still believe in a God of love when you see all this suffering around you?" he asked. Yet when I mentioned my anger with God to my father, he said, "Why are you angry? God is the potter and does what he wants with his clay", but that almost made it worse! I felt that a God who could allow such horror was not the God of love I knew and trusted.

This was C. S. Lewis's problem as he struggled with his grief following the death of his wife from cancer. In *A Grief Observed* he wrote, "Not that I am (I think) in much danger of ceasing to believe in God. The real danger is of coming to believe such dreadful things about him. The conclusion I dread is not 'So there's no God after all,' but, 'So this is what God's really like. Deceive yourself no longer.'" He then asks, "Is it rational to believe in a bad God? Anyway, in a God as bad as that? The cosmic Sadist, the spiteful imbecile?"

It was also Gerald Sittser's problem following the death of his wife, mother and daughter in a car crash:

> There appear to be two possible answers: Either God is powerful but not good, and thus a cruel God who causes suffering; or God is good but not powerful and thus a weak God who cannot prevent suffering, though he would like to. Both answers have problems because they appear to undermine what we want to believe about God, namely that he is both powerful and good.

This is the universal question of suffering Christians. How can we continue to believe in a God who is both all-loving and all-powerful?

Sittser helpfully explores this question in the chapter called "The absence of God". He came to three new perspectives which helped him, and me, to come to terms with this problem:

A   How do we view God's sovereignty?

He described the common view that many people have about God. "I was inclined to believe that God simply pulled the strings and manipulated the events of our lives as if we were marionettes on a string and God was a puppeteer controlling us completely. Such a view is obviously deterministic, as if life happens to us as dictated by God. He sets the course, and we have to follow it." As he questioned this view of God, he realized that it was too simplistic and belittling to God.

> His sovereignty encompasses all of life — for example, not simply tragic experiences but also our responses to them. It envelops all of human experience and integrates it into a greater whole. Even human freedom, then, becomes a dimension of God's sovereignty, as if God were a novelist who had invented characters so real that the decisions they make are genuinely their decisions. As the novelist, God stands outside the story and "controls" it as the writer. But as characters in the novel, humans are free to act and to determine their own destiny. God's sovereignty, then, transcends human freedom but does not nullify it. Both are real — only in different ways and on different planes. Belief in God's sovereignty thus gives us the security of knowing God is in control, but it also assigns to us the responsibility of using our freedom to make wise choices and to remain faithful to him. It assures us that God is transcendent without cancelling out the important role we play.

I have found this a helpful picture which has enabled me to begin to understand the interaction of our human freedom and God's sovereignty. As I study the Scriptures, I see the way God has allowed human beings freedom, even to disobey him, yet at the same time he has always worked to restore their situations. Thus David had the freedom to commit adultery and murder, but Nathan was sent to challenge him. David had the freedom to kill the unwelcome messenger as many Eastern potentates would have done, or to accept the rebuke and repent deeply as Psalm 51 shows that he did. Adam and Eve were truly free to obey God or to listen to the voice of the tempter. But in the moment of sinning and rebellion, God had a solution in place. Genesis 3:15 shows that God was already planning for a deliverer who would crush Satan's head at the same time as his heel was bruised — the first hint of the cross. I believe that, conversely, Jesus, as true man, was free to listen to the tempter's voice, as "he was tempted in every way just as we are" (Hebrews 4:15), yet he chose to obey his Father in every respect. Our God is not a deterministic God, manipulating our actions. We genuinely have free will. He will never coerce us into faith, but he loves us with an everlasting love and longs to forgive our sins and heal our wounds, so he works to mend the situations we have created by our wrongful actions.

Philip Yancey, in his book, *Where is God When it Hurts?*, asks the question, "What do we expect God to do when accidents happen?"

> Does God reach down, slightly twist the wheels of school buses and watch them career through the guardrails? Does he draw a red pencil line through a map of Indiana to plot the exact path of a tornado? "There, hit that house, kill that six-year-old, skip over the next house..." Does God programme the earth like a video game, constantly experimenting with tidal waves, seismic tremors and hurricanes? Is that how he rewards and punishes us, his helpless victims? Posing the questions so brazenly may sound sacrilegious. But they've long haunted me, and in various forms have been tossed at me by agnostic friends.

Like C. S. Lewis, who said in *The Problem of Pain* that it is only a problem to those who believe in a loving God, Yancey says:

> Faith in God offers no insurance against tragedy. Nor does it offer insurance against feelings of doubt and betrayal. If anything, being a Christian complicates the issue. If you believe in a world of pure chance, what difference does it make whether a bus from Yuba City or one from Salina crashes? But if you believe in a world ruled by a powerful God who loves you tenderly, then it makes an awful difference.

Given the spirit of unforgiveness prevailing in Rwanda, given the manipulations of the leaders, what did we expect God to do to prevent the genocide? Everyone involved had, and has, genuine free will to turn to him in repentance and ask for his forgiveness and help in forgiving others — or to reject his love and continue a policy of hate.

B The relationship between God's sovereignty and the incarnation

Sittser says,

God's sovereignty means that God is in ultimate control of everything. The Incarnation means that God came into the world as a
vulnerable human being. [...] The sovereign God came in Jesus
Christ to suffer with us and to suffer for us. He descended deeper
into the pit than we will ever know. His sovereignty did not protect him from loss. If anything, it led him to suffer loss for our
sake. God is therefore not some distant being who controls the
world by a mysterious power. God came all the way to us and lived
among us.

I have always found such comfort in this aspect of God's sovereignty. The God we serve is not remote like *Imana* of traditional
Rwandan belief, but the God who became man and shared our
sorrows and suffering from the inside. Consider Jesus praying
in agony in the garden of Gethsemane. He simply could not face
the fact of the cross with all that it entails. Thankfully, he was
able to say, "Thy will be done," but not before he had faced the
fact that he did not want it. His struggle in the garden helps us
as we face things that seem too difficult for us to go through.

Just before I left for Rwanda in September 1995, I was leading a meditation on the cross. A member of the group said, "I
can see that Jesus suffered terribly on the cross — but no more
than many another has suffered since. And his sufferings only
lasted for three hours. Many people suffer agonies that go on for
months or even years. What was so unique about his suffering?"
At one level there was nothing unique about it. He shared the
pain of every human being on a purely human level. But on
another level it was totally unique, as Isaiah 53:4-6 shows:

> Surely he has borne our griefs and carried our sorrows; yet we
> esteemed him stricken, smitten by God, and afflicted. He was
> wounded for our transgressions, he was bruised for our iniquities,
> upon him was the chastisement that has made us whole, and with
> his stripes we are healed. All we like sheep have gone astray; we
> have turned every one to his own way and the Lord has laid on
> him the iniquity of us all (RSV).

When Jesus cried out on the cross, "My God, my God, why have
you forsaken me?" it was a genuine cry of horror because, for
the first time in his sinless existence, God could not look upon
his beloved Son who had become sin for us (2 Corinthians 5:21).

Isaiah says that the iniquity of us all was laid on him. This was the uniqueness of the suffering of Jesus, as he bore not only my sin and yours, but also the hatred and unforgiveness of every murderer in Rwanda and Bosnia and Northern Ireland. Not only that, but Isaiah says that he bore all our griefs and sorrows. The sorrows of every person who has ever suffered loss — every bereaved person in Rwanda and every lost child, or person bewildered by the loss of an arm or leg. Jesus carries our sorrows, not to take them away necessarily, but to share them. The grief still has to be worked through but Jesus is alongside, suffering with each one and longing to share his peace with them in the midst of their suffering.

C   The sovereignty of God and faith

Sittser writes:

> I have wondered for a long time why faith is so essential. Why did not God make his divine nature more obvious? Why did God not make it easier to believe? It seems to me that we know enough to believe but not so much that we are compelled to believe. [...] We can live normal productive lives on earth and dismiss God. We can be atheists and get away with it. The point is that we have a choice. More than anything, God covets our love. But real love can never be forced. Freedom is what makes love possible in the first place. That is why God will never coerce us into a relationship. Faith allows us to choose God in freedom.

There is so much that I have learned from my Rwandan friends who continue to believe in a God who cares for them even when they are struggling for their very existence. They have a simple trust and a joy in the Lord which challenges me at every turn. In the West we have so much in terms of material wealth that we no longer have to trust God for our next meal. Here they never question God's sovereignty as I do. They choose to love and trust him in the way that I believe he longs that all of us would.

VII How could people pray all night and then take up a machete in the morning to kill?

There are two questions involved in this one. The first is to do with the nature of faith and its relationship to daily living. The second is to do with prayer, what it is and how it works.

Often in Rwanda, as in Britain, I think that people consider that faith is a matter of ritual and Sunday worship which has no relationship to daily living. As Antoine Rutayisire has pointed out, the early missionaries dismissed the Rwandan beliefs as "nonsense", so they connected to God in an intellectual way, but their emotional well-being and daily living connected to the spirit world. There is, therefore, a serious dichotomy between what they say they believe, and how they live it out.

A story I have often used when I teach or preach, was of a man who went to a prayer meeting in Kigali, where he listened to a man praying fervently. He said to himself, "This man certainly knows his Lord, he knows how to pray so well." Next morning he happened to see the same man in the market-place yelling at someone in anger. He went to him and said, "Didn't I see you praying last night? Is this the way a Christian should act before all these non-believers?" His reply staggered him. "You can't bring Jesus into the market-place!" I was equally staggered in Britain when I refused to go back on my word when selling my house. My estate agent was a leading member of our church council, but he said, "Oh, you can't bring Christianity into the house-selling business." Unless our lives are consistent with what we say we believe, then I believe all the prayers we offer are worth nothing.

This is what God told his people through the prophet Amos. They thought that all God required was ritual worship and sacrifices. They were content to offer him that, but considered that how they lived for the rest of the day was their business, so they stole and lied and cheated, trampling on the poor and denying justice to the needy who could not bribe them. God said to them:

> I hate, I despise your religious feasts; I cannot stand your assemblies. Even though you bring me burnt offerings and grain offerings, I will not accept them. Though you bring choice fellowship offerings, I will have no regard for them. Away with the noise of your songs! I will not listen to the music of your harps. But let jus-

tice roll on like a river, righteousness like a never-failing stream! (Amos 5:21-24).

In other words, God takes no delight in the most wonderful worship services that we can devise, unless our lives are lived in accordance with his wishes. There is no point in praying all night, as they delight to do in Rwanda, unless they bring Jesus into the market-place.

Having said that, I believe that true prayer is vital. In Revival days, the first house to be built on new mission stations was the *kazu* where people could meet to study God's word and to pray in harmony. As we have seen, it was in the *kazu* that God first started to work in a new way at Kigeme in 1970, and I am encouraged by the fact that, in Byumba, between 20 and 50 people turn up every weekday morning at 6 a.m. to pray for an hour before going to work. As I have said, I believe there is a struggle going on in heavenly places for the soul of this nation, and God's people need to join in the fight as they pray.

I have spent time discussing the sovereignty of God. Something that staggers me is that, although without God we can do nothing, yet God has chosen to do nothing without our prayers. He has so limited himself that he will not act without our prayers. And amazingly, our prayers are effective, sometimes even to the point of changing God's mind over what he had planned to do. Moses interceded for his people and God changed his mind and did not destroy them (Numbers 14). That inadequate prophet, Jonah, preached God's vengeance on Nineveh, the king instructed his people to pray in penitence before God, and God did not bring the declared judgement (Jonah 3).

In Ezekiel 22:23-29, God describes the wickedness of Israel which has brought him to declare judgement on her. Then he says,

> I looked for a man among them who would build up the wall and stand before me in the gap on behalf of the land, so that I would not have to destroy it, but I found none. So I will pour out my wrath on them and consume them with my fiery anger, bringing down on their own heads all they have done, declares the Sovereign Lord (Ezekiel 22.30-31).

Even at that stage of Israel's history, if an Abraham or a Moses had interceded on behalf of his people, it seems that God would not have brought the Babylonians upon them in judgement. He looked for a man to intercede and found none, and so the judgement stood.

I do not understand why God needs our prayers before he will act, but this seems to be the only conclusion one can reach. Why were so many people that I prayed for miraculously saved? Was it just coincidence? Archbishop Temple said, "Coincidences happen when I pray — and they don't when I don't!" If God is not a puppeteer, pulling the strings, how do my prayers affect him? If I don't expect him to jerk us out of the way of danger, then what is the point of prayer?

In some way that I do not understand, when we seek to align our wills with God's will, we join in the spiritual battle, and we co-operate with God in what he is doing. As I prayed for my friends in Rwanda, who knows how they were protected? Frederick hid in the roof with blood from his wound smearing the wall as he climbed up. Did my prayers help to blind the soldiers so they did not see the blood? John and Viviane fed on mushrooms that grew where they do not normally grow — did my prayers help that process? Denis forbade the killers to touch his wife "in the name of Jesus". Was his courage a result of my prayers? I am not suggesting that I was the only one who was praying, nor that I know how prayer works. All I know is that God chooses to work in answer to our prayers, and that thousands of people are still praying for the healing of this land — and God seems to be doing a new thing here.

Yet some of those for whom I was praying did die. What am I to say about my prayers in those instances? Why are some of those for whom we pray healed, often in spectacular ways, and others die, often very painfully? First of all, we must affirm our belief in the sovereignty of God. I cannot presume to dictate to him what he should do. He knows all the circumstances and allows things to happen which we, from our perspective, find incomprehensible. I am frequently challenged by the final verses of Hebrews 11, that great chapter about faith. In verses 32-35a the writer describes miraculous escapes from appalling trials, all "by faith". Yet in verses 35b-38 others were not rescued, they were imprisoned and tortured, stoned, sawn in half, again all "by faith". Second, it is important to remember that, for a Christian, death is not the end. Indeed, ultimate healing comes for all of us when we die, for sin and pain no longer exist. As I have said earlier, there were visions in the SU camp preceding the genocide, of rivers of blood and people being taken into heaven in clouds of glory. Why some were taken and others left, I do not know, but they were ready for it. Finally, I am comforted by what my friend, Jacqueline, said following the killing of her husband. "God said to me, Simon-Pierre's work is done and I have taken him home." Ultimately that is the only answer to why some died and others lived. In God's economy, their work was done and he took them home where the glory they experience blots out completely any suffering that they had on earth.

At the end of every year, the staff of African Evangelistic Enterprises spend a few days in fasting and prayer, as they seek God's will for the coming year. In 1996 they prayed that the refugees in Zaire and Tanzania would return without bloodshed — it happened. In 1997 they felt that God was telling them to focus their prayers on those who had been involved in the bloodshed, for conviction of sin, for confession and a willingness for victims to forgive. It is happening — although there is a very long way to go. In 1998 their target was to raise an army of intercessors trained in spiritual warfare, to pray for the healing of this land.

Antoine wrote a letter which was quoted in *The Peacemaking Power of Prayer* by John D. Robb and James A. Hill. He said that the Lord had revealed to AEE as they prayed, that the return of the refugees would result in a period of instability in the county. And indeed there was a terrible time in Ruhengeri and Gisenyi préfectures, which spilled over into Byumba and Gitarama préfectures, throughout 1997 and 1998. AEE intercessors went to Ruhengeri to pray for the people there in a week of prayer and fasting with the Christians of the area. He wrote:

The Lord revealed to us that the region was plagued by demons of rebellion in links with the Nyabingi female demon that has been given the northern part of the country as its dominion. [...] The Lord also revealed that evil spirits Fear, Hatred and Terror have been dominating the area as can be seen in the names they give to their children. Names like Ntibanyendera (they don't wish me well), Ntahondi (I'm on my own), Ntanshuti (no friends) and others of that spirit are common in that area. [...] We were led to bind all those evil spirits if we were to see results in the region in terms of peace and stability.

He returned in May for a further three days of prayer and fasting and found a totally different atmosphere, something I can confirm when I visited the area in February 1999. I was astounded by the sense of peace and hope, when all I had felt on my previous visit was despair. Antoine quoted from a letter from a Christian leader in the region telling how God had answered their prayer. "Recently, many of those who had been kept captives by the rebels in the forests started to return to their home communes. They continue to come back every day. Besides, rebels are surrendering to the security forces and are asking for forgiveness, and this happens daily." Antoine adds:

> Wonderful reports were given during that time of people inviting Christians to destroy the shrines of Nyabingi, of rebels surrendering, of people getting converted, and churches resuming their activities. Today, the whole region is at peace. Maybe the politicians do not acknowledge the impact of prayer on the turn of events, but we as intercessors know, and I still have my notebooks with all the promises of what is going to happen. What a mighty God we have!

(Sadly, in June 2001 there was another outburst of violence in that area as several of the hard-core *interahamwe* had left the war in Congo and attempted to get back into Rwanda. With nothing to lose, their aim was to overthrow the government or die in the attempt. Unlike the horror of the fighting in 1998, this time things were different because there was little or no support from the local people and the army appeared to be in control, although no one knows what the final outcome will be. I asked Antoine what his reactions to these events were, and he said he had gone back to the notebooks which he wrote at that time and found that peace had only been promised for a season, but that ultimately there would be complete peace.)

Antoine then turned to another area which he and his team had been covering in prayer.

We now have around 150,000 people in jail because of participation in the genocide. It has been evaluated that it would take more than 300 years if those people are to be judged fairly. The Lord has told us to pray for repentance (recognition of the sin, confession of the sin, asking for forgiveness and restitution) on the part of offenders and healing and a spirit of forgiveness on the part of the offended. This has been the most difficult topic to pray for. The wounds on the hearts of the people are still very fresh and that's probably why the results are still meagre. But we have seen some wonderful miracles in that area, too. Many prisoners are now repenting and asking for forgiveness and even some of the survivors of the genocide who are healed now go to the prisons to extend their forgiveness.

My prayer is that those who read this will feel called by God to join the intercessors in Rwanda as we work together with him to bring a deep healing to the wounds of this land.

VIII Is it possible to repent on behalf of one's ethnic group, or is true repentance only individual?

I have made mention already of Dr Rhiannon Lloyd who has made several visits to Rwanda since 1995 at the invitation of AEE. She has done much to help people face the agony of what they went through in 1994, and also to help them to find it in their hearts to forgive those who have sinned so terribly against them. She finds that some have repented of not doing more to help Tutsi in their time of need because of fear for their own lives which would have been at risk if, for instance, they had hidden Tutsi in their homes.

But this is not her whole message. She has also helped people, both Hutu and Tutsi, face the consequences of their tribal sin. On the last evening of each seminar, three of the leaders, as European, Tutsi, and Hutu, each confess on behalf of their tribe for sins done to others. Rhiannon usually begins, as a European.

I feel this is important as they are blaming us anyway, so I need to diffuse their anger towards Europeans and give them the chance to forgive us before they are free to deal with their sins against each other. It's not just repenting for what we did in '94 but for helping to sow the seeds of hatred between the tribes earlier in this century, using the division so that we could "divide and rule". Actually, I start even earlier with slavery and all the ways in which Europe has exploited Africa for its own benefit.

This has usually paved the way for a deep work of the Holy Spirit in healing and restoring those who have attended her seminars. (I wish I could say that I have been to one but I have spoken to many who have been greatly blessed at them.)

There have also been several books written on the subject of identificational repentance in recent years, notably *The Sins of the Fathers* by Brian Mills and Roger Mitchell, and *Healing America's Wounds* by John Dawson. While not endorsing all that has been written, I do feel that there is much in the concept of identificational repentance which needs to be explored and applied, particularly in Rwanda.

What is identificational repentance?

Rhiannon describes it as "standing in the gap" and exercising our priestly role on behalf of our people. She says,

> If we have harboured hatred, resentment, prejudice or judgement against someone from another ethnic group, we need to repent of our attitudes, thoughts or actions. We need to take responsibility for our own sins. But the Bible talks about collective as well as individual responsibility, corporate as well as personal guilt. For corporate guilt, there is another kind of repentance which can also be very powerful in bringing about healing and reconciliation. It is called Identificational repentance.

Numbers 16:43-48 gives a very powerful picture of Aaron in his priestly role, running into the midst of his rebellious people who are under God's judgement, carrying his censor of incense. "He stood between the living and the dead, and the plague stopped" (16:48). In the Bible, incense is a picture of the prayers of God's people. On another occasion, when God said that he would blot out the people and make a new start with Moses, Moses interceded for the people, saying that this would not be in accordance with God's character and would bring disrepute on his name, and pleading with him not to destroy them. His plea changed God's mind. One of the saddest verses in the Bible is Ezekiel 22:30 where God looks for someone in Judah to "stand before me in the gap on behalf of the land, so that I would not have to destroy it, but I found none", and as a result the land was destroyed and the people taken into captivity for 70 years. This seems to imply that if only one person had been acting in a priestly way as both Aaron and Moses did, pleading on behalf of their people, God would not have destroyed their land.

In 1 Peter 2:9, Christians are called a "royal priesthood" and so are expected to perform a priestly role in interceding for the people, or standing in the gap on behalf of the land. Another verse much quoted by those who teach about identificational repentance is 2 Chronicles 7:14: "If my people, who are called by my name, will humble themselves and pray and seek my face and turn from their wicked ways, then will I hear from heaven and will forgive their sin and will heal their land."

Thus far, all the verses I have quoted are to do with intercession, but there are some specific examples where people confess not only their own sin but also that of their fathers. Nehemiah and Daniel both repent of sins which "I and my father's house" have committed, even though they were not born when the sins bringing judgement on the people were committed. (See Nehemiah 1:5-7 and Daniel 9:4-19.) God acted again, restoring the people to the land, as Daniel had prayed, and enabling Nehemiah to return to Jerusalem and fortify her against her enemies. Jeremiah also repented on behalf of his people (Jeremiah 14:20), but in his case God said it was too late, the judgement would have to stand, but that God would strengthen Jeremiah himself so that he would not be destroyed (chapter 15). This would imply that Ezekiel 22:39 had been written earlier, perhaps before Ezekiel and the 10,000 leaders of the nation were taken into captivity, and that Jeremiah's prayer was after this judgement had already begun.

I believe that Jesus identified with his people, when he was baptized by John. He had committed no sin, yet he accepted the baptism of John "for repentance of sin" in anticipation of that time when he would bear the sins of the whole world on the cross.

C. Peter Wagner, in a leaflet called *The Power to Change the Past*, says that identificational repentance is done in the same way as personal repentance. First, there is an acknowledgement of specific sins committed by the group. In America, in recent years, Christians have been confessing the sin of racism, exemplified in the slaughter of native Americans, and the mass importing of slaves. In Britain, many Christians acknowledge the sins which accompanied the evangelization of the world in the wake of colonization, so that the two were not distinguished. At the root of the colonization was the desire of the English to dominate. They had already dominated Wales and Scotland, and their inherent sense of superiority was something that the Lord had to deal with among the missionaries in Rwanda. Christians in Britain are beginning to repent of these attitudes on behalf of their land.

Second, there is the need to confess these corporate sins. For example, in Rwanda, at the seminars run by Rhiannon, she has confessed the sins of the white community who abandoned Rwanda to its bloodbath instead of intervening at an earlier stage, and who supplied many of the arms with which the killing was prolonged, even after the genocide was over. Then a Hutu has confessed the sins committed in the genocide against the Tutsi, and then a Tutsi has confessed the arrogance and disregard they had towards the Hutu before the revolution of 1959.

Thirdly, there is an acknowledgement that the blood of Jesus was shed for the sins of the whole world, including the sins just confessed.

Finally, there is a determination to walk in new ways. As a Hutu has confessed the sins of his tribe, a Tutsi will grant him forgiveness on behalf of his tribe, and so on. Rhiannon says that at this point there is often a breakthrough in her seminars as people start hugging each other across tribal divides, often with tears, and healing begins.

Rhiannon points out that confessing sin on behalf of a tribe, does not absolve individuals from confessing their own sin. She says,

> They must confess before God on their own behalf. It does mean that the people who hear our confession are able to let go of their judgements and bitterness and find grace to forgive. Our confession does not change the past but it does help to change the present and the future. [...] Confession, repentance and reconciliation

must become a way of life. We, as Christians representing the local church, are God's hope for healing the nation and have a chance to live out these principles in a unique way. It is God's plan that His church and his people adopt this way of life and become priestly reconcilers to hurting people.

She says that standing in the gap "does not absolve the guilty of their responsibility; does not mean that criminals can avoid punishment so that justice is averted; does not mean that we are representing our tribe in some official capacity." What it does do is release those there to receive the healing they need from the Holy Spirit. As these seminars take place around the country, many have testified to healing from anger, bitterness and hatred as they forgave those of the opposite tribe. I pray that this work will continue until all seeds of hatred are destroyed so that this land will never again go through the experiences of the past few years.

IX Revival was individual — it never tackled social issues.

Roger Bowen, then general secretary of MAM, said in his J. C. Jones Lecture of 1995,

> The Church in Rwanda has operated with a very privatized and inadequate view of sin. The challenge to repentance has usually focussed on a fairly limited range of private morality — lying, stealing, adultery, drunkenness. However there is little awareness of the solidarities of sin that we are embedded in as members of society. [...] Ironically, the Revival doctrine of sin underestimates the power and depth of evil, and by focussing on personal/private morality is quite inadequate to tackle the hideous strength of structural evil and corporate sin manifested in an act of genocide.

It is quite true that the early missionaries saw the corruption within public life and advised Christians not to get involved in it, thus leaving the field to Satan, as Antoine Rutayisire said to my father in 1995. I said something like this in a talk I gave soon after I returned to England in 1995. A former missionary stood up and said, "While I repent of my attitudes now, we have to understand that we were acting from the light as we saw it at the time." As Roger points out in the same lecture, the missionaries who founded the Anglican Church in Rwanda were:

> heirs of theological controversy at home which focussed around the authority of Scripture and attitudes to Biblical criticism. [...] The more conservative attitude to Scripture and the associated controversy, led to an emphasis on evangelism rather than any engagement with the public life of the nation or critique of the socio-political context.

It is so easy to be critical in hindsight. I remember the shock waves within the evangelical community in Britain, in the 1960s, when the newly started Evangelical Alliance Relief Fund (Tear Fund) wrote a book called *They Cannot Live on Prayer*. Up to that point, evangelicals had tended to despise those involved with a "social gospel" rather than evangelism. It has taken a long time but most Christians now recognize that social action is an essential partner to evangelism. It has taken even longer to recognize the need to challenge political structures, as Jubilee 2000 did, or embedded evil within societies in the West, so it is hardly surprising that the early missionaries put their focus on evangelism.

Having said that, as I hope I have shown in the main body of this book, one deep-rooted evil which was tackled in the Revival was the evil of racism. Where people were truly committed to the Lordship of Christ, there was no room for division on ethnic grounds — there were no Hutu or Tutsi, black or white, Burundians or Rwandan. The same was true in South Africa as Desmond Tutu said,

> My passionate opposition to apartheid stems from my understanding of the Bible and the Christian faith. If anyone can prove that apartheid is consistent with the teachings of the Bible and Jesus Christ then I will burn my Bible and cease forthwith to be a Christian. Praise to God that no one can do that!" (*The Words of Desmond Tutu*, by Naomi Tutu.)

One person who was much influenced by the Revival movement in Uganda was Archbishop Luwum who saw it as his job on behalf of Christians in Uganda to challenge President Amin. He was shot, but his example lives on. Sadly, although several terrible things happened in the years leading up to the genocide, many of the church leaders were too closely involved with the previous government to exercise their prophetic role in challenging what they were doing. My fear is that a similar thing may be happening again with the new government!

There are several comments I want to make about this issue of church and society:

(a) It is true that the early missionaries concentrated on evangelism. But to say that they did not tackle social issues is not true. They started hospitals and schools as a means of improving the health and economic state of the people. Indeed, my father was advised by Pawulo Rutwe and Sira Kabirigi about accepting the Belgian government grants for Shyogwe School, despite the subsequent lack of freedom to choose their own staff. They said, "If you can send away your own children to get a good education, you are morally obliged to let the children in Rwanda get the best education they can get." Put in those terms, my father had no hesitation about accepting the grants.

(b) The education system in Rwanda, following the rather authoritarian Belgian teaching methods, but also because of the lack of buildings, books and equipment, has tended to rely on the teacher writing essential information on a blackboard, the student writing it down, learning it by heart and then reproducing it in exams. This has led to an uncritical acceptance of all that the teacher says, often because they have no means of checking it out. This uncritical acceptance of those in authority is also seen in church and political circles. One of my main burdens, as I teach church leaders, is how to get my students to think for themselves in evaluating biblical texts. Often I will teach about two opposing doctrines, both of which can be supported by Scripture. "Which is the right one?" I will be asked. They find it really hard to handle when I tell them to evaluate the texts for themselves and come to their own conclusions!

(c) The pietist background of most of the missionaries who came to Rwanda before and since the Revival, and the

Christian education left to the African church leaders was "inadequate to deal with Church-State issues," according to Roger Bowen. He added that their theology led to "one of two reactions: either the withdrawal from the public life of the nation into a spiritual ghetto, or a naive and uncritical support of whoever is in power with biblical justification being frequently drawn from Romans chapter 13. Both these reactions are discernible within the life of the Anglican Church in Rwanda."

(d) The emphasis on evangelism has meant that most preaching has been with a view to calling people to "repent and believe the gospel". When teaching the church leaders, I am concerned to ensure that they will see this, not as the end of their preaching, but the beginning, and that they learn how to train their church members in Christian living.

(e) Because of the authoritarian nature of society in Rwanda, people find it easier to follow a list of rules, rather than to work out principles to enable them to decide how to act in different circumstances. As a result, the church in Rwanda is extremely legalistic, often following customs decided by those in Revival days who were really in tune to the Spirit's leading for their time and generation. Modern Christians still follow these traditions without thinking through the rationale for them in different circumstances today.

(f) As Antoine Rutayisire has pointed out, there was a dismissal of traditional beliefs as "nonsense", but no attempt to help people fight their very real fears about spirit attack. My mother says that only latterly in her missionary life did she have any idea about spiritual warfare, and in the early days at Shyogwe had no way to fight back against spiritual attack. It is only recently that there has been any real teaching about our authority in Christ to fight against the spirits of darkness which are so much part of life in Rwanda.

While all that is true of Rwanda before the war, it is equally true that many Christians in the West do not see it as part of their role to get involved in politics or to seek to right injustice. Partly this is because we feel so helpless in the face of grim need throughout the world, we feel that we would be trying to empty the ocean with a teaspoon, but also it is because so little teaching is given in churches about God's attitude to injustice. Gary Haugen, who was the director of the UN genocide investigation in Rwanda and is now president of International Justice Mission, has written a book called *Good News about Injustice* (IVP, 1999) in which he challenges Christians to get involved.

He describes injustice as the abuse of power. Looking at what the Bible says about injustice, he comes up with this definition: "Injustice occurs when power is misused to take from others what God has given them, namely, their life, dignity, liberty or the fruits of their love and labour" (p 72). "I saw the tears of the oppressed and they have no comforter; power was on the side of their oppressors" (Ecclesiastes 4:1).

He says:

As Christians we have learned much about sharing the love of Christ with people all over the world who have never heard the gospel. We continue to see the salvation message preached in the far corners of the earth and to see indigenous Christian churches vigorously extending Christ's kingdom on every continent. We have learned how to feed the hungry, heal the sick and shelter the homeless.

But there is one thing we haven't learned to do, even though God's Word repeatedly calls us to the task. We haven't learned how to rescue the oppressed. [...] It is perhaps more accurate to say that as people committed to the historic faith of Christianity, we have <u>forgotten</u> how to be such a witness of Christ's love, power and justice in the world. In generations past the great leaders of Christian Revival in North America and Great Britain were consumed by a passion to declare the gospel and to manifest Christ's compassion and justice. But somewhere during the twentieth century some of us have simply stopped <u>believing</u> that God can actually use us to answer the prayers of children, women and families who suffer under the hand of abusive power or authority in their communities. We sit in the same paralysis of despair as those who don't even claim to know a Saviour — and in some cases, we manifest even <u>less</u> hope.

I confess that when I hear about a child being raped or a widow having her land seized unlawfully, I feel helpless, but this book has challenged me to be more involved by showing me how God views injustice. Consider the following verses from the Bible:

> Why does the wicked man revile God? Why does he say to himself, "He won't call me to account?" But you, O God, do see trouble and grief; you consider it to take it in hand. The victim commits himself to you; you are the helper of the fatherless (Psalm 10:13-14).

> For I, the Lord, love justice; I hate robbery and iniquity (Isaiah 61:8).

> For the Lord is righteous, he loves justice (Psalm 11:7).

> This is what the Lord says: "Let not the wise man boast of his wisdom or the strong man boast of his strength or the rich man boast of his riches, but let him who boasts boast about this: that he understands and knows me, that I am the Lord, who exercises kindness, justice and righteousness on earth, for in these I delight," declares the Lord (Jeremiah 9:23-24).

> Evil men do not understand justice, but those who seek the Lord understand it fully (Proverbs 28:5).

> He has showed you, O man, what is good. And what does the Lord require of you? To act justly and to love mercy and to walk humbly with your God (Micah 6:8).

> The Lord works righteousness and justice for all the oppressed (Psalm 103:6).

> If you take your neighbour's cloak as a pledge, return it to him by sunset, because his cloak is the only covering he has for his body. What else will he sleep in? When he cries out to me, I will hear, for I am compassionate (Exodus 22:26-27).

> Look! The wages you failed to pay the workmen who mowed your fields are crying out against you. The cries of the harvesters have reached the ears of the Lord Almighty (James 5:4).

From these and other verses we can see God's passionate concern for all victims of injustice and his desire that his people should feel a similar passion. In Jesus, God entered this suffering world and himself suffered injustice. Gary Haugen writes:

> In Rwanda, where I had to bear the burden of digging through the twisted, reeking remains of horrific mass graves, I tried to imagine, for just a minute, what it must have been like for God to be present at each of the massacre sites as thousands of Tutsi women and children were murdered. Frankly, the idea was impossible to bear...

So often we pay lip-service to the God of justice, considering that righting injustice is his business, not ours. Yet he has chosen to work through us. In the same way that people hear the good news of the gospel because people preach it, or the hungry are fed or the sick are healed because men and women of compassion go in the name of Christ to feed and heal, so victims of injustice are helped through us.

I have quoted Ezekiel 22:30 in the context of intercessory prayer, but reading it in its context from verse 25 we see that what God was looking for was someone to intervene in situations of injustice. Or see Isaiah 59:15-16a, "Truth is nowhere to be found, and whoever shuns evil becomes a prey. The Lord looked and was displeased that there was no justice. He saw that there was no-one, he was appalled that there was no-one to intervene."

Gary Haugen summarizes:

> ... three promises of God on which we base all our hope for bringing about justice: (1) Ours is a God of justice, a God who hates injustice and wants it to stop; (2) God desires to use his people as his instruments for seeking justice and rescuing the oppressed; and (3) God does not give his people a ministry that he won't empower.

As we step out in faith to do the things we believe God is calling us to do, we will find the way God uses us to fight injustice in the world he loves. Not all have the expertise to fight injustice in the streets, but we can all seek to be informed, we can all pray, we can all support those involved in the fight, and where injustice comes to our notice we can bring it to the attention of others.

There were many failures in the church in Rwanda before the genocide. I pray that we all will be prepared to step out in faith to fight injustice in the future, so that never again will we hear people say, "God is dead, we can do what we like", or "I can do what I like today; tomorrow I will repent and God will forgive me." Psalm 10:10-11 describes this attitude of the oppressor: "His victims are crushed, they collapse; they fall under his strength. He says to himself, 'God has forgotten; he covers his face and never sees.'"

Had the church not kept silent in the face of the assassinations which led up to the genocide, or the injustice for the forgotten refugees in Uganda who eventually invaded as the RPF, the horror of the war and the genocide might never have happened. "You hear, O Lord, the desire of the afflicted; you encourage them, and you listen to their cry, defending the fatherless and the oppressed, in order that man, who is of the earth, may terrify no more" (Psalm 10:17-18).

Bibliography

History of the Ruanda Mission (MAM) and Revival

A Grain of Mustard Seed, Lindesay Guillebaud (Oxford, Church Army Press, 1959).

An African Apostle, Penny Relph, publisher unknown.

Breath of Life, Patricia M. St John (London, Norfolk Press, 1971).

Fire in the Hills, H. H. Osborn (Crowborough, Highland, 1991).

God Has Ears, Doreen Peck (Southwell, Penelope Young, 1999).

Only One Weapon, Harold Adeney (Ruanda Mission, 1963).

Pioneers in the East African Revival, H. H. Osborn (Winchester, Apologia, 2000).

Quest for the Highest, Dr J. E. Church (Exeter, Paternoster Press, 1981).

Ruanda's Redemption, Dr Stanley Smith and Dr Len Sharp (out of print).

The Coming of the Rain, Katharine Makower (Carlisle, Paternoster Press, 2000).

The Road to Revival, Dr Stanley Smith (out of print).

History of the genocide

A People Betrayed: The Role of the West in Rwanda's Genocide, L. R. Melvern (London, Zed, 2000).

Faith under Fire, Antoine Rutayisire (Essex, African Enterprise, 1995).

Leave None to Tell the Story, Human Rights Watch.

Rwanda Crisis: History of a Genocide, Gerard Prunier (London, C. Hurst, 1995).

Rwanda: Death, Despair, Defiance, African Rights (London).

Season of Blood: A Rwandan Journey, Fergal Keane (London, Penguin, 1995).

The Colour of Darkness, Lesley Bilinda (London, Hodder & Stoughton, 1996).

Walk This Way: The Journey of a Rwandan Refugee, Joseph Ndereyimana (Carolyn L. R. Neville, 1999).

We Wish to Inform You That Tomorrow We Will Be Killed with Our Families, Philip Gourevitch (London, Picador, 1999).

Afterthoughts

I   J. C. Jones Lecture, 1995, Roger Bowen, quoted as an appendix in *Faith under Fire*, Antoine Rutayisire (Essex, African Enterprise, 1995).

        The Peacemaking Power of Prayer, John D. Robb and James A. Hill (Nashville, Broadman and Holman, 2000).

II   *A Grace Disguised: How the Soul Grows through Loss*, Gerald Sittser (Grand Rapids, Zondervan, 1995).

        God and the Victim: Theological Reflections on Evil, Victimization, Justice and Forgiveness, Lisa Barnes Lampman (ed.), et al. (Grand Rapids, Wm B. Eerdmans, 1999).

        No Future Without Forgiveness, Desmond Tutu (London, Rider, 1999).

        Once Saved, Always Saved?, David Pawson (London, Hodder & Stoughton, 1996).

        Struggling to Forgive, Brian Frost (London, HarperCollins, 1998).

III   *Finding God in Unexpected Places*, Philip Yancey (Milton Keynes, Summit, 1995).

IV   *Once Saved, Always Saved?* David Pawson (London, Hodder & Stoughton, 1996).

V   *The Peacemaking Power of Prayer*, John D. Robb and James A. Hill (Nashville, Broadman and Holman, 2000).

VI   *A Grace Disguised: How the Soul Grows through Loss*, Gerald Sittser (Grand Rapids, Zondervan, 1995).

        A Grief Observed, C. S. Lewis (Bantam Doubleday Dell, 1976).

        The Problem of Pain, C. S. Lewis (London, Simon & Schuster, 1996).

Where is God when it Hurts?, Philip Yancey (London, Marshall Pickering, 1998).

VII   *The Peacemaking Power of Prayer*, John D. Robb and James A. Hill (Nashville, Broadman and Holman, 2000).

VIII   *Healing America's Wounds*, John Dawson (Virginia Woodard [Editor] Gospel Light Publications, 1997).

The Power to Change the Past, C. Peter Wagner.

The Sins of the Father, Brian Mills and Roger Mitchell (Kent, Sovereign World, 1999).

IX   *Good News about Injustice*, Gary A. Haugen (Leicester, IVP, 1999).

J. C. Jones Lecture, 1995, Roger Bowen, quoted as an appendix in *Faith under Fire*, Antoine Rutayisire (Essex, African Enterprise, 2000).

Guillebaud Family: Summary

Harold Guillebaud (29th September 1889 – 22nd April 1941) married **Margaret Edwards** (8th October 1889 – 10th July 1961) on 5th September 1912. In 1925 they responded to a call by Dr Sharp for a Bible translator and sailed for Africa with their three older daughters. Harold worked with Samsoni Inyarubuga on the translation while Margaret set up home in Kabale, Uganda. They returned to England for six months in 1928, taking the whole family back to Uganda with them. During that time Margaret had an exhibition of her sketches shown at the Belgian Colonial Office in Brussels. On 23rd November 1931 the New Testament in Kinyarwanda was completed. They returned to England in 1932 for the education of the family. Harold bought a house in Cambridge and got involved with students of the Christian Union, particularly through "Sunday lunches". Harold wrote *Why the Cross?* and *Some Moral Difficulties in the Bible.* He also edited the first three of the series *Search the Scriptures* and was a founding member of Tyndale House, Cambridge. In May 1936 he returned to Africa alone to continue translation work, leaving Margaret to keep home for their daughters. She and Lindesay joined him there in July 1937 and they travelled back together, celebrating their silver wedding en route. In 1940 he was asked to become archdeacon of Ruanda-Urundi and made the difficult journey out in wartime, accompanied by Margaret and their daughters Rosemary and Lindesay. In November that year he was made archdeacon in Namirembe Cathedral, Kampala, but died in Matana on 22nd April 1941. Margaret remained at Matana teaching Bible classes to women and starting "*Intore za Yesu*" — a youth group. She also started a small printing press at Matana which was replaced in 1952 by a larger bookshop and printing room which was a memorial to Harold. In August 1956 she retired due to ill heath, and set up home in Cambridge with Lindesay. She died there on 10th July 1961.

Peter Guillebaud (19th April 1914 – 7th November 1996). Eldest child of Harold and Margaret. He was eleven when his parents sailed for Africa leaving him at Monkton Junior School, near Bath. In June 1928 he travelled to Africa with the whole family. During his time abroad he was tutored by his father. In January 1929, he was confirmed in Namirembe Cathedral, but this only made him feel guilty, until a year later at Monkton Combe Senior School, when he made a commitment to Christ, helped by his friend Harold Adeney. In 1932 he went to St John's College, Cambridge, to study mathematics, graduating with a First in 1935. He then went to the Cambridge Teacher Training College for Men. In 1936 he became engaged to **Elisabeth Sutherland** (11th January 1915 – 12th September 2001) who was studying history at Girton College. She also went on to teacher training college while he went to teach at Seaford College, Sussex. On 24th December 1938 Elisabeth sailed for Burundi with the Sharps while Peter completed his two years of teaching and then went to the Missionary Training Colony. On 23rd November 1939 Peter sailed for Africa with the Adeneys. He settled at Buye, teaching the deacons and building their house while waiting for the wedding. Elisabeth, meanwhile, was starting a primary school at Buhiga, having learned the language and taught at Matana. Peter and Elisabeth were the first trained educationalists to join the mission, and, between them, started most of the schools where the mission worked. On 12th April 1940 Peter and Elisabeth were legally married at a civil ceremony in Kampala, and on 24th April 1940 they held the church wedding at Matana. They set up house at Buye where Elisabeth taught at the primary school and Peter trained primary school teachers. Following the death of Peter's father at Matana on 22nd April 1941, they visited Mukono in Uganda and were helped into a fuller fellowship in Revival. In 1946 they started a secondary school at Shyogwe and remained there for the next few years with trips to England, time at Shyira and Kigeme, but most often at Shyogwe. Peter compiled a hymn book in Kinyarwanda during those years and Elisabeth started a teacher training school both there and at Shyira. In 1959 there was revolution in Rwanda. Peter and Elisabeth helped in a large displaced persons' camp at Hanika while at the same time he was schools inspector. They were told that it would be advisable to leave the country and transferred to Burundi, where he continued as schools inspector but Elisabeth started a secondary school at Matana. They then moved to Bujumbura where they ministered in a slum area. In 1964 Elisabeth left Peter there with his sister, Rosemary, while she went to England to provide a home for their teenage children. After six months he joined her and they lived in London doing various jobs, but always involved with overseas students until returning to Rwanda in 1969, this time with Scripture Union during the heady days of Revival in secondary schools. In 1979, due to retire, Peter was asked to coordinate a team of Bible translators for an ecumenical translation of the Bible in modern language. Elisabeth set up home in Kigali and taught Kinyarwanda to missionaries. In 1986 they finally retired to England, but after watching on television the awful events of 1994, they returned for a year to Kigali, listening to stories and preaching reconciliation through the cross of Jesus. They returned to England in February 1996, and on 7th November 1996 Peter died in Bradfield, near Reading. Elisabeth returned to Rwanda with her daughter, Meg, and was involved with helping widows and orphans at Byumba until her death there on 12th September 2001. She had also just finished translating from Kirundi into Kinyarwanda Rosemary's commentary on Hebrews.

Rosemary Guillebaud (b 4th June 1915). Eldest daughter of Harold and Margaret, she first came to Africa with her parents in 1925 when she was ten years old. With her sisters, she helped her father with his translation work by reading the Bible to him in English while he checked the Kinyarwanda. She became fascinated by the process of Bible translation. In 1932 the family returned to England and she studied modern languages at Newnham College, Cambridge. The War Office allowed her to accompany her parents to Burundi in 1940. She went to Kigeme to learn Kinyarwanda and had passed the first language exam when her father died on 22nd April 1941. She was asked by Dr Stanley Smith to take over her father's work of translation.

Helped by a skilled team of translators, she managed to complete the Kirundi New Testament with Psalms by 1951, and she was able to give her mother the completed Bible manuscript as Margaret was dying in 1961. She returned to Burundi where she assisted the shoemaker, Joel Abekyamwale, to translate the New Testament into Bembe (spoken by a large tribe in Congo). She also wrote a commentary on Hebrews in Kirundi. She finally retired in 1979 to a bungalow in Cambridge which she shared with her sister, Philippa, until Philippa's death on 10th October 2000. She still lives there.

Lindesay Guillebaud (16th November 1917 – 16th December 1971). Second daughter of Harold and Margaret, she accompanied her parents and two sisters to Kabale in 1925. She had a nasty experience when a dog bite went gangrenous and she nearly died, and she was also very ill with dysentery, but survived the two trips to Africa while gaining a love for the people. She experienced another illness in England which prevented her from completing her studies. As a result she was free to accompany her mother to Africa in 1937 to meet her father, and then for all three to return together. In 1940 she accompanied her parents and Rosemary to Burundi, and stayed at Matana while Rosemary went to Kigeme to study Kinyarwanda. She supported her mother in the traumatic months following her father's death, keeping house for her and Rosemary, while at the same time launching out in ventures of her own. She first started a kindergarten and then began to train girls to teach the little ones. She also started a brides' school for those about to get married. Later, Lindesay also supervised all the schools in her area. In August 1956 she returned to England with her mother, keeping house for her in Cambridge, until Margaret's death there in 1961. A year later she became candidates secretary for CMS and rented a flat in London. Later she became personal assistant to the general secretary of CMS, John V. Taylor. In 1971, after several months of ill health, she died of heart failure.

Philippa Guillebaud (13th December 1918 – 10th October 2000). Philippa travelled to Kabale with her parents and two elder sisters in 1925, and again in 1928. She went to teacher training college in Cambridge and spent the war years there.

She then went to the Sudan with CMS in 1945 where she ran a girls' school in Yei. In 1962, Philippa was expelled from the Sudan because the government could see no merit in Bible translation and settled in Gulu, northern Uganda, where she completed the translation with the help of refugees. She retired to Cambridge in 1980. She had increasing ill health and was confined to a wheelchair during her later years, finally dying of cancer in 2000.

Mary Stockley (née Guillebaud) (15th June 1921 – 8th January 1999). Mary was left in England with her twin sister, Veronica, when her parents and three elder sisters travelled to Uganda in 1925. They both became very withdrawn and unhappy. In 1928 she went to Uganda with the whole family, returning in 1932 when she went to school in Cambridge. She then studied the piano at the London School of Music and gained her LRAM, but at the outset of war she opted to train as a nurse at St Thomas' Hospital, London, where she met Dr Tom Stockley, whom she married on 31st March 1950. They settled in Cambridge where Tom was a GP, until his sudden death from a heart attack in 1964. They had five children. Mary then taught piano, mainly from her home. When the family grew up, she trained as a counsellor with Marriage Guidance, later Relate. She died in Cambridge of a brain tumour in 1999.

Veronica Madeley (née Guillebaud) (b 15th June 1921). With Mary, Veronica was left in England when her parents travelled to Uganda in 1925. In 1928 she went to Uganda with the whole family, returning in 1932 when she went to school in Cambridge. She learned to type so that she could help her father with Bible translation, but then the War Office would not permit her to leave England — three members of one family being too many to leave at war time. She worked with George Sutherland at the LNER offices until she was called up and joined the WAAF. She became a wireless mechanic for the duration of the war. In 1950 she went to Rwanda to help Mrs Stanley Smith run the Home Protestant for Protestant Boys at the large secondary school in Astrida (later Butare) and to type the Bible manuscript for Dr Stanley Smith. She returned to England in 1952 and married Dick Madeley on 29th August 1953. They had three children. She became very involved with the Christian Alliance and the Bible Society, and now lives near Oxford.

John Guillebaud (b 19th January 1941). The eldest child of Peter and Elisabeth, John was born in Buye, Burundi. He was educated in Africa until he was ten when he went to school in England. He went to Cambridge University and trained as a doctor at St Bartholomew's Hospital in London. He is now professor of family planning and reproductive health at University College, London as well as medical director of the Margaret Pike Family Planning Centre. On 15th April 1972 he married Gwyn Jones, and they have three children. He is very involved with the conservation movement and travels the world speaking on planned parenthood and environmental issues, and teaching family planning methods. He has authored and co-authored a number of books, including *The Pill*, and written numerous articles for medical and Christian journals.

Margaret (Meg) Guillebaud (b 12th October 1943). Meg was born at Buye, Burundi, the second child of Peter and Elisabeth. She went to school in Africa until she was fifteen and then to Clarendon School, North Wales. After obtaining a degree at Edinburgh University she did Voluntary Service Overseas in Malawi for fifteen months from 1966. She then joined the Metropolitan Police from 1968 until 1977 when she went to All Nations Christian College for two years. In 1979 she did a year at Cranmer Hall, Durham, before being ordained deaconess in June 1980. She was ordained deacon in Norwich Cathedral in 1987 and priest in Bristol Cathedral in 1994. She went to Rwanda with her parents in 1995 for a month, and returned, having resigned her job in England, later that year to teach in Byumba. She accompanied her parents to Britain again in January 1996, applied to MAM and returned in July that same year to teach deacons and then catechists in Byumba diocese. Following the death of her father in November 1996 she returned to England, but went back to Byumba the following January, accompanied by her mother. They supported each other in their ministries until her mother died in September 2001. She still lives in Byumba, teaching church leaders in the diocese.

David Guillebaud (b 20th February 1946). David was born at Buye, Burundi, and educated in Africa until he was twelve when he attended school in England. He went to university in London where he studied French and German, and met Peta Steele whom he married on 30th March 1968. They have four children. He is a management consultant who has worked in the oil industry, in economic development overseas, in travel, and latterly in e-commerce. The family have lived in Algeria, France and England. He is now active in various consulting and e-business ventures based in Burnham, near Slough in England.

Christine Paterson (née Guillebaud) (b 26th June 1950). Christine, born in Buye, Burundi, is the youngest child of Peter and Elisabeth. She was educated at various schools in Africa before attending Clarendon School, North Wales, followed by the North London Collegiate School. She went to York University where she studied linguistics. She then had a year at St John's College, Nottingham, followed by two years as a travelling secretary for Universities and Colleges Christian Fellowship (UCCF). On 26th April 1975 she married Ross Paterson and joined him in Taiwan. With Mainland China opening up in the late 1970s, they returned to England to focus on ministry into China. Based in York, Ross founded the Chinese Church Support Ministries (also known as Antioch Missions) and Derek Prince Minstries, China. In 1994 they moved to Singapore with their five daughters. Ross, with Christine, has written several books, including *Heartcry for China* and *The Antioch Factor*. They now split their time between Singapore and England to be near their daughters in school.

Simon Guillebaud (b 22nd March 1973). Simon, the second child and only son of David and Peta, born in England, is the fourth generation of Guillebauds to work in Rwanda and Burundi. Educated in France, he is bilingual in French and English. He also went to Harrow School and Loughborough University, where he graduated in languages and politics. After a brief period working in marketing, he travelled extensively in Africa before becoming certain of the Lord's leading to Burundi. Since January 1999 he has worked as a youth evangelist with Scripture Union in Bujumbura, where he plans to live for the long term.

Key Personnel

Joel Abekyamwale (p 160). A young shoemaker, from the Bembe tribe in Congo, who translated Mark's Gospel into Bembe from Swahili. Rosemary revised it with him and together they translated the whole New Testament into Bembe.

Harold Adeney (pp 43, 88, 97-98, 99, 141, 150, 261, 271). Married to Isobel. Both served as doctors and missionaries from 1939. Harold was instrumental in leading Peter to faith while at school. Newly married in 1939, Harold and Isobel travelled to Burundi with Peter. They returned to England in 1966 and Harold became general secretary of the Ruanda Mission until 1972. He returned to Burundi to plant a church at Gitega and was ordained in Burundi in 1975. They returned to England in 1966. He and Isobel were joined by Elisabeth for a trip around Burundi in 1997.

M. Anet (pp 32, 37, 38). Head of Belgian Protestant Mission, based in Brussels, Belgium, which took over all the German Protestant stations after 1919. He supported and encouraged Harold in his work, and strongly advised the Belgian government to allow CMS to work in Rwanda.

Rev. Lawrence Barham (pp 36, 93, 118). Joined the Ruanda Mission in 1928, training men for the ministry at Kabale until 1938 when he moved to Buye, Burundi. In 1931 he married Julia. He became archdeacon of Ruanda-Urundi in 1957. He retired in 1959 and became general secretary of the Ruanda Mission. In 1964 he was asked to become the first bishop of the separate diocese of Ruanda-Urundi to pave the way for the new national bishops of the two separate diocese of Rwanda and

Burundi who were consecrated in 1965. Lawrence then retired to parish ministry in England. He died in 1973. His wife, Julia, died in 1984. His son, Ken, also became a bishop, in Cyangugu, southern Rwanda.

Rev. Jim Brazier (p 77). Founded the new station at Shyira in 1930 before moving to Kigeme in 1934 soon after marrying Joan. Following the deaths in 1940 of Archeacon Pitt-Pitts and then a year later Harold Guillebaud, he became the third archdeacon of Ruanda-Urundi and moved to Buye, Burundi. In 1951 he was consecrated bishop of Ruanda-Urundi, which was still not a separate diocese, so he became assistant bishop of Uganda. He retired to England in 1964 and died in 1989.

Rev. Bill Butler (pp 92, 102, 113, 123, 124). Bill was at Monkton School with Peter. They were then together at the Missionary Training Colony, and Bill was Peter's best man at his wedding in April 1940. Bill went as a CMS missionary to Uganda where he was ordained in November 1940 and sent as chaplain to Mukono Theological College. He was strongly influenced by William Nagenda, who was there as a student, and was transferred for sympathizing with the expelled students in 1941. He married Nancy and worked at Kako in Uganda for many years. He retired in 1962 and became general secretary of Ruanda Mission before returning to parish ministry in 1966. He died in 1995 while Peter and Elisabeth were in Kigali.

Yohana Bunyenyezi (pp 57, 118). Harold and Margaret's cook-boy at Kabale. Yohana accompanied Blasio Kigozi to Gahini, where he accepted the Lord Jesus as his Saviour. He went to Mukono to be trained for ordination but was expelled for involvement in Revival in 1941. He went to Bujumbura as a missionary in 1944 and also worked in Bukavu. Later he was ordained. He died in 2000.

Dr Bill Church (pp 62, 68, 71). The brother of Joe Church, he came to help his brother at Gahini in 1931. In 1935 he walked to Buhiga in Burundi with Kosiya Shalita and established a hospital there with 30 volunteers from Gahini. Kosiya went on to Matana and Bill frequently travelled south in that first year to encourage him. He married Janet Casson in 1937 and together they worked at Buhiga and then back at Gahini until they retired in 1957. He then became a GP at Little Shelford, outside Cambridge, sharing a practice with Tom Stockley who married Mary Guillebaud. Following the death of Janet in 1972 he married Mildred Forder, a friend of Janet, in 1977, who had herself been a nurse for many years at Gahini. He died in Cambridge in 1979.

Dr Joe Church (pp 37, 45, 46, 48, 50, 55, 56, 57, 58, 59, 60, 62, 63, 65, 66, 69, 70, 87, 112, 113, 115, 116, 124, 125). Married to Decie: doctor and missionary evangelist from 1927. Moved to Gahini in 1928 and with Simeoni Nsibambi was instrumental, by the power of the Holy Spirit, in bringing about the Revival in Rwanda. He had to leave Rwanda in October 1961. He went to Kabarole in Uganda where his son, Robin, was building a hospital, and he helped in the construction for three years. In 1964 he retired to Lweza on Lake Victoria and then moved to Kampala, Uganda. In June 1972 he retired to Little Shelford, near Cambridge, where his brother, Bill, was the GP. He wrote several books including *Quest for the Highest* and *Every Man a Bible Student*. He died on 29th September 1990, aged 90. His wife, Decie, followed him on 30th March 1991, aged 86.

Margaret Clayton (p 86). A missionary from 1938, Margaret was teaching at Matana when Elisabeth arrived there in 1939. She moved to Uganda where she was involved with the Mothers' Union. She lives in England in retirement.

Niyi Daramola (pp 221, 262). A Nigerian working in the offices of Scripture Union in Nairobi, Kenya. He took over as head of SU Africa on the retirement of Dr Mutombo.

Denis (pp 222, 223). Denis's whole family was killed in the 1960s, leaving him with a five-year-old niece to look after. She was adopted by Meg's church in Lowestoft. Denis later married Venantie and was ordained as a Baptist pastor. In 1994 he forbade the killers to touch his wife "In the name of Jesus". He was appointed *conseilleur* of the camp at Byumba. Later he became president of the Baptist Church in Rwanda, but resigned to study theology in Uganda.

M. Durand (pp 31, 37, 38, 131). A member of the Belgian Protestant Mission in Rwanda, who was won over by Harold's scholarship at the Kirinda conference, but later denied his agreement with the conference decisions and resigned from the consultative committee. Later he helped Peter revise the Kinyarwanda hymn book.

Edison (pp 185, 186, 187, 188). A student at Shyogwe who accused Pastor Geoffrey and killed the *assistant médical*, Helene's husband, at Shyogwe. He was later converted at Kigali. In 1994 he rescued Tutsi, and later saw Helene and asked for forgiveness. They testified together in the stadium in Kigali.

Edith (pp 233-235). Christine's friend at Shyogwe. Her husband and members of her family were killed at Hanika. Edith fled, and the Lord saved her at one of the barriers. She visited the killer of her husband in prison, and later her aunt's killer asked for her forgiveness. She was trained in trauma counselling by Dr Rhiannon Lloyd, and is now a teacher at Hanika School.

Ephraim (pp 204-205, 208, 256, 267-268). A soldier and musician, married to Francine. Francine was miraculously saved during the RPF attack on Ruhengeri. Peter gave Ephraim his accordion. Ephraim is now a chauffeur and choir master at Byumba. Francine helped Elisabeth in the girls' sewing school.

Fidele and **Yvonne (pp 220, 223, 234).** A couple who saved many Tutsi in 1994. Yvonne escaped to Nairobi after finding that all her family had been killed in Gitarama, but Fidele was taken to Byumba where he disappeared, believed killed.

John Gakwandi (pp 175-176, 183-184, 194-195, 230-232). An *assistant médical* at Kigeme, whose family were made homeless in 1959, and again in 1963. He was converted in 1970, but lost his job in 1972. In 1977 he married Viviane, who had been converted at Kigeme on 13th January 1970. They and their children were miraculously preserved in 1994 in the house of **Marianne Schmeling**, a German living in Kigali. He now runs Solace Ministries to help widows in Rwanda.

Pierre Gakwandi (pp 228-230). A Presbyterian pastor, and one of the team of translators of the Bible working with Peter from 1980 to 1991, when Pierre returned to Butare to pastor a church. He and his wife, Rosa, were preserved in their home in Butare in 1994. In 1995 he returned to Kigali to get a new team together to continue with the Bible translation. Once this was done, he pastored a church in Kigali while his wife started a ministry to help orphans. He had a stroke in 1999 but has made a good recovery.

Joy Gerson (pp 66, 85, 87). A missionary from 1936 to 1952, she had just arrived as a teacher at Gahini Girls' School when Revival broke out there in 1936. From 1938 to 1948 she was headmistress of Kigeme Girls' School and then went to start another school at Shyira. In 1952 she married Rev. B. W. M. Berdoe and resigned from the mission.

Major General Juvenal Habyarimana (pp 189, 190, 191, 192, 193, 195, 203, 205, 206, 207, 209, 216, 242, 245). On 5th July 1973, he took over the government in a bloodless coup, deposing **President Kayibanda**. Next morning he announced over the radio that the killing must stop. In 1974 he created a single party system (MRND) for the country. For many years there was stability and the economy improved although his regime was oppressive. By the end of the 1980s his wife had surrounded herself with a powerful élite called the *kazu* which was taking control. She was known as Kanjogera. In October 1990, when the RPF invaded Rwanda, Habyarimana allowed an anti-Tutsi campaign to unite the Hutu. In August 1993 he signed the Arusha peace accords agreeing to share power with the RPF, but delayed implementing. On 4th June 1994 he flew to a meeting in Dar-es-Salaam where he was urged to have no further delay. On his return on 6th June his plane was shot down and he was killed. This gave rise to the genocide.

Harriet (pp 227-228). Marian Kajuga's niece, whose husband, Silas, was killed in Butare. She escaped through the help of a Hutu friend and is now a member of parliament.

Israel Havugimana (pp 186, 194, 195, 212, 214, 217, 242, 251). Israel was converted through SU camps. He was a schoolboy at Shyogwe who protected Tutsi in 1972. Later, at university at Butare, he was persecuted for not accepting the initiation rights. In 1977 he married Jacqueline, who died after the birth of their third child. He became head of African Evangelistic Enterprise (AEE) in Rwanda and worked for reconciliation between the tribes from 1990 to 1994. He was killed the day after the president's plane came down, having warned Bishop Rwaje to stay indoors.

Helene (pp 186-187, 188, 237). Helene's husband was the *assistant médical* at Shyogwe, who was killed by schoolboys in 1972. She fled to Kabgayi where she was seen by Peter and Elisabeth. She then went to Burundi, returning in 1995. She met Edison, one of her husband's killers, who asked her forgiveness, and together they testified to the power of Christ in their lives. She is living in Israel Havugimana's house and looking after the two granddaughters of **Geoffrey and Chloë Kinyanza**.

Godfrey Hindley (pp 112, 149, 156, 279). Married to Phyllis, and a doctor at Shyira from 1935. He was the field secretary when Peter and Elisabeth were advised to leave Rwanda in 1962. The following year he and Peter attempted to stop the invasion of Rwanda by refugees. He retired in 1985 and died in 1996. Phyllis still lives in England. Chris, their son, was personnel secretary when Simon Guillebaud applied to MAM.

Geoffrey Holmes (pp 22, 37, 63). A pioneer missionary from 1924 to 1940, Geoff was an ex-captain in the British army who came to Kabale in 1924. He found Gahini a suitable place to start a hospital, but returned to Gatsibo to give Dr Joe Church a free rein at Gahini. He married Ernestine Carr in 1930 and was ordained in December of that year. He started the work at Kigeme in 1932, retired in 1940 and died in England in 1964.

M. Honoré (pp 37, 38, 39, 43, 44, 80). A missionary with the Belgian Protestant Mission at the Presbyterian station of Remera in Rwanda, who collaborated with Harold in his translation work, revising the work with him. His daughter, Lillette, was a partner with MAM from 1955 to 1996.

Samsoni Inyarubuga (pp 24-25, 27, 28, 29, 30, 35, 43, 44, 47, 59, 69, 78, 82). Grandson of **King Rutarindwa** of Rwanda, married to Lindesay. He had to flee Rwanda when **Musinga** came to the throne and was unable to return until Musinga was deposed in 1932. He was Harold Guillebaud's chief assistant in translating the Bible into Kinyarwanda and was blessed during the Revival.

Jacqueline (pp 247, 249-250). Married to Simon-Pierre, who was the schools worker for Scripture Union. Because they were of different tribes, both parents opposed their marriage but eventually they agreed. He was killed at a barrier, but she and her two little girls were sent home. She lived with Peter and Elisabeth in the SU dormitories in 1995 and travelled with them, giving her testimony in churches.

Jennifer (pp 176-177, 195-196). Having been converted at Kigeme, Jennifer travelled with Peter and Elisabeth to schools in the 1970s. She was expelled from the Anglican Church because she was baptised by immersion. She married a Pentecostal pastor who was falsely accused, in 1998, of involvement in the genocide. He led many fellow prisoners to the Lord, and died of meningitis in 2001, still in prison.

Carl and Eleanor Johnson (p 271). Carl and Eleanor were Brethren missionaries in Bujumbura, Burundi. Christine lived with them while she attended a Belgian school in Bujumbura. They refused to leave Burundi when told to do so by the government, and, although both were well into their 80s, they found themselves looking after a large displaced persons camp around their home in 1997. Carl died in February 2001, but Eleanor is still looking after the needy people in the camp.

Mabel Jones (pp 125, 169, 170, 171, 172, 253, 260). A teacher at Shyogwe from 1950, Mabel was headmistress at Kigeme School when Revival came in 1970. Later she founded a home for girls who wanted to serve the Lord at Shyogwe. She retired in 1984. She returned to speak at the "oldies' camp" in 1995 and spoke at Peter's funeral. She lives in retirement in England.

Kabera (p 35). The brother of **Kanjogera**, who plotted with her to defeat Rutarindwa. He ruled with her during Musinga's minority.

Sira Kabirigi (pp 117, 118, 120, 128, 143, 234). Converted at Gatsibo through the ministry of Geoffrey Holmes, Sira went to Gahini school where he was filled with the Holy Spirit. He was in the first class of those learning to be teachers at Buye and was with the **Stanley Smiths** when the decision was taken to develop Shyogwe. He was the only unmarried man in the team of those who started Shyogwe, but married a nurse, Geraldine, a few years later. He was imprisoned and beaten up in the troubles following the king's death in 1959. He died of natural causes before the events of 1994, but Geraldine was thrown into a longdrop at Shyogwe where she died.

Paul Kagame (pp 192, 208, 239, 278). President of Rwanda from 2000. He had been a refugee in Uganda, and in 1981 he joined Yoweri Museveni in an attempted coup against Milton Obote, Uganda's president. He and **Fred Rwigyema** remained with Museveni's guerrilla army until they captured Kampala in January 1986. He remained as a senior officer in the army, but after **Fred Rwigyema** was sacked as army c-in-c, together they developed the RPF. He was in America when the RPF invaded Rwanda in October 1990 and Rwigyema was killed. He flew back and took control of the RPF. He was in command of the successful army which finally won control of Kigali. He became the vice-president of the government of national unity, and when the president, Pasteur Bizimungu, resigned in 2000, he was elected president.

Eustace and Marian Kajuga (pp 68, 111, 118, 119, 120, 159, 203, 206, 207, 216, 217, 225-227, 228, 238, 239, 253, 259).

Both were converted as schoolchildren at Gahini in 1936. Eustace had been among the first intake of students that Peter trained as primary school teachers. He had returned to Gahini to teach and there he had married Marian in 1943. She had trained as a nurse and had worked at Kigeme before returning to Gahini. They joined Peter at Shyogwe in 1946 as they founded the new school there. Later, Eustace went to Buye to train as a pastor, being ordained in 1960. They stayed at Buye, helping with the thousands of refugees from Rwanda, until Eustace was asked to go to Nyamata to replace **Yona Kanamuzeyi** following his death in 1964. In 1968 Eustace went to Kigali as pastor and then to Gahini to train pastors. In Kigali, their son, Richard, was killed on his motor-bike. They retired from active ministry in 1988 and lived near Gahini. In 1994 Marian went to Congo for her son-in-law's funeral, leaving Eustace with their eldest son, Husi. Next morning Eustace, Husi and his wife were all killed. Marian returned to Rwanda, with her son, Wilberforce, later that year, and met Peter and Elisabeth in 1995. She still lives with Wilberforce in Kigali.

Husi Kajuga (pp 120, 127, 203, 216, 225-226). Eustace and Marian's eldest child, Husi was Mcg's close friend when they were children. When he grew up he worked for the water company in Kigali but lost his job because of discrimination against Tutsi. He then started trading in Cyangugu where he was joined by his younger brothers who had been thrown out of school. He married a Belgian, Annie, and had three children. He was converted at a Billy Graham rally in Bujumbura. By 1994 he was doing well in his trading company. He and Annie, together with his father Eustace, were all shot the day after the president's plane went down. Their youngest son, Frederick, managed to escape and was evacuated to Belgium where he joined his brother and sister.

Robert Kajuga (pp 203, 206, 207, 217, 225, 228). The youngest son of Eustace and Marian Kajuga who became the general of the killers called *interahamwe*. He was shot while retreating to Cyangugu and died of his wounds in Kinshasa, Congo, where his mother saw him just before he died.

Wilberforce Kajuga (pp 203, 225-227, 235, 238-239, 256). The second son of Eustace and Marian Kajuga, who in 1972 was thrown out of school and joined his older brother, Husi, building up a very prosperous trading company. He married Nora and had five children. He was with his mother at the funeral of his brother-in-law when the genocide started. His wife and three middle children were killed on the first day. His eldest son, John, was in Nairobi studying, and so escaped. His daughter, Celine, walked to various orphanages, and was eventually reunited with her father. Wilberforce has since remarried and had two other children. John has also married and has a son.

Yona Kanamuzeyi (pp 64, 65, 69, 70, 125, 144, 145, 156-158, 159). Yona was influenced by Blasio Kigozi but did not make a deep commitment to Christ at the time. As a church teacher he was disciplined for immorality and drunkenness. Touched by the Revival in 1939, he went to Shyogwe as the church teacher, following **Gideon Kabano** in 1950. After the revolution of 1959 he volunteered to go to Nyamata with his family to care for the displaced Tutsi who had been resettled there. He was killed as a Tutsi sympathizer in 1964. The account of his death prompted the dean of St Paul's Cathedral to write his name in the book of modern martyrs. His wife, Mary, fled with the children to Uganda where she was welcomed on the tea estate run by Christians called Namutamba, near Kampala. She died there before the RPF invaded Rwanda. One of her sons invaded with the RPF and is now a minister in the government of Rwanda.

Kanjogera (pp 35, 39-42, 206). Also known as **Nyirayuhi** (the mother of Yuhi). Appointed by **King Rwabugiri** as regent for his son Rutarindwa, instead she conspired with her brother, Kabera, to kill Rutarindwa and place her son, Musinga, on the throne. She was co-regent with Kabera during her son's minority and always a power behind his throne. Madame Habyarimana was nicknamed Kanjogera after her.

Gregoire Kayibanda (pp 141, 148, 150, 172, 182, 183, 185, 189). Secretary to the Roman Catholic Archbishop at Kabgayi, he was a prime mover in the revolution in 1959. He became president of the Republic of Rwanda. He was deposed by Major-

General Habyarimana. He was imprisoned and his fate, thereafter, is not known.

Emmanuel Kayijuka (pp 173, 218, 221, 235, 238, 249, 252, 253, 259, 262). General secretary of Scripture Union. He was converted at Gahini following a visit of some girls from Kigeme school in 1970. Initially, during the fighting around Kigali, the Scripture Union staff, together with several refugees, stayed on the premises, but following the death of the schools worker, Simon-Pierre, they realized it was time to go. Emmanuel escaped with his family to Bukavu where SU arranged for him to get to Nairobi. For some months he organized SU meetings in the refugee camps around Rwanda but knew that he had to return to Rwanda to continue in this job. He returned in January 1995 with Niyi Daramola and then on a more permanent basis with Peter and Elisabeth in February 1995. He shared their accommodation in the SU dormitory until they were able to get the SU house back in 1996. Julienne was able to join him in 1997 and they are still continuing the work in Kigali.

Bishop Norman Kayumba and **Madeleine (pp 210-212, 240, 248, 279-280).** Both Norman and Madeleine came to faith in the 1970s. He was one of the new bishops controversially consecrated in 1991, and was re-consecrated with the others on 5th June 1992 when he became bishop of Kigeme. He remained there most of 1994, protecting as many Tutsi as he could. He left briefly when the fighting drew near, but returned as soon as possible at the end of 1994. Madeleine remained in Kenya studying theology. She returned in 1997 and was ordained as a pastor. She died in October 1998 and soon afterwards Bishop Norman went to England to make a home for his children. He resigned as bishop of Kigeme and is now assistant bishop of Coventry, England.

Blasio Kigozi (pp 57, 58, 59, 60, 63, 64, 65, 67, 68, 69, 119, 145). Simeoni Nsibambi's younger brother, from a wealthy family in Uganda. In 1929, he went to Gahini as a result of God's call, where he was headmaster of the Boys' School. He was ordained deacon in 1934 and led the Evangelists' Training School. He was filled with the Spirit in 1935 and became gripped with a sense of urgency. He was en route to a synod of the Church of Uganda, where he planned to challenge the Church's spiritual apathy, when he fell ill with tick fever and died in Mengo Hospital, Kampala, on 25th January 1936.

Yosiya Kinuka (pp 58, 59, 67, 90, 91, 93, 96-97, 113, 125). Son of a chief in Ankole, Uganda, he was treated for tropical ulcers at Kabale. While there he learned to read and write and then trained to become a hospital assistant. He was baptized in 1924 and sent to Mengo for training. He married Dorcas in May 1928 and a month later went to Gahini as head hospital assistant. He was led to the Lord by Simeoni Nsibambi in 1931 and became a key figure in the East African Revival. He was among the first Rwandans ordained at Buye in 1941. Following independence of Rwanda in 1962, Yosiya and Dorcas returned to Uganda to minister to Rwandan refugees near the Rwanda border. In 1966 he retired to Rugando in his native Ankole where he died in 1975. His wife, Dorcas, died in February 1998.

Geoffrey Kinyanza (pp 145, 185, 187, 216, 217, 235-237). Born at Gatsibo and named after Geoffrey Holmes. He was converted through the influence of Blazio Kigozi. His wife, Chloe, was one of the girls at Gahini school when the Holy Spirit descended on it in 1936. Ordained in 1950 and sent to Shyogwe as pastor in 1960. In 1972 he was accused of teaching sedition by Edison, but the president told the church to move him and no further action was taken. He became pastor in Kigali. Welcomed Edison as a brother when he was converted ten years later. In 1994 he was beaten up and left for dead, but was nursed back to health by Chloe and a neighbour. All their children were killed, but two granddaughters survived, now being cared for by Helene. Geoffrey stayed in a very poor neighbourhood in Kigali "living the gospel" until illness and age forced him to accept a diocesan house near the cathedral, where he died in February 1997, followed by his wife in December 2000.

Hilda Langston (pp 85, 87). A teacher at Shyira from 1937, she retired in 1962 and died in England in 1988.

Dr Rhiannon Lloyd (pp 254-255). A medical doctor who is also qualified in psychiatry, Dr Lloyd has spent several years working in countries where there is ethnic conflict, trying to help people recover from their mental scars. She has run several seminars in Rwanda to help traumatized people find healing, and training people in trauma counselling.

Jacqueline Lugtenborg (pp 172, 173). A Dutch missionary with the Belgian Protestant Mission (SBMP), a teacher at Remera in 1970, who was filled with the Spirit in those days. She later worked with Mabel Jones both in Rwanda and later in England. They share a house in retirement.

Marie (p 246). Adopted the child of her Tutsi friend who had dreamed about the events before they happened. She is now helping Rose Gakwandi in her orphan work.

Michel and Immaculée (pp 247-249). Tutsi who were sheltered by a succession of Hutu in the Kigeme area. In 1995 they shared the dormitory accommodation at Scripture Union with Peter and Elisabeth. Michel started a society called Moucecore whose main aim is to preach the gospel as a means of bringing reconciliation between the tribes.

Misaki Mvuningoma (pp 57, 145-146, 148). Chosen to go to Bufumbira to teach Blasio Kigozi Kinyarwanda. He was converted at Gahini during the Revival and later went to Mukono where he was ordained. He married Dorothy and was pastor at Hanika when 6,000 Tutsi arrived needing help. When that camp was closed down, he fled to Tanzania. He returned to Gahini with his wife in 1995 and died there in 2001.

M. Monnier (pp 36, 37, 43, 44). A missionary with the Seventh Day Adventists in Rwanda, he supported Harold in his translation work, although there were a number of disputes over questions of theology.

Dr Kenneth Moynagh (pp 132, 137). He married Wendy in 1942. He was the doctor at Matana from 1947. He retired for his family's sake in 1964 and became doctor to the doctors at St

Bartholomew's Hospital, London. He died in 1972. Wendy still lives in Bromley and spoke of her long friendship with Elisabeth at her thanksgiving service in 2001.

Dr Mutombo (pp 218, 219). General secretary for Scripture Union in Africa, who visited Peter and Elisabeth in 1994 and encouraged them to return to Rwanda. He resigned in 1996 and his place was taken by Niyi Daramola.

Yuhi V. Musinga (pp 24, 35, 36, 39-42, 63, 78, 138). The last autocratic king of Rwanda. He became king following the defeat of his half-brother, Rutarindwa, when he was only a boy. His mother, Kanjogera, and uncle, Kabera, ruled as regents. He never accepted Christianity and was deposed by the Belgians in 1931 in favour of his son, Rudahigwa. He died in exile in Congo.

Muzungu (pp 212, 213, 217, 268-269). The archdeacon of Byumba in the 1990s, who was accused of distributing weapons to *interahamwe*, when, in fact, it was a consignment of agricultural tools and seeds for displaced persons who were returning home to Byumba. He spent four years in the camps not knowing whether his wife had survived, but was reunited with her in 1997. He is at present one of four archdeacons in the Byumba diocese.

Nathan and Helene (pp 174, 180, 193, 194, 195, 196, 201). Chosen as the first national staff worker for Scripture Union, Nathan, with Helene, first worked alongside Peter and Elisabeth, and then took over in 1979. He was succeeded by Emmanuel Kayijuka, when he went to Kenya to do further study, and has still not returned.

William Nagenda (pp 66, 69, 70, 92, 102, 113, 115, 125). A Ugandan, son of a chief, who was converted through **Simeoni Nsibambi**, and was trained at Budo School and Makere University, and became a government clerk. He wanted to train for the Anglican ministry but was asked instead to go to Gahini to replace Blasio Kigozi who had just died. He and Blasio had married sisters: his wife was Sara. In 1936 he began leading the Evangelists' Training School, but recognizing that he still did not have the power of the Holy Spirit to change his life, he spent a week praying and meeting with God in a new way. He became one of the leaders of Revival and travelled with teams, usually including Yosiya Kinuka and Joe Church, all over the world. He was in the group of 26 students who were expelled from Mukono in 1941, so he never was ordained. In 1964 he started to show signs of what today would probably be diagnosed as Alzheimer's disease. In 1966 he felt called by God to work among students in England, so he and Sara worked for three years at the Overseas Hostel Association in Oxford until his health became too poor. In December 1971, thinking that perhaps his illness was Parkinson's disease, he flew to Germany for treatment, but suffered a mild heart attack. They then flew back to Uganda where he died on 8th January 1973.

Kigeri V. Ndahindurwa (pp 140, 143). Nephew of King Rudahigwa who was nominated to succeed him in 1959 but never came to the throne. He was exiled when President Kayibanda took power.

Simeoni Nsibambi (pp 56, 57, 58, 147). A high-born Ugandan working with the public health department, in Kampala. In 1929 he joined Joe Church to search the Bible for references to the Holy Spirit. He soon left government service and became a full-time evangelist. He was instrumental in leading to the Lord two of the main evangelists from the East African Revival, Yosiya Kinuka and William Nagenda.

Doreen Peck (pp 125, 159). A teacher at Shyogwe from 1947, in 1962 she went to Nyamata to help Yona Kanamuzeyi with the refugees and stayed on with Eustace Kajuga. In 1967 she became the first official worker for the Mothers' Union in Rwanda. She returned to England in 1970 to lecture at All Nations Christian College where she was still teaching when Meg attended the college. In 1978 she left and was appointed CMS area secretary for the Dioceses of Sheffield and Southwell. She died in 2000 having just published her book *God Has Ears*.

Arthur Pitt-Pitts (pp 62, 92, 110). A contemporary of Harold Guillebaud and the Mission founders at Cambridge. He served as a CMS missionary in Uganda from 1917, where he married Rosalind Carr in 1922. He then became secretary to the mission in Kenya in 1930, before being asked to become the first archdeacon of Ruanda-Urundi in 1935. His wisdom was much needed during the early, heady days of Revival. He was never robust in health and suffered acutely from arthritis of the spine, which was not improved by all the travelling on bad roads. In February 1940, having chaired his first diocesan council meeting at Buye in Burundi, he went to Kenya for treatment. There he developed a rare blood disease and died after a short illness in Nairobi on Good Friday 1940.

Mr Roome (pp 30-31, 37). A representative of the Bible Society in East Africa, he encouraged Harold in his translation work and convened a conference at Kirinda to gain the cooperation of other missionaries in Rwanda.

Mutara III Rudahigwa (pp 35, 121, 137, 138, 139, 140). King of Rwanda from 1931 when his father, Musinga, was deposed until his death under suspicious circumstances in 1959. His death led to revolution, and Rwanda became a republic under President Kayibanda.

Pawulo Rutwe (pp 87, 88, 154, 193-194). After being saved in the Revival at Matana, he helped Elisabeth to learn the reality of her faith. He married Dorotiya, a Rwandan teacher from Shyogwe, and went to Bujumbura as evangelist in 1962, working there with Peter and Elisabeth. He was later ordained, and had a tremendous ministry as an evangelist in Burundi. He died in Nairobi still preaching in hospital in 1992. His wife, Dorotiya, still lives in Bujumbura.

Antoine Rutayisire (pp 191, 224-225). General secretary of African Evangelistic Enterprise, who was preserved through the genocide. He has written a book of testimonies of those who survived the fighting called *Faith under Fire*. He is doing all he can to promote reconciliation in the country.

Rutarindwa (pp 24, 35). Nominated as king of Rwanda following his father, Rwabugiri's death. His step-mother, Kanjogera, was appointed regent, but she conspired with her brother, Kabera, to kill him and enthrone her own son, Musinga. Rutarindwa was defeated in a bloody battle near Shyogwe in 1898.

Fred Rwigyema (pp 192, 193, 207-208). A Tutsi refugee in Uganda who, with Paul Kagame, joined Museveni in his struggle against Milton Obote, gaining much experience in fighting and earning the trust of Museveni. In January 1986 they took Kampala and Fred Rwigyema was made the commander-in-chief of the Uganda army and minister of defence in the new government. He was sacked at the end of 1989 and together he and Paul Kagame started strengthening the RPF. They invaded Rwanda on 1st October 1990 and the next day he was killed. Paul Kagame then took over as leader and eventually became president of the country.

Kigeri IV Rwabugiri (p 35). King of Rwanda who died in 1896. He succeeded in conquering much of central Rwanda.

Onesphore Rwaje (pp 186, 194, 211, 212, 213, 214, 251-252, 259, 272). Converted in 1970, he was a schoolboy at Shyogwe who, together with ten fellow Christians, did their best to protect Tutsi who were under attack. He married Josephine, a Presbyterian from Kirinda who had also been converted in the 1970s. He was ordained in 1985 and became the diocesan secretary at Kigali in 1987. He went to study at New College, Edinburgh, in 1990, where he received a telegram to return to be consecrated bishop of the new diocese of Byumba in November 1991. He did much to sort out the infighting between bishops which was going on at the time, but was unable to attend the re-consecration of the bishops because he was searching for his wife and family who had been caught up in the fighting in Byumba. In 1994 he stayed quietly in his house, protecting those who came to his door, but keeping a low profile until the RPF took the city. He became a refugee in Bukavu, Nairobi and Tanzania, but came back to Rwanda within a month. He then went to a meeting in Botswana, and on the way back he had a serious accident. He returned to Byumba as soon as he could in 1995 and invited Meg to train catechists in his diocese. As dean of the Province of Rwanda, he had to sort out the difficulties of the bishops of the Anglican Church until new bishops were consecrated and Archbishop Kolini was enthroned in January 1998. He is still bishop of Byumba with the declared priority of training and development in his diocese.

Robert Serubibi (pp 50, 51, 81, 86, 95, 97, 107, 108, 132, 252). Married to Eseri. Robert was originally the Guillebauds' head houseboy. With Harold's help, he studied at Budo and became a church teacher at Seseme in Bufumbira. With his family, they walked to Burundi where he was a missionary near Matana. He was trained at Mukono Theological College in 1941 and was ordained in 1945. Posted to Rweza, near Matana, he died there in December 1946. Eseri continued at Matana, running the brides' school with Lindesay before retiring to Kabale in 1959. She often joined Peter and Elisabeth on Scripture Union trips, and died at Kabale in 1999.

Dr Len Sharp (pp 21, 22, 24, 25, 26, 59, 63, 82, 84, 85, 93, 97, 98, 99). Doctor and pioneer missionary in Ruanda-Urundi from 1921-1955. Len married Esther, sister of Zoe Stanley Smith. Founded the Ruanda Mission (CMS) with his brother-in-law, **Dr Algie Stanley Smith** in 1921. They worked in Kabale until the way opened for them to start a hospital at Gahini, Rwanda. When work began in Burundi, he built the hospital at Matana and practised there for many years, before moving back to Uganda and starting leprosy work on an island in Lake Bunyoni. He bought another island where he built a house for his own use, to which he retired in 1955. In 1958 he founded Kisiizi Hospital in Uganda with his son, John. He and Esther retired to Mombasa, Kenya in 1960. It was here that they both died, Esther in 1962 and Len in 1976.

Kosiya Shalita (pp 37, 50, 61, 62, 63, 81, 82, 83, 93, 98, 107). First Rwandan clergyman. He was educated in Uganda, his family having fled the wrath of Musinga. He accompanied Geoff Holmes to choose the site at Gahini where he stayed to assist Joe Church, and was ordained in Uganda in 1933. In 1934 Kosiya became the first missionary to Matana, Burundi. In 1957 he was consecrated bishop of Ankole in Mbarara, Uganda. He died in 1993.

Dora Skipper (pp 45, 66, 67, 68, 69). Teacher and missionary in Rwanda (1930-1958). Dora was the headmistress of the Girls' School at Gahini. Previously she had been a CMS missionary in Uganda.

Dr Algie Stanley Smith (pp 21, 25, 43, 51, 56, 59, 60, 61, 63, 71, 99, 101, 102, 112, 114, 117, 119, 124, 132, 151). Doctor and pioneer missionary in Ruanda-Urundi, he married Zoë, sister of Esther Sharp, and founded the Ruanda Mission (CMS) with his brother-in-law, Dr Len Sharp. Worked with Dr Sharp at Kabale and helped him start the hospital at Gahini. When Archdeacon Guillebaud moved to England and then to Burundi, he took over the translation of the Old Testament into Kinyarwanda. He and his wife looked after Protestant students studying at the senior schools in Butare. In 1955 he retired to Mbarara, Uganda, where he translated the Bible into Lunyankole, which is very similar to Kinyarwanda. Their daughter brought them back to England in 1978, where Algie died in 1979 and Zoë in 1980.

Sylvester (pp 222, 245, 253). Emmanuel's second-in-command at SU, who met the Guillebauds on their arrival at Kigali in 1995. He had preserved many of Emmanuel Kayijuga's belongings. About 300 people were killed in his community, but his whole family survived. He is a Baptist pastor still working at SU.

Rev. Eric Townson (pp 168, 188). Eric, with his wife Ruth, were youth evangelists who arrived in Rwanda in 1969 and lived next door to Peter and Elisabeth in Kigali, and were much used when Revival hit in the 1970s. They returned to parish ministry in England. Eric died in September 2001.

Rev. Jack Warren (pp 22, 25). Jack came to Kabale in 1924, hoping the mountain air would heal a lung disease, and supervised all the small churches in South-West Uganda for four years. Returned to England at the end of 1928 where he died on 29th January 1929.

William (p 185). A Murundi who fled to Rwanda when his father was killed in the Burundi fighting of 1972, he was expected to join the killing of Tutsi in Rwanda in revenge, but the only night he went with the gang they did not kill anyone. He used to travel with Peter and Elisabeth, giving his testimony in schools during their time with Scripture Union. In 1994 he saved some Tutsi in his house, but was accused of involvement in the genocide and removed from his job as a lay preacher in the Presbyterian church. In 1999 he went to Uganda looking for work and disappeared. It was assumed that he was killed by burglars.

Rev. Giles Williams (pp 204, 228, 230). Giles took over from Peter when he retired in 1986, and co-ordinated the Bible translation team for the Old Testament. He was in Rwanda when the president's plane came down, having just left the master disks of the Bible in the office. They were miraculously preserved, and he discovered them intact when he returned as soon as the fighting had stopped. He asked Pierre Gakwandi to get a team of translators together, and for the next six years he combined life in a busy parish in England with travelling to Rwanda every few months to revise the work the team had done. The Bible was published early in 2002.

Appendix C

Chronology

1861	John Hanning Speke camps on the river Kagera but does not cross it into Rwanda.
1875	Stanley tries to cross the Kagera but is greeted by a hail of arrows.
1884	Conference of Berlin assigns Ruanda-Urundi to Germany as part of German East Africa.
1896	Death of King Kigeri IV Rwabugiri which is followed by a power struggle between his nominated successor, his son, Rutarindwa, and Kanjogera.
1897	Battle between the king and queen mother near Shyogwe. Kanjogera wins and rules the country in the name of her son, King Musinga. Samsoni Inyarubuga, later Harold's translator, who is related to Rutarindwa, flees to Uganda. The Germans enter Rwanda and rule through Kanjogera and her brother, Kabera, in the name of the king and his chiefs.
1912	Bloodshed in the Ruhengeri area as the northern Hutu princedoms are forced to accept the rule of the king.
5th September 1912	Harold and Margaret Guillebaud get married.
1913	Four gospels translated into Kinyarwanda by K. Roehl and published by Bible Society.
1919	Drs Stanley Smith and Sharp approach the CMS Committee for support in Ruanda-Urundi. Belgium takes over from Germany as the colonial governors of Ruanda-Urundi.
1921	Britain asks Belgium for a large section of Eastern Rwanda, in order to build a railway from the Cape to Cairo.
1922	Ruanda Mission establishes several outposts in Rwanda, including Gahini.
October 1923	Eastern Rwanda was handed back to Belgium.

1924	Dr Sharp returns to England seeking more help. Harold and Margaret respond.
25th June 1925	Harold and Margaret sail for Africa with their three older daughters. He starts translating Mark's gospel with Samsoni Inyarubuga.
May 1926	Harold baptizes the first Rwandan converts at Gahini.
11th April 1927	Bible Society conference at Kirinda. Harold is told to continue translating.
3rd September 1927	Harold and Margaret return to England for the rest of their family.
1928	Exhibition of Margaret's sketches at the Belgian Colonial Office.
June 1928	Harold and Margaret return to Kabale with their whole family. On a safari to Rwanda they visit the royal court at Nyanza and meet King Musinga and his mother, Kanjogera. Dr Joe Church arrives at Gahini.
1928-1929	Famine in Eastern Rwanda.
1929	Peter returns to England to attend Monkton Senior School, where he makes a commitment to Christ.
	Robert and Eseri Serubibi get married in Kabale.
September 1929	Dr Joe Church and Simeoni Nsibambi meet for prayer and Bible study on the Holy Spirit in Kampala.
5th March 1930	First draft of New Testament completed.
19th May 1930	Joe and Decie Church get married in Kampala.
1930	Yosiya Kinuka converted.
1931	King Musinga is deposed by the Belgians and his son, Rudahigwa, made king in his place.
23rd November 1931	New Testament in Kinyarwanda arrives in Kabale.
February 1932	Harold returns to England for the education of the family. During his years in England he publishes *Why the Cross?* and *Some Moral Difficulties in the Bible*, edits the first three of the series *Search the Scriptures*, and is a founding member of Tyndale House, Cambridge.
1932	Peter goes to St John's College, Cambridge, to study mathematics.
1933	Elisabeth Sutherland goes to Girton College, Cambridge, to read history.
	Census of Rwandans ordered by the Belgians. Identity cards issued and tribes fixed.
	Kosiya Shalita ordained as the first Rwandan clergyman.

27th May 1934	Blasio Kigozi ordained deacon at Namirembe Cathedral.
1934	Dr Bill Church and Kosiya Shalita walk to Burundi as missionaries, Bill at Buhiga and Kosiya at Matana.
1935	Peter graduates with a First. Goes on to study at the Cambridge Teacher Training College.
25th January 1936	Blasio Kigozi dies.
1936	Peter gets engaged to Elisabeth. He then goes to teach at Seaford College while Elisabeth does a teacher training course at Cambridge.
May 1936	Harold Guillebaud returns to Africa alone to continue translation work at Kigeme.
June 1936	Joe Church leads a team to Mukono Theological College.
29th June 1936	The Holy Spirit descends in power on Gahini Girls' School. Over the next few days many believe in Jesus Christ, among them Eustace and Marian Kajuga, Chloe Kinyanza and Margaret Kabano.
End of 1936	William Nagenda arrives in Gahini.
Easter 1937	Dora Skipper and Joe Church are publicly reconciled in Christ.
July 1937	Harold returns to England with his wife and Lindesay, who had joined him in Burundi in May 1937.
1937	Gideon Kabano converted. Robert and Eseri Scrubibi walk to Matana as missionaries.
1938	Peter goes to the Missionary Training Colony.
24th December 1938	Elisabeth sails for Africa with the Sharps.
1939	Yona Kanamuzeyi converted at Gahini.
23rd November 1939	Peter sails for Africa where he settles at Buye, teaching the deacons and building their house while waiting for the wedding.
12th April 1940	Peter and Elisabeth have civil wedding in Kampala.
24th April 1940	Peter and Elisabeth get married at Matana.
3rd August 1940	Harold leaves England with his wife and two older daughters for Burundi.
November 1940	Harold made archdeacon of Ruanda-Urundi in Namirembe Cathedral, Kampala.
9th February 1941	Ordination of first Rwandans in Rwanda, among them Yosiya Kinuka.
22nd April 1941	Harold dies at Matana, Burundi.

October 1941	The Mukono incident when 26 students, among them William Nagenda and Yohana Bunyenezi, are expelled.
1942	Death of George Sutherland, Elisabeth's father.
March 1943	Rosemary's appointment as official translator of the Bible into Kirundi confirmed.
1943	Eustace marries Marian Kajuga at Gahini.
1944	Yohana Bunyenyzi goes to Bujumbura as a missionary.
27th June 1945	Robert Serubibi ordained in Uganda.
1945	Philippa Guillebaud goes to teach in the Sudan. Mutaho conference healing divisions among missionaries followed by the first Kabale convention.
1946	Peter, together with Eustace and Marian, Gideon and Margaret and Sira, starts Shyogwe School.
28th June 1946	Opening of Shyogwe School.
1946	United Nations Trusteeship for Ruanda-Urundi rules that they must move slowly towards self-government.
3rd January 1947	Robert Serubibi dies.
1947	Peter and Elisabeth on leave, spreading the news of Revival in England.
November 1951	Kirundi New Testament with Psalms in print.
1953	Peter and Elisabeth on leave, first in England and then doing the Cours Colonial in Brussels.
1954	King Rudahigwa begins gradual land reform in Rwanda.
1955	Both Dr Stanley Smith and Dr Sharp retire to Uganda.
August 1956	Margaret retires due to ill health. Sets up home in Cambridge with Lindesay.
1956	Peter compiles a hymn book in Kinyarwanda.
1957	Kosiya Shalita consecrated bishop of Ankole in Mbarara, Uganda. Peter and Elisabeth on leave for six months — return with John.
1959	Eseri Surubibi retires to Kabale.
June 1959	Chrissie Sutherland, Elisabeth's mother, dies, and Peter and Elisabeth return to England to sort out her affairs.
24th July 1959	King Rudahigwa of Rwanda dies in Bujumbura.
October 1959	Revolution begins in Rwanda.
January 1960	Meg leaves Rwanda for school in England.

1960	Yona Kanamuzeyi, with his family, moves to work among refugees at Nyamata. Geoffrey and Chloe Kinyanza move to Shyogwe.
10th July 1961	Margaret Guillebaud dies in Cambridge.
August 1961	Refugees flock to Hanika Church. Peter and Elisabeth join other missionaries in helping the pastor, Misaki, and his wife, Dorothy.
October 1961	Republic of Rwanda declared. Dr Joe Church obliged to leave Rwanda.
1962	Peter and Elisabeth relocate to Matana, Peter as schools inspector and Elisabeth to try to re-start Matana Secondary School. Lindesay Guillebaud begins work with CMS as candidate secretary.
1st July 1962	Rwanda and Burundi become two independent countries.
November 1962	Philippa Guillebaud expelled from the Sudan. Yosiya and Dorcas Kinuka go to work among Rwandan refugees in Uganda.
October 1963	Peter and Elisabeth join Pawulo and Dorotiya Rutwe in Bujumbura.
December 1963	An attempted coup in Rwanda leads to many Tutsi being killed.
January 1964	Elisabeth leaves Peter to keep house with Rosemary and flies back to England.
23rd January 1964	Yona Kanamuzeyi is killed at Nyamata. Eustace and Marian move there to take his place.
May 1964	Tom Stockley, Mary's husband, dies.
1965	Rosemary starts learning Bembe and revising Mark's gospel with Joel Abekyamwale. Peter resigns from the Mission and starts working with overseas students through the IVF.
1966	Meg graduates from Edinburgh University and goes to Malawi with VSO.
1968	Meg back from Malawi, John back from six months in Brazil, David marries Peta Steele, Christine goes to York University. Eustace Kajuga becomes the first pastor of Kigali.
1969	Peter and Elisabeth return to Rwanda, seconded to Scripture Union.
13th January 1970	A new wave of Revival starts among secondary school students at Kigeme.
16th December 1971	Lindesay Guillebaud dies in London.
15th April 1972	John marries Gwyn Jones.
April 1972	An attempted coup in Burundi leads to massive slaughter of educated Hutu and a renewed wave

	of attacks on Tutsi in Rwanda throughout 1972. Jean Gakwandi loses his job, Geoffrey Kinyanza is forced to leave Shyogwe and Helene's husband is killed there.
1973	Death of both William and Sara Nagenda.
5th July 1973	In a coup-d'etat Major-General Juvenal Habyarimana becomes president of Rwanda.
1974	Single party government, almost all Rwandans became members of the *Mouvement Révolutionnaire National pour le Développement* (MRND).
1975	Christine Guillebaud marries Ross Paterson and moves to Taiwan. Death of Yosiya Kinuka in Uganda.
1976	Meg Guillebaud visits Rwanda and feels the Lord calling her to work there.
1977	Meg resigns from the police and goes to All Nations Christian College. Spate of Christian weddings encouraged by Scripture Union.
1979	Peter hands over Scripture Union to Nathan. Rosemary and Philippa retire to Cambridge.
June 1980	Meg ordained deaconess in Southwark Cathedral, and soon afterwards Peter and Elisabeth return to Kigali to co-ordinate a new Bible translation.
1981	Yoweri Museveni, with the help of Fred Rwigyema and Paul Kagame, among others, attempt a coup against President Obote of Uganda. Obote allows persecution of Rwandan refugees, many of whom die in camps in no man's land between the borders of Rwanda and Uganda.
26th January 1986	Yoweri Museveni ousts Milton Obote and becomes president of Uganda. Fred Rwigyema becomes the commander-in-chief of the Ugandan army and minister of defence in the new government.
1986	Collapse of world coffee prices with knock-on effect on the Rwandan economy. Rwandan refugees in Uganda are refused permission to return to Rwanda. The modern New Testament complete, Peter and Elisabeth finally retire.
1988	Colonel Mayuya murdered, followed by many other killings.
November 1989	Fred Rwigyema sacked as commander-in-chief of the Ugandan army and minister of defence.

1990	Peter and Elisabeth have a Golden Wedding trip to Rwanda. The *interahamwe* become active in political violence. President Habyarimana is forced by international pressure to allow opposition parties, which are largely formed on tribal lines.
29th September 1990	Death of Dr Joe Church, followed a few months later by his wife, Decie.
1st October 1990	The RPF attack Rwanda from the north. Fred Rwigyema is killed next day.
November 1990	RPF defeated and re-gathers in the Virunga Mountains led by General Paul Kagame.
23rd January 1991	RPF attack Ruhengeri, releasing prisoners and killing soldiers at the camp. Ephraim's wife, Francine, is preserved. The attack is followed by revenge massacres on both sides. In-fighting in the Anglican Church results in several bishops being consecrated illegally.
24th November 1991	Bishop Onesphore Rwaje is consecrated in the new diocese of Byumba.
5th June 1992	Re-consecration of the new bishops. Bishop Rwaje searches for his wife, Josephine, who had fled when Byumba was attacked by the RPF the day before.
1992	Byumba prefecture has most of its people in displaced persons camps. Peace talks begin in Arusha, Tanzania.
August 1993	Arusha peace accords signed. Bishop Kosiya Shalita dies in Uganda.
21st October 1993	Murder of the first Hutu president of Burundi, followed by massacres of Hutu and Tutsi alike. Many Hutu refugees flee to Rwanda, prompting further killings of Tutsi there. Radio Mille Collines encourages racial hatred.
6th April 1994	The presidents of Rwanda and Burundi are both killed when their plane is shot down at Kigali. The killing starts immediately.
7th April 1994	Eustace Kajuga and Husi, Israel Havugimana, Prime Minister Agathe Uwilingiyimana and ten Belgian soldiers with UN, all killed with many others.
10th April 1994	Belgian paratroopers arrive to help evacuate all *bazungu* over the next few days and then the UN troops withdraw from the country.
11th April 1994	Battle for Kigali begins.
4th July 1994	Meg ordained in Bristol Cathedral.

19th July 1994	RPF capture Kigali.
July 1994	A new government of national unity with the Hutu president Pasteur Bizimungu and Tutsi vice-president Paul Kagame is sworn in. An end is announced of identity cards declaring tribe. The government army flees towards Cyangugu and Goma. Geraldine Kabirigi, among others, is killed at Shyogwe. Killing still goes on in the vast refugee camps outside the country where the killers control the population and refuse to let any return to Rwanda. The new government begins the slow and painful process of rebuilding the country.
19th February 1995	Peter, Elisabeth and Meg fly for Nairobi and ten days later to Kigali.
March 1995	Meg returns to England, resigns from her parish and comes back as a volunteer with MAM six months later to teach catechists in Byumba diocese.
January 1996	Peter, Elisabeth and Meg return to Bradfield, near Reading. Meg applies to MAM as a full mission partner.
July 1996	Meg returns to Byumba to teach deacons.
7th November 1996	Peter dies in Bradfield. Meg flies back for the funeral. That same evening there is a mass movement of refugees back to Rwanda.
13th January 1997	Meg and Elisabeth return to Byumba, Meg to teach catechists and Elisabeth to start work among widows and orphans.
⸱bruary 1997	Death of Geoffrey Kinyanza.
⸱ril 1997	Visit of Deborah Paterson and Simon Guillebaud, and a trip back to Burundi.
May - December 1997	Installation of new bishops in vacant dioceses in Rwanda.
Easter 1998	Simon goes to Cambodia.
October 1998	Simon goes to Byumba to learn the language.
January 1999	Simon starts work in Bujumbura as a youth evangelist with Scripture Union.
April 2000	Resignation of President Bizimungu and election of General Paul Kagame as president of Rwanda.
December 2000	Death of Gideoni Kabano and then Chloe Kinyanza.
12th September 2001	Elisabeth dies at Byumba.